"Joclyn Oats has invaluably assembled a fascinating compilation celebrating the art of furniture history and design. She provides a look into the drawing archives of notable practitioners and exceptional presentation of her own eloquent visual and textual literacy. A beautifully crafted inspiring resource, sure to cultivate a desire to learn and create."
—*Clemenstien Love, Art + Design Director, THE cre.æ.tive ROOM*

"A revelatory way to gain a deep understanding and instinctive feel for furniture, Joclyn Oats' *An Illustrated Guide to Furniture History* lights the path toward a level of understanding that simple memorization of facts and dates simply can't achieve. Using sketching and other simple learning tools, Oats shares what is probably the most effective and enjoyable method available to develop a true sensitivity for furniture styles and characteristics."
—*Zurich Esposito, Hon. AIA*

"Joclyn Oats has written an exceptionally engaging book that will delight the reader who is on a journey to learn the history of furniture. Designers and students of design will thoroughly enjoy the beautiful images and historical context."
—*Denise Rush, ASID, IIDA, IDEC, Dean and Faculty, School of Interior Architecture, Boston Architectural College, USA*

An Illustrated Guide to Furniture History

An Illustrated Guide to Furniture History provides upper-level students and instructors with an alternative visual analytical approach to learning about furniture history from Antiquity to Postmodernism. Following an immersive teaching model, it presents a Nine-Step Methodology to help students strengthen their visual literacy and quickly acquire subject area knowledge.

Moving chronologically through key periods in furniture history and interior design, such as the Renaissance, the Arts and Crafts Movement, and Modernism, it traverses Europe to America to present a comprehensive foundational guide to the history of furniture design.

Part I addresses furniture within the context of the built environment, with chapters exploring the historical perspective, construction principles, and the categorization of furniture. In Part II, the author visually depicts the structural organization of the methodological process, a three-category framework: History, Aesthetics, and Visual Notes. The chapters in this part prepare the reader for the visual analysis that will occur in the final section of the book. The book is lavishly illustrated in full color with over 300 images to reinforce visual learning and notation.

A must-have reference and study guide for students in industrial and product design, interior design, and architecture.

Joclyn M. Oats is a tenured Associate Professor in the Design Department at Columbia College Chicago, USA. Joclyn has practiced architecture and interior design and served the College in an administrative capacity as coordinator and director for the BFA, Interior Architecture, MFA, Architectural Studies, and the MFA, Interior Architecture programs for over a decade. Her teaching has covered a wide range of courses for both graduate and undergraduate levels: studio courses, technical courses, and architecture and design history surveys.

An Illustrated Guide to Furniture History

Joclyn M. Oats

LONDON AND NEW YORK

First published 2022
by Routledge
2 Park Square, Milton Park, Abingdon, Oxon OX14 4RN

and by Routledge
605 Third Avenue, New York, NY 10158

Routledge is an imprint of the Taylor & Francis Group, an informa business

© 2022 Joclyn M. Oats

The right of Joclyn M. Oats to be identified as author of this work has been asserted by her in accordance with sections 77 and 78 of the Copyright, Designs and Patents Act 1988.

All rights reserved. No part of this book may be reprinted or reproduced or utilised in any form or by any electronic, mechanical, or other means, now known or hereafter invented, including photocopying and recording, or in any information storage or retrieval system, without permission in writing from the publishers.

Trademark notice: Product or corporate names may be trademarks or registered trademarks, and are used only for identification and explanation without intent to infringe.

Every effort has been made to contact and acknowledge copyright holders, but the author and publisher would be pleased to have any errors or omissions brought to their attention so that corrections may be published at a later printing.

British Library Cataloguing-in-Publication Data
A catalogue record for this book is available from the British Library

Library of Congress Cataloging-in-Publication Data
Names: Oats, Joclyn M., author.
Title: An illustrated guide to furniture history / Joclyn M. Oats.
Description: Abingdon, Oxon ; New York : Routledge, 2021. | Includes bibliographical references and index.
Identifiers: LCCN 2021000516 (print) | LCCN 2021000517 (ebook)
Subjects: LCSH: Furniture–History.
Classification: LCC NK2270 .O28 2021 (print) | LCC NK2270 (ebook) | DDC 749.09–dc23
LC record available at https://lccn.loc.gov/2021000516
LC ebook record available at https://lccn.loc.gov/2021000517

ISBN: 978-0-367-40655-4 (hbk)
ISBN: 978-0-367-40656-1 (pbk)
ISBN: 978-0-367-80829-7 (ebk)

Typeset in Univers
by Apex CoVantage, LLC

Contents

List of illustrations ix
Introduction xxvii

PART I FURNITURE AND THE BUILT ENVIRONMENT 1

1 A historical perspective 3

2 Construction principles 12

3 Piece categorically 42

PART II UNDERSTANDING THE PIECE 121

4 The Analysis of Form: Nine-Step Methodology 123

5 A graphic narrative 155

PART III OBJECT OF DESIRE: FURNITURE PERIODS, MOVEMENTS, AND STYLES, FROM ANTIQUITY TO THE 20TH CENTURY 179

    Introduction 179

6 Antiquity: Egypt, Greece, and Rome 181

7 Renaissance: Italy, France, and England 196

8 18th century: Italy, France, England, and America—Late Colonial 214

■ Contents

9   Precursors to Modernism: Europe Arts and Crafts Movement,
    Art Nouveau, and Viennese Secession (or Wiener Werstätte),
    and American Arts and Crafts   238

10 Modernist movements: Deutscher Werkbund, Bauhaus, De Stijl,
    International Style   261

11 Early Modernist designers and architects: Pierre Chareau
    (1883–1950), Eileen Gray (1878–1976), Jean Prouvé
    (1901–1984), Charlotte Perriand (1903–1999)   280

12 Modernism in America and the European connection   305

13 Movements after Modernism: High-tech, Postmodermism,
    Deconstructivism   326

14 Conclusion   343

Index   352

Illustrations

TIMELINES

1.1	Pictorial timeline (all sections)	6
1.2	Pictorial timeline—Antiquity, Renaissance	8
1.3	Pictorial timeline—18th–20th century: Europe, America	9
1.4	Pictorial timeline—20th century: Europe, America	10
4.1	Furniture pictorial timeline—18th century	127
6.1	Pictorial timeline—Antiquity: Egypt, Greece, and Rome	181
7.1	Pictorial timeline—Renaissance: Italy, France, and England	196
8.1	Pictorial timeline—18th century: Italy, France, England, and America—Late Colonial	214
9.1	Pictorial timeline—Precursors to Modernism: Europe Arts and Crafts Movement, Art Nouveau, and Vienna Secession (or Wiener Werstätte), and American Arts and Crafts	238
10.1	Pictorial timeline—Modernist movements: Deutscher Werkbund, Bauhaus, De Stijl, International Style	261
11.1	Pictorial timeline—Early Modernist designers and architects: Pierre Chareau (1883–1950), Eileen Gray (1878–1976), Jean Prouvé (1901–1984), Charlotte Perriand (1903–1999)	280
12.1	Pictorial timeline—Modernism in American and the European connection	305
13.1	Pictorial timeline—Movements after Modernism: High-tech, Postmodernism, Deconstructivism	326

TABLE

4.1	The Analysis of Form: Nine-Step Methodology	125

PLATES

2.1	Detail drawings of furniture joinery from XVIIIth Dynasty Egyptian furniture. Collège Boulle, Paris	15
2.2	Detail drawings of furniture joinery. Collège Boulle, Paris	16

Illustrations

2.3	French, Louis XIV, XV, XVI furniture	29
2.4	18th-century English Queen Anne furniture	30
2.5	17th- and 18th-century American furniture	31
2.6	Picker's selection: antique headboards and posts	39
2.7	Four-image grid of Leonards' designs and restoration work	40
3.1	Metropolitan Museum of Art. The Boiserie from the Hôtel de Varengeville Period Room, French, Paris, ca. 1736–1752	51
3.2	Sheraton Sideboard, Kittinger Furniture Company Inc. furniture catalog. Sheraton Dining Table, Kittinger Furniture Company Inc.	71
3.3	George Hepplewhite Sideboard, Kittinger Company Inc. furniture catalog. George Hepplewhite chest of drawers, Kittinger Furniture Company Inc. furniture catalog	72
4.1	Author's drawing Visual Notes Exercise 1, High Chest of Drawers	137
4.2	Author's drawing Visual Notes Exercise 2, French Armchair	145
4.3	Author's drawing Visual Notes Exercise 3, Marshmallow Sofa	153
6.1	Cubiculum (bedroom) from the Villa of P. Fannius Synistor at Boscorealeca. 50–40 B.C.	192
7.1	The Gubbio Studiolo, ca. 1478–1482. From Ducal Palace in Gubbio. Entrance of the studiolo with walls using illusionistic intarsia panels depicting latticed cupboards holding a variety of books, scientific and musical instruments, and other objects. Room view with visible window	211
8.1	Dining Room from Kirtlington Park, 1748, Oxfordshire, England, Design by John Sanderson for Sir James Dashwood, 1st Baronet. Rococo decoration (plaster work) and Neoclassical interior architecture	234
9.1	The Salle à Manger Masson, 1903–1904, Nancy, France. Designed by Eugène Vallin. Artwork, the work of Victor Prouvé. Installed at the Musée de l'Ecole de Nancy	258
10.1	Interior space designed for "Inner Equipment of a Home," at the 1929 Fall Salon. Design by Le Corbusier, Charlotte Perriand, and Pierre Jeanneret. View 2, Interior space designed for "Inner Equipment of a Home," 1929 Fall Salon. Designed by Le Corbusier, Charlotte Perriand, and Pierre Jeanneret	276
10.2	Villa Tugendhat, 1929, Brno, Czech Republic. Designed by Ludwig Mies van der Rohe and Lilly Riech, Living area looking towards curved wall of dining area, with Barcelona and Tugendhat chairs. Dining area with Brno tubular chairs at round dining table	277
11.1	E-1027 Interior, 1929, Roquebrune-Cap-Martin, France. Designed by Eileen Gray. Photograph of the main living space restored. Managed by Cap Moderne	301
12.1	Virginia Museum of Fine Arts Membership Suite, 1950s, and Rare Book Room, Library. Member's lounge area, Rare Book Room	322

13.1	Schuppich Sporn & Winischhofer, Renovation 1983–1988, Vienna, Austria. Designed by Coop Himmelb(l)au Architects	340

FIGURES

2.1	Mortise-and-tenon joints A–D	17
2.2	Mortise-and-tenon joints, furniture detail examples	17
2.3	Dovetail joints A–D	18
2.4	Dovetail joints—drawers	18
2.5	Dovetail joints—Bombé Desk	18
2.6	Edge joint A–D	19
2.7	Edge joint furniture details	19
2.8	Spline joint A–D	20
2.9	Spline joint interior details	20
2.10	Da Vinci sketches	22
2.11	Lathe design and tools from *Mechanick Exercises* (1701), Joseph Moxon	22
2.12	Lathe design and tools from *Mechanick Exercises* (1703), Joseph Moxon	22
2.13	Two-axis lathe design	23
2.14	Two-axis lathe furniture design details	23
2.15	English 18th-century chair leg development	25
2.16	English chair leg design, early Neoclassical	27
2.17	French chair leg design, late Neoclassical	27
2.18	Ball-and-claw carving, 2014	33
2.19	Leonards' Company headboard shapes, a–f	37
2.20	Leonards' production overview	37
3.1	18th-century French Rococo bergère	42
3.2	18th-century French fauteuil	43
3.3	Fauteuil details. Cartouche back, cabriole leg, scroll foot	44
3.4	Louis XV bergère	44
3.5	Louis XV fauteuil located in the Boiserie from the Hôtel de Varengeville Period Room. French, Paris, ca. 1736–1752	44
3.6	Fauteuil evolution A–D, Régence through transitional Louis XV–XVI	45
3.7	18th-century French commode and console table	46
3.8	18th-century French hardware	46
3.9	Commode, ca. 1765–1770, French. Attributed to Léonard Boudin and Pierre-Antoine Foullet. Veneered marquetry with gilt-bronze mounts	47
3.10	Console table, ca. 1700–1725, Rome, Italy. Gilded linden and gilt-bronze, with green porphyry stone. Size 38½″ × 69¼″ × 27¾″	48

Illustrations

3.11	Louis XV Canepé from Annexes of the Chateau of Versailles. Detail of wood carved Canepé leg and base trim	48
3.12	Sofa etching by Jean-Charles Delafosse (1734–1791). Beechwood sofa with original pink and white paint, possibly German	49
3.13	Garden elevation of the Hôtel de Varengeville at no. 217 boulevard Saint-Germain. Floor plan of the first floor of the Hôtel de Varengeville	52
3.14	Hôtel de Varengeville view opposite direction of Plate 3.1. Author's drawing of a similar arabesque Boiserie wall panel detail of the Hôtel de Varengeville	52
3.15	Bureau plat and details A–C. Located in the Boiserie Hôtel de Varengeville, Period Room. Maker Gilles Joubert (French, ca. 1689–1775), date 1759. Lacquered oak, gilt-bronze mounts, lined with modern leather. H 31¾" × W 69¼" × D 36"	53
3.16	Gaetano Brunetti pier table etchings, ca. 1736	55
3.17	Brumetti's Rococo chair etching. Author's rendition of the original etching	56
3.18	Splat back chair detail	56
3.19	Chippendale chair back designs. Enlarged chair, author's rendition	57
3.20	George Hepplewhite shield-back chairs. From his book *The Cabinet-Maker and Upholsterer's Guide*, (Plate 4), 1788 and 1794	58
3.21	Thomas Sheraton, plate from *The Cabinet-Maker and Upholsterer's Drawing Book*	59
3.22	Thomas Sheraton, rectangular chair back designs	59
3.23	English chair splat design variations	60
3.24	George Hepplewhite, shield-shape chair back	60
3.25	Samuel McIntire rectangular back armchair	61
3.26	Dumfries House, front exterior view	61
3.27	Dumfries House, Family Parlour	61
3.28	Dumfries House, Blue Drawing Room	62
3.29	Thomas Chippendale, elbow chair for Dumfries House	62
3.30	Chinese Chippendale rosewood breakfront bookcase	63
3.31	Chippendale George III dining chair, Neoclassical design	63
3.32	Rococo "ribband-back" side chair, ca. 1755–1760. After the design of Thomas Chippendale. Mahogany with upholstered seat. One of a pair	63
3.33	Thomas Chippendale design, gilt gold armchair, 1765, for Sir Lawrence Dundas residence, 19 Arlington Place, London	64
3.34	Author's illustration, Chinese Chippendale chair, Victoria and Albert Museum collection	64

3.35	English commode, ca. 1760, mahogany, serpentine shape, carved edge detail, bracket feet	65
3.36	George III Chippendale period mahogany serpentine chest, ca. 1770, England. Details—bracket feet, drawer pulls, dovetail joints	65
3.37	Commode features 1–5	65
3.38	Sofa in Chippendale's drawings Vol. 1, 1759, black ink and gray wash	66
3.39	English camelback sofa with damask upholstery	66
3.40	Marlborough leg styles of Thomas Chippendale	66
3.41	Harewood House, Yorkshire, England, front façade	67
3 42	Harewood House Music Room	67
3.43	Harewood House Yellow Drawing Room	68
3.44	Harwood House Music Room settee	68
3.45	Harewood House Music Room chair	68
3.46	Harwood House Yellow Drawing Room settee	68
3.47	Harwood House Yellow Drawing Room chair	68
3.48	Thomas Chippendale watercolor plate of giltwood carved sofa for Sir Lawrence Dundas	69
3.49	One of a pair of giltwood sofas designed by Robert Adam, workshop Thomas Chippendale, ca. 1763, for Sir Lawrence Dundas	69
3.50	Kittinger Georgian Breakfront, SKU: KC3701, Kittinger Furniture Co., Inc.	73
3.51	Mahogany breakfront bookcase design by Robert Adam. Workshop of Thomas Chippendale, 1764, for Sir Lawrence Dundas, 19 Arlington Place, London	73
3.52	Photograph, Sir Lawrence Dundas breakfront bookcase design of Robert Adam, workshop of Thomas Chippendale, 1764, for Sir Lawrence Dundas, 19 Arlington Place, London	74
3.53	Queen Anne chair	76
3.54	Philadelphia highboy	78
3.55	Philadelphia lowboy depicting a typical aesthetic and form for the Philadelphia lowboy	78
3.56	American Chippendale ball-and-claw variations A–E	79
3.57	Flat-top secretary, Newport, Rhode Island	80
3.58	Flat-top secretary, Newport, Rhode Island—details	81
3.59	Attributed to John Townsend, chest of drawers, ca. 1765 (block-front chest), Newport, Rhode Island	82
3.60	Attributed to John Townsend, bureau table, ca. 1765, Newport, Rhode Island	82
3.61	Classification of Newport, block-front chest construction and aesthetic details	83

■ Illustrations

3.62	Classification of Newport, block-front chest construction and aesthetic details	84
3.63	Dressing table, ca. 1750–1755. Probably Christopher Townsend. Mahogany, yellow poplar, eastern white pine	85
3.64	Ball-and-claw with undercut talon	85
3.65	Label from tall clock case, John Townsend's workshop	85
3.66	Slant-front desk from Benjamin Frothingham's shop	86
3.67	Slant-front desk open with view of interior. Detail of pigeonholes, Benjamin Frothingham's shop	86
3.68	Paper label used by Benjamin Frothingham's shop	86
3.69	Queen Anne bonnet-top secretary, ca. 1750. Attributed to Benjamin Frothingham. Interior displaying pigeonholes. Detail of pigeonholes	87
3.70	American case piece top configurations, 18th century	87
3.71	Queen Anne bonnet-top replica, Statton Furniture Mfg. Co Catalog image	88
3.72	Queen Anne bonnet-top, 1760–1785, Charlestown, Massachusetts. Designed by Benjamin Frothingham Jr. Medium subicu, mahogany, white pine, and red pine	88
3.73	Thomas Jefferson original writing table/lap desk designed by Benjamin Randolph, Smithsonian Museum. Replica of Benjamin Randolph's desk. Work of craftsman Lon Schleining	90
3.74	Benjamin Randolph Queen Anne, mahogany card table, Philadelphia, ca. 1765. Detail of carved knee. Author's illustration of prominent knuckle ball-and-claw foot	90
3.75	Chippendale-style card table, Philadelphia, ca. 1770. Attributed to Benjamin Randolph. Mahogany, oak, pine, with gadroon trim at apron and animal paw foot (32″ × 28½″ × 15⅝″)	90
3.76	Philadelphia carved marble slab table. Author's rendition	91
3.77	Benjamin Randolph Chippendale-style side chair, Philadelphia	92
3.78	Chippendale Rococo-style side chair, Philadelphia, 1770. Attributed to Benjamin Randolph. With intricately pieced carved splat and surface scrollwork. Mahogany, white cedar Made for John & Elizabeth Lloyd. Carved by Hercules Courtenay. View from the back, splat detail (37″ × 24¼″ × 22½″)	93
3.79	Upholstered armchair, Chinese Chippendale style with Gothic arches, fret work, and marlborough legs, ca. 1766. Attributed to Thomas Affleck	93
3.80	Chinese Chippendale-style upholstered armchair, ca. 1770. Attributed to Thomas Affleck. Similar to Figure 3.79	94
3.81	Marlborough chair leg styles with Chippendale Chinese fret work	94
3.82	Philadelphia card table, 1769–1770. Attributed to Thomas Affleck	95
3.83	Gadroon detail at apron	95
3.84	Card table, one of a pair, Philadelphia, ca. 1770. Attributed to Thomas Affleck for John Cadwalader residence	95

3.85	Side chair, ca. 1769. Attributed to Benjamin Randolph, possibly carved by Hercules Courtenay, Philadelphia, Pennsylvania. Mahogany, northern white cedar, with intricately carved pierced splat and surface scrollwork. Same as Figure 3.78 and Figure 3.85	96
3.86	Side chair with details, 1769–1770. Attributed to Thomas Affleck. Mahogany with intricately carved pierce splat and surface scrollwork	97
3.87	Clothes press, ca. 1760–1790. Attributed to Thomas Affleck, Philadelphia, Pennsylvania. Classical style derivative form—with pediment resembles a Classical temple	98
3.88	Chest-on-chest, 1770–1775. Attributed to Thomas Affleck, Philadelphia, Pennsylvania. The intricate carvings attributed to James Reynolds. Classically derivative form—swan neck pediment with lattice screen within and center carved bird finial. Mahogany, mahogany veneer, white cedar, yellow pine, tulip poplar	98
3.89	William Savery side chair design for Independence Hall, Philadelphia (1743–1750), replica. A historical reproduction by craftsman Robert Whitely	99
3.90	Rush-seat chair, ca. 1745, William Savery. Medium, maple and rush	99
3.91	The Governor's Chamber, Independence Hall, Philadelphia, Pennsylvania. View depicting William Savery's four original side chairs (1743–1750) and Robert Whitley's four replicas of the William Savery side chairs	100
3.92	William Savery tilt-top mahogany tea table, 1745–1750	100
3.93	Philadelphia tassel-back armchair and details. Author's rendition	101
3.94	Philadelphia Chippendale-style mahogany tassel-back side chairs, 1765. Made for Justice Samuel Chase.	103
3.95	High chest 1760–1780, Philadelphia, Pennsylvania. Walnut and yellow poplar, 96¾" × 45½" × 23 11/16"	104
3.96	Philadelphia high chest, 1765–1780. Swietenia, tulip poplar, oak, yellow pine, and cedar, H 90¼"	105
3.97	High chest, 1765–1775. Philadelphia. Mahogany, Mahogany veneer, tulip poplar, yellow pine, white cedar, 91¾" × 44⅝" × 24⅝"	106
3.98	Tilt-top tea table, 1765–1775, Philadelphia. Medium mahogany, size H 29", Diam. 37"	106
3.99	Slab table, ca. 1770, Philadelphia. Mahogany, marble, and yellow pine, L 48¼". Slab table detail of cabriole leg and knee	107
3.100	Historic image of Thomas Elfe house and shop, front façade, 54 Queen Street, Charleston, South Carolina. Contemporary image of Thomas Elfe house, front façade	109

■ Illustrations

3.101	Double chest, Charleston, 1765–1775. Not credited to Thomas Elfe but similar design elements as Elfe's work. Mahogany veneer, pierced work pediment with rosettes and globe	110
3.102	Drop-leaf mahogany table. This replica is a table design attributed to Thomas Elfe. It is seen in various historic house museums, Heyward-Washington House, South Carolina, and Middleton Place House Museum, South Carolina. Tim Killen, detailed SketchUp design 3D	111
3.103	Sketches of table examples showing a variety of stretcher conditions and thumbnail of rule joint	111
3.104	Historic image, Heyward-Washington House front elevation (façade), Charleston, South Carolina. Contemporary, Heyward-Washington House Museum front elevation (façade), Charleston, South Carolina	111
3.105	Heyward-Washington House chimney piece	112
3.106	Historical image, Heyward-Washington House Museum Drawing Room with view of chimney piece. Heyward-Washington House Museum Drawing Room with view of chimney piece	112
3.107	Double chest of drawers with desk drawer, 1765–1775, Charleston, South Carolina. Mahogany and mahogany veneer primary; cypress and mahogany secondary. H 78″ × W 46½″ × D 25⅛″. Courtesy of Museum of Early Southern Decorative Arts (MESDA) Acc. 946	112
3.108	Double chest of drawers, 1765–1775, Charleston, South Carolina. Mahogany and mahogany veneer primary; cypress, tulip poplar, and mahogany secondary, H 76″ × W 45¼″ × D 24″. Courtesy of Museum of Early Southern Decorative Arts MESDA, MRF 8018. Acc. HF 368	112
3.109	Chest-on-chest, ca. 1770, Charleston, South Carolina. Mahogany and cypress with brass hardware 74½″ × 44¼″ × 24⅛″	113
3.110	Thomas Chippendale book Plate LXVII, second edition of the *Gentleman and Cabinet-Maker's Director* (1754 and 1755), or third edition 1762, Plate XCIII	114
3.111	Breakfront bookcase, Charleston, South Carolina. Bookcase and details A–C	115
3.112	Breakfront bookcase, Charleston, South Carolina, color photograph	116
3.113	Breakfront bookcase, Charleston, South Carolina, details, front and back, A–E. Black and white photographs	116
3.114	Port Royal Parlor. View in front of the fireplace. Winterthur Museum, Garden and Library	117
3.115	Parlor Royal Parlor expanded view. Winterthur Museum, Garden and Library	117
4.1	High chest of drawers. American, Philadelphia, 1750–1760. Mahogany, yellow pine, and tulip poplar, 256.7 × 113.1 × 59.1 cm	128

4.2	Author's drawing, for Visual Notes STUDY 1, High Chest of Drawers	129
4.3	High chest of drawers, American, Philadelphia, 1750–1760. Mahogany, yellow pine, and tulip poplar, 256.7 × 113.1 × 59.1 cm	130
4.4	Author's drawing, for Visual Notes STUDY 2, High Chest of Drawers	131
4.5	High chest of drawers, American, Philadelphia, 1750–1760. Mahogany yellow pine, and tulip poplar, 256.7 × 113.1 × 59.1 cm	132
4.6	Author's drawing, for Visual Notes STUDY 3, High Chest of Drawers	133
4.7	High chest of drawers, American, Philadelphia, 1750–1760. Mahogany yellow pine, and tulip poplar, 256.7 × 113.1 × 59.1 cm	134
4.8	Author's drawing, for Visual Notes STUDY 4, High Chest of Drawers	135
4.9	High chest of drawers, American, Philadelphia, 1750–1760. Mahogany, yellow pine, and tulip poplar, 256.7 × 113.1 × 59.1 cm	136
4.10	French armchair (Louis XV fauteuil), located in the Boiserie from the Hôtel de Varengeville, Period Room, French, Paris, ca. 1736–1752	138
4.11	Author's drawing, for Visual Notes STUDY 1, French Armchair	139
4.12	French armchair, (Louis XV fauteuil), located in the Boiserie from the Hôtel de Varengeville, Period Room, French, Paris, ca. 1736–1752	140
4.13	Author's drawing, for Visual Notes STUDY 2, French Armchair	141
4.14	French armchair (Louis XV fauteuil), located in the Boiserie from the Hôtel de Varengeville, Period Room, French, Paris, ca. 1736–1752	142
4.15	Author's drawing, for Visual Notes STUDY 3, French Armchair	143
4.16	French armchair (Louis XV fauteuil), located in the Boiserie from the Hôtel de Varengeville, Period Room, French, Paris, ca. 1736–1752	144
4.17	Marshmallow Sofa, George Nelson. Designed for Herman Miller Furniture Company, 1956–1965. Painted tubular steel, with vinyl-covered latex foam circular pads	146
4.18	Author's illustration, Visual Notes STUDY 1, Marshmallow Sofa	147
4.19	Marshmallow Sofa, George Nelson. Designed for Herman Miller Furniture Company, 1956–1965. Painted tubular steel, with vinyl-covered latex foam circular pads	148
4.20	Author's drawing, Visual Notes STUDY 2, Marshmallow Sofa	149
4.21	Marshmallow Sofa, George Nelson. Designed for Herman Miller Furniture Company, 1956–1965. Painted tubular steel, with vinyl-covered latex foam circular pads	150
4.22	Author's drawing, Visual Notes STUDY 3, Marshmallow Sofa	151

■ Illustrations

4.23	Marshmallow Sofa, George Nelson. Designed for Herman Miller Furniture Company, 1956–1965. Painted tubular steel, with vinyl-covered latex foam circular pads	152
5.1	Ron Arad, sketch studies for "Well Tempered Chair"	157
5.2	Ron Arad, Sketch study for "Well Tempered Chair"	157
5.3	Studio K Creative, Bellemore custom Round banquet, plan and elevations. Sketch by Michael Regan	158
5.4	Studio K Creative, Bellemore, custom Round banquet three-dimension. Sketch by Michael	158
5.5	Studio K Creative, GT Fish & Oyster custom Rope chandelier (Concept 1). Sketch by Michael Regan, 3D modeler	159
5.6	Studio K Creative, GT Fish & Oyster custom Rope chandelier (Concept 2). Sketch by Michael Regan, 3D modeler	159
5.7	Studio K Creative, Maple & Ash custom Necklace chandelier. Sketch by Michael Regan, 3D	159
5.8	Florence Knoll office sketches. Desk with Barcelona chairs and table, desk and credenza, sofa, and Barcelona table and stool	160
5.9	Florence Knoll office sketches. Seating area chairs and table, open office view with work surface, return, storage bins above, and two-drawer pedestal	161
5.10	Chris Koules, CJK Design Custom Woodworking. Sketch and photo Oak Reading Side Table designed to accommodate a book or laptop in a lift up compartment. Lower shelf is designed to vertically store books. Sketch and photo of Chair Round Side Table (pair). These tables are designed curved as an alternative to the traditional rectangular side table. The table provides hidden lower storage. The medium is oak bead board which was a popular decorative material used in early 20th-century architecture	162
5.11	Chris Koules, CJK Design Custom Woodworking, Red Oak Radiator Cover and photo. This piece is in the American Arts and Crafts tradition. The two-part piece is designed to allow air flow through all sides of the slatted base. The top portion provides shelving for books and or decorative art pieces	162
5.12	Krueck and Sexton Architects, sketch of seating piece black in on white paper	163
5.13	Krueck and Sexton Architects, sketch of seating piece, reverse reading, white on black	163
5.14	Krueck and Sexton Architects, rendered sketch of table on yellow tracing paper	164
5.15	Gary Lee, graphite sketch of the Campbell Bench, from the Chai Ming collection; Campbell Bench rendering; Campbell Bench photograph, Chai Ming Studios	164
5.16	Thomas Pheasant, ink sketch of Athens Lounge Chair, for Baker Furniture Thomas Pheasant. Collection	165

5.17	Giancarlo Piretti, ideation sketches for the Strive chair, Krueger International, KI	167
5.18	Jean Prouvé sketch, ink and colored pencil, Cité Chair, 1930, Paris. Sketched for his class at The Conservatoire National des Arts et Métiers (CNAM), Paris, France	169
5.19	Karim Rashid, vignette sketch of the Oh Chair with table and stool	170
5.20	Deborah Rogers, graphite drawing, floor plan for the Goodgold family room built-in bookcase; graphite drawing of the west elevation of built-in bookcase; graphite drawing, north elevation of Built-in bookcase; Goodgold family room photograph of the built-in bookcase installed	171
5.21	Hjördís Sigurgísladóttir & Dennis Jóhannesson, ARK|HD, Reykjavík, Iceland, Hjördís' sketch of the "Swing" chair, front view, 100% recyclable steel	172
5.22	Hjördís Sigurgísladóttir & Dennis Jóhannesson, ARK|HD, Hjördís' sketch of the "Swing" chair back view, 100% recyclable steel	172
5.23	Morlen Sinoway, sketch studies for Bob Messerly's desk	174
5.24	Morlen Sinoway, sketchbook, two-page study for a jewelry dresser	175
6.1	Egyptian bed or chair legs. Bull leg, ca. 2960–2770 B.C. Animal leg, ca. 3100–2650 B.C.	183
6.2	Hatnefer's chair, New Kingdom, ca. 1492–1473 B.C., 18th Dynasty, Egypt	184
6.2a	Hatnefer's chair back detail of deity Bess in the center, tit-amulet on either side and djed-pillar at the ends.	184
6.3a	Reniseneb's chair back detail incised decoration depicting owner seated on a chair of identical form with accompanying text	185
6.3	Chair of Reniseneb, New Kingdom, ca. 1450 B.C., Egypt	186
6.3b	Author's illustration of back chair back detail similar to Renisenbe's chair	186
6.4	Gravestone of Xanthippos, Athens, Greece, ca. 420 B.C.	187
6.5	Klismos chair replica. Designer, Terrance Harold Robjohn-Gibbings. Manufacturer, Eleftherios Saridis, Athens, Greece, 1961	188
6.6	Ink sketch by designer Thomas Pheasant, Athens Lounge Chair, Lounge chair, Baker Furniture Thomas Pheasant Collection	188
6.7	Roman banquet couch, 1st century B.C. (Late Hellenistic–Early Imperial), wood and brass	190
6.7a	Roman banquet couch detail showing the leg with brass fittings and fulcra	190
6.8	Roman couch and footstool, A.D. 1st–2nd century, wood and bone reassembled from fragments	191
6.8a	Roman couch detail of the corner showing carved bone leg and crescent shape fulcra, carved head above lion pantome (animal head)	191

Illustrations

6.8b	Footstool detail of wing cupids and leopards	191
7.1	Cassone with reliefs of Caesar, the Slaying of Niobe's sons. Italy, third quarter of the 16th century, walnut on pine	199
7.2	Savonarola chair, Italy, 16th century, 38⅜" × 25" × 21"	199
7.3	Sgabello chair, Italy, 16th Century, 41 5/16" × 11⅞" × 16¾"	200
7.3a	Sgabello chair detail back crest area with a fleur-de-lis-like design flanked right and left with rosettes	200
7.3b	Sgabello chair detail view of the back of the chair showing a carved monogram "A.D."	201
7.4	Walnut cupboard, two-part, French cabinet (*meuble à deux corps*), ca. 1570, with 19th-century additions, walnut, approximate size, top and bottom, 6" × 5" × 2"	203
7.5	Caquetoire armchair, France, second half of 16th century and 19th century, walnut, cut silk cushion	204
7.6	Standing livery cupboard, England, ca. 1585, walnut with ebony, cedar, and holly inlays, oak interior and back panels	207
7.7	Bed—Great Bed of Ware, Ware, England, 1590–1600, oak, carved and originally painted, with panels of marquetry	209
7.7a	Bed—Great Bed of Ware, dressed with bedlinens	209
8.1	Console table, Italian, Rome, ca. 1700–1725. Gilded linden and poplar, green porphyry, gilt-bronze, 38½" × 69¼" × 27¾"	218
8.2	Armchair, Italian, ca. 1730–1740. A set of four. Carved, gessoed, and gilt walnut with upholstery, 55¼" × 33½" × 34¾"	219
8.3	Desk (secretary) Italian, Venice, ca. 1730–1735. Fall front, mirrored glass. Pine, carved, painted, gilded and varnished linden wood decoration with colored decoupage prints. Overall: 102" × 44" × 23". Desk with doors open and fall front down	220
8.4	Console table, ca. 1700–1725, Italian, Rome. Gilded linden and gilt-bronze, with green porphyry stone. Size 38½" × 69¼" × 27¾"	222
8.5	French armchair, 18th century, Louis XV, Rococo, ca. 1753. One of two made for Baron Johann Ernst Bernstorff, Dutch Ambassador to the court of Versailles. Beech wood, gilded gold frame, Beauvais tapestry upholstery	223
8.6	Commode, ca. 1765–1770, French. Attributed to Léonard Boudin and Pierre-Antoine Foullet. Veneered marquetry with gilt-bronze mounts	223
8.7	Neoclassical giltwood sofa. One of a pair designed by Robert Adam. Workshop of Thomas Chippendale, 1765, for Sir Lawrence Dundas	226
8.8	Mahogany breakfront bookcase design by Robert Adam. Workshop of Thomas Chippendale, 1764, for Sir Lawrence Dundas, 19 Arlington Place, London	227

8.9	English Rococo ribbon-back chair, ca. 1755–1760. After the design of Thomas Chippendale	228
8.10	Queen Anne bonnet-top secretary, ca. 1750, Boston, Massachusetts, Attributed to Benjamin Frothingham. Primary wood sabicu and mahogany	230
8.11	Chest of drawers, ca. 1765 (block-front-chest). Attributed to John Townsend, Newport, Rhode Island. Mahogany, tulip poplar, pine, and chestnut	232
8.12	Side chair, ca. 1769, Pennsylvania. Attributed to Benjamin Randolph, possibly carved by Hercules Courtenay. Mahogany, northern white cedar, with intricately carved pierced splat and surface scrollwork	233
9.1	Large buffet cabinet, 1897, Arts and Crafts, Isle of Man. Designed by Mackay Hugh Baillie Scott for the dining room at Glencrutchery House. Oak with repoussé copper panel and gilt inlay	241
9.2	High-back chair with oval back-rail (Argyle Chair), 1898, Glasgow, Scotland (Arts and Crafts, Scotland). Designed by Charles Rennie Mackintosh for the Argyle Tea Rooms, Argyle Street, Glasgow, Scotland	243
9.3	Display cabinet, ca. 1900, Art Nouveau, France. Louis-Désiré Eugène Gaillard. Walnut, gilt bronze, and glass	246
9.4	Side chair, 1900–1913, Art Nouveau. Designed by Hector Guimard. Pearwood and tooled leathe.	247
9.5	Side Chair, Model No. 371, ca. 1906, Vienna Secession, Vienna, Austria. Designed by Josef Hoffmann. Beech and wood laminate	250
9.6	Armchair No. 8, Vienna Secession, Vienna, Austria. Designed by Otto Wagner. Polished walnut, mother-of-pearl, and brass with leather seat	251
9.7	Side chair, 1910, Prairie Style, Chicago, Illinois (American Arts and Crafts). Designed by George Grant Elmslie. Oak, laminated oak, horsehair	255
9.8	Settle, 1909, Craftsman Furniture, Eastwood, New York (American Arts and Crafts). Designed by Gustave Stickley. Oak and leather upholstery (replacement)	256
10.1	Side chair, 1902, Germany, Deutscher Werkbund. Designed by Peter Behrens. Ebonized oak and woven rattan	265
10.2	Wassily Chair, 1925, manufactured ca. 1927–1928. Design by Marcel Breuer (American, b. Hungary, 1902–1981). Probably manufactured by Standard-Möbel (Dessau, Germany). Chrome-plated steel, canvas H 72.8 × W 77 × D 68 cm	268
10.3	Cesca Armchair, 1928, Germany. Designed by Marcel Breuer. Polished tubular steel frame, and black painted beechwood, with woven cane seat	268

■ **Illustrations**

10.4	Red/Blue Chair, ca. 1918, Netherlands. Designer Gerrit Thomas Rietveld. Plywood construction, painted red, blue, black, and yellow	270
10.5	Barcelona Chair, 1929, Germany. Designed by Ludwig Mies van de Rohe. Bent chrome-plated flat steel frame with leather strap supports for leather back and seat cushion. Back and seat cushions are tufted	272
10.6	MR Chair, 1927, Germany. Designed by Ludwig Mies van de Rohe and Lilly Reich. Nickel-plated bent tubular steel frame. Without arms, leather seat and back; with arms, rattan continuous seat and back	273
10.7	LC 1 Sling Chair (Fauteuil Basculant No. B 301), 1928, Paris. Designed by Charles-Édouard Jeanneret-Gris, Charlotte Perriand, and Pierre Jeanneret. Chrome-plated bent tubular steel and leather upholstery	273
10.8	LC 2 (Fauteuil Grand Comfort), 1928, Paris. Designed by Charles-Édouard Jeanneret-Gris, Charlotte Perriand, and Pierre Jeanneret. Chrome-plated bent tubular steel with seat, back, and arm cushions upholstered in leather	274
10.9	LC 4 Chaise Lounge (B 306 Chaise Lounge), 1928, Paris. Designed by Charles-Édouard Jeanneret-Gris, Charlotte Perriand, and Pierre Jeanneret	275
10.10	Charlotte Perriand resting on the chaise lounge, LC 4 Chaise Lounge (B 306 Chaise Lounge), 1928. Designed by Le Corbusier, Charlotte Perriand, and Pierre Jeanneret	275
11.1	Armchair, 1924–1926, France. Designed by Pierre Chareau. Rosewood veneer with metal bun feet	284
11.2	Armchair, 1925, France. Designed by Pierre Chareau. Bleached mahogany, fully upholstered	284
11.3	Table Model SN 3, ca. 1927, France. Designed by Pierre Chareau. Metal work by Louis Dalvet (French, 1885–1950). Cut mahogany and wrought iron	285
11.4	Black Lacquered Block Screen, ca. 1922–1923, France. Pierre Bobot. Wood blocks, with black lacquer and aluminum connectors	288
11.5	Table (Black & White), ca. 1922–1924, France. Designed by Eileen Gray. Oak and sycamore, painted black and white	289
11.6	Transat Chair, "Fauteuil Transatlantique," 1925–1927, France. Designed by Eileen Gray. Wood, lacquer, and chromed brackets	289
11.7	Bibendum Chair, 1926, France. Designed by Eileen Gray. A semi-circular form, comprised of three stacked fully leather upholstered tire-like rolls which define the chair back and arms, with a chrome-finished steel base	290
11.8	Adjustable Table, 1927, France. Designed by Eileen Gray. The frame is polished chromium-plated tubular steel with glass in-set top	290

11.9	Cité Armchair, 1930, France. Designed by Jean Prouvé. The frame consists of powder-coated steel runners and leather belt armrest with fully wood seat and backrest. The Vitra collection offers a variety of woods and colors for the steel frame	294
11.10	Standard Chair, 1934/1950, France. Designed by Jean Prouvé. Steel frame, flat and tubular with a wood seat and backrest. The Vitra collection offers a variety of woods and colors for the steel frame	295
11.11	Guéridon Table, 1949, France. Designed by Jean Prouvé. The table is constructed entirely of wood. Triangulated legs are organized in a triangle formation, inherently rigid. The connectors are powder-coated steel struts	295
11.12	EM Table, "Entretoise Métallique," 1950, France. Designed by Jean Prouvé. The medium is sheet metal and wood. The top is supported by metal triangulated legs which are turned out in a diagonal slant and braced with a metal tie creating a visually balance piece	296
11.13	Revolving Armchair (LC 7), 1928, France. Designed by Charlotte Perriand. Chrome-plated tubular steel with leather upholstered crest rail and seat	298
11.14	Bookcase, Maison de Tunisie, 1952, France. Designed by Charlotte Perriand and Jean Prouvé. The medium is mahogany, aluminum, pine, canvas, and lacquer, with color variations	299
11.15	Wall Cabinet, 1939, France. Designed by Charlotte Perriand for the office of Georges Blanchon, Administration du Bureau Central de la Construction, Paris. The medium is fir, aluminum, and lacquered mahogany	300
12.1	Swag Arm Chair, 1956, U.S., Herman Miller Furniture Company, produced 1958–1964. Designed by George Nelson (1908–1986). The shell is fiberglass-reinforced plastic, with legs which are steel 16-gauge adjustable glides	310
12.2	Coconut Chair, 1958, U.S., Herman Miller Furniture Company. Design by George Mulhauser (1922–2002), for George Nelson Associates. Seat formed of fiberglass-reinforced polyester with steel legs	311
12.3	DCW (Dining Chair Wood), Herman Miller Furniture Company, ca. 1946. Designed by Charles Eames (1907–1978) and Ray Eames (1912–1988). The medium is molded birch plywood, rubber, steel, and resin	312
12.4	670/671 Lounge Chair and Ottoman, 1956, U.S., Herman Miller Furniture Company. Designed by Charles Eames (1907–1978) and Ray Eames (1912–1988). The medium is molded plywood and rosewood veneers, case aluminum, black leather-covered latex foam, and down upholstery	313

Illustrations

12.5	Sofa, The Girard Group, 1965, U.S. Designed by Alexander Girard (1907–1993) for Braniff Airline. Re-created in 1967 for Herman Miller Furniture Company. The outer shell may come in a variety of fabrics or painted, and the welt selected from one of three colors. The inner shell and cushion may be upholstered in a variety of fabrics. The shell rests on steel legs with a circular disk pad for the floor	314
12.6	Chair, The Girard Group, 1965, U.S. Designed by Alexander Girard (1907–1993) for Braniff Airline. Re-created in 1967 for Herman Miller Furniture Company. The outer shell may come in a variety of fabrics or painted, and the welt selected from one of three colors. The inner shell and cushion may be upholstered in a variety of fabrics. The shell rests on steel legs with a circular disk pad for the floor	315
12.7	Fabrics designed by Alexander Girard for the Herman Miller Furniture Company. Demonstrating his signature designs and color palette *(left)* Circles—Barberpole, 1957 *(right)* Palio, 1964	315
12.8	Sofa, Knoll Lounge Collection, 1954, U.S., Knoll International. Designed by Florence Knoll (1917–2019). Modern rectilinear form, angular profile. With six legs in heavy gauge steel with polished chrome finish. Seat and back covering is tufted and covered with a polyester fiber fill	318
12.9	Lounge Chair, Knoll Lounge Collection, 1954, U.S. Designed by Florence Knoll (1917–2019). Modern, rectilinear form, angular profile. Metal base is heavy gauge steel. The chair frame is wood construction. The back and seat cushions are tufted	319
12.10	Side Chair, Knoll International, Pedestal Collection (Tulip), 1956, U.S. Designed by Eero Saarinen (1910–1961). Its medium is an aluminum base, with a fused plastic finish, molded plastic shell reinforced with fiberglass, and an upholstered seat cushion	319
12.11	Coffee Table, Pedestal Group Collection (1955–1956), U.S., Knoll International. Designed by Eero Saarinen (1910–1961). The Collection's medium is an aluminum base with a fused plastic finish, molded plastic shell reinforced with fiberglass, and an upholstered seat cushion	320
12.12	Knoll International, Side Chair, 1955. Designed by Harry Bertoia (1915–1978). The medium is a steel frame with black lacquered metal and plastic	320
12.13	Knoll International, Small Diamond Chair, after 1952. Designed by Harry Bertoia (1915–1978). The medium is a steel frame, covered in vinyl, with upholstered Naugahyde cushions	321
13.1	Beaubourg Desk Chair, ca. 1976, France. Designed by Michel Cadestin and Georges Laurent. Galvanized steel-wire frame, steel star-shape base, and leather seat	328

13.2	Seconda Chair, 1980, Italy. Prima Chair, 1982, Italy. Designed by Mario Botta. The medium for both chairs is a metal frame with perforated metal seat and polyurethane foam cylinder back rollers	329
13.3	Dr. Sonderbar Chair, ca. 1983, France. Designed by Philippe Starck for XO Design. The medium is nickel-finish tubular steel frame and perforated steel seat and welded fabrication	330
13.4	Reading Room Chair, ca. 1978, U.S. Designed by Richard Meier for Aye Simon Reading Room, Solomon R. Guggenheim Museum, New York City. The chair became part of the "Richard Meier Collection" for Knoll. The medium is wood with a black lacquered finish	331
13.5	Rocking Chaise, 1982, U.S. Designed by Richard Meier for the "Richard Meier Collection" for Knoll. The medium is wood with a black lacquered finish	331
13.6	Carlton Room Divider, 1981, Italy. Designed by Ettore Sottsass for the Memphis Group. A seminal Postmodern furniture piece. Manufactured by Memphis Milano. The material is medium-density fiber board (MDF) and plastic laminate	334
13.7	First Chair, 1983, Italy. Designed by Michele De Lucchi for the Memphis Group. A Postmodern design. The medium is powder-coated steel with lacquered wood	334
13.8	Bel Air Chair, 1982, manufactured, 1984, Italy. Designed by Peter Shire for the Memphis Group. A Postmodern design. The medium is a wood frame with cotton upholstery over foam and painted wood	335
13.9	Sunar Hauserman Loveseat, 1980, U.S. Designed by Michael Graves for the Sunar Hauserman company. A Postmodern design. The medium is a bird's eye maple frame, with ebony inlays and vibrant peacock-blue upholstered back and seat	336
13.10	Parrot Chair, 1980, U.S. Designed by Michael Graves. Manufactured by Sawaya Moroni, Milan. A Postmodern design. The medium is curly maple, with black lacquered rolled arms and burgundy leather seat	336
13.11	Arcadia Table, 1990, Italy. Designed by Michael Graves. Manufactured by Meccani Arredamenti, Italy. A Postmodern design. The medium is arcadia, in arable with ebony inlays, and black lacquered wood columns	337
13.12	Side Chair "Easy Edges," 1971, U.S. Manufactured ca. 1982. Designed by Frank Gehry. Design emphasis Deconstructivism	338
13.13	"Cross Check" Chair, 1989–1991, U.S. Designed by Frank Gehry for Knoll Associates, 1989. The chair was part of a collection and series. The medium is laminated strips of bent maple	339

Illustrations

14.1	Grass Armchair, 21st century, U.S. Windmark Collection for Landscape Forms, designed by Margaret McCurry. The medium is aluminum steel with a powder-coat paint finish	344
14.2	Gingko Leaves Armchair, 21st century, U.S. Windmark Collection designed by Margaret McCurry. Outdoor furniture Armchair, the medium is aluminum steel with a powder-coat paint finish, color: buttercup	344
14.3	Almodington Bench, ca. 1750, Somerset County, Maryland. "Garden seat" for Almodington Plantation. Medium yellow pine, paint. Dimension LOA 96¼", HOA 45½", DOA 28"	347
14.4	Munder-Skiles Outdoor Funiture replica, Almodington Bench, ca. 1750, Somerset County, Maryland	347
14.5	Windsor Chair, "Sack Back." Similar to the design as the chair at Carpenter's Hall, 1774	348
14.6	Adirondack Chair, East Coast, U.S. Similar to the design of the early 20th-century traditional Adirondack Chair	348
14.7	Westport Chair, Westport, New York. Similar to the design of an early 20th-century original Westport Chair	348

Introduction

The premise of this book, *An Illustrated Guide to Furniture History*, was to develop an appropriate teaching tool and alternative way to learn about furniture history other than via the conventional semester survey course. I have held on to the notion of a textbook publication for many years. Its origins date back to the 1990s when I was charged with designing a two-day undergraduate course titled "The History of Furniture Seminar." This nonconventional seminar approach emphasizes the immersion-learning model. The paramount feature of this model is to gain knowledge of the subject—furniture history—in several weeks instead of in a 15-week semester course.

An Illustrated Guide to Furniture History to a certain degree emulates "The History of Furniture Seminar" course—in essence, it is a seminar. Simultaneously, students or adult learners will strengthen their visual literacy through participation in this immersion-learning model and prescribed methodological approach—the Analysis of Form: Nine-Step Methodology. The ninth step and crucial part of the process is the use of visual notes. This step is the connective tissue between learning furniture history and visual literacy. The concept of visual notes has roots in design disciplines such as architecture, interior architecture, interior design, industrial design, and landscape architecture. Visual notes are a convention whereby analytical documentation is recorded graphically rather than with words, so sketching, drawing, diagramming, and rendering collectively become the analysis tool.

Graphic communication is intrinsic to the pedagogical construct for design disciplines. Using this methodological approach—working through this process will imprint on one's mind the findings—key features of the furniture piece are chosen to investigate. It is the idea of interaction between brain and hand, memory and muscle memory that will facilitate recall and recognition—an imprint in the student's memory. Recent studies about memory conducted by theorists have been done in relation to the process involved in remembering. These studies demonstrated the intrinsic relationship between drawing and memory. At the end of Chapter 14, you will find a listing of theorist names and experiments/studies for your reference and further investigation.

Part I—Furniture and the built environment—is the foundation for the rest of the material in the book and addresses furniture within the context of the built environment. The first chapter is dedicated to the historical perspective, the second examines construction principles, and the third chapter looks at the categorization of furniture. Part II—Understanding the piece—will prepare the reader for the visual analysis that will occur in Part III—Object of desire: Furniture periods, movements and styles, from Antiquity to the 20th century. Therefore, Part II, Chapter 4 and Chapter 5, will address visual representation and how to develop and utilize visual notes as an analysis tool.

In Chapter 4—The Analysis of Form—the author depicts visually the structural organization of the methodological process, a three-category structure: History, Aesthetics, and Visual Notes, with visual notes being the ninth step and a crucial part of the process. The two key aspects critical to the Nine-Step Methodology are practice examples and visual notes exercises. These aspects are integral parts for Step 9, and indelibly linked to the final drawing—the *Visual Notes Exercise*. In Chapter 4, the author will use practice examples to demonstrate how to work through the Nine-Step process. The examples will address each step by using drawings/sketching and written notes when appropriate.

The intent of Chapter 5—A graphic narrative—is to prepare the student and adult learner for Part III. As mentioned previously Part III could be considered analogous to a survey course. For each chapter in Part III, the student will survey the "pictorial timeline" applying the Analysis of Form: Nine-Step Methodology, Steps 1–9. The student will need a sketchbook on hand to use for sketching; the recommended type and size is a hardcover, 8″ × 11″ or 9″ × 12″. Here the student or adult learner will sketch practice examples and visual note studies. The preparation for Part III will occur in this chapter through reviewing sketch techniques and methods of design professionals. Design professionals use sketching as a tool for communicating their design process, research, investigation and analysis. The author has selected furniture sketching examples from local Chicago practitioners—architects and designers—and other notable design professionals spanning the globe and decades. These examples will serve as a guide for your own practice examples and visual note studies you chose to investigate on the pictorial timeline. The end goal and apex of your analysis—the final *Visual Notes Exercise*, evidence of having grasp the essence of the pictorial timeline piece.

For Part III, the pictorial timeline furniture pieces are representative of conventional cannons pertaining to Western civilization. Once one arrives at Part III, the student or adult learner will survey the pictorial timeline for each chapter, select their desired pieces to analyze, and apply the Analysis of Form: Nine-Step Methodology, Steps 1–9 by using their sketchbook as well as referring to the professional examples from Chapter 5 to use as models for their own work.

To conclude this Introduction a few last thoughts. Graphic communication is intrinsic to the pedagogical construct for design disciplines. I firmly believe that for those who are captivated and interested in the visual world and the objects that define its richness, there isn't a more appropriate way to learn about furniture history than through visual means, using graphic communication as the primary tool for learning.

PART I

Furniture and the built environment

1 A historical perspective

Furniture is an integral part of architecture and interior design. An awareness of how fundamentally furniture is integrated into the built environment is crucial to understanding its design and development—remembering that at certain points in history, furniture was often designed apart from its need to function. Inseparable from social, political, and economic influences, furniture design and its history reflect the changing living conditions and lifestyles of developing civilizations.[1] Exactly defining furniture styles can be arduous because furniture styles evolve in a historical continuum, each reflecting the one preceding it and incubating the one to follow, running concurrently and interweaving or overlapping in both time and place.[2] For individuals interested in understanding furniture design and its history, placing furniture in a historical context—time period, social and political factors, including wars, religions, dynastic marriages, etc.—is important. The context allows one to see how each design grew out of a design that had gone before. The concept of designing began only 400 or so years ago.[3] Design comes from the Italian noun, *disegno*, meaning drawing or design; it's a term used during the 16th and 17th centuries to designate a form and discipline required for representation of the ideal form of an object in visual arts.[4]

Regarding furniture physiognomics in a historical continuum, this book uses a "pictorial timeline" for reference. This chapter introduces the pictorial timeline in Timeline 1.1—the complete timeline from Antiquity through to the 20th century. Timeline 1.1 provides the complete time range of the furniture covered in Chapters 6–13. On the subsequent pages, the pictorial timeline is enlarged and divided into three sections for visual clarity, Timeline 1.2, Timeline 1.3, and Timeline 1.4.

The pictorial timeline will assist the student or adult learner in understanding the evolution of furniture design and styles and is intrinsic to the premise of this book's nonconventional approach, immersion-learning model, and prescribed methodology—the Analysis of Form: Nine-Step Methodology. For the pictorial timeline, a small selection of furniture pieces that are indicative of the period and capture the aesthetic spirit of the time has been chosen. The timeline isn't extensive in the number of pieces chosen but selects what are deemed paramount examples. The pictorial timeline moves chronologically, but not century by century, spanning from Antiquity to the 20th century. This pictorial timeline consists of critical points in time that define the Western canons pertaining to furniture history and interior design; the goal, as mentioned in the Introduction, is for the student or adult learner to gain knowledge about furniture history through the use of visual notes (Chapters 6–14), simultaneously reinforcing visual literacy. Using this type of timeline for investigation of furniture design and history exposes the relationship between the physical form of furniture and social concepts of class, status, and gender. This indelible timeline should facilitate a visual understanding of design changes through history, a journey from Antiquity to the 20th century, noting furniture's evolution from functional and utilitarian to decorative-arts status, or "object of desire." By the end of the book, the reader will possess a basic understanding of furniture history and will have developed a foundation of knowledge that will facilitate continued learning of the subject if he or she chooses.

There will be some unevenness content-wise with respect to the canons. In-depth coverage will be dedicated to periods that have a stronger impact on furniture, such as the historical periods defined by monarchs, specifically 18th-century England during the reigns of George I through George III; in France, in the period of Louis XIV through Louis XVI; and comparable periods in American history. Briefer coverage will be given to Antiquity—Egypt, Greco-Roman classicism, Renaissance, and Baroque.

Important to understanding a furniture piece historically is gaining familiarity in the various ways of furniture making—ways in which furniture has been constructed. Chapter 2, Construction principles, will focus on 18th-century furniture construction because of the advancement in technology at the time. This chapter centers on the salient 18th-century furniture pieces, those that represent technological advancements in furniture assembly. Examples from France, England, and America are reviewed. In Chapter 2, the main focus is on wood construction methods and the role of the cabinetmaker, who was responsible for design conception and production. Also discussed is the role of the craftsmen who assisted in the production—turner, joiner, *ebéniste*, etc. This chapter reviews tools and equipment, such as the turning wheel and lathe, and detailed furniture examples that have been designed and shaped using these tools. Other examples indicate assembly methods (e.g., mortise-and-tenon connections, dovetail joints, rabbet joints, scarf joints) and furniture pieces representing these methods, including chairs with turned legs, stile backs, table legs, etc.

As mentioned in the Introduction, due to the book's premise, immersion-learning model, and nine-step methodological approach, all chapters pay particular attention to the visual images. Serving as guides and tools that reinforce this learning model, the images represent a range of delineation methods, techniques, and illustrative approaches, and include quick sketches, tightly delineated drawings, or refined rendered drawings. Examples representing a range of rendering techniques (e.g., watercolor, colored pencils, markers, oil pastels) are also included throughout the book.

Becoming familiar with 18th-century construction principles in Chapter 2 will provide the platform for understanding how to categorize a piece within a timeframe and place of origin. Chapter 3, Piece categorically, describes how to do this by examining 18th-century French, English, and American furniture examples to show how furniture can be categorized and identified by specific physical features. The chapter explores ubiquitous pieces of this period (e.g., chairs, bureaus, case pieces) and how certain pieces possess anthropomorphic qualities, such as a back, leg, arm, foot, or knee. Additionally, the importance of provenance and the impact it has on a piece of furniture's physical characteristics is discussed. These characteristic examples range from the form of a piece, type of joinery, material, and the finish—in essence, the overall aesthetic quality. This section emphasizes important questions to consider regarding provenance (i.e., time period, country of origin, and cabinetmaker) and the physical considerations that speak to regional and cultural influences, such as chair-back variations and various leg forms, and tops of case pieces and high chests. These questions are an integral part of the Analysis of Form: Nine-Step Methodology, introduced in Chapter 4.

On the following pages are the pictorial timeline sections. It is recommended that you spend some time perusing the timelines, familiarizing yourself with the selections and periods. Remember each chapter will have its own enlarged section once the reader gets to Chapters 6–13. A reminder: The timeline consists of only a small selection of pieces indicative of the period—capturing the aesthetic spirit of the time and representing critical points in time that define the canons pertaining to furniture history. The timeline reads from left to right; headings and labels identify the period, movement and/or style, and country. To reiterate, the organization through time references three countries: France, England, and America. The timeline begins with Antiquity—Egypt, Greece, and Rome—then moves past many centuries to the 16th and 17th centuries, Renaissance and Baroque, Italy and France; next to 18th-century America, France, and England; and ends with the late 19th- to 20th-century America, France, and England.

■ An Illustrated Guide to Furniture History

Pictorial Timeline: country, period, movement, style

Antiquity

Egypt New Kingdom 1567–1320 | Greece 4th–5th cent. | Rome Early Imperial Period 1st–2nd cent.

Pictorial Timeline: country, period, movement, style

Renaissance

Italy, circa 14th–16th c. | France, circa 15th–17th c. | England, Late 15th–Early 16th c.

Pictorial Timeline: country, period, movement, style

Europe *Early 20th century*

Deutscher Werkbund 1907–1934 | De Stijl, ca 1917–1931 | International Style ca 1920s–1930s | Bauhaus 1919–1933

Pictorial Timeline: country, period, movement, style

Europe *Early 20th century*

Pierre Chareau (1883–1950) | Eileen Gray (1878–1976) | Jean Prouvé (1901–1984) | Charlotte Perriand (1903–1999)

1.1
Pictorial timeline (all sections)

A historical perspective

Pictorial Timeline: country, period, movement, style

18th Century

Italy, Baroque–Rococo ca. 1725–1774 | France, Rococo ca. 1723–1774

Pictorial Timeline: country, period, movement, style

Europe 19th and 20th century

England, Georgian Period – George Hill | England & Scotland Arts and Crafts 1860–1929 | France Art Nouveau 1890–1900 | Austria Vienna Secession (or Wiener Werkstätte) 1897–1906

America 19th and 20th century

America – Late Colonial ca. 1720–1780 | America Arts and Crafts – Prairie Style 1893–ca. on Craftsman Style 1895–1920

Pictorial Timeline: country, period, movement, style

America – Early–Mid 20th century

Herman Miller Furniture company (1923 –) | Knoll International (1938 –)

Nelson (1908–1986) | Hans G. Knoll (1914–1955) Florence Knoll Bassett (1917–2019)
George Mulhauser (1922–2002) | Eero Saarinen (1910–1961) Harry Bertoia (1915–1978)
Alexander Girard (1907–1993)
Charles Eames (1907–1978) Ray Eames (1912–1988)

Pictorial Timeline: country, period, movement, style

America – Late 20th century

Late Modernism High-Tech Movement | Postmodern Movement | Deconstructivism Movement
Michael Graves (1934–) | Frank Gehry (1929–)
George Nelson (1942–) | Peter Shire (1947–)
Mario Botta (1943–)
Richard Meier (1934–)

1.1 (Continued)

An Illustrated Guide to Furniture History

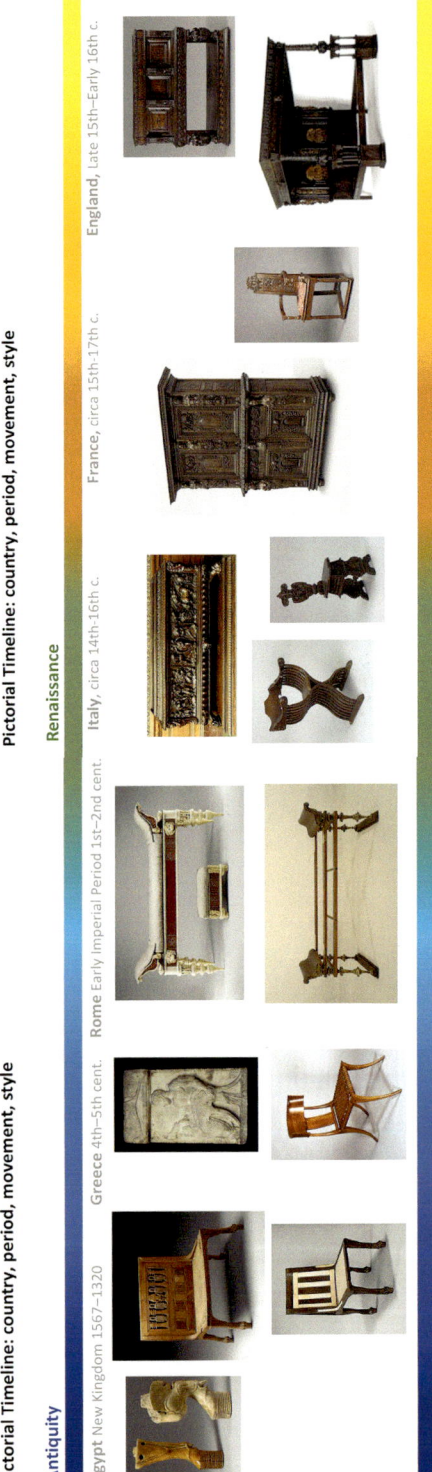

1.2
Pictorial timeline—Antiquity, Renaissance

A historical perspective

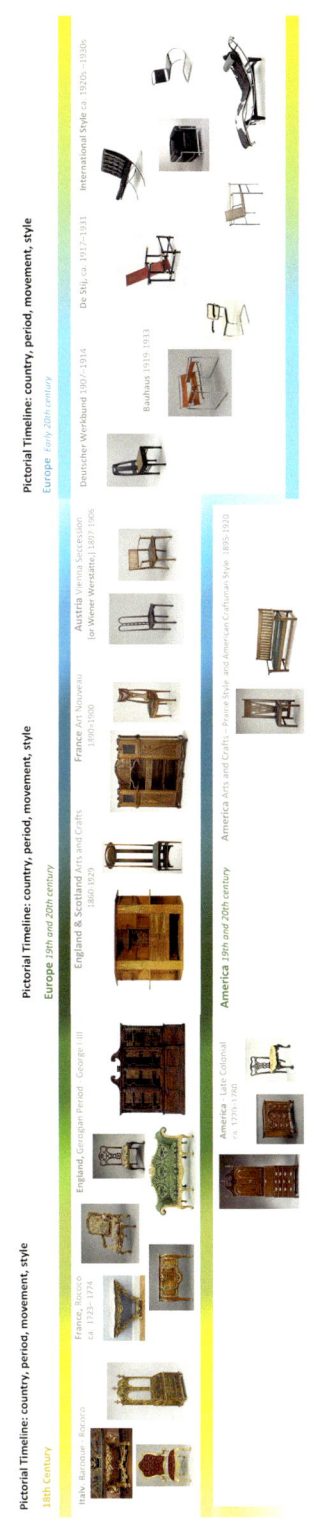

1.3
Pictorial timeline — 18th–20th century: Europe, America

An Illustrated Guide to Furniture History

1.4
Pictorial timeline—20th century: Europe, America

NOTES

1. Treena Crochet, *Designer's Guide to Furniture Styles* (New Jersey: Prentice Hall, 1999), Preface, p.XI.
2. H.D. Molesworth and John Kenworthy-Browne, *Three Centuries of Furniture in Color* (A Studio Book, Viking Press, 1972), Prefatory Note.
3. Judith Gura, *The Guide to Period Styles for Interiors From the 17th Century to the Present* (New York: Fairchild Books, Bloomsbury, 2016), Introduction, p.XI.
4. www.ductuibart.cin/browe/disegno.

2 Construction principles

With respect to 18th-century French, English, and American furniture, the discussion on construction principles must begin with the assiduous cabinetmaker and his shop. The term *cabinetmaker* in England and the American colonies refers to one who doesn't necessarily produce only cabinets, but furniture (e.g., case pieces, chairs, tables, desks) in a workshop, or atelier, where the production takes place. In 18th-century France, the term used for *cabinetmaker* is *ébéniste* (originally rendered in the 17th century)—one who works with ebony. Specific to chair design, the French term is *menuisier*, which denotes a woodcarver or chair maker.[1]

    The nascent 18th-century cabinetmaker's shop was a place of both creativity and productivity. The name of the business was that of the owner, who was the determiner of design and aesthetic direction. Typically, these shops flourished through generations—father, son, grandson, and great-grandson. The generational continuation of the trade and business applied not only to the owner but also to the craftsman/artisan and his descendants. In regard to job hierarchy in this line of work, there was master, or master craftsman; journeyman; and apprentice. If not an inheritor of the business or connected through family, one could be hopeful to work upward through the hierarchy, eventually becoming a workshop owner. The craftsman should not be thought of as a laborer but as an artisan, each with his own specialty in the design and production process—turning, carving, and finishing—making each piece special, adding subtleties, thoughtfulness, and refinements. In England from the mid- to late Georgian period, the leading cabinetmakers were known as the "big three": Thomas Chippendale, George Hepplewhite, and Thomas Sheraton. However, one should not forget during the later part of the 18th century the contribution of the Scottish Adam brothers: Robert, James, and John. The notable American cabinetmakers of the mid- to late 18th century were emigrants from Europe, such as John Townsend and John Goddard (Newport, Rhode Island); Benjamin Frothingham (Charlestown, Massachusetts); Benjamin Randolph, Thomas Affleck, and William Savery (Philadelphia); and Thomas Elfe (Charleston, South Carolina). The leading 18th-century French *ébénistes*—during the reigns of Louis XIV through Louis XVI—were André-Charles Boulle for the Garde-Meuble of Louis XV; Gilles Joubert; Jean-François Oeben, who worked extensively for Madame de Pompadour; and German emigrants Jean Henri Riesener (Johann Heinrich Riesener) and David Roentgen, Marie-Antoinette's favorite cabinetmakers.

When it comes to successfully joining wood, whether building a house or a chair, there are few construction principles. The greatest challenge is joining the wood components at right angles to one another. In the cabinetmaker's workshop, a critical role was that of "joiner," who worked his craft of joinery. Through joining pieces of wood, the joiner helped bring designed furniture pieces such as chairs, tables, bookshelves, breakfronts, and case pieces to fruition. The types of joinery found in the earliest archaeological examples from the ancient world are also found in the 18th century and today. Many of these ancient methods were still found after the advent of metal fasteners (nails, screws, etc.) simply because the joints had proven to be so strong.[2] The function of a joint is to make frames and increase the length and surface of solid wood. This section discusses four important joint forms in furniture design and construction: mortise-and-tenon, dovetail, edge, and spline, which are illustrated in Figure 2.1 through Figure 2.9.

Furniture framing consists primarily of joining pieces at right angles. The strongest joint for joining wood at right angles is the *mortise-and-tenon* joint. This ancient joint is found in Egyptian furniture thousands of years old.[3] The joint is a square peg (the tenon) fitted precisely to a square hole (the mortise). The mortise-and-tenon joint comes in many variations, each suited to a particular purpose or craft tradition. This chapter illustrates the most common. The typical tenon is rectangular in cross-section, as is the mortise.[4] This gives great resistance to twisting forces. The tighter the fit, and the longer and taller the tenon, the stronger the joint will be. The so-called *through-tenon*, which completely penetrates the mortise-bearing member, is the strongest of all. It is important that the tenon does not slide out of the mortise. The most common means to secure the tenon is with a peg, which fits into a hole near the opening of the mortise, in combination with lashing (binding, wrapping, or fastening), as well as with wedges, which spread the tenon in the mortise and prevent the tenon from being pulled out of the mortise.

The joint typically seen in box or drawer construction is the *dovetail joint*. The term "dovetail joint" can refer to one tail or many in a row, such as those used on the side of a drawer. The joint is a wedge-shaped tenon, or the "tail," on one component, which overlaps a corresponding wedge-shaped slot in a second component. The "pin" is the portion of wood surrounding these slots. Except in decorative joinery, all the pins are on one board, and all the tails are on another. Like the mortise-and-tenon joint, the strongest dovetail joint is made when the pins and tails go all the way through the joint.[5]

The *edge joint* joins the long edge of boards together to make a panel. This is another ancient technique. These joints increase the width of the wood surface, such as for a tabletop whose edges are glued together. Simple edge gluing requires that absolutely straight and square surfaces be prepared. Historically, glues prepared from animal skin were the most common; comparable glues are used today. More elaborate joinery, such as tongue-and-groove (a modified mortise-and-tenon), is used only for alignment of the matching surfaces. Veneering can also be thought of as a specialized form of edge joint, whereas the wood veneer sheets are glued.[6]

■ An Illustrated Guide to Furniture History

The *spline joint* is used to increase length. An example of these fundamental joints can be found in 18th-century case furniture construction, such as a "high boy," or "high chest." A high boy is a cabinet with a lower-case and upper-case section of drawers. Typically, the lower case, a mortise-and-tenon frame with legs, would be a box joined by dovetails at the corners. Doors of frame and panel construction would enclose the case. The frames would be joined by mortise-and-tenon joints, with panels (perhaps two or more edge-glued boards) fitted into a groove on the inside edge of the frame. In the best mortise-and-tenon and dovetail joinery, no glue is required.[7]

On the following page are copies of detailed drawings from antiquity illustrating furniture joinery of a typical ancient Theban chair from Upper Egypt (Plate 2.1 and Plate 2.2). The Theban Necropolis is a necropolis on the west bank of the Nile, opposite Thebes (Luxor). The area was used for ritual burials for much of the Pharaonic period, especially during the New Kingdom.[8]

These studies are made directly from furniture in the Louvre under the direction of M. Garnier from the Collège Technique Boulle in Paris. These images illustrate the variety of joints that existed and were used for necropolis furniture (Plate 2.1).

Here are more studies of the same period, illustrating joint variety from the Theban Necropolis. These drawings were also made in the Louvre and documented under the supervision of Garnier (Plate 2.2).

The following drawings on the next several pages are examples of the four important joint forms in furniture design and construction discussed earlier: mortise-and-tenon, dovetail, edge, and spline (Figure 2.1–Figure 2.9).

Construction principles

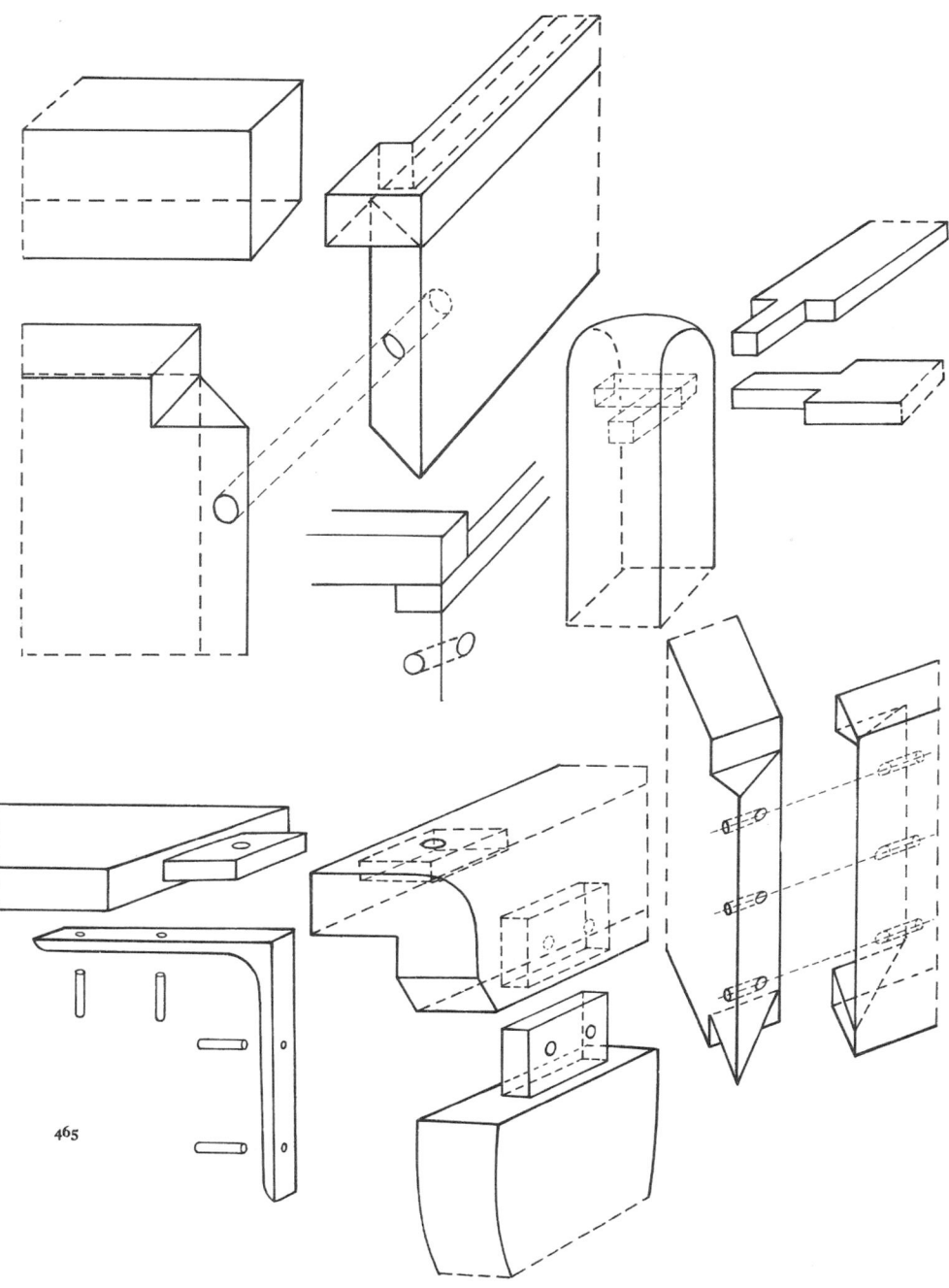

Plate 2.1
Detail drawings of furniture joinery from XVIIIth Dynasty Egyptian furniture. Collège Boulle, Paris.
Source: Hollis S. Baker, *Furniture in the Ancient World: Origins and Evolutions 3100–475 B.C.* (New York: Macmillan Company, 1966), p.305.

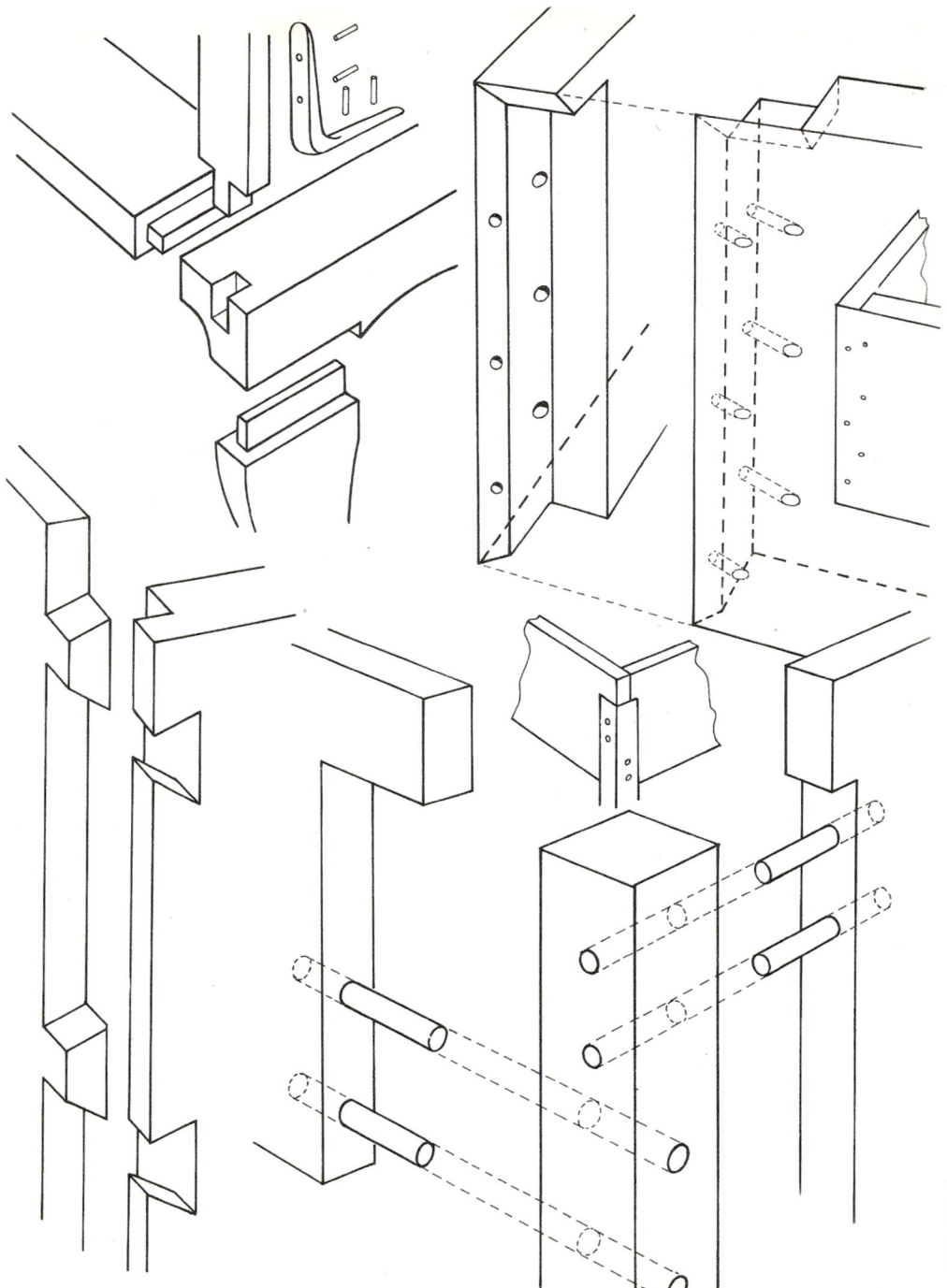

Plate 2.2
Detail drawings of furniture joinery. Collège Boulle, Paris.

Source: Hollis S. Baker, *Furniture in the Ancient World: Origins and Evolutions 3100–475 B.C.* (New York: Macmillan Company, 1966), p.306.

Construction principles

Figure 2.1
Mortise-and-tenon joints A–D.

Author's illustration.

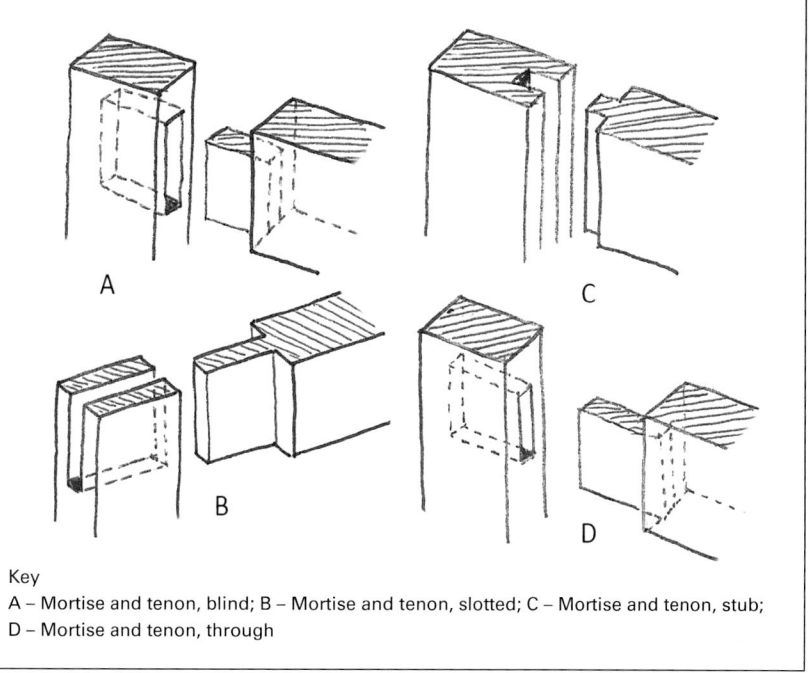

Key
A – Mortise and tenon, blind; B – Mortise and tenon, slotted; C – Mortise and tenon, stub;
D – Mortise and tenon, through

Figure 2.2
Mortise-and-tenon joints, furniture detail examples.

Author's illustration.

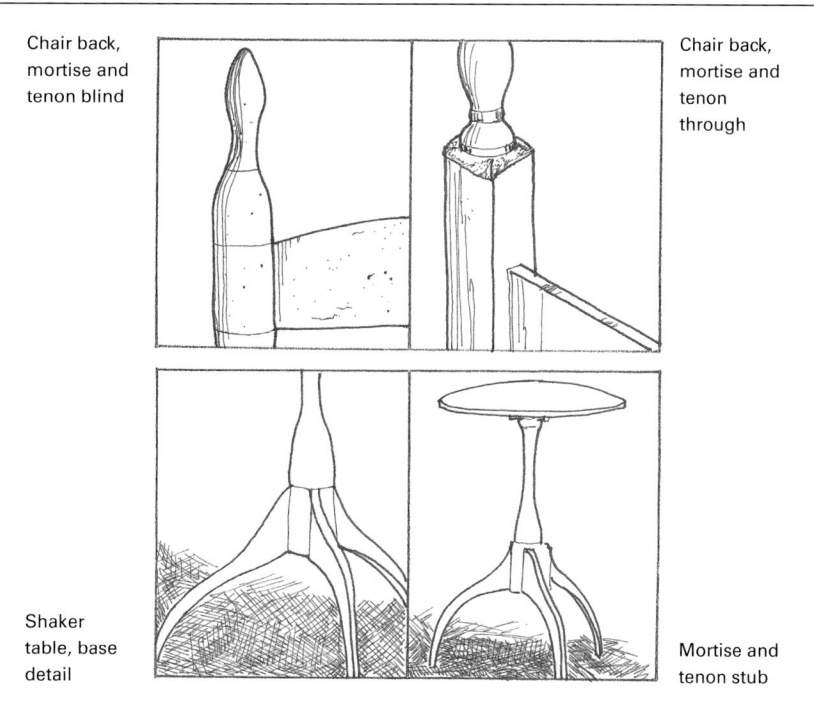

Chair back, mortise and tenon blind

Chair back, mortise and tenon through

Shaker table, base detail

Mortise and tenon stub

■ An Illustrated Guide to Furniture History

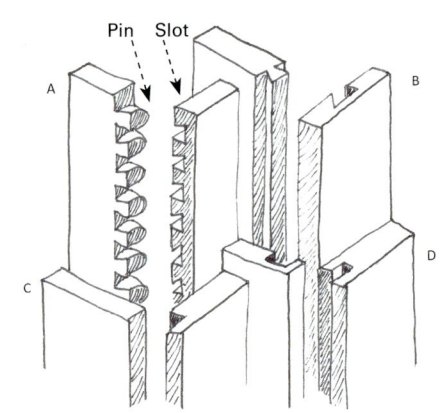

Figure 2.3
Dovetail joints A–D.
Author's illustration.

Key
A – Dovetail
B – Dovetail dado
C – Dovetail rabbet
D – Dovetail lock

Handmade dovetail
drawing by Author

Figure 2.4
Dovetail joints—drawers.

Machine made dovetail
drawing by Author

Sketch by Author, Kindel
Furniture Bombé Desk,
Winterthur Museum Collection

Figure 2.5
Dovetail joints—Bombé Desk.

Kindel Furniture Company employee
Bobby Owens finishing dovetail
joints, Massachusetts Bombé Desk,
Winterthur Museum Collection

18

Construction principles

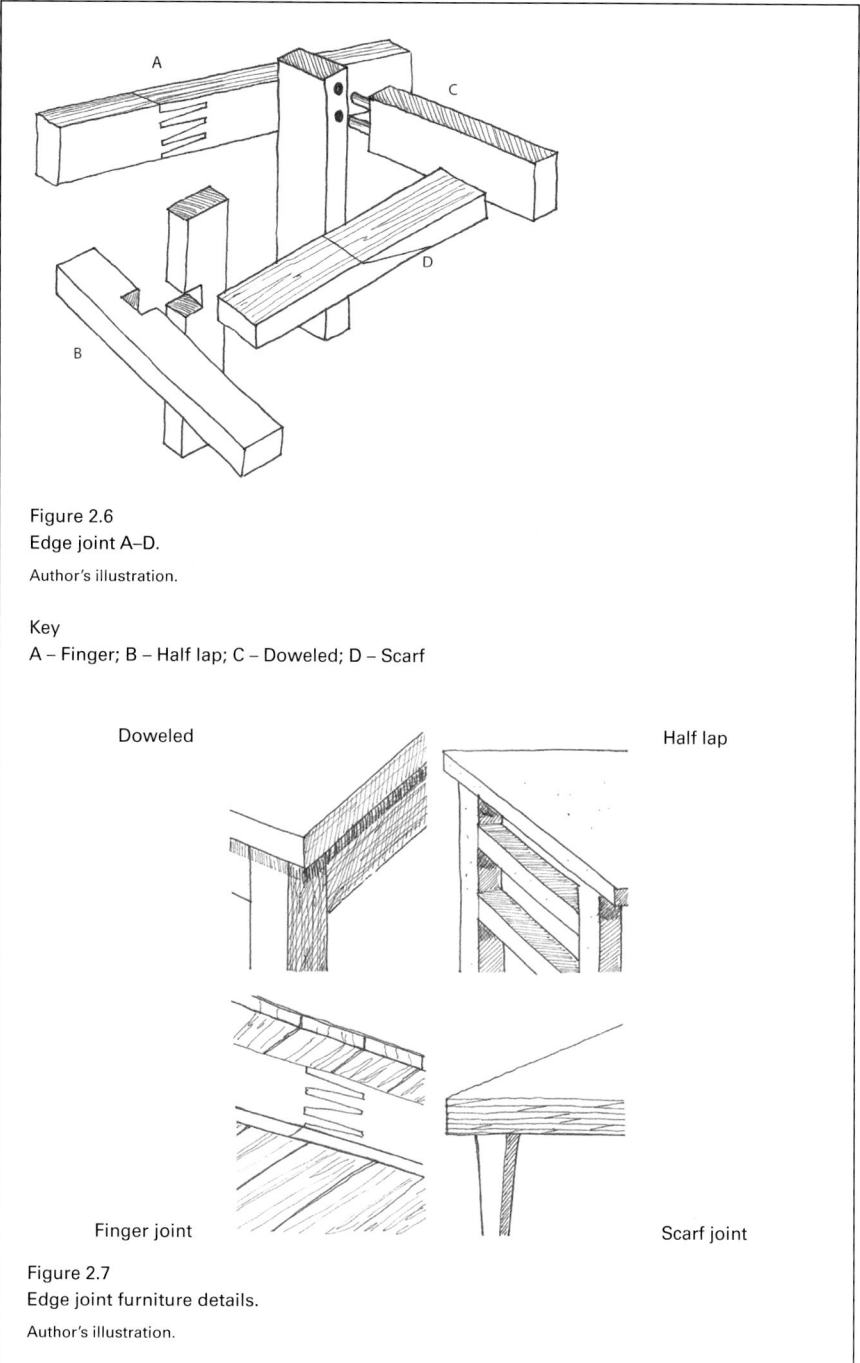

Figure 2.6
Edge joint A–D.
Author's illustration.

Key
A – Finger; B – Half lap; C – Doweled; D – Scarf

Figure 2.7
Edge joint furniture details.
Author's illustration.

■ An Illustrated Guide to Furniture History

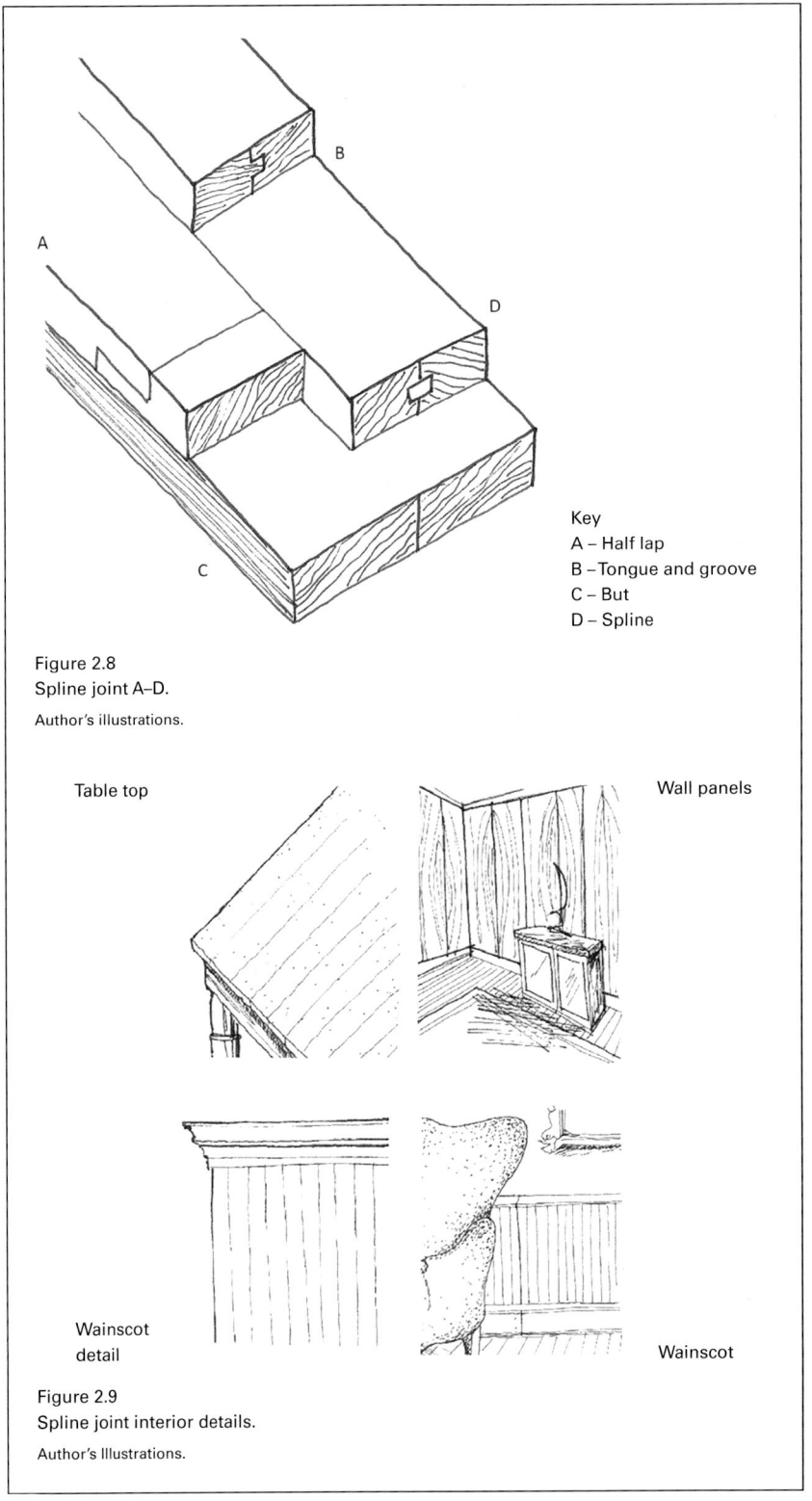

Key
A – Half lap
B – Tongue and groove
C – But
D – Spline

Figure 2.8
Spline joint A–D.
Author's illustrations.

Table top

Wall panels

Wainscot detail

Wainscot

Figure 2.9
Spline joint interior details.
Author's Illustrations.

Moving from right angles and right-angle joinery to the opposite cylindrical forms with respect to construction principles is also important. In the workshop, the "turner," who worked his craft of turning, was valued equally as the "joiner." Turning is a process in which a cutting tool describes a helix toolpath linearly while the work piece rotates. The tool's axes of movement may be a straight line or along some set of curves or angles, but they are essentially linear forms with an axis, and therefore can be held from either end and turned. The tool that allows for an axial piece of wood to be held in place at two ends and gouged into shape is a *lathe*. The lathe is an ancient tool believed to have been created by the ancient Egyptians, and known to be used in Assyria, India, and ancient Greece. The lathe was very important to the Industrial Revolution. Known as the mother of machine tools, it was the first machine tool, which led to the invention of other machine tools.[9] There are various types of lathes. Today, two primary types are used for metal or woodworking; however, woodworking lathes are the oldest type.

The earliest woodworking lathe dates back to around 1300 B.C. when the ancient Egyptians first used a two-person lathe. One person turned the wood piece with a rope, while the other person used a sharp tool to carve into the wood's surface. These simple machines are believed to be the first machine tools created. The simple design was later improved by the Romans who replaced the rope with a bow to improve the turning process.[10]

Later, during the Middle Ages, a foot pedal was introduced and hand operation was replaced. This style of machine is known as a spring pole and was commonly used until the early 20th century. This was a major advantage to the wood craftsman because he could now use both hands to hold and guide tools.[11]

The first continuously revolving mechanical lathe on record was depicted in a sketch by Leonardo Da Vinci, ca. 1480. A *treadle lathe* with a crankshaft and a large wooden flywheel, is shown in his sketch images depicted in Figure 2.10.

The use of the lathe allowed the cabinetmaker to design compound curves, elaborate shapes, and intricate designs for chair and table legs, chair backs, pediment scrolls, and finials, as well as other architectural interior details. On the next several pages are shown two versions of 18th-century lathe machine design, followed by drawings illustrating the wide variety of furniture details and pieces designed through use of the lathe. The lathe examples are etchings from Joseph Moxon, *Mechanick Exercises*, Winterthur Museum, Garden & Library (Figure 2.11 and Figure 2.12). Moxon's *Mechanick Exercises* was published between 1677 and 1684, in two volumes, giving instructions on metalworking, woodworking, bricklaying, printing, etc. The next example, a drawing from Stuart King, History *of the Lathe*, depicts a lathe that is set up for two-axis turning (Figure 2.13). Following are four American Early Colonial furniture details illustrating design variations of turned forms (Figure 2.14).

■ An Illustrated Guide to Furniture History

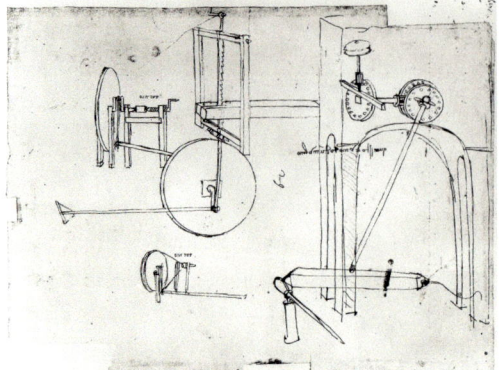

Figure 2.10
Da Vinci sketches.

Source: Science Museum/Science and Society Picture Library, UK.

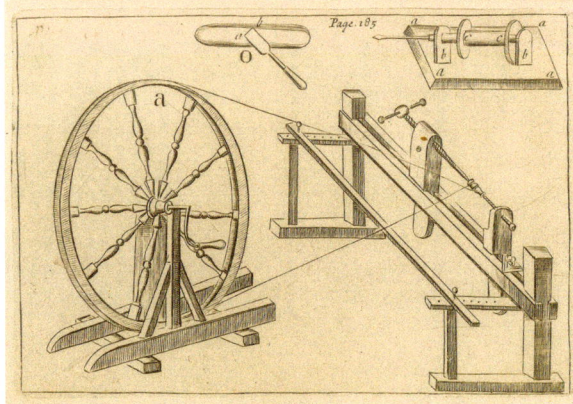

Key
a – Great wheel drill-bench [in right corner]
O – Chisel lying aslant
a–b – Cutting angle
a–a – Thick board
b–b – Stiles
c–c – Rowler

Figure 2.11
Lathe design and tools from *Mechanick Exercises* (1701), Joseph Moxon.

Source: Courtesy, the Winterthur Library: Printed Book and Periodical Collection.

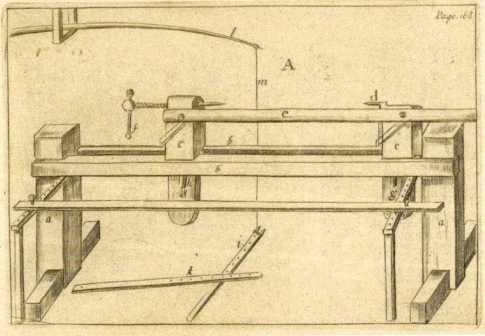

Key
a – Legs or stiles
b – Checks [side]
c – Puppets
d – Pile
e – Ren
f – Handle and the crew
g – Tennats of the puppegs
h – Wedge
i – Treddle
k – Cross-treddle
l – Pole
m – String

Figure 2.12
Lathe design and tools from *Mechanick Exercises* (1703), Joseph Moxon.

Source: Courtesy, the Winterthur Library: Printed Book and Periodical Collection.

Construction principles

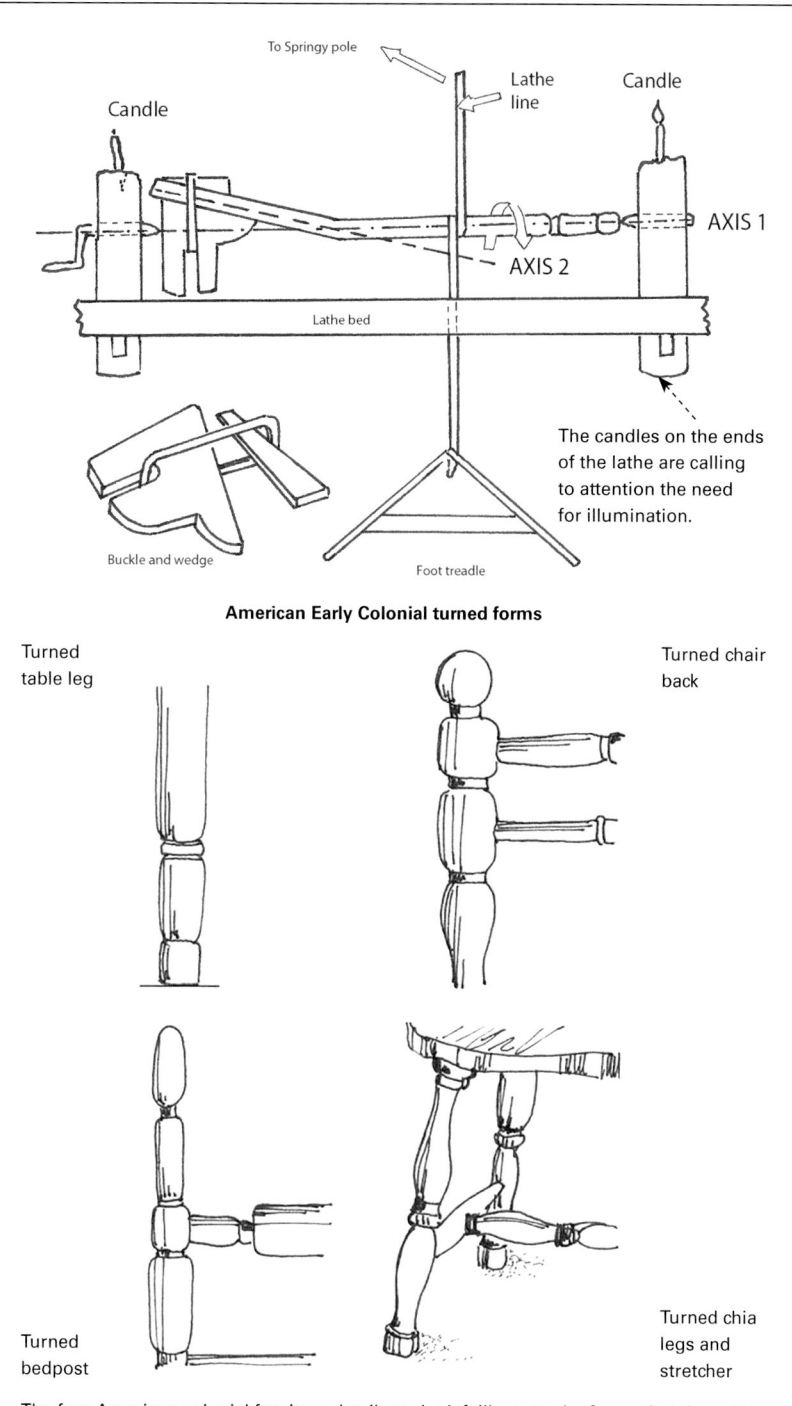

Figure 2.13 Two-axis lathe design

Source: Courtesy of Stewart King, Master Woodworker, UK.

Figure 2.14 Two-axis lathe furniture design details.

Source: Author's illustrations.

The four American colonial furniture details to the left illustrate the forms that the cutting tool can gouge into shape while held in place at two ends. To reiterate, the turning describes a helix toolpath linearly while the work piece rotates. Recognized in these for examples is that the tool's axes of movement were along a set of curves.

■ **An Illustrated Guide to Furniture History**

On the following page are six examples depicting 18th-century leg development (Figure 2.15). These English turned-leg and gouged shapes are simpler than the Early Colonial American examples on the previous page. The leg design is a *cabriole*. The cabriole leg was ubiquitous in the 18th century throughout France, England, and America and used for chairs, tables, commodes, high chests, etc.

When a cabinetmaker wanted to express an elaborate cabriole leg design, the foot would be shaped as a claw-and-ball or scroll. A less elaborate shape is a club-foot. The knee portion of the leg, if elaborate, would often be carved as a stylized acanthus leaf. A less elaborate leg would have no carved detail, as seen in the three straight-leg types on the lower row. With respect to lathe use, these lower three represent a straight-line axis.

Construction principles ■

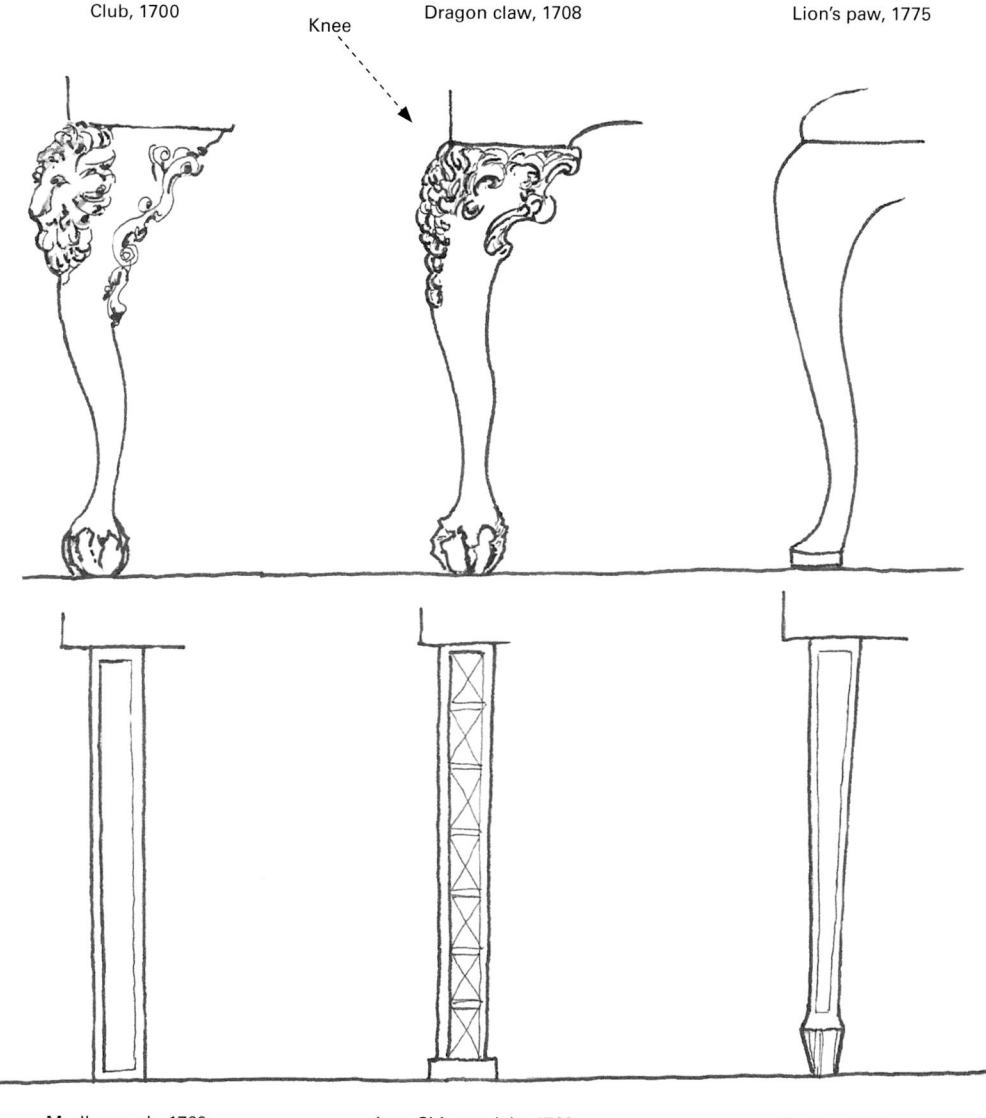

Figure 2.15
English 18th-century chair leg development.
Author's illustrations.

Intricate lathe turning involved the use of compound geometry such as combining cylindrical, rectilinear, and angled shapes in one form. This is visible in the examples of French and English Neoclassical designs on the following page (Figure 2.16 and Figure 2.17). A more complicated type of gouging—in essence, sculpting—was applied in shaping the female body for the figural leg design seen below in French Late Neoclassical design.

Construction principles ■

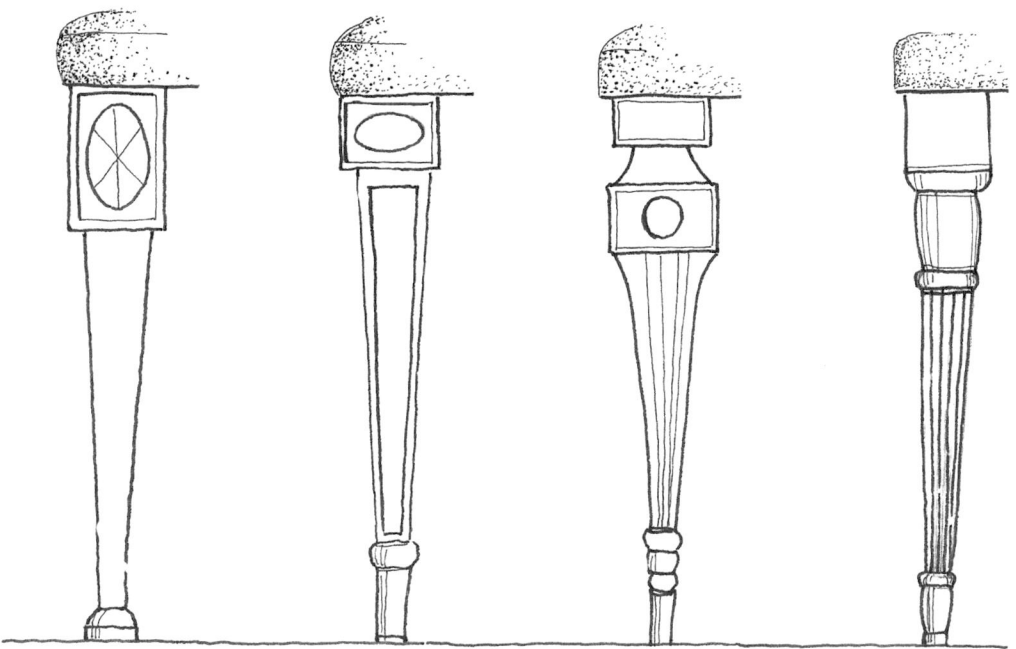

Sheraton-style quadrangular and round tapered leg forms

Figure 2.16
English chair leg design, early Neoclassical.
Author's illustration.

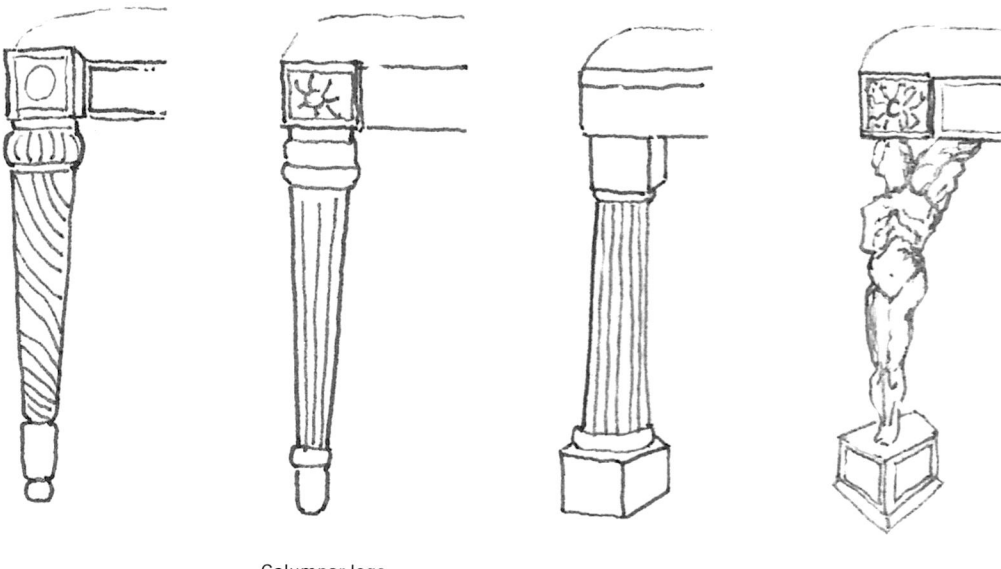

Columnar legs   Figural leg

Figure 2.17
French chair leg design, late Neoclassical.
Author's illustration.

■ **An Illustrated Guide to Furniture History**

On the next several pages, French, English, and American period furniture (18th century) are from Franklin Gottshall's book, *How to Design and Construct Period Furniture*, 1989 (Plate 2.3, Plate 2.4, and Plate 2.5). Take note of the illustrative manner in which furniture is depicted to accentuate the form, shape, and detail from lathe technology. The plates are representative of various designs from the cabinetmaker's shop and the skill of his craftsmen.

Plate 2.3
French, Louis XIV, XV, XVI furniture.

Source: Joseph De Chiara, Julius Panero, and Martin Zelnik, *Time-Saver Standards for Interior Design and Space Planning* (New York: McGraw-Hill Education, 1990), p.41.

An Illustrated Guide to Furniture History

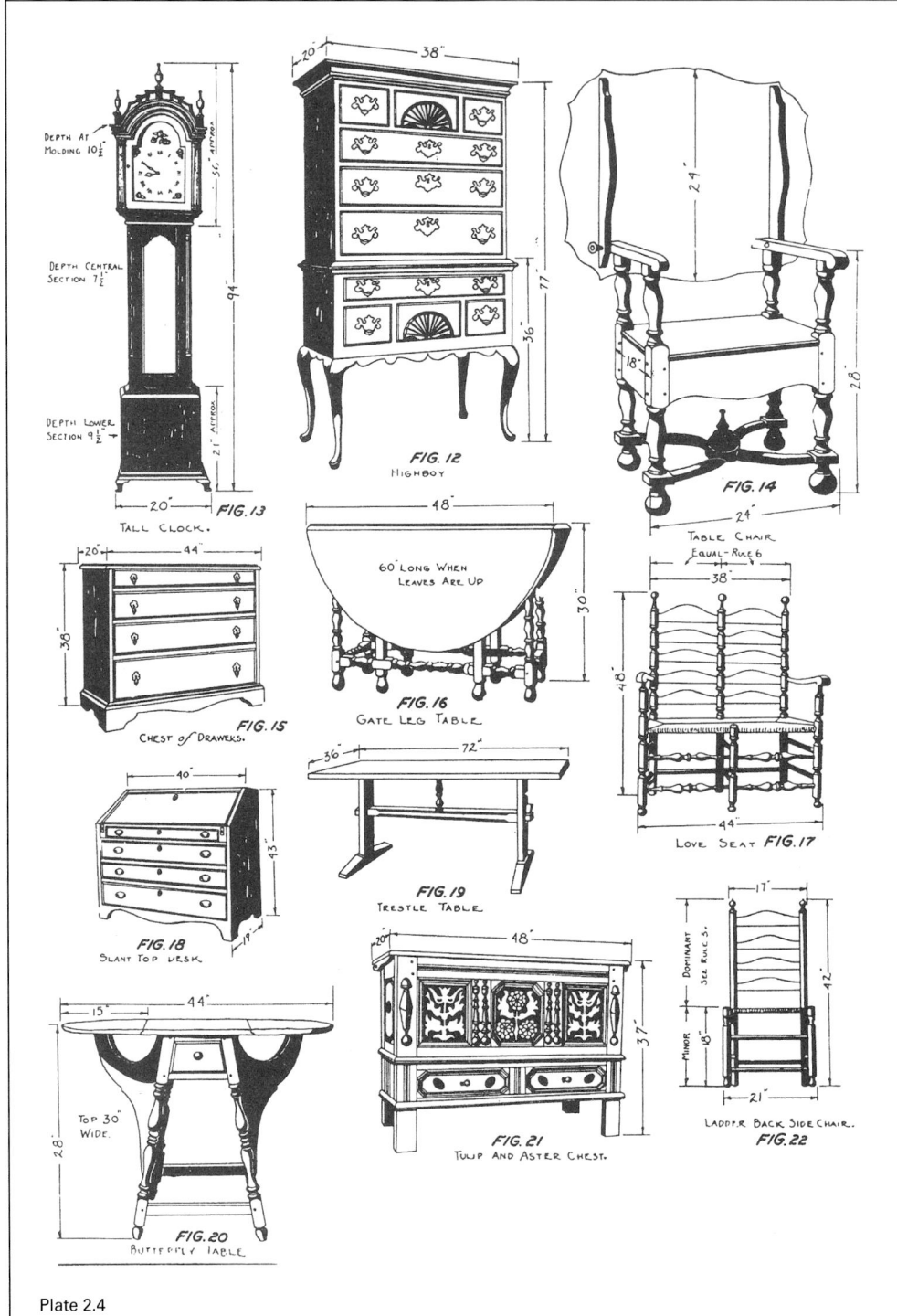

Plate 2.4
18th-century English Queen Anne furniture.

Source: Joseph De Chiara, Julius Panero, and Martin Zelnik, *Time-Saver Standards for Interior Design and Space Planning* (New York: McGraw-Hill Education, 1990), p.35.

Construction principles

Plate 2.5
17th- and 18th-century American furniture.
Source: Joseph De Chiara, Julius Panero, and Martin Zelnik, *Time-Saver Standards for Interior Design and Space Planning* (New York: McGraw-Hill Education, 1990), p.30.

■ **An Illustrated Guide to Furniture History**

Discussed thus far has been furniture construction with respect to assembly methods and the type of equipment used that reflect the customs and traditions of 18th-century cabinetmakers, tracing technology, tools and approach to joinery back to antiquity. These customs and traditions are still used and seen today, and on the next several pages, we view contemporary examples of these construction practices as applied to 21st-century furniture design and construction.

Over the next several pages are six video images photographed at the Art Institute of Chicago, American Furniture Gallery 167 (Figure 2.18). These video images demonstrate a 21st-century craftsman using a lathe to shape (turn) a leg with a claw-and-ball foot.

Walking through this process, step 1 depicts the craftsman securing the leg axially in the lathe at both ends for shaping. In step 2, after the leg is shaped, the pattern is drawn with pencil outlining the claw form. In step 3, the pattern is visible, and one can see the craftsman chisel (gouge) the wood, following the pattern. In step 4, the form is defined, leaving positive and negative areas; although rough, the claw is revealed. Refinement occurs in step 5, as the knuckle joints of the claw are formed; and in step 6, near completion, the features are the most refined and the artistry is revealed.

Construction principles

Step 1: Phil Lowe carves a ball and claw.

Step 2: Phil Lowe carves a ball and claw.

Figure 2.18
Ball-and-claw carving, 2014.

Source: Courtesy of Peabody Essex Museum.

Courtesy of the Peabody Essex Museum, Salem, Massachusetts. Phil Lowe carves a ball and Claw, 2014. Video, In Plain Sight: The Art of Nathaniel Gould—Revolutionary War-era joiner's shop in Duxbury, Massachusetts.

Step 3: Phil Lowe carves a ball and claw.

Step 4: Phil Lowe carves a ball and claw.

Figure 2.18
(Continued)

Construction principles

Step 5: Phil Lowe carves a ball and claw.

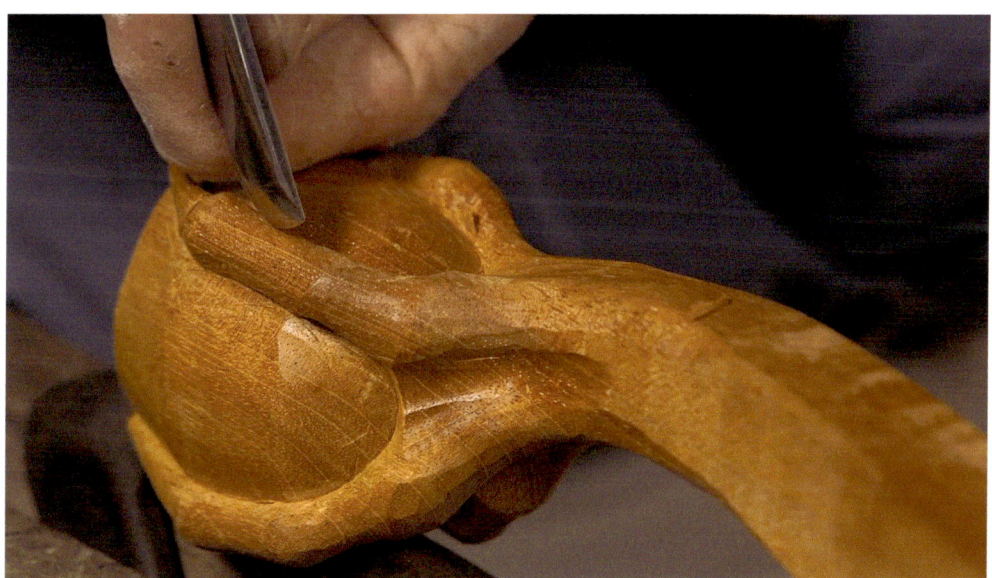

Step 6: Phil Lowe carves a ball and claw.

Figure 2.18
(Continued)

Another contemporary example of these construction practices being applied in the 21st century is Leonards—an 85-year-old family-owned antique company founded in 1933 in Seekonk, Massachusetts. The Jenkins family represents three generations working for the company, similar to 18th-century cabinetmaking practices.[12]

Leonards refurbishes, recycles, and custom designs antique furniture, and provides interior design services. The company's specialty is bed design (Figure 2.19). The beds are either refurbished or custom designed based on historical examples. Today the furniture is still manufactured by hand, not mass-produced (Figure 2.20). In 1974, there were seven or eight elderly European cabinetmakers. These European cabinetmakers are no longer at the firm, yet craftspeople still earned their trade on-site.[13]

Construction principles

Figure 2.19 Leonards' Company headboard shapes, a–f.

Author's illustrations.

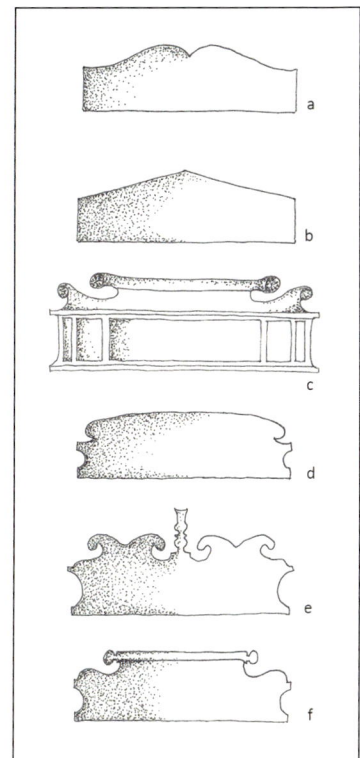

Key
a – Sweetheart
b – Peak
c – Rolltop w/panel
d – Ram's ear
e – Folk Art
f – Roll top

Figure 2.20 Leonards' production overview.

Source: "Bedtime Story," *Country Living*, May 2008, p.134. Photographer, Ryan Benyi.

Worker turning a post

Worker using tool

37

■ **An Illustrated Guide to Furniture History**

Today it is normal for antique businesses to work with "pickers." On the next page is a variety of antique headboards, footboards, and posts from a "picker" awaiting approval from company president Jeff Jenkins. Antique picking is the art of buying antiques at auctions and through sales and individuals, and selling them at a profit to antique shops. Typically, pickers comb areas of the country—the Atlantic Coast, the Ohio Valley, the South—for furniture they hope to sell (Plate 2.6).

Plate 2.7 (p. 40) represents examples of Leonards' design and restoration work and collection of historical elements restored, refurbished, and/or redesigned, such as rosettes, bedpost, finials.

Plate 2.6
Picker's selection: antique headboards and posts.

Source: "Bedtime Story," *Country Living*, May 2008, p.133. Photographer: Ryan Benyi.

■ An Illustrated Guide to Furniture History

Plate 2.7
Four-image grid of Leonards' designs and restoration work.

Source: "Bedtime Story," *Country Living*, May 2008, p.136. Photographer: Ryan Benyi.

Next, Chapter 3—Piece categorically—will cover the concept of learning how to classify furniture with respect to place of origin by looking specifically at 18th-century furniture from three countries.

NOTES

1 https://en.wikipedia.org/wiki/Ébéniste.
2 www.si.edu/MCI.
3 Ibid.
4 Ibid.
5 www.si.edu/mci/english/learn_more/taking_care/fundconst.html.
6 Ibid.
7 Ibid.
8 https://en.wikipedia.org/wiki/Theban_Necropolis.
9 https://en.wikipedia.org/wiki/Lathe.
10 www.machinesales.com/blog/2012.
11 Ibid.
12 "Bedtime Story," *Country Living*, 2008, p.132.
13 Ibid.

3 Piece categorically

When learning about furniture and its history, categorizing furniture and the importance of provenance—possessing the ability to categorize and classify a furniture piece as to its place of origin and within a timeline—are equally as important as construction priciples. Chapter 3 will walk the student or adult learner through this process, using examples from 18th-century France, England, and America.

Figure 3.1
18th-century French Rococo bergère.
Author's illustration.

FRANCE

Furniture produced in 18th-century France during the reign of Louis XV (1723–1774) had an obvious and distinct style referred to as *Rococo*. Interiors and furniture during this period are very distinquishable, making the period ideal for discussing how to categorize a piece physically with respect to its origin and timeline. This style originated in France but spread throughout the rest of Europe during the 18th century. The next several pages will introduce some of the most recognizable furniture pieces of the French Rococo style.

The colored pencil-rendered drawing above is of a *bergère*, an enclosed upholstered armchair with an over-upholstered seat frame (Figure 3.1). This chair was specifically designed for comfort and to move about the suite (*meuble courant*).

The wood frame could be beech, fruitwood, walnut, or mahogany. The frame is typically decorated with carved relief and is painted or gilded.

Louis XV enabled a prodigious development of the arts. His reign is considered the golden age of French furniture. During his reign, the interior emphasis was on the ensemble; painters and sculptors helped define the decorative arts and had an impact on architecture and interior design. This period established an aesthetic of lightness and comfort, and a sense of intimacy. It is associated with femininity in both scale and decorative motifs. This aesthetic was the opposite of that of Louis XIV, for whom furniture had to express a feeling of power.

The term *Rococo* originates in the combination of two French words: *rocaille*, originally referring to rockeries, artificial grottoes, and rustic treatments; and *coquille*, meaning cockleshell. These qualities visually translated into the Rococo aesthetic vocabulary, defined by exuberance. This quality is visible in plasterwork and metalwork decoration with curvilinear shapes of intertwining *C*- and *S*-forms, stylized leaves and shells, sinuous and fluid repetitive lines visible on both furniture and all interior wall planes. The French Rococo period's correlation to architecture and visual arts is concurrent with the "Late Baroque Period."

Another seating piece of the period is a *fauteuil* (Figure 3.2). The fauteuil is designed as an open-arm chair, but can be without arms, as shown in the pencil-rendered drawing below. No matter the design, the seat and back are upholstered. The scale of the fauteuil is smaller than the bergère, yet the wood frame is treated the same—carved with relief ornament and gilded or painted. Additionally, the same type of wood is used for the frame: beech, fruitwood, walnut, or mahogany.

Figure 3.2
18th-century French fauteuil.
Author's illustration.

Other interesting physical features beyond the gilded or painted relief wood frame is the design of the chair back and legs. The shape of the chair back is referred to as a *cartouche*. It resembles a rounded, convex surface and is usually surrounded with carved ornamental scrollwork for receiving painted or low-relief decoration. At the crest of the cartouche, in the center, will be a carved motif—flowers, stylized leaves, or a scallop shell.

The shape of the chair leg is a *cabriole*. As mentioned in Section 1.1 Construction principles, this leg is formed and shaped with a lathe. The form is partially *S*-shaped, and the knee portion often carved relief. For the French Rococo chair, the foot configuration is typically a scroll.

On the following page are enlarged line drawings of these specific details: cartouche back, cabriole leg, and scroll foot (Figure 3.3).

The photographs of a bergère and a fauteuil are from two excellent sources recommended to facilitate your understanding of furniture history (Figure 3.4 and

■ An Illustrated Guide to Furniture History

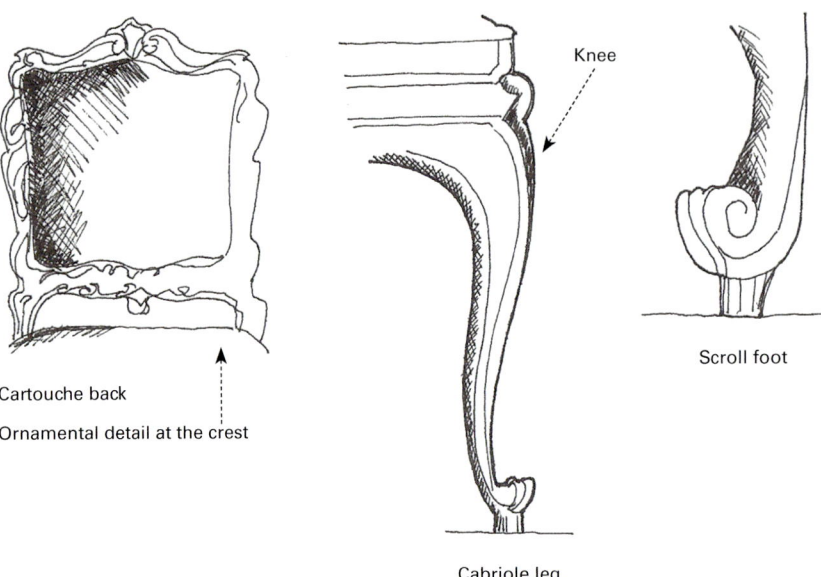

Figure 3.3
Fauteuil details.
Author's illustration.

Cartouche back
Ornamental detail at the crest

Knee

Scroll foot

Cabriole leg

Figure 3.5). The bergère is from *Chairs: A History*, by Florence de Dampierre (Harry N. Abrams, 2006), and the fauteuil is from *Period Rooms in the Metropolitan Museum of Art* (Metropolitan Museum of Art, 1996) by the museum's curatorial team. These chairs are some of the finest examples of their type. The photographs help depict with realistic clarity the three-dimensional features discussed in the rendered drawings on the previous pages.

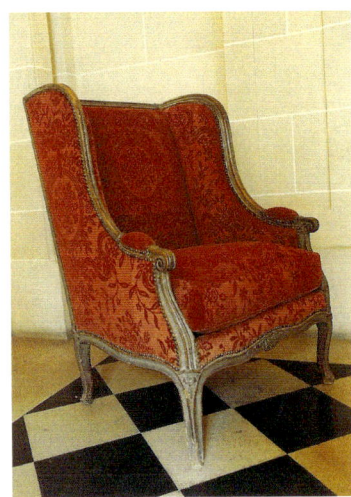

Figure 3.4
Louis XV bergère.

Source: Florence deDampierre, *Chairs: A History* (New York: Abrams, an imprint of Harry N. AbramsInc., 2006), p.187.

Figure 3.5
Louis XV fauteuil located in the Boiserie from the Hôtel de Varengeville Period Room. French, Paris, ca. 1736–1752.

Source: The Metropolitan Museum of Art, Public Domain, OA [Open Access]. Period Room.

44

Below are four chair examples that show the evolution of fauteuil design from the reign of Louis XV through Louis XVI (Figure 3.6). Chairs A and B are Régence-style chairs (1715–1723), which was a transition from the primarily rectilinear forms of Louis XIV to the curvilinear contours of Louis XV. Chair C, during Louis XV's reign, depicts a lighter form, with more graceful curves used for the cabriole leg, padded arms, and a cartouche-shaped back. Chair D is indicative of the transition from Louis XV through Louis XVI; one can see it is less curvilinear and appears more upright, emphasizing a round arch, and beginning to reflect the Greco-Roman influence which becomes popular aesthetically in the late 18th century. With chair D, the shape of the cabriole leg expresses less of a curve, eventually becoming straight under Louis XVI, and the change to a Classical aesthetic.

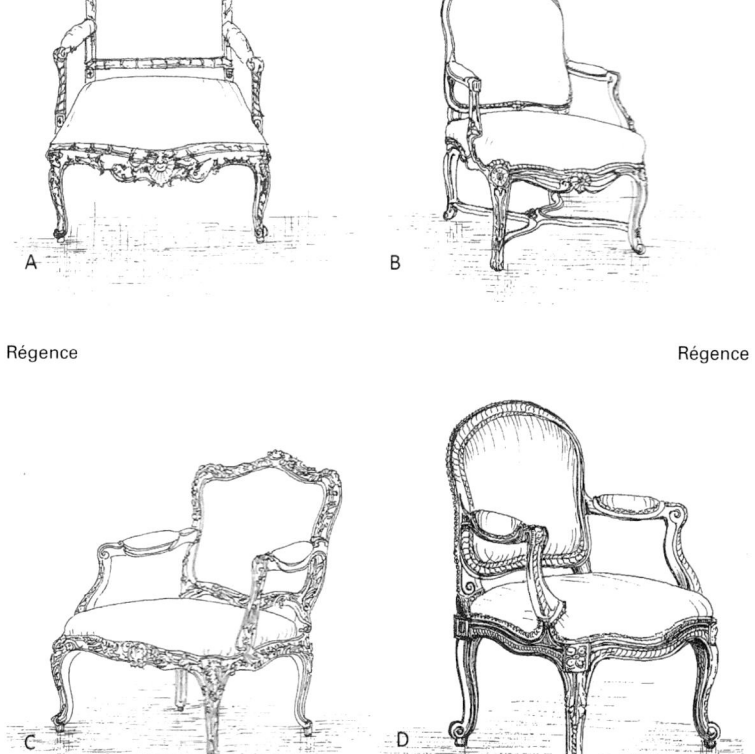

Figure 3.6
Fauteuil evolution A–D, Régence through transitional Louis XV–XVI.

Source: Robbie G. Blakemore, *History of Interior Design & Furniture, From Ancient Egypt to Nineteenth-Century Europe* (New York: John Wiley & Sons, Inc., 2006), p. 239. Copyright © 2006 by Robbie G. Blakemore. All rights reserved.

The discussion now moves away from chairs and toward storage and display—nascent commode and console design of the mid- to late 18th century (Figure 3.7). The physiognomies of the *commode* and *console table* are salient representatives of the Rococo style in France. Commodes of mid-18th-century France were both decorative and useful. During this period, the word *commode* meant a cabinet or chest of drawers for storing personal items (that meaning will apply in this book). However, the evolution of this word is an example of semantic drift—a gradual change in the meaning of a word as it becomes used in changing context.[1]

 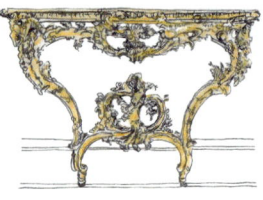

Commode   Console table

Figure 3.7
18th-century French commode and console table.
Author's illustration.

The physical form of the 18th-century commode was low, wider than it was tall, and placed on short cabriole legs. It was meant to stand against a wall. Earlier commodes had a *bombé*, or convex, shape, as in the drawing in Figure 3.7; later forms had serpentine tops and fronts, with tops often made of marble. In addition, the front was elaborately decorated with inlaid wood (marquetry). Commodes were displayed prominently in the home and typically paired with mirrors and matching chairs, or rooms had a matching pair of commodes.

Commode derives from the French word for "convenient" or "suitable." With respect to semantic drift, the word went on to refer to a particular type of cabinet that held chamber pots, then to a piece of wooden chair-like furniture that held the chamber pot. In its final iteration, the term was used to refer to the porcelain plumbing fixture that replaced the chamber pot altogether—the toilet.[2]

The 18th-century French *console table* is a side table placed against a wall and normally fixed. The legs support only the front of the top portion, which is usually made of marble. This table is viewed only from the front or side. The legs and apron are elaborately carved gilded or painted wood. The asymmetrical Rococo decorative approach is exemplified here: the ubiquitous Rococo decorative motifs, sinuous *S*- and *C*-shapes, and stylized acanthus leaves, flowers, and scallop shells. Below are asymmetrical details of *ormolu* hardware in typical Rococo design. Ormolu is a gilded bronze that results from a gilding technique in which a finely ground, high-carat gold-mercury amalgam is applied to a bronze object. The French refer to this technique as *bronze doré*. Using ormolu hardware was prevalent during the Rococo period (Figure 3.8).

Figure 3.8
18th-century French hardware.
Author's illustration.

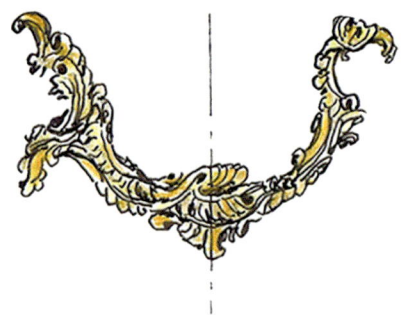

Ormolu drawer pull   Ormolu escutcheon

The photographic images of the commode and console on this page and the next will assist in visualizing the pieces' three-dimensional features discussed in the author's rendered drawings with realistic clarity (Figure 3.9 and Figure 3.10). However, there is a difference in commode type. The author's rendering (Figure 3.7) is a specific form of commode called a *commode en tombeau*. The name derives from tomb/sarcophagi design. The form is voluminous and bombée-shaped, with a marble top and generously covered with ormolu decoration, in the trim, relief elements, escutcheons, and handles. Figure 3.9 corresponds with the explanation above describing the typical 18th-century physical form—low, wider than it was tall, and placed on short cabriole legs, designed with the purpose of standing against a wall.

The console table, ca. 1735 Paris, France, is representative of an early French Rococo piece (Figure 3.10). Although it has features that are no doubt Rococo, such as the serpentine marble top and curvilinear carved ornament and use of the *C*-scrolls and *S*-scrolls shaping the apron, legs, and stretcher. The earlier indicator is that the form is less curvaceous, not as delicate of scale, and the ornament is symmetrical.

The last piece discussed in this section is an elegant sofa made out of elaborately carved wood known as a *canapé* (Figure 3.11). The canapé emerged in the 18th century during the reigns of both Louis XIV and Louis XV. The overall shape of the canapé is distinct: elegant yet leggy, with the latter quality giving the sofa the appearance of weightlessness—visually delicate with upholstered open arms, back, and seat resting lightly on shapely cabriole legs. Precious hardwoods, such as walnut, cherry, and mahogany, were used for the frame, and most often would be carved relief, gilded, or painted.[3]

Notice the delicate and weightless quality of the form, the way in which the three-cartouche-shaped back and single-cushion seat relate to the open arms and cabriole legs. This is an excellent example that visually explains my general perception of canapés. This piece is a Louis XV sofa from the annexes of the Chateau of Versailles in France, ca. 1760. This hand-carved eight-leg canapé has a gilt finish and restored Aubusson tapestry, and measures H 47" × W 87" × D 31".

Figure 3.9
Commode, ca. 1765–1770, French. Attributed to Léonard Boudin and Pierre-Antoine Foullet. Veneered marquetry with gilt-bronze mounts.

Source: Metropolitan Museum of Art, New York. Public Domain, OA [Open Access]. Robert Lehman Collection, 1975.

■ An Illustrated Guide to Furniture History

Figure 3.10
Console table, ca. 1700–1725, Rome, Italy. Gilded linden and gilt-bronze, with green porphyry stone. Size 38½" × 69¼" × 27¾"

Source: Art Institute of Chicago, Department, European Decorative Arts. Creative Commons Zero (CC0).Gift of K. Wrigley through The Antiquarian Society.

Figure 3.11
Louis XV Canepé from Annexes of the Chateau of Versailles, *(below)* detail ofwood carved Canepé leg and base trim.

Source: Courtesy of Country French Interiors, Dallas, TX.

The two beatific Rococo canapés below are fascinating (Figure 3.12). The exuberant character of both designs is imaginative and projects an animate quality. The first is an etching by French architect Jean-Charles Delafosse, and the second is thought to be a German design, originally with a pink-and-white painted wood frame. The cabriole legs evoke a feeling of energy and movement. This animate quality is further defined on both pieces by the use of stylized leaves and shell motifs formed by *S*- and *C*-shapes, moving fluidly from horizontal and vertical parts of the cartouche back cushions. This sinuous and asymmetrical patterning of motifs exemplifies Rococo design.

The ideal way to understand the relationship of an individual piece to the space in which it belongs is to view historical furniture in context. Since the late-19th century, museums have been a primary source in making this happen through the installation of period rooms. As the 21st century approached, the concept and practice as to the role and purpose of the period room has been debated. In his *New York Times* article "Gilding the Ancien Régime," former *Boston Globe* art critic Ken Johnson expresses a provocative thought and explanation:

> The period room is a paradoxical museum animal. Though consisting of original materials like carved wood wall panels, fireplace mantels, beds, chandeliers,

Figure 3.12 *(above)* Sofa etching by Jean-Charles Delafosse (1734–1791). *(below)* Beechwood sofa with original pink and white paint, possibly German.

Source: Florence deDampierre, *Chairs: A History*. (New York: Abrams, an imprint of Harry N. AbramsInc., 2006), p.191.

An etching of a sofa by Jean-Charles Delafosse (1734–1791), whose ornamental designs for chairs were highly influential and contributed to the dissemination of the *goût antique*. Metropolitan Museum of Art, New York City *(below)* label to the left image—Beech wood sofa originally with pink and white painted frame has similarities to the etching by Delafosse above. This piece also recalls drawings by the German rococo decorator and furniture-designer Johann Michael Hoppenhaupt (1709–69). L' Antiquaire & The Connoisseur, Inc.

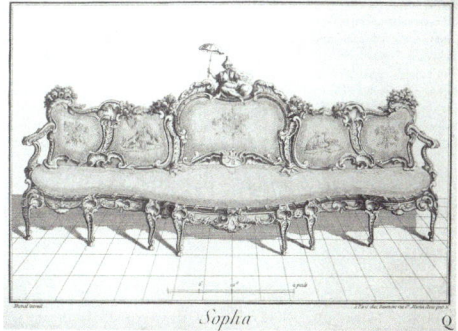

paintings and sculptures, it is usually less an intact piece of the past than a creative reconstruction, a historical fantasy that requires much stagecraft to work its magic.[4]

The statement has merit; however, as one who teaches design history, the period room as a learning tool is irreplaceable. With respect to the built environment (i.e., interior design and architecture), it provides a three-dimensional reality for envisioning decorative objects in their time and place that reading materials and classroom lectures cannot.

On the next page is a period room at the Metropolitan Museum of Art (the Met) in New York City that I regularly visited with my graduate students (Plate 3.1). It served as an immeasurable tool for learning about 18th-century French Rococo style *d'hôtel particulier*. The room, Hôtel de Varengeville, ca. 1736–1752, is located in the Wrightsman Galleries for French Decorative Arts. Yes—it can be viewed as "less an intact piece of the past and creative reconstruction," as Johnson said, yet the attribute to behold is a marvel to the eye and superb example of *d'hôtel particulier*. Not all the pieces in the space are necessarily original but are representative of what would have been in a salon. Its provenance—Paris, Left Bank, no. 217 boulevard Saint-Germain, originally (no. 16 rue Saint-Dominique) built for Charlotte Angélique Courtin by architect Jacques Gabriel. The photographer, Joseph Coscia, captures the most recent curation of the room (2007) with the lighting set to depict evening at twilight.

The question might arise: How did this Rococo interior get to the Met? Early in the 20th century, wealthy patrons/benefactors of the arts frequented auctions for purchases. In the same manner as purchasing artwork, parts of a room(s) or an entire room from grand residences would be purchased, deconstructed, and reconstructed in the desired place of the buyer, often to be later bequeathed to a museum or foundation. The Wrightsmans, long-time Met benefactors, purchased the paneling of the Hôtel de Varengeville in the early 1960s and presented it to the Met not long after.

On the next page is the photographic view most often taken of the hotel. The furniture and "decorative art pieces" are arranged in a fashion like that of salons during this period. The wall paneling, as mentioned, is original to the hotel. The *bureau plat* (or writing table) is from Louis XV's office in the Palace of Versailles. The matching fauteuils in the front lower left and far right are part of a set of 12 armchairs and two settees ordered in Paris in 1753 by Baron Johann Ernst Bernstorff, a Dutch ambassador to the court of Versailles, for the tapestry room at his palace in Copenhagen. The armchairs are covered with the original wool-and-silk Beauvais tapestry, woven with animal and bird subjects. This work is modeled after Jean-Baptiste Oudry (1686–1755), known for his artistry in the use of animal and bird subjects.[5]

The room exemplifies French Rococo interior, defined by tripartite volume—wall paneling (dado, central plane, and cornice), trimmed with stylized leaves formed into *S*- and *C*-shapes and shell motifs, moving fluidly between vertical and horizontal planes on walls and furniture. Interior wall colors of this period were usually a light hue; here, it is off-white. Lastly, the use of ormolu mounts on furniture constructed of beechwood, fruitwood, oak, and mahogany pieces, sometimes lacquered such as the *bureau plat* (writing table) in this room so typical of the style.

Plate 3.1
Metropolitan Museum of Art. The Boiserie from the Hôtel de Varengeville Period Room, French, Paris, ca. 1736–1752.

Source: Metropolitan Museum of Art, New York. The Boiserie from the Hôtel de Varengeville Period Room. French, Paris, ca. 1736–1752.

To the right is an exterior garden elevation and floor plan (Figure 3.13). Over the centuries, the interior has been altered and the top floor was added after 1877.[6] The plan is of the first floor, and it is not known which room originally contained the paneling now in the museum. The photograph is a view looking in the opposite direction from the previous one, depicting the room in a daylight setting. The detail is of similar *boiserie* (sculptured paneling) showing a central arabesque motif (Figure 3.14).

 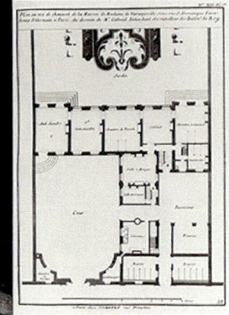

Figure 3.13
(left) Garden elevation of the Hôtel de Varengeville at no. 217 boulevard Saint-Germain. *(right)* Floor plan of the first floor of the Hôtel deVarengeville.

Source: Garden Elevation Hôtel de Varengeville. The Metropolitan Museum of Art, European Sculpture and Decorative Arts Archives. The Metropolitan Museum, NewYork,N.Y., U.S.A.
(right) Jacques-François (1705–1771), Architecture Françoise, 4 Volume, 1752–56, Gift of Mrs. Alexander Mcmillan Welch,1946 (46.52.3(1-4)). The Metropolitan Museum, NewYork, N.Y., U.S.A.

Image copyright ©The Metropolitan Museum of Art, Image Source: Art Resource, NY.

<--- arabesque

Boiserie (panel) sketch similar to the wood panelsof Hôtel de Varengeville. This type of panel was ubiquitousin mid-18th-century French Rococo Hôtelinteriors. The decorative plaster work, trim, cornice, and arabesque are gildedin gold also typical of this period.

Boiserie (panel) sketch similar to the wood panelsof Hôtel de Varengeville. This type of panel was ubiquitousin mid-18th-century French Rococo Hôtelinteriors. The decorative plaster work, trim, cornice, and arabesque are gildedin gold also typical of this period.

Figure 3.14
(left) Hôtel de Varengeville view opposite directionof Plate 3.1. *(right)* Author's drawing of a similar arabesque Boiserie wall panel detail of the Hôtel de Varengeville.

Source: Boiserie from the Hôtel de Varengeville.18th century (ca.1735 and later). Oak, Mr. and Mrs. Charles Wrightsman Gift, 1963 (63.228.1). The Metropolitan Museum of Art.

Image copyright ©The Metropolitan Museum of Art, Image Source: Art Resource, NY.

As mentioned previously, the *bureau plat* (writing table) as seen in this period room, was commissioned by Louis XV for his study in Versailles. The maker was Gilles Joubert. The table remained at Versailles until 1786, when it was replaced by a marquetry version commissioned by Louis XV. A close examination of the desk and details shows its brilliant crimson lacquered finish and pseudo-Asian landscape scenes in gold (Figure 3.15).

A – Center frontlacquered panel and ormolu mounts

B – Cabriole legdetail and ornamental knee detail

C – Decorative motif, lacquer and gold leaf on modern leather

Figure 3.15
Bureau plat and details A–C. Located in the Boiserie Hôtel de Varengeville, Period Room. Maker Gilles Joubert (French, ca. 1689–1775), date 1759. Lacquered oak, gilt-bronze mounts, lined with modern leather. H 31¾" × W 69¼" × D 36".

Source: Metropolitan Museum of Art, Public Domain, OA [Open Access]. The Boiserie Hôtel de Varengeville, Period Room.

No doubt the debate about the role and purpose of the period room will continue. Regarding teaching and learning, and whether the period room is a paradoxical museum animal, as Johnson states, the paradox, in my opinion, is that the animal has assumed the role of trainer. As I said at the beginning of this section, as a learning tool, the period room is irreplaceable and provides a three-dimensional reality for envisioning decorative objects in their time and place in a way that reading materials and classroom lectures cannot.

ENGLAND

Comparable to the reigns of 18th-century France monarchs, Louis XV through XVI, the reigns of England's George I through III also produced furniture with an obvious and distinct style. Like that of Louis XV, the reigns of George II (1727–1760) and George III (1760–1820) was a time when interiors and furniture had highly distinguishable charcteristics. The mid- through late Georgian period is ideal for discussing how to categorize furniture physically with respect to place of origin and timeline. At this time in England, the importation of mahogany, which ended the common use of walnut, can be atributed to a monumental and significant change in furniture design features. The term *Georgian* refers both to the monarch reign and aesthetic quality—Georgian style. The timeframe is designated as early, middle, and late. The aesthetic quality is designated the same way. It is fitting to begin this discussion with the three renowned cabinetmakers of the time (the "big three") mentioned previously: Thomas Chippendale (1718–1779), George Hepplewhite (1727–1786), and Thomas Sheraton (1751–1806). However, before reviewing how to place their work categorically, a discussion about the development of the pattern book is important for context. The "big three" promulgated the concept of pattern books for furniture design. These books influenced interior design and decoration, and the practice of using them grew during the course of the century. The pattern book offered a choice to the patron and a model for the craftsman, which could be varied at will.

Initially, pattern books issued by architects and builders contained engraved designs for doors, ceilings, doorways, and chimneypieces, and gradually included devices.[7] One of the earliest to be published was *The Gentlemens* [sic] *or Builders Companion*, in 1739, by architect William Jones. Both drawings and engravings for the pattern books provided valuable evidence of the gradual development of the Rococo style in England,[8] which coincides with Chippendale establishing himself as a cabinetmaker.

Although Chippendale's workshop interpreted the Rococo aesthetic with less exaggeration than French designs, during the early Georgian period, several English designers and decorators produced work that closely resembled the French exuberance. The depiction of the rendered English Rococo chair is an enlarged rendered drawing by the author of Gaetano Brunetti's engraving of a Rococo chair design, ca. 1736 (Figure 3.17). His etching is seen in the lower-right corner. Brunetti was a painter and decorator, and produced impressive engraving and designs for Rococo furniture in Britain around 1730 and in Paris around 1739 (Figure 3.16 and Figure 3.17). These designs featured wood gilded in gold and were bold in color or pattern upholstery as shown in the rendition by author. The etching (ca. 1736) of Brunetti's designs for pier tables illustrates the exuberance that was characteristic of the French Rococo style.

English cabinetmakers

The eldest of the "big three," Thomas Chippendale was born in June 1718 in Yorkshire, England, at the beginning of the Georgian period. His father, John

Figure 3.16
Gaetano Brunetti pier table etchings, ca. 1736.

Source: Royal Academy of Arts, Picture Library, United Kingdom.

Chippendale, was a joiner (joyner). The Chippendale family had long been in the woodworking trade. He apprenticed in York and then moved to London, setting up shop and designing furniture before the mid-Georgian period. As French Rococo came to England and quickly became the style of choice, Chippendale's work reflected this style, and by the late Georgian period, he was influenced by the Chinese aesthetic *chinoiserie*—Chinese Chippendale. His furniture pieces often are referred to as English Rococo no matter if they were produced in the early or late Georgian period. His reputation was impeccable, and after publishing *The Gentleman and Cabinet-Maker's Director*, in 1754, he became renowned. His designs throughout reflected 18th-century British furniture fashion of the time and, in the realm of traditional/historical furniture, is still being produced today.[9]

Figure 3.17 *(top left)* Brumetti's Rococo chair etching *(bottom right)*, author's rendition of theoriginal etching upper left.

Source: Douglas Ash... [et al.], *World Furniture, An Illustrated History.* New York, London, Sydney, Toronto: Hamlyn Publishing Group Limited, 1976), p.132.

The image on the next page (top three) are engravings from a page in *The Gentleman and Cabinet-Maker's Director* and reflect options for a splat-back chair (Figure 3.19). The splat is the central back portion of a chair and can be solid or carved—see the sketch below (Figure 3.18).

The center chair has been enlarged and rendered by the author to depict the wood tone and upholstery choice for this period. As mentioned previously, mahogany replaced walnut, and upholstery was brightly colored damask or tapestry.

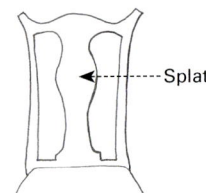

Figure 3.18
Splat back chair detail.
Author's illustration.

Figure 3.19
Chippendale chair back designs. Enlarged chair, author's rendition.

Source: Metropolitan Museum of Art, Public Domain, OA [Open Access]. Drawings and Prints.

The Rogers Fund, 1920.

Throughout the 18th century, splat design had a variety of forms, such as fiddle, vase, ribbon, oval, shield, heart, lattice, lyre, and chinoiserie.

During the late Georgian period, of the "big three," both Hepplewhite's and Sheraton's work was inspired by Greco-Roman designs. Their design aesthetic is referred to as Classical or Neoclassical.

Documentary evidence about the life of Hepplewhite is sparse.[10] He was a furniture designer and cabinetmaker who, by 1760, had established himself in London. One of the most notable features of his design is he replaces the splat back with a shield shape and, at times, a heart-shape form. This shape is dubbed the shield-back chair, as seen on the following page (Figure 3.20). Hepplewhite's furniture guided and defined the Neoclassical vocabulary of late 18th century. The language included urns, anthemion, vases rosettes, wheat ears, festoons, husk, and swags—all common Greco-Roman motifs from Antiquity. His furniture designs incorporated these motifs in a distinctive way: light and elegant. This aesthetic became the fashion between about 1775 and 1800. Below is an etching of the shield-back chairs from his book *The Cabinet-Maker & Upholsterer's Guide*, published after his death by his widow, Alice, in 1788.[11]

Also during the late Georgian period, Hepplewhite's peer Sheraton worked with the Neoclassical vocabulary. Sheraton's design approach became the most powerful source of inspiration for furniture design of the time. His work was characterized as similar to Hepplewhite's but with a layer of feminine refinement and rectilinear expression. He began his career no differently than other cabinetmakers of the day, starting as an apprentice, then becoming a journeyman cabinetmaker until he moved to London in 1790 at age 39. Once in London, his career trajectory is unusual. His erudite approach proved successful for his reputation as a cabinetmaker.

He set himself up as a professional consultant and teacher. He taught perspective, architecture, and cabinet design for craftsmen. He became a prolific publisher, publishing four volumes of *The Cabinet-Maker and Upholsterer's Drawing-Book* in 1791. The book was widely influential over a large part of the country since the community of cabinetmakers and joiners subscribed to this book.[12] On the following page are two sheets from *The Cabinet-Maker and Upholsterer's Drawing-Book*. The top sheet illustrates the use of the perspective convention for drawing chair frames, and the second sheet depicts six chair-back variations for a patron to consider (Figure 3.21 and Figure 3.22).

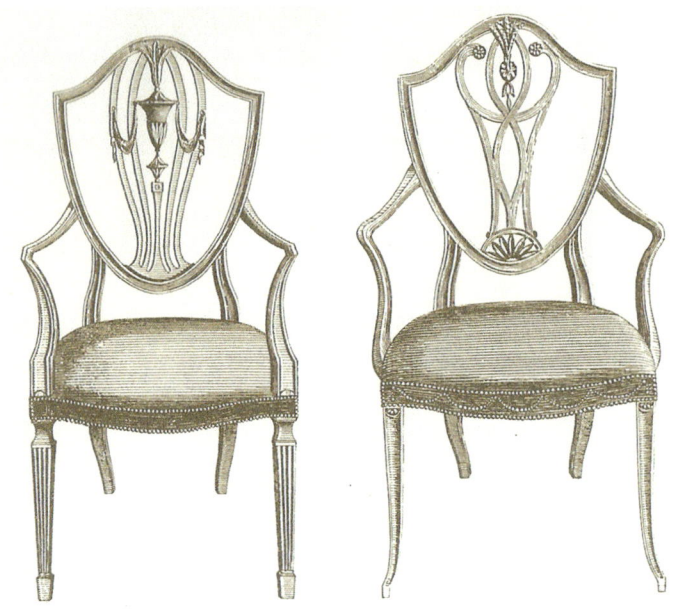

Figure 3.20 George Hepplewhite shield-back chairs. From his book *The Cabinet-Maker and Upholsterer's Guide*, (Plate 4), 1788 and 1794.

Source: Douglas Ash... [et al.], *World Furniture, An Illustrated History* (New York, London, Sydney, Toronto: Hamlyn Publishing Group Limited, 1976), p.141.

Piece categorically

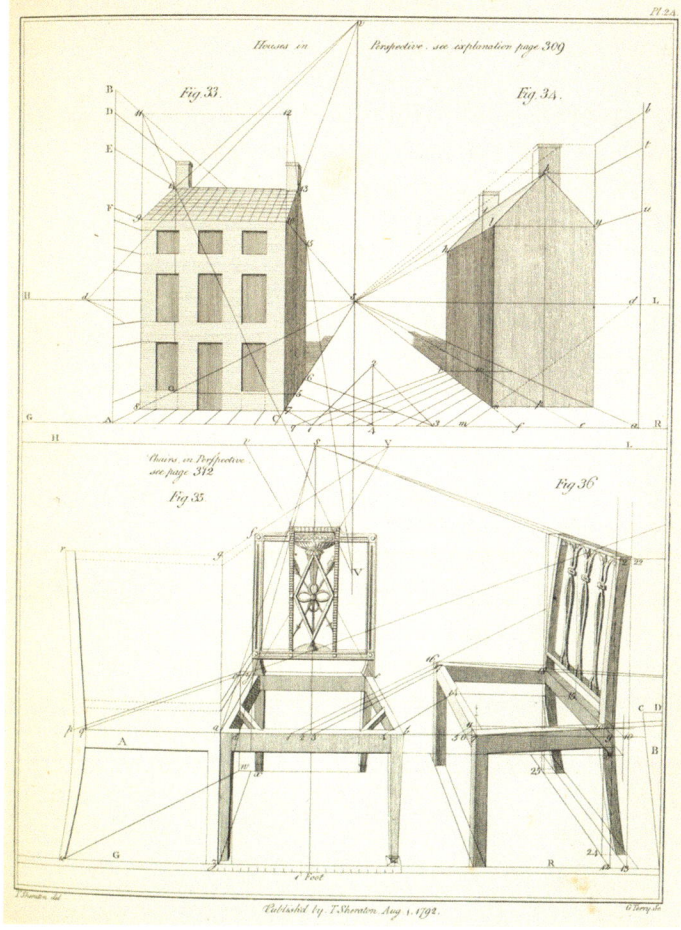

Figure 3.21 Thomas Sheraton, plate from *The Cabinet-Maker and Upholsterer's Drawing Book*.

Source: Royal Academy of Arts, Picture Library, United Kingdom.

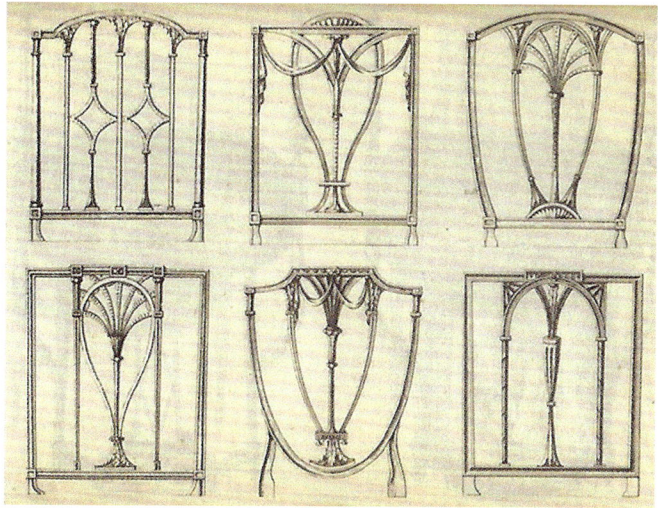

Figure 3.22 Thomas Sheraton, rectangular chair back designs.

Source: Judith Gura, *The Guide to Period Styles for Interiors: From 17th Century to the Present* (New York, London: Fairchild Books, An Imprint of Bloomsbury Publishing, Inc., 2016), p.115.

Interestingly, it is an established fact among academics and professionals (i.e., museum curators, antique experts, dealers, collectors, etc.) that there are no known documented pieces by George Hepplewhite that exist today, and few pieces actually built by Thomas Sheraton have survived.

On the right are other common 18th-century English splat-back designs; the two on the top row depict solid spats, and the three examples below depict yoke backs (Figure 3.23). The yoke back derives its name from two *S*-shape curves thought to resemble an ox yoke.

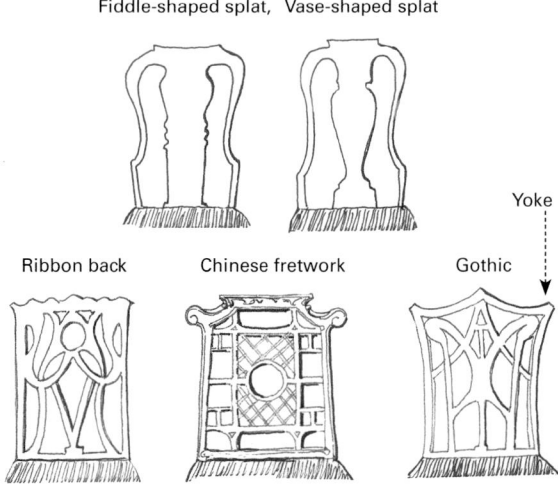

Figure 3.23
English chair splat design variations.
Author's illustrations.

The chairs on the following page are from the Metropolitan Museum of Art, American Wing. The shield-back chair is similar to Hepplewhite's pattern book design seen several pages back (Figure 3.24). Given the scale of the chair, it seems Hepplewhite-inspired. Sheraton's shield-back designs are more diminutive. However, the Greco-Roman features that inspired both cabinetmakers are evident in the use of the urn and swag design motifs.

The chair below is attributed to Samuel McIntire, ca. 1757 (Figure 3.25). The design definitely resembles qualities of plate 33 from Sheraton's *The Cabinet-Maker and Upholsterer's Drawing-Book* on the previous page.

McIntire was an American architect and cabinetmaker during the Federal period in America, which coincides with the late Georgian period in England (during the reign of George III). McIntire's work is shown here to compensate for original Hepplewhite and Sheraton chairs not being available. These two chairs, although not made in England, are superb examples representing pattern-book designs of Hepplewhite and Sheraton.

Figure 3.24
George Hepplewhite, shield-shape chair back.

Source: Mark Hinchman, *History of Furniture a Global View* (New York, New York: Fairchild Books, 2009), p.284.

After reviewing 18th-century English furniture pieces individually, it will be beneficial to look at such pieces in context. Dumfries House, an 18th-century Palladian villa in Ayrshire, Scotland, is a superb residence to view for this purpose. It is the work of renowned architect Robert Adam and his brothers, James and John, with furnishings from the workshop of Thomas Chippendale. Dumfries House contains a world-class collection of British Rococo furniture, including some 50 examples

Figure 3.25 Samuel McIntire, rectangular back armchair.

Source: Metropolitan Museum of Art, Public Domain, OA [Open Access]. Department, The American Wing.

by Thomas Chippendale.[13] Over the next several pages this world-class collection is seen in context. This furniture was ordered straight from the craftsman's workshop in 1759 by the fifth Earl of Dumfries, who commissioned the house.[14]

Dumfries House teetered on the verge of sale and dispersal, but thanks to the leadership of His Royal Highness the Prince of Wales—one of his foundations allied with other sources—Dumfries was acquired by a specially created trust and saved. This was not only a feat for the British people, but also for anyone who cares about great architecture and the decorative arts. The front exterior view and family parlor with Chippendale furniture give one an idea of Dumfries House's splendor (Figure 3.26 and Figure 3.27).

Figure 3.26 Dumfries House, front exterior view.

Source: Courtesy of the Prince's Foundation, Dumfries House, Ayrshire, Scotland.

Figure 3.27 Dumfries House, FamilyParlour.

Source: Courtesy of the Prince's Foundation, Dumfries House, Ayrshire, Scotland.

■ An Illustrated Guide to Furniture History

The family parlor includes Chippendale elbow chairs and card tables, camelback sofa by Alexander Peter, and harpsicord by Jacob Kirkman.[15] The blue drawing room was supplied with elbow chairs by Chippendale in 1759; he also created the rare rosewood breakfront bookcase (Figure 3.28, Figure 3.29, and Figure 3.30). The Murano-glass chandelier is original to Dumfries House, the chinoiserie mirror is by William Mathie, the gilt-wood pier table is the work of George Mercer, and the portraits are on loan from a private collector.

Figure 3.28 Dumfries House, Blue Drawing Room.

Source: Room interior looking at the fireplace flanked by settees and armchairs

Reverting back to look at 18th-century pieces individually here are examples of Chippendale's Neoclassical, Rococo, and chinoiserie either designed or supplied by his studio. The left chair, ca. 1772, is identical to the chair in the Met Chippendale collection; it is part of a suite of 14 chairs and was auctioned at Christie's recently (Figure 3.31). Chippendale executed this set of Neoclassical mahogany dining chairs for Goldsborough Hall in Yorkshire. The design is that of architect Robert Adam. The Classical approach to this mahogany chair is apparent in the carved laurel wreath and swag at the top of the splat and the carved bell-flower motif in front of the legs. To the right, also from the Met's collection, is a good example of a chair in the manner of Thomas Chippendale Rococo style "ribband-back" chair (1755–1760) or ribbon back, as expressed

Figure 3.29 Thomas Chippendale, elbow chair for Dumfries House.

Source: Courtesy of the Prince's Foundation, Dumfries House, Ayrshire, Scotland.

Figure 3.30 Chinese Chippendale rosewood breakfront bookcase.

Source: Courtesy of the Prince's Foundation, Dumfries House, Ayrshire, Scotland.

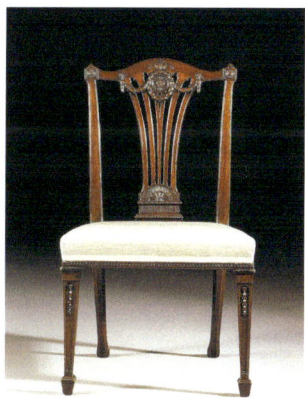

Figure 3.31 Chippendale George III dining chair, Neoclassical design.

Source: Florence de Dampierre, *Chairs: A History* (New York: Abrams, an imprint of Harry N. Abrams Inc., 2006), p.201.

Figure 3.32 Rococo "ribband-back" side chair, ca. 1755–1760. After the design of Thomas Chippendale. Mahogany with upholstered seat. One of a pair.

Source: Metropolitan Museum of Art, Public Domain, OA [Open Access]. Department, European Sculpture and Decorative Arts. Gift of Irwin Untermyer, 1964.

with a ribbon-like pierced splat, which forms the yoke back, scrollwork-carved cabriole legs, and scroll feet (Figure 3.32).

The next chair discussed is a massive gilded gold elbow chair from a project in which Robert Adam and Thomas Chippendale worked jointly for Sir

Lawrence Dundas, 19 Arlington Place, London (Figure 3.33). The designs were conceived by Adam and executed by Chippendale. This chair has characteristics of both French Rococo and Neo-classicism. Evident is the curvilinear Rococo chair form overlaid with a Classical border of foliage-wrapped reeding and centered with anthemia ending in sunflower double rosettes, carved seat-rail with the central shell framed by griffins and the legs framed by sphinxes.

Figure 3.33 Thomas Chippendale design, gilt gold armchair, 1765, for Sir Lawrence Dundas residence, 19 Arlington Place, London.

Source: Private Collection Photo © Christie's Images/Bridgeman Images.

The Chinese Chippendale chair below the gilded gold elbow, from the Victoria and Albert Museum collection, is not attributed to Chippendale but is an excellent example of his aesthetic (Figure 3.34). As stated in the museum literature, this chair is one of a set of at least 16 chairs, possibly for a dining room. The design is directly from *The Gentleman and Cabinet-Maker's Director* (1754). It reveals fretwork replacing the splat, with a yoke resembling a Chinese pagoda. Chippendale produced many pieces in this chinoiserie style (Chinese Chippendale) such as the rosewood breakfront bookcase at Dumfries House, as seen on the previous pages.

Figure 3.34 Author's illustration, Chinese Chippendale chair, Victoria and Albert Museum collection.

Source: Reference for sketch, On-line image from Public Domain.

Similar to French commode design, mid-18th-century English commode design, ca. 1760, had a bombée form, serpentine fronts, and softly curved outlines (Figure 3.35). By the 1770s, the shape of commodes universally became plainer and more linear in design, such as the George III Chippendale period mahogany chest (Figure 3.36). This chest, ca. 1770s, is unusual: the mahogany base molding is japanned and rests on four original shaped feet. By the 1790s, ormolu mounts were rare and plain handles and escutcheons were used. In Britain, the commode evolved into a plainer rectilinear box form—a chest of drawers that graduated in drawer size. The decorative quality by the late 18th century consisted of the serpentine front, with plinth base and brackets (Figure 3.37).

Eighteenth-century English seating pieces extend beyond armchairs and side chairs. The settee—bench-like in form, offering a seat for two or more persons, with a back and typically with all-wood arms—should not be forgotten. By the late

Figure 3.35 English Commode, ca.1760, mahogany, serpentine shape, carved edge detail, bracket feet.

Author's illustration.

Figure 3.36 *(Top)* George III Chippendale period mahogany serpentine chest, ca.1770, England. Details *(bottom left)* Bracket feet, drawer pulls, dovetail joints.

Source: Courtesy of Alexander George Fine Antiques Limited, UK.

18th century, the settee became synonymous with a contemporary sofa. In Chippendale's pattern books, what evolved was a settee with an arched back that rises to a higher point or peak in the middle and again slightly at the sides; the frame consisted of exposed wood, with taut upholstery for the seat and arms, which were often rolled or scroll-shaped, and lacked a separate back cushion. These sofas are referred to as camelback style (camelback sofa). The historic black-ink and gray-wash drawing is what would have been produced at the time for the furniture pattern book. The 1759 drawing is from Chippendale's workshop and can be found in the Met's collection (Figure 3.38).

Figure 3.37 Commode features 1–5.

Author's illustrations.

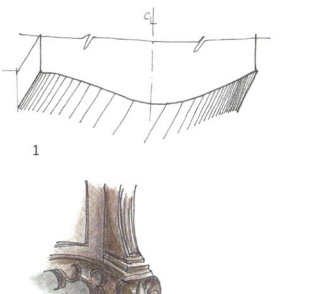 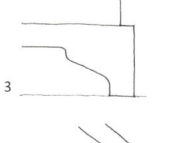 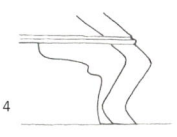 

Key
1 – Serpentine front, compound curve with a convex section between two concave ones
2 – Bracket food with carved fleur-de-lis
3 – Plinth base with bracket foot
4 – Ogee bracket foot
5 – Drawer pull

■ An Illustrated Guide to Furniture History

Figure 3.38 Sofa in Chippendale's drawings Vol. 1, 1759, black ink and gray wash.

Source: The Metropolitan Museum of Art, Public Domain, OA [Open Access]. Department of Drawings and Prints. Rogers Fund, 1920.

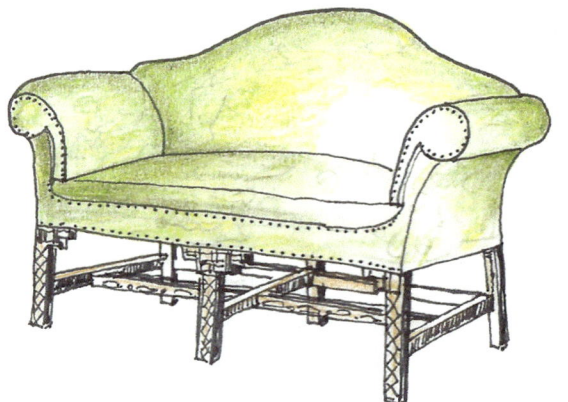

Figure 3.39 English camelback sofa with damask upholstery.

Author's illustration

By the late 18th century, camelback sofas were ubiquitous seating pieces in the residences of the aristocracy. The rendered drawing below is a Chinese Chippendale–inspired camelback sofa (Figure 3.39). The Chinese fret pattern on the marlborough leg and at the corners show the chinoiserie influence (Figure 3.40). By the mid- to late Georgian period, the marlborough leg for settees and other furniture pieces was a favored style.

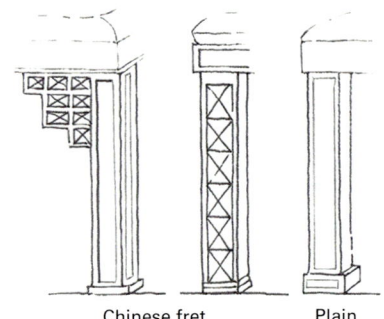

Chinese fret   Plain

Figure 3.40 Marlborough leg styles of Thomas Chippendale.

Author's illustration

Stylistically, the camelback sofa can range from simple to elaborate. Robert Adam's camelback designs for Harewood House are filled with such examples.

66

Edwin Lascelles, 1st Baron Harewood, had the country home built between 1759 and 1771, and employed the finest craftsmen of the time to work on the exterior and interior. Architect John Carr was commissioned to design the house; architect Robert Adam, the interiors; and Thomas Chippendale, the furniture. It took approximately 12 years to complete the house and its interiors. By 1765, the home was largely completed and, by 1771, all complete. Harewood House is considered one of the finest country houses in Yorkshire, England. Visible is the exterior front façade, music room, and the yellow drawing room (Figure 3.41, Figure 3.42, and Figure 3.45). The sofa designs for the music room and yellow drawing room will be discussed on the next several pages.

The circular-designed music room is considered to be the most complete example of Adam's interiors at Harewood House. Chippendale's shop was responsible for

Figure 3.41
Harewood House, Yorkshire, England, front façade.
Source: Reproduction by courtesy of Harewood House Trust. Photographer: Simon Warner

Figure 3.42
Harewood House Music Room.
Source: Reproduction by courtesy of Harewood House Trust.

Figure 3.44
Music Room chair.
Source: Courtesy of Harewood House Trust.

Figure 3.43
Harwood House Music Room settee.
Source: Courtesy of Harewood House Trust.

Figure 3.45
Harewood House Yellow Drawing Room.
Source: Reproduction by courtesy of Harewood House Trust.

executing the furniture. The interior architectural quality for both rooms is Neoclassical, which is revealed in the treatment of the wall and ceiling planes. The furniture is also Neoclassical. The music room's gilded gold camelback sofa (settee) is restrained with regard to applied ornament, yet the detail applied in the trim as well as the carved detail is what one would see in Greco-Roman designs (Figure 3.44). The legs are not cabriole but straight and fluted as a Classical column would be. The upholstery is possibly a French Aubusson tapestry. The suite of furniture included matching chairs (Figure 3.45). The yellow drawing room's settee is similar to the music room. Yet the settee and chairs possess an even more Neoclassical aesthetic (Figure 3.46 and Figure 3.47). Their applied ornament is more

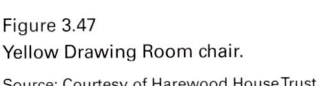

Figure 3.46
Harwood House Yellow Drawing Room settee.
Source: Courtesy of Harewood House Trust.

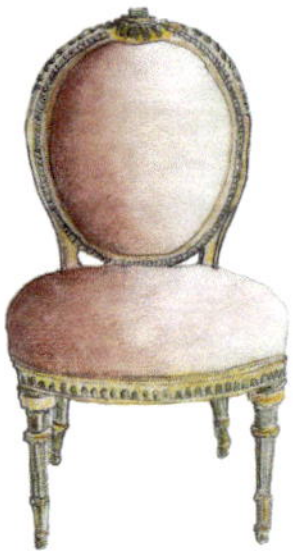

Figure 3.47
Yellow Drawing Room chair.
Source: Courtesy of Harewood House Trust.

restrained. The finish is painted and gilded, and the legs end with casters, which is an interesting feature.

Adam and Chippendale worked on Sir Lawrence Dundas's residence at 19 Arlington Street in London. It appears Adam and Chippendale's collaboration on the Dundas residence mirrored their collaboration on Harewood House. Dundas hired Adam to furnish the home, and Adam engaged Chippendale to execute his furniture designs. The furniture for this project is unmistakably Neoclassical.

The plate below is a watercolor rendering of the sofa design made for Dundas (Figure 3.48). The execution of the piece by Chippendale translates somewhat differently in reality, as you can see in Dundas's sofa below, ca. 1765 (Figure 3.49). Christie's specialist succinctly explains the Neoclassical quality: they believe this suite to be the finest Neoclassical seating Chippendale's shop produced. The specialists mention the sofa's voluptuous Rococo form, the graceful quality of the serpentine back and cabriole legs—what makes it unique is the successful overlaying of Classical motifs to the Rococo form; cresting bordered with foliage-wrapped reeding and centered with anthemia ending in sunflower double rosettes, seat-rail carved with central shell framed by griffins and sphinxes framing the legs. The cabriole legs are headed by anthemia issuing ribbon-tied interlaced descending wreaths, ending on hairy-paw feet ringed by beaded girdles. The primary wood used for construction is

Figure 3.48
Thomas Chippendale watercolor plate of giltwood carved sofa for Sir Lawrence Dundas.

Source: Private Collection Photo © Christie's Images/ Bridgeman Images.

Figure 3.49
One of a pair of giltwood sofas designed by Robert Adam, workshop Thomas Chippendale, ca.1763, for Sir Lawrence Dundas.

Source: Private Collection Photo © Christie's Images/ Bridgeman Images.

lime wood gilded gold; the original upholstery was a crimson damask. Christie's professionals believe this to be the most expensive suite of furniture Chippendale made.

To conclude this section, it is important to speak about non-upholstered furniture, furniture bearing some resemblance to a storage component, a *case piece* or *case goods*. The case piece includes bookcases or cabinets with breakfronts, high chests, buffets, sideboards, etc. By the later part of the 18th century, as with architecture, furniture moved away from the robust undulating and curvilinear form of Rococo and began to mimic the Classical forms of Greece and Rome. Furniture legs became straight, resembling Classical columns, with the edges sometimes tapered and fluted. Other Classical details such as swags, festoons, ribbons, feathers, and urns were used, carved in light relief or painted designs. The use of contrasting veneers replaced mahogany and included a wide range of species: maple, popular tulipwood, birch, and rosewood. As important as the design-motif change is the change in the scale of furniture pieces. The pieces were slighter and delicate, more rectilinear than protruding.

Of the "big three," Hepplewhite and Sheraton, as mentioned earlier in this section, popularized the Neoclassical style, which became omnipresent in the late 18th century. Stylistically, this aesthetic transferred well for case-piece design. It is said that Hepplewhite and Sheraton's 18th-century pattern books influenced architect Robert Adam's Neoclassical designs in the late 18th century. It is fascinating to think that these books are still influencing the furniture design of leading traditional furniture companies, such as Kittinger Furniture Company; Baker, Knapp & Tubbs Company; Statton Furniture Company; Henredon Company; Hickory Chair Furniture Company; and Century. These companies produce furniture derived from the pattern books of the "big three." On the following pages are some 21st-century classic case-piece examples from the Kittinger Company recalling the work of Sheraton and Hepplewhite.

In their publication *American Furniture: 1620 to Present*, authors Jonathan L. Fairbanks and Elizabeth Bates characterize Sheraton's designs succinctly as "a fiercely rectilinear silhouette."[16] This silhouette is visible in the Kittinger Furniture Company's catalog collection of Sheraton reproductions beginning on the following page (Plate 3.2, Plate 3.3, and Figure 3.50). The catalog description has been included to show how contemporary furniture companies explain historic reproduction furniture.

The Sheraton dining table on the following page has one of the most notable features of his design: the tripod base made of three somewhat delicate looking arched legs caped with casters or other metal detail. This design feature became as important to Sheraton's design repertoire as the shield-shape chair became to Hepplewhite's design repertoire.

Concluding this section is a photograph of a Chippendale George III mahogany breakfront, ca. 1764, auctioned in 2008 at Christie's, London (Figure 3.51). To mark the 300-year anniversary of Chippendale's furniture production, on July 5, 2018, Christie's UK released an excellently crafted and informative video (www.christies.com/features/How-to-spot-a-genuine-Thomas-Chippendale-9281-3.aspx). In the video, specialists reveal some of Chippendale's telltale innovations, designs, and techniques. Orlando Rock, chairman of Christie's UK, states, "Chippendale

Kittinger Company
www.kittingerfurniture.com

KC3812 • Sheraton Sideboard

This sideboard has crotch mahogany on door and drawer fronts, front legs detailed with boxwood inlay and a stringing bellflower motif and medallion, drawers and cupboards that lock, center drawer with a silver insert, and solid brass hardware. Shown with optional banding on top and doors.

Dimensions:
W 66" D 25" H 36 ¾"

Weight: 300

KT3210 • Sheraton Dining Table

Swirl mahogany with ribbon cut mahogany banding ebony inlay. Three 12" leaves. Length when open 108".

Dimensions:
L 72" W 48" H 30"

Plate 3.2
(above) Sheraton Sideboard, Kittinger Furniture Company Inc. furniture catalog. *(below)* Sheraton Dining Table, Kittinger Furniture Company Inc.
Source: Kittinger Furniture Co., Inc., Buffalo, N.Y.

■ An Illustrated Guide to Furniture History

Kittinger Company
www.kittingerfurniture.com

KC5207 • George Hepplewhite Sideboard

This Hepplewhite sideboard is of mahogany and mahogany veneer inlaid in boxwood. The top locking center drawer is partitioned for silver and a large linen drawer is hidden below. This sideboard has a door on the left end, a drawer on the right end and solid brass hardware.

Dimensions:
W 78 5/8" D 23 ½ " H 39"

Weight: 250

KC2551 • Hepplewhite Chest

This Hepplewhite chest of drawers with mahogany and mahogany veneer has five drawers banded by satinwood with holly and ebony inlay, and solid brass hardware.

Dimensions:
W 38 " D 21 " H 34 "

Weight: 180

Plate 3.3
(above) George Hepplewhite Sideboard, Kittinger Company Inc. furniture catalog. *(below)* George Hepplewhite chest of drawers, Kittinger Furniture Company Inc. furniture catalog.
Source: Kittinger Furniture Company, Inc. Buffalo, N.Y.

Figure 3.50
Kittinger Georgian Breakfront, SKU: KC3701, Kittinger Furniture Co., Inc.

Source: Kittinger Furniture Company, Inc. Buffalo, N.Y. at the base.

Figure 3.51
Mahogany breakfront bookcase design by Robert Adam. Workshop of Thomas Chippendale, 1764, for Sir Lawrence Dundas, 19 Arlington Place, London.

Source: Private Collection Photo © Christie's Images/ Bridgeman Images.

is a name synonymous with the greatest works of art created out of timber by a man in England. We really know him now because of his celebrated book *The Gentleman and Cabinet-Maker's Director*, through which he disbursed his ideas to regional cabinetmakers, to patrons, and also internationally." Chippendale was incredibly bold in embracing new styles and new techniques, influenced often from France and the Continent.[17] Robert Copley, international head of furniture at Christie's London, elaborates, "I suppose what we love about Chippendale is the incredible, fanciful furniture that he designed: the Chinoiserie cabinets that he's known for, but also the evolution from the Rococo to the Neoclassical. He was obviously an extremely good draughtsman and designer, and his enduring appeal is not only the great designs, but also their beautiful execution."[18] The black-and-white photograph is of this mahogany breakfront bookcase in a room flanked by two chairs prior to the Christie's auction (Figure 3.52). As recorded by Christie's UK, its provenance—supplied to Sir Lawrence Dundas, between 1763 and 1766, for the Library, 19 Arlington Street, London, and by descent.

Figure 3.52
Photograph, Sir Lawrence Dundas breakfront bookcase design of Robert Adam, workshop of Thomas Chippendale, 1764, for Sir Lawrence Dundas, 19 Arlington Place, London.

Source: Country Life Picture Gallery, Farnborough, England, United Kingdom.

AMERICA

The third and last country to be discussed with regard to categorizing furniture based on place of origin and timeframe is 18th-century America—specifically, the 13 colonies. This period in America corresponds with the later part of Louis XIV's reign and the reigns of Louis XV and Louis XVI in France, and with the reigns of George I, George II, and George III in England. The Colonial American periods follow European examples of design, yet the style arrived across the Atlantic after an interval of about 15 years.[19] The furniture timeline for 18th-centry America is divided as follows: Early Colonial American style, ca. 1640–1720s, ending with King William III and Queen Mary II; and Late Colonial American style, defined by Queen Anne, ca. 1720–1780, Chippendale style, ca. 1750–1790, and Rococo style ca. 1750–1777 (or Chippendale/Rococo style). By the end of the century, the Federal style arrives, referencing Neoclassicism and the work of George Hepplewhite and Thomas Sheraton.

Early Colonial furniture pieces recall the Jacobean and Carolingian periods of English history—massive in size and heavy and solid, with straight, simple lines and little ornamentation. Early settlers made their own modest pieces of furniture—benches, stools, tables, beds, and chests. Having survived the rigors of settling in a new nation, Americans were steadily gaining ground, both in the amenities of day-to-day living and in stylishness and sophistication.[20] Virgin forests of pine, oak, maple, cherry, and other native trees were abundant, and the settlers were able to use the finest quality of wood for furniture making. Handmade furniture gave way to skilled cabinetmakers, many who relocated to the New World from Europe, and the cabinetmaker's shop was born. By the 18th century, furniture styles generally followed that of England.

In respect to the timeline for American furniture, this section will begin with the Late Colonial America 1720–1780s. By the mid-18th century, life in the colonies was becoming increasingly settled.[21] From the earliest settlements, North American communities were principally middle class, in both economic reality and social ideology. With the emergence of a prosperous class of merchants and shipbuilders, and the arrival in the colonies of European-trained craftsmen, more people were able to afford fine furnishings, and more specialists were available to make them. This was an advantage for the cabinetmaker in the New World.[22]

The middle-class colonists were freemen who owned property but were not as rich as the gentry were. The middle class worked at skilled jobs, such as teacher or craftsman, or ran small stores and businesses, such as cabinetmaking. Colonial aristocracy in the South was made up mostly of the larger rice and tobacco planters; in the Mid-Atlantic and New England regions, rich merchants were the social leaders. Few of the settlers had been aristocrats in England, but as they became wealthy, they patterned their social lives after the aristocrats of the Old World. The wealthy wanted their homes to reflect the country homes and estates of England and other parts of Europe. The middle class wanted their homes to reflect the wealthy class in the New World.

The middle class sought after higher-grade furnishings and materials. Furniture, like architecture, was a universal art form used by all classes and thus became an important barometer for mainstream taste.[23] The furniture construction followed European traditions. Specific joinery techniques were used; the work of the joiner (joyner) and the use of the lathe enabled complicated turned shapes by the turner. Also similar to the European model, these businesses included multi-generations of a family, and the craftsman and artisan followed the same type of hierarchical structure as in Europe, working from apprentice to journeyman to master.

The physical form of 18th-century American furniture is intrinsically linked to national identity and region. The regions of the 13 colonies (New England, Mid-Atlantic, and South Atlantic) were settled by specific national groups. mid-16th-century Spaniards settled in St. Augustine, Florida; early 17th-century Swedish colonists settled in the Mid-Atlantic region; the Dutch settled in Connecticut, the Connecticut River Valley, Western Pennsylvania, and the southern tip of New York, and Virginia. The English and the Scots settled throughout the 13 colonies. Furniture can be categorized in relation to these national groups and the regional differences, driven by their cultural rituals and traditions. However, cabinetmakers' success was not linked to national identity, but in financial success and earning a living. In the New World, furniture making tended to concentrate in the port cities: Newport (Rhode Island), Boston, Philadelphia, New York City, Baltimore, and Charleston (South Carolina).

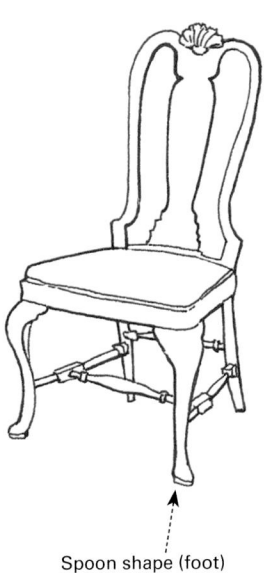

Figure 3.53
Queen Anne chair.
Author's Illustration

There were two styles of furniture that were predominant during the Late Colonial period: Queen Anne and Chippendale/Rococo. With respect to physiognomies, American Queen Anne furniture was based on the *S*-curved form of English designs but differs in several important areas: the mass/scale of the American case piece is slimmer, and the cabriole legs are elongated with a pronounced knee, which gently curves and tapers at the ankle, terminating with a club or spoon foot. By the 1730s, Boston as a leading colonial city and its furniture makers developed a standard chair form with a vase-shaped splat and *S*-curved cabriole legs.[24] Later, the archetypical Queen Anne chair was made in Philadelphia.[25] The line drawing on the right depicts the chair style of the Boston and Philadelphia (Figure 3.53).

Spoon shape (foot)

Chippendale furniture or Chippendale/Rococo is seen in America after copies of Thomas Chippendale's publication *The Gentleman and Cabinet-Maker's Director* made their way to the colonies within the first year of publication.[26] The American adaptation of Rococo focused almost exclusively on the style's ornamental motifs—shells and rocaille, scrollwork, acanthus leaves (raffles), and other flora and fauna, often in asymmetrical compositions.[27] Leading urban craftsmen enthusiastically applied these elements to furniture, in addition to architectural interiors, engravings, and silver. The form of these pieces is linear; England's Queen Anne furniture emphasizes the curve. There is an emphasis on the claw-and-ball foot and the ornamental carving was robust but less three-dimensional than English chairs. A prevalent detail for Chippendale chairs is the intricately pierced, heavily carved openwork splat back.

A particular invention of American furniture in which an upper-case piece sits on a lower-case piece can be referred to by several names: high chest, highboy, tallboy, or simply a chest-on-chest. These forms often were raised up on legs—for convenience and a graceful, taller silhouette—with the lower case called a lowboy (Figure 3.54 and Figure 3.55). The form continued until after the American Revolution and became the most important item of furniture in most colonial homes.[28] There was a relationship between this case piece and Classical architecture—the Classical temple. The temple has a base, central section, and pediment; the case piece has a base, central section, and top/cornice. The drawing of the Chippendale Philadelphia highboy illustrates the boldness of scale and details; the heavily carved pediment, cabriole legs, shell motifs, and overall mass and scale of the piece communicates a Georgian vocabulary instead of Queen Anne.

Reiterating the emphasis of the furniture foot, important to note are the claw-and-ball variations used for furniture throughout colonial regions: New England, Mid-Atlantic, and South Atlantic (Figure 3.56).

This section discusses the physical character—the architype of furniture produced by cabinetmakers regionally (New England, Mid-Atlantic, and South Atlantic). Regarding physical form, what becomes apparent is how Colonial American furniture design, like European furniture design, assumes qualities that are architectural in nature. Greco-Roman Classicism influenced case-furniture design form, scale, proportion, and details. Richly upholstered chairs and sofas emphasized flowing, curved outlines decorated with scrolls, anthemion, acanthus leaves, and shells emulating carved decorative motifs of Classical architecture. This "serpentine line of beauty," also prevalent in portraiture, was later described by English painter William Hogarth in his *Analysis of Beauty* (1753) as the overriding aesthetic of the age.[29]

Beginning with New England, we'll first examine case furniture. The 18th-century American case piece typically had carved light relief, flower motifs, or lunettes, shells, scrolls, anthemion, and acanthus leaves. In the early 18th century, many pieces, especially chest pieces, were painted (black, red, and yellow). For seating pieces, fabrics included tapestries and brocades, velvet, silks, and linen; carpets were likely an Oriental or Aubusson. For the room itself, architectural features for the interior included woodwork and trim throughout the house, comprising wood mantels and surrounds, corner cupboards, dining rooms, wainscot and crown molding at the ceiling, and case trim around the doors and windows.

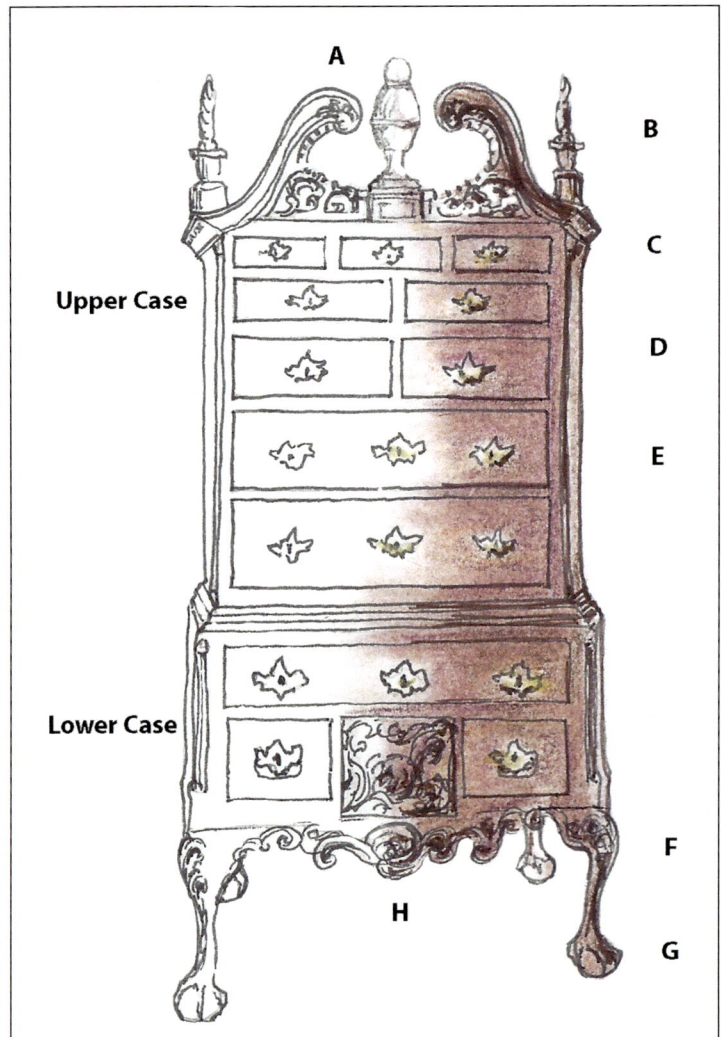

Figure 3.54 Philadelphia highboy.

Author's illustration.

Key
A – Scroll-top pediment
B – Finial urn
C – Chamfer corners
D – Drawer with brass escutcheons diminishing in size
F – Cabriole leg with carved knee
G – Ball-and-claw feet
H – Scallop edge

Figure 3.55 Philadelphia lowboy depicting a typical aesthetic and form for the Philadelphia lowboy.

Author's illustration.

Figure 3.56
American
Chippendale
ball-and-claw
variations A–E.

Source: Photo by
Jim Postell. Jim
Postell, *Furniture
Design* (Hoboken,
New Jersey: John
Wiley & Sons, Inc.
2007), p.291.

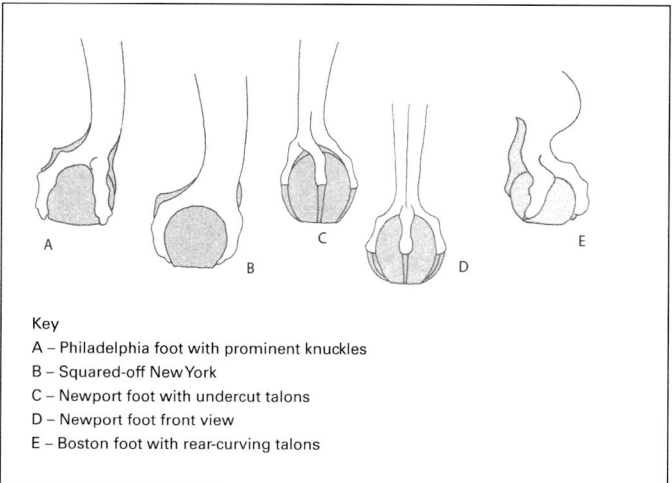

Key
A – Philadelphia foot with prominent knuckles
B – Squared-off New York
C – Newport foot with undercut talons
D – Newport foot front view
E – Boston foot with rear-curving talons

Reinterpretation of pattern books by Chippendale, Hepplewhite, and Sheraton was ubiquitous during this time.

New England is the oldest clearly defined U.S. region settled by Puritans fleeing religious persecution in England. Establishing the first colony in 1620, a large influx of Puritans populated New England during the puritan migration (1620–1640), settling largely in the Boston and Salem areas. Around the 1680s, the next group to flee religious persecution and come to New England was the Quakers, who were in search of economic opportunities and a more tolerant environment. The intent of the Quakers was to build communities of "holy conversation." They founded thriving communities in Delaware Valley and in the three colonies—West Jersey, Rhode Island, and Pennsylvania—and established themselves politically in these areas. The Quaker William Penn established West Jersey and Pennsylvania. Because of the religious nature of New England's origins, the culture is described as being reserved and proper, but equally industrious and fastidious about finance. Eighteenth-century New England had excellent harbors and became a fishing, shipbuilding, and commercial center. At one time, it was the most prosperous region in the New World, and it became possible for the middle-class merchant to rise to affluence and employ architects to design large residences, which aided a busy cabinetmaking industry in the region.

New England

Newport, Rhode Island

The drawing below left is from *Sutton Fine Furniture Company, Furniture Glossary* (Figure 3.57). Sutton Fine Furniture was responsible for fine reproductions licensed by the British National Trust, the Smithsonian Institute, the Henry Ford Museum, and the Museum of Early Southern Decorative Arts. The flat-top secretary (writing table) below is a good example of Newport design—straightforward in its approach, with very little applied ornament or carving. In the 18th century, Quaker

■ An Illustrated Guide to Furniture History

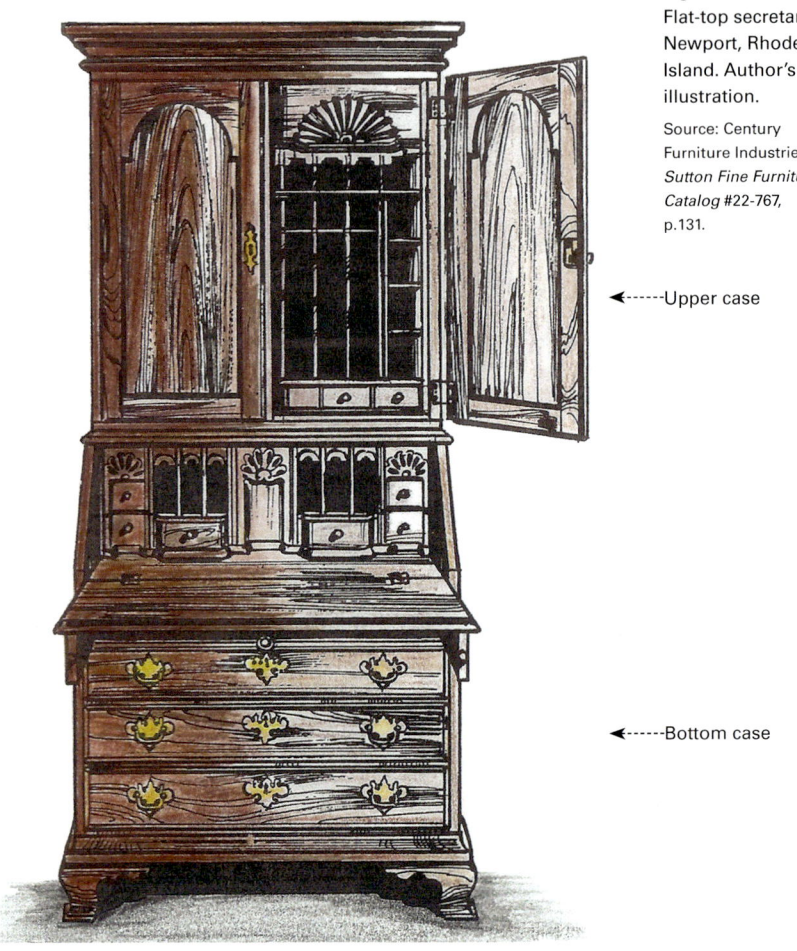

Figure 3.57
Flat-top secretary, Newport, Rhode Island. Author's illustration.

Source: Century Furniture Industries. *Sutton Fine Furniture Catalog #22-767*, p.131.

◄------Upper case

◄------Bottom case

cabinetmakers set up shop in Newport. One of the best-known establishments was John Townsend and John Goddard. The work will be seen on the next several pages. This secretary (writing table), reserved in character, is a typically Newport piece. The aesthetic quality has as much to do with the materiality—wood grain— as with applied decorative motifs. This furniture type was common for Newport households. The secretary consisted of an upper-case and a lower-case piece, each possessing certain features (Figure 3.58). The upper case had a flat top with crown molding and an incised shell as the decorative motif central to each door opening. The lower case had a drop-front with drawers graduating in size, with robust-shaped escutcheons and pigeonholes for storage

The Townsend and Goddard families lent their names to an extensive body of New England furniture made in and associated with Newport in the second half of the 18th century. The families were joined through marriages and were part of a large cabinetmaking community centered in The Point neighborhood of Newport,

Piece categorically ■

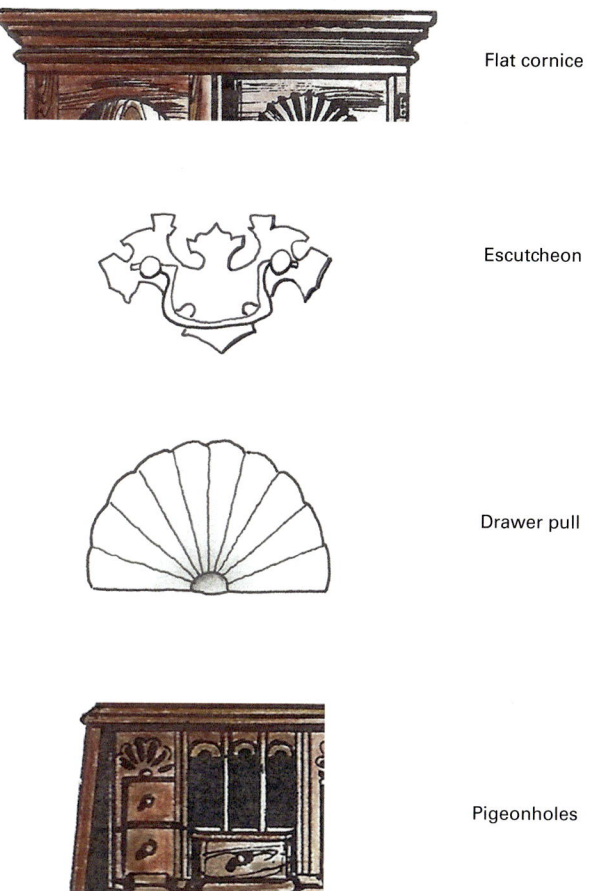

Figure 3.58
Flat-top secretary, Newport, Rhode Islanddetails.Author's illustrations
Source: Century Furniture Industries. Sutton Fine Furniture Catalog #22-767, p.131.

which was predominately Quaker. John Townsend and John Goddard founded the Newport School of Furniture, and the families became a cabinetmaking dynasty.

The furniture associated with Townsend and Goddard can be identified by several unique features. Their block-front furniture became known as the block-and-shell. The term *block-front* refers to a particular type of furniture front (façade) divided into three vertical panels: the center one is slightly concave, and the outer ones are slightly convex. The block-and-shell reference refers to the carved cockleshell ornament above each vertical section. This design is particularly evident in the chest of drawers on the left and in the bureau table to the right, with its deeper recessed center section, typical of bureau tables. This approach to block-fronts falls within the "Townsend and Goddard School," the set of design principles practiced by Newport cabinetmakers. Their aesthetic includes an ogee-curve foot, a bracket foot, or a distinct claw-and-ball foot, in which there is an open space carved between the talon and ball. The claw-and-ball foot form is thought to be unique to Newport, though not unique to the Townsend and Goddard families. These particular pieces of furniture are designed with ogee feet.

In the Met collection are excellent examples of two of Townsend's block-front pieces, ca. 1765 (Figure 3.59 and Figure 3.60). The chest of drawers on the left is made of mahogany and secondary woods (tulip poplar, pine, and chestnut), and the bureau table on the right is also made of mahogany and secondary woods (chestnut and tulip poplar).

Block-front furniture captured the imagination of New England cabinetmakers and their wealthier patrons for almost 100 years[30] and was characterized by richness, rationality, classic proportions, and compromising symmetry. Newport construction techniques as well as design principles fused with the native product to produce a wholly distinctive style. This includes a block-front façade, a shell that terminates the blocking, use of a blocked desk lid that is square rather than the slightly rounded corners on the blocking of the top drawer, and the use of a flat mahogany strip at the bottom of the case.

Figure 3.59 Attributed to John Townsend, chest of drawers, ca.1765 (block-front-chest). Newport, Rhode Island.

Source: Metropolitan Museum of Art, The American Wing Public Domain, OA [Open Access]. Rogers Fund, 1927.

On the next several pages are drawings that graphically explain the specific block-front details that classify a piece as belonging to Newport (Figure 3.61 and Figure 3.62).

On the following page is a Townsend and Goddard dressing table (Figure 3.63). It is an excellent example of the "Townsend and Goddard School," that school of thought and design practiced by Newport cabinetmakers—again, a straightforward approach, minimal applied

Figure 3.60 Attributed to John Townsend, bureau table, ca.1765. Newport, Rhode Island.

Source: Metropolitan Museum of Art, The American Wing. Public Domain, OA [Open Access]. Gift of Mrs. Russell Sage, 1909.

ornamentation, and design motifs. The decorative quality often results from the pattern of the wood grain and the shape of the constituent parts of the whole piece. This dressing table is considered Chippendale style. The wood is primarily mahogany, with secondary wood of yellow poplar and white pine used for the drawers and backs. The shape is oblong, with a dramatic scalloped front skirt.

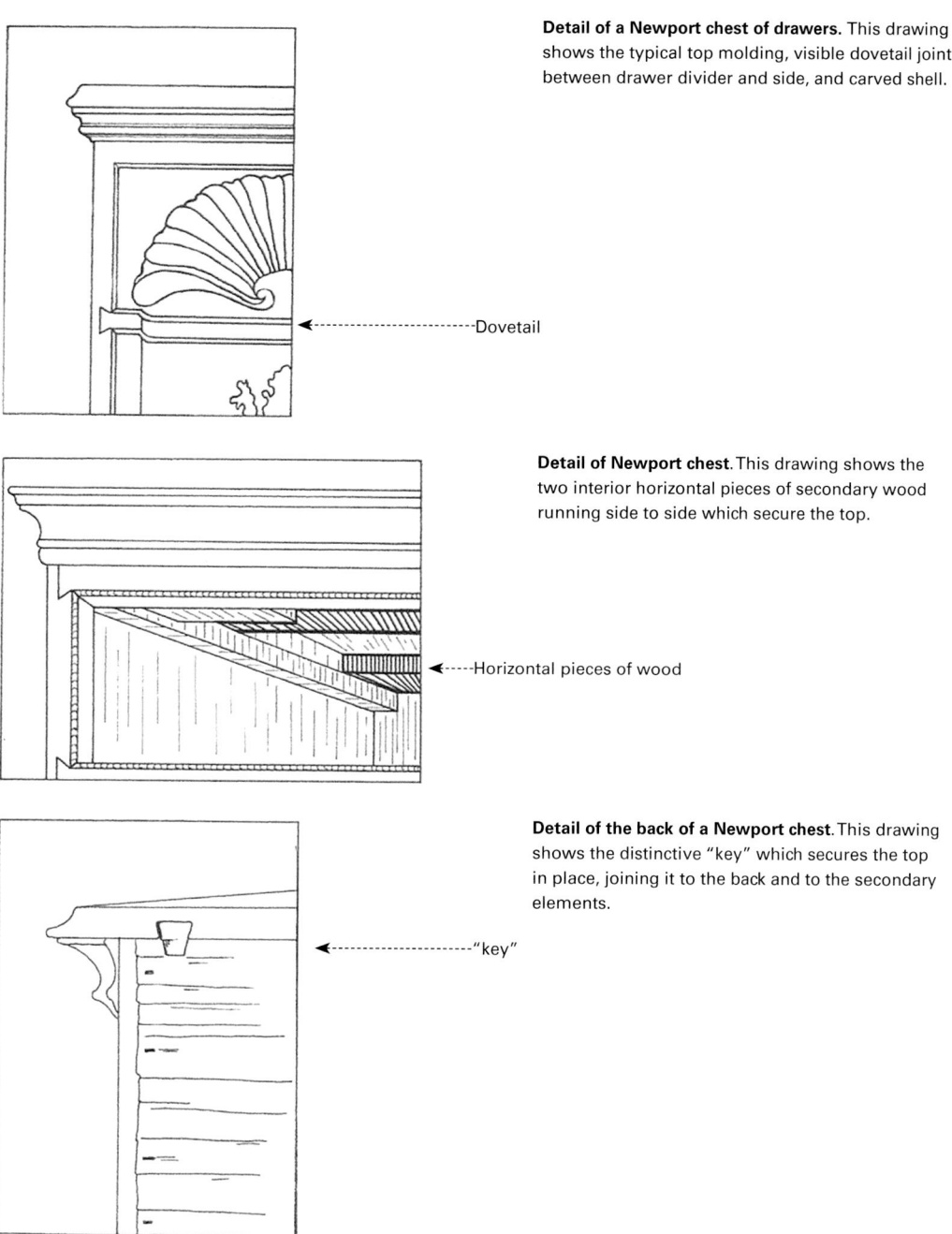

Detail of a Newport chest of drawers. This drawing shows the typical top molding, visible dovetail joint between drawer divider and side, and carved shell.

Dovetail

Detail of Newport chest. This drawing shows the two interior horizontal pieces of secondary wood running side to side which secure the top.

Horizontal pieces of wood

Detail of the back of a Newport chest. This drawing shows the distinctive "key" which secures the top in place, joining it to the back and to the secondary elements.

"key"

Figure 3.61
Classification of Newport, block-front chest construction and aesthetic details.
Source: Margaretta Markle Lovell, "Boston Blockfront Furniture," *Boston Furniture of the Eighteenth Century*, published by the Colonial Society of Massachusetts, 1972, vol. 48, pp.84, 85, and 87.

■ An Illustrated Guide to Furniture History

Detail of Newport chest with bottom drawer removed. This drawing shows the typical form of case construction (horizontal mahogany strip behind the molding is flat in back and occasionally is supported by a small strip of secondary wood; case bottom is about two inches below the top edge of the molding).

Case bottom ------▶

Detail of Newport case and drawer construction. This drawing shows the typical form of drawer construction (the end of the drawer bottom is often visible from the side with a runner applied beneath), and visible joint between drawer divider and case side

Visible joint ------▶

Detail of typical Newport foot. Ogee curved feet are common.

Ogee foot ------▶

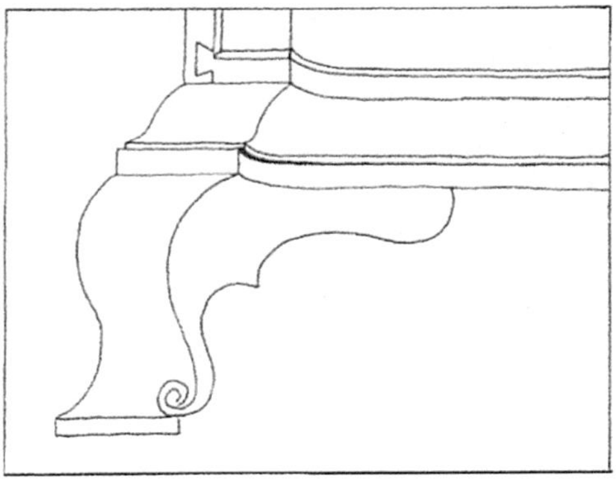

Figure 3.62
Classification of Newport, block-front chest construction and aesthetic details.
Source: Margaretta Markle Lovell, "Boston Blockfront Furniture," *Boston Furniture of the Eighteenth Century*, published by the Colonial Society of Massachusetts, 1972, vol. 48, pp.85, 87, and 88.

Figure 3.63
Dressing table, ca. 1750–1755. Probably Christopher Townsend. Mahogany, yellowpoplar, eastern white pine.

Source: Museum of Fine Arts Houston, The Bayou Bend Collection.

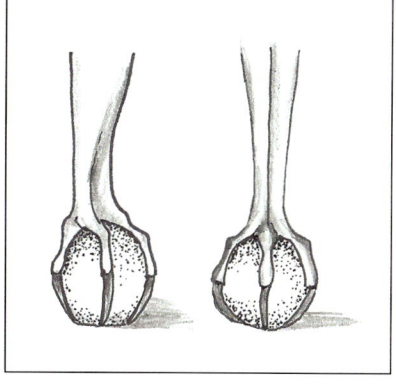

Figure 3.65
Label from tall clock case, John Townsend's workshop.

Source: Metropolitan Museum of Art, Public Domain, OA [Open Access]. The American Wing. Rogers Fund, 1927.

Figure 3.64
Ball-and-claw with undercut talon *(left)* front view, *(right)* side view.

Author's illustration.

The lone motif, a central scallop shell incised half-circle, gives this central area hierarchy. The drawers are complimented with brass drawer pulls and escutcheons. The legs are reminiscent of the French cabriole shape, yet much more angular at the knees. The ankles are deeply carved with claws and undercut talons, grasping spherical ball feet (Figure 3.64). All cabinetmakers had their mark or label for pieces they designed and made. Shown is the paper label used by John Townsend's workshop. This label is from a tall clock case made by John Townsend. The clock is in the collection at the Metropolitan Museum of Art in New York (Figure 3.65).

Benjamin Frothingham (1734–1809) of Charlestown, Massachusetts, was also known for his design of block-front furniture. His slant-front desk (ca. 1770–1775) depicts the difference between his form and that of the Newport cabinetmakers (Figure 3.66 and Figure 3.67). His was rounder than the Newport block-fronts produced by Townsend and Goddard. Notable characteristics of his furniture include a delicate ogee bracket foot or pronounced claw-and-ball foot, and for his high chest, crisp corkscrew finials rising from an urn. His aesthetic quality, not unlike the Quaker designs, emphasized the grain of the wood. For the slant-top desk below, he chose a highly figured mahogany wood grain for the block façade, visible on the drop-front panel and drawer fronts. The interior lower left has three reverse-blocked sections with carved fans separated by a single blocked drawer and double pigeonholes.

The black-and-white image on the right is a view of the front (façade), with the three reverse-blocked sections visible also seen in the photograph below. The interior double pigeonholes have rounded arches that reflect the scallop shells left, right, and center. The hardware, drawer pulls, and escutcheons are brass.

The slant-front desk is made of mahogany, with secondary wood of pine; has brass drawer pulls, and escutcheons; and is supported by a pronounced ogee curve with claw-and-ball feet. The size of the piece is H 49¼" × W 25½" × D 15½".

The provenance—made for Colonel Churchill Williams of Philadelphia, in Frothingham's shop, in Charlestown, Boston Massachusetts. The paper labels of Frothingham's shop identifying the maker are more ornate than Townsend (Figure 3.68).

Frothingham's Queen Anne bonnet-top secretary, ca. 1750, expresses his preference of design features—his trademark (Figure 3.69). The upper case of the secretary features arched raised-panel doors and a bonnet top with corkscrew finials. The lower case is supported by bracket feet and features drawers with flat façades that decrease in size, and brass pulls and escutcheons. Other typical New England features seen in this piece are fall-front, panel doors, drawers that decrease in size, pigeonholes, and brass escutcheons. Mahogany and sabicu are the primary woods for this piece, and, the secondary wood is pine.[31] The overall dimensions are H 98¾" × W 38½" × D 22".[32] There was a variety of bonnet-shape configurations for case piece tops as well as a few other shapes (Figure 3.70).

The final Frothingham piece to be discussed is another Queen Anne bonnet-top high chest, ca. 1765 (Figure 3.71). This image is a replica of the original. Colonial American furniture, as with historical English furniture in the 21st century, is also produced as historical reproduction pieces. Statton Furniture Company in Hagerstown, Maryland, has produced historical handcrafted reproductions for more than 80 years and has been a leader in handcrafted traditional solid cherry furniture. Statton's furniture catalog (Statton Old Towne) refers to this piece as a

Figure 3.66
Slant-front desk from Benjamin Frothingham's shop.

Source: Historic Deerfield, Photo by Penny Leveritt.

Figure 3.67
Slant-front deskopen with view of interior. *(below)* Detail ofpigeonholes, Benjamin Frothingham's shop.

Source: Historic Deerfield, Photo by Penny Leveritt.

Figure 3.68
Paper labelused by Benjamin Frothingham's shop.

Source: Historic Deerfield, Photo by Penny Leveritt.

Figure 3.69 Queen Anne bonnet-top secretary, ca. 1750. Attributed to Benjamin Frothingham. *(right)* Interior displaying pigeonholes. *(below right)* Detail of pigeonholes.

Source: Courtesy of Bernard & S. Dean Levy, Inc. Antique Store, New York, New York.

Figure 3.70 American case piece top configurations, 18th century.

Author's illustrations.

Key
A – Double bonnet or hooded pediment; D – Swan neck pediment; B – Bonnet or hooded pediment; E – Bonnet top pediment; C – Flat cornice pediment

bonnet-top highboy; it is considered one of the most distinguished reproductions ever produced by Statton craftsmen (Figure 3.72).

In general, the Late Colonial American Queen Anne high-chest characteristics include the *S*-curved form of English design, carved shell motifs, acanthus leaves, cabriole leg, and diminutive scale. The quality of this piece is specific to Frothingham—his overall careful and delicate approach to details, such as the unique carved shell without the surrounding acanthus leaves, limited molding trim at the bonnet top, lightness of the corkscrew finials rising from the urns, slightness in the scale and curve of the cabriole leg, petite upturned spoon foot, and, lastly, the delicate teardrop finials at the base. The scale of this piece is slight, barely over six feet tall. The overall size: H 79" × W 39½" × D 20", with the center finial height at 84". In closing the discussion, it is important not to forget the material. Frothingham did not solely work in mahogany, as this piece is made from solid cherry and cherry veneer, for which Statton is most renowned.

■ An Illustrated Guide to Furniture History

Figure 3.71
Queen Anne bonnet-top replica, Statton Furniture Mfg. Co Catalog image.
Source: T. Hunt Hardinge, Former Preseident of Statton Furniture Mfg. Co.

Figure 3.72
Queen Anne bonnet-top, 1760–1785, Charlestown, Massachusetts. Designed by Benjamin Frothingham Jr. Medium subicu, mahogany, white pine, and red pine.
Source: Courtesy of Winterthur Museum, #1967.1445 Gift of Henry Francis du Pont.

Mid-Atlantic America

Philadelphia

For many years, the central hub for Late Colonial furniture production was Boston, yet the second half of the century is known as Philadelphia's golden age for furniture production. Philadelphia reigned supreme among the American colonies: it was the nation's first capital, from 1789 to 1800, as well as the state capital until 1799. During the 1750s, while the population of Boston remained static at about 15,000, that of Philadelphia first exceeded New York's and then continued to grow, reaching approximately 19,000 in 1760 and 28,500 in 1774.[33] Situated next to the Delaware River and Schuylkill River, Philadelphia had unparalleled access to the vast hinterlands of the middle colonies. Commerce and trade in the region's abundant natural produce made Philadelphia rich at precisely the time that Rococo fashion in England was at its height.[34] The number of immigrants from Europe rose quickly in the mid-1700s. As a result, the need for household goods and the craftsmen to make them intensified.

The first intimations of the Rococo or Chippendale style began to appear in Philadelphia furniture in the early 1750s.[35] Characteristics that later defined these pieces as Philadelphia Chippendale or Philadelphia Rococo included naturalistic carving; cabriole leg with leafy ornament at the knee; frilly-edged rocaille shells flanked by streamers of foliage; asymmetrical scrollwork; pierced and openwork; and use of the shield, cartouche, and finial.

The city had a large contingent of woodworkers. The names of 172 who were active between about 1730 and 1760 are known. Many of the craftsmen were native born, but there were also numerous immigrants. The city also attracted an influx of trained woodworkers, most notably carvers from London during the 1760s. One of the most prominent of all the native cabinetmakers was Benjamin Randolph (1720–1791), who was born in New Jersey but had settled in Philadelphia by 1762. His surviving ledgers refer to a variety of business ventures. Some of this work will be seen on the next several pages. Another cabinetmaker who rose to prominence came to the country with the influx of artisans in the 1760s, Thomas Affleck (1740–1795) from Aberdeen, Scotland. He had apprenticed in Scotland before moving to London in 1760, and then on to Philadelphia, ca. 1763. A third cabinetmaker who gained prominence in Philadelphia was William Savery, with Benjamin Franklin being an early patron. After a seven-year apprenticeship, Savery opened his shop on Second Street, just south of High (now Market) Street in Philadelphia. Two Savery-attributed pieces actually descended through Franklin's family. William Savery was known for his Queen Anne and Philadelphia Chippendale styles. Most notably, his shop designed the chairs for the Governor's Council Chamber in Philadelphia's Independence Hall. Four of the original chairs exist today.

On the next several pages, the work of these Philadelphia craftsmen, Randolph, Affleck, and Savery, will be discussed with respect to Mid-Atlantic physiognomy and categorization.

Benjamin Randolph set up his shop Philadelphia around 1764. He made Queen Anne and Philadelphia Chippendale/Rococo–style furniture that was the fashion for the time. Randolph is sometimes referred to as "the Chippendale of Colonial America" for his exquisite examples of Chippendale-style furniture. His highboys, along with William Savery's, incorporated Chippendale characteristics and were considered as handsome as anything made by Chippendale himself. One of Randolph's clients was Thomas Jefferson, for whom he made the lap desk on which Jefferson wrote the Declaration of Independence. The mahogany wood original (Figure 3.73, left) is in the Smithsonian Institution. The closed version of the lap desk (Figure 3.73, right) is the craftsmanship of Lon Schleining, as shown in the *Fine Woodworking* publication. This article provided instruction for how to design and build the writing desk.

Below is a Randolph card table, 1760s, from the Winterthur Museum, Garden & Library collection (Figure 3.74). The primary wood is mahogany, with secondary wood of oak, white pine, tulip poplar, and brass. The piece exhibits both American Queen Anne characteristics visible in the center detail (elongated cabriole leg with a pronounced knee—with a diminutive scale leg), including Chippendale characteristics and carving on the knee, but not heavy relief, as one might typically expect with Chippendale pieces. The left detail is a very defined claw-and-ball foot: the Philadelphia foot with prominent knuckle. Lastly, the center drawer with brass escutcheon expresses that this is the front, when placed against a wall.

■ An Illustrated Guide to Furniture History

Figure 3.73
(left) Thomas Jefferson original writing table/lap desk designed by Benjamin Randolph, Smithsonian Museum. *(right)* Replica of Benjamin Randolph's desk. Work of craftsman Lon Schleining.

Source: *(left)* Division of Political and Military History, National Museum of American History, Smithsonian Institution.

Source: *(right)* The Tauton Press, Thomas Jefferson's writing desk replica. Work of craftsman Lon Schleining. Photo credit, Michael Pekovich, Fine Woodworking Magazine, Oct. 2000.

Figure 3.74
(left) Benjamin Randolph Queen Anne, mahogany card table, Philadelphia, ca. 1765.
(center) Detail of carved knee, *(right)* Author's illustration of prominent knuckle ball-and-claw foot.

Source: Winterthur Museum, Gardens & Library Card table, Benjamin Randolph, Philadelphia, 1765–1775, Mahogany, 1958.0085.001, Museum purchase, Courtesy of Winterthur Museum.

On the right is another of Randolph's card tables from the Philadelphia Museum of Art, made approximately ten years after the previous table discussed (Figure 3.75). This design is quintessential Chippendale. The long S-profile, characteristic of American Queen Anne style is gone. There is visual strength in the cabriole leg and heftier knee that isn't in the 1760 card table. Instead of a drawer defining the front of the table, here a sweeping wood grain pattern of the mahogany, with its varied tonal expression. The use of the gadroon trim at the bottom of the apron moving onto the cabriole leg adds to the leg's three-dimentional quality. Notice that Randolph does not use a claw-and-ball foot, but instead a furry animal paw foot. This move supports the visual weight of the

Figure 3.75 Chippendale-style card table, Philadelphia, ca. 1770. Attributed to Benjamin Randolph. Mahogany, oak, pine, with gadroon trim at apron and animal paw foot (32″ × 28½″ × 15⅝″).

Source: Philadelphia Museum of Art, 125th Anniversary Acquisition. Gift of the McNeil Americana Collection, 2007-65-11.

table. Lastly, the use of the gadrooning helps extenuate the mahogany panel front. The secondary wood is oak and pine, the dimensions H 32″ × W 28½″ × D 15⅝″.

The drawing on the right is a table authentic to Philadelphia—the slab table (Figure 3.76). Its name refers to the marble top. This table is visually similar to a card table but functions differently. It is usually found in parlors, also positioned against a wall, similar to the card table. It has been recorded that slab tables were used as serving tables because of the indestructible surface of their marble tops. When necessary, food and beverages would be placed on top. The size of the slab table was typically four to five feet in length, and the legs were either cabriole or marlborough shape. The drawing is an illustration from *Sutton Fine Furniture Glossary*.

Figure 3.76 Philadelphia carved marble slab table.

Author's rendition

Source: Century Furniture Industries. *Sutton Fine Furniture Catalog* #22-410M, p.134.

The Winterthur Museum collection chair is a fine example of Randolph's Philadelphia Chippendale. This museum, also mentioned earlier, is an important institution for American Colonial decorative arts (Figure 3.77). Academics, heritage-study experts, and museum scholars considered Winterthur a national treasure for American heritage. Its history began nearly 60 years ago, when collector and horticulturist Henry Francis du Pont (1880–1969) opened Winterthur, his childhood home, to the public. Today, Winterthur is a premier museum of American decorative arts, with an unparalleled collection of nearly 90,000 objects made or used in America between about 1640 and 1860. The collection is displayed in the magnificent 175-room house, much as it was when the du Pont family lived there, as well as in permanent and changing exhibition galleries.[36] Winterthur is an interdisciplinary center for collections-based scholarship and conservation, and has well-established graduate and research fellowship programs.

The visible Chippendale feature in Randolph's chair at Winterthur is the carving but it is less three-dimensional than that of an English Chippendale piece. The carving here is incised instead of heavy relief. However, other features identical to Chippendale—intricate curved and looped splat; scallop seat front; cabriole leg; and carved acanthus leaf knee—all appear to be from Chippendale's publication *The Gentleman and Cabinet-Maker's Director*. Additionally, the treatment of the yoke back—exaggerated with stylized carving on the surface—is also from the pattern book. What is original to Randolph and Philadelphia cabinetmakers is the termination of the leg with the prominent Philadelphia knuckle claw-and-ball foot.

■ An Illustrated Guide to Furniture History

Figure 3.77
Benjamin Randolph Chippendale-style side chair, Philadelphia.

Source: Winterthur Museum, Gardens & Library. Side chair, Benjamin Randolph, Philadelphia, 1760–1775. Mahogany and Atlantic white cedar, 1961.0803.003. Gift of Henry Francis du Pont. Courtesy of Winterthur Museum.

The last piece of Randolph's discussed here is the mesmerizing mahogany side chair, ca. 1769, shown below from the Philadelphia Museum of Art's American collection (Figure 3.78). This particular chair design has a presence in multiple museum collections, which, as part of a furniture suite, is not necessarily unusual, but what is perplexing is that the authorship varies among the different institutions. The Metropolitan Museum of Art, American Wing, possesses the chair of the same design also attributed to Randolph. Additionally, this chair design exists in Winterthur Museum's Colonial collection but is attributed to Thomas Affleck. Affleck's chair will be considered in the next several pages.

The chair below, attributed to Randolph, is a splendid example of Philadelphia Chippendale Rococo. The features fearlessly reveal Chippendale's design vocabulary, defined by the intricately pierced carved splat with compound curves and surface scrollwork moving upward to form the yoke. The virtuosity of the carved design motifs—unbridled stylized acanthus foliage seen on the skirt connecting to the cabriole leg—is wonderfully three-dimensional. The relationship between the parts of the chair create this formally refined and elegant piece of furniture. The wood is mahogany, with a secondary wood of northern white cedar. The upholstery at this time would have been silk damask, as shown in the chair below. In her publication *Chairs: A History*, Florence de Dampierre states, "These chairs

92

Figure 3.78 Chippendale Rococo-style side chair, Philadelphia, 1770. Attributed to Benjamin Randolph. With intricately pieced carved splat and surface scrollwork. Mahogany, white cedar. Made for John & Elizabeth Lloyd. Carved by Hercules Courtenay. *(right)* View from the back, *(below)* splat detail (37" x 24¼" x 22½").

Source: Philadelphia Museum of Art, Gift of the McNeil Americana Collection, 1991-74-1.

Figure 3.79 Upholstered armchair, Chinese Chippendale style with Gothic arches, fret work, and marlborough legs, ca. 1766. Attributed to Thomas Affleck.

Source: Metropolitan Museum of Art, Public Domain, OA [Open Access]. The American Wing. Purchase, John Stewart-Kennedy Fund and Rogers Fund, by exchange, 2007.

represent the highest achievement of Philadelphia chair making."

Thomas Affleck is considered by many scholars to be the leader of the Philadelphia cabinetmakers. A successful businessman, Affleck kept detailed records and account books from which many of his furniture pieces can be traced to the wealthy and most important citizens of Philadelphia.

Attributed to Thomas Affleck is this Philadelphia armchair design, ca. 1766, from the Met's American Wing collection, which features a 40-inch-wide chair, analogous to a contemporary lounge chair (Figure 3.79).

The chair has stretchers on three sides to support its size. Homage to Chinese Chippendale style is visible in its use of the marlborough front legs and fret at the front corners. The fully upholstered chair has a tufted back and seat, which is unique. Similar to wood chair design, the chair has a slight yoke back, but now upholstered. The frame is mahogany. The upholstery type for this period was damask.

Also attributed to Affleck, ca. 1770, and from the Met collection is a very similar design (Figure 3.80). This chair is wider, 43 inches, upholstered in damask, which was not unusual. It has a similar intricate fret pattern at the corner of the legs, but there is an extra stretcher added to the back for support. Lounge chairs such as these would have been in the parlors of Late Colonial American homes.

The sketches depict other variations for Chippendale marlborough legs and stretchers (Figure 3.81).

The card table on the right attributed to Thomas Affleck, Winterthur Collection, records Affleck's role as joiner (Figure 3.82). The table is made of mahogany, with secondary woods of pine and white oak. The table dates from 1769–1770.

Figure 3.80 Chinese Chippendale-style upholstered armchair, ca. 1770. Attributed to Thomas Affleck. Similar to Figure 3.79.

Source: Metropolitan Museum of Art, Public Domain, OA [Open Access]. The American Wing. Purchase, John Stewart-Kennedy Fund and Rogers Fund, by exchange, 2007.

The card table is characteristic of Philadelphia cabinetmakers in its design approach: the graceful, elongated cabriole leg and elaborately carved acanthus leaf knee, terminating with the prominent knuckle claw-and-ball foot. Card tables at this time were designed to be placed

Figure 3.81 Marlborough chair leg styles with Chippendale Chinese fret work.

Author's illustrations

against a wall and brought forward in a room and flipped open when ready to use; therefore, the carved gadrooning around the apron is on the front and sides only. A gadroon is a motif originally used in silver and furniture resembling ruffles. It is created by fluting and/or reeding, also referred to as nulling and knurling (Figure 3.83)

The next card table below, ca. 1770, is one of a pair of tables documented (Figure 3.84). Affleck's bill lists two parlor "commode card tables" for John Cadwalader's house on Second Street. This table is an exquisite example of Philadelphia Rococo style. Carving is on all surfaces, with enlacing motifs, scrollwork, acanthus leaves, edge trim, and carved patterns recalling French Rococo design. Instead of gadrooning, the apron is defined with a carved serpentine skirt and asymmetrical shield in the middle; the legs end with hairy-paw feet instead of claw-and-ball feet.

In addition to Affleck's documentation, there is documentation indicating that Randolph's shop worked on Cadwalader's residence on Second Street. It is apparent that Cadwalader employed the finest cabinetmakers in Philadelphia to furnish his home.

Piece categorically ■

Figure 3.82
Philadelphia card table, 1769–1770. Attributed to Thomas Affleck.

Source: Winterthur Museum, Garden & Library. Card table, Thomas Affleck, Philadelphia, 1769–1770. Mahogany, hard pine and white oak, 1952.0257. Gift of Henry Francis du Pont. Courtesy of Winterthur Museum.

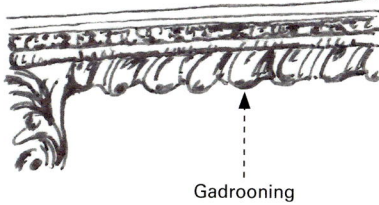

Figure 3.83
Gadroon detail at apron.
Author's illustrations.

Figure 3.84
Card table, one of a pair, Philadelphia, ca. 1770. Attributed to Thomas Affleck for John Cadwalader residence.

Source: The Dietrich American Foundation, Pittsburg, Pennsylvania.

Revisiting the chair seen earlier, the chair below, ca. 1769 (Metropolitan Museum of Art Accession Number 1974.325s), is also attributed to Randolph (Figure 3.85). However, as the author continued research for the book, the same chair, as mentioned previously, was found in the collection of the Winterthur Museum (Museum Object Number 1958.2290), this time credited to Affleck. Further investigation found that authors Morrison H. Heckscher and Leslie Greene Bowman, in their publication *American Rococo, 1750–1775: Elegance in Ornament*, attribute this chair to Affleck as well, based on written documentation found (Affleck's bill, for work completed between October 13, 1770, and January 14, 1771, for Cadwalader's parlor furniture for the house at Second Street).[37] A bill from autumn 1770 mentions a suite of chairs, credited to this same design. The documents were meticulously rendered in a copperplate hand, with separate charges for his carvers.[38] The rooms of the residence were designed and executed as an ensemble and were said to be some the finest designed rooms in Philadelphia.

Figure 3.85 Side chair, ca. 1769. Attributed to Benjamin Randolph, possibly carved by Hercules Courtenay, Philadelphia, Pennsylvania. Mahogany, northern white cedar, with intricately carved pierced splat and surface scrollwork. Same as Figure 3.78 and Figure 3.85

■ An Illustrated Guide to Furniture History

Figure 3.85
Side chair, ca. 1769. Attributed to Benjamin Randolph, possibly carved by Hercules Courtenay, Philadelphia, Pennsylvania. Mahogany, northern white cedar, with intricately carved pierced splat and surface scrollwork. Same as Figure 3.78 and Figure 3.85.
Source: Metropolitan Museum of Art, New York, New York. Public Domain, OA - Open Access. The American Wing. Purchase, Sansbury-Mills and Rogers Funds, Emily Crane Chadbourne Gift, Virginia Groomes Gift, in memory of Mary W. Groomes, Mr. and Mrs. Marshall P. Blankarn, John Bierwirth and Robert G. Goelet Gifts, The Sylmaris Collection, Gift of George Coe Graves, by exchange, Gift of Mrs. Russell Sage, by exchange, and funds from various donors, 1974.

On the following page is the chair from the Winterthur Museum collection attributed to Thomas Affleck. This discrepancy as to who authored the chair is a good lesson with regard to history and provenance. History—studying past events as a whole series connected with someone or something—is not an exact science (i.e., who made the piece, where it was made, for whom it was made, etc.). If no bill or label identifying cabinetmaker or shop exists, then there can be discrepancies between well-established institutions regarding provenance and authorship.

The details below make it easier to see the quality of the carving for the splat and cabriole leg and knee for this Winterthur Museum chair (Figure 3.86). This chair is mesmerizing in the virtuosity of the carved design motif, unbridled yet formally refined. The result is a deftly designed and elegant piece of furniture. I concur with Florence de Dampierre: this suite of chairs does appear to be a high achievement for Philadelphia chair making.

To conclude this discussion of Affleck's work, we'll look at two case pieces, both of which are located in the Met's American Wing (Figure 3.87 and Figure 3.88). Affleck used a different aesthetic approach for each example. The high chest on the left is Classical in nature, reminiscent of a Stoic temple. The rectilinear form has an architecture quality and is closely related to an English George II piece. The use of the robust wood grain to accentuate the four door panels was well conceived. Used here are multiple secondary woods: yellow pine, eastern white cedar, tulip poplar. Its size is large—H 91⅜" × W 44⅜" × D 24¾"—but not as tall as the chest-on-chest to its right. This functions as a secretary—notice the

Figure 3.86
Side chair with details, 1769–1770. Attributed to Thomas Affleck. Mahogany with intricately carved pierce splat and surface scrollwork.

Source: Winterthur Museum, Gardens & Library Side chair, Thomas Affleck, Philadelphia, 1769–1770, Mahogany and cedar, 1958.2290. Gift of Henry Francis du Pont, Courtesy of Winterthur Museum. Photo by Gavin Ashworth.

center horizontal area with pull-out, like a table. The door panels are interesting: raised planes with pattern wood grain and juxtaposing geometry for the top and bottom. This piece has perfect proportions, balanced and harmonious. The broken pediment, appearing as if just removed from a building, is a spectacular way to terminate the height.

Chest-on-chest, 1770–1775. Attributed to Thomas Affleck, Philadelphia, Pennsylvania. The intricate carvings attributed to James Reynolds. Classically derivative form—swan neck pediment with lattice screen within and center carved bird finial. Mahogany, mahogany veneer, white cedar, yellow pine, tulip poplar

The chest-on-chest on right, a bit later in date, is a very tall piece of furniture, about 8 feet tall—H 97½″ × W 46⅞″ × D 24¼″. Due to the height of the 18th-century high chest, the pediment was detachable. This was done for moving convenience—to preserve the integrity of the piece; therefore, the assembly of the chest-on-chest always involved three components. A spectacular feature of this

■ An Illustrated Guide to Furniture History

Figure 3.87
Clothes press, ca. 1760–1790. Attributed to Thomas Affleck, Philadelphia, Pennsylvania. Classical style derivative form—with pediment resembles a Classical temple.

Source: Metropolitan Museum, The American Wing. Public Domain OA [Open Access]. Rogers Fund, 1950.

Figure 3.88
Chest-on-chest, 1770–1775. Attributed to Thomas Affleck, Philadelphia, Pennsylvania. The intricate carvings attributed to James Reynolds. Classically derivative form—swan neck pediment with lattice screen within and center carved bird finial. Mahogany, mahogany veneer, white cedar, yellow pine, tulip poplar.

Source: Metropolitan Museum of Art, The American Wing. Public Domain OA [Open Access].

Metropolitan Museum of Art. Purchase, Friends of the American Wing and Rogers Funds; Virginia Groomes Gift, in memory of Mary W. Groomes, and Mr. and Mrs. Frederick M. Danziger, Herman Merkin and Anonymous Gifts, 1975.

chest-on-chest is the tightly scrolled broken pediment with lattice screen, and the center bird finial described as a phoenix (the carver is believed to be James Reynold of Philadelphia).[39] The manner in which the mahogany and mahogany veneer grain pattern is orchestrating the patterning, texture, and tonal quality on the flat drawer façades is pivotal. This high chest also has several secondary woods—white cedar, yellow pine, tulip poplar. Although this chest-on-chest is a large piece, the constituent parts create a visually pleasing whole. The scale is reduced by the stepped horizontal molding at the lower case and upper case, outlining the base and cornice and creating a visual balance between the chamfered corner and ogee curved feet.

William Savery is the final Philadelphia cabinetmaker to be discussed. He worked for seven years as an apprentice in Philadelphia before opening his shop in 1742 on Second Street, just south of High (now Market) Street in Philadelphia. Benjamin Franklin was an early patron. Two Savery-attributed pieces descended in Franklin's family. Savery is noted for his furniture in Philadelphia Queen Anne and Philadelphia Chippendale styles. In addition to working with mahogany and walnut, Savery manufactured large numbers of maple rush-seated chairs, as shown on the right.

A notable project for Savery was Independence Hall in Philadelphia, where he produced a set of eight Queen Anne–style chairs. Four originals remain, and the others have been replaced (Figure 3.89). The replaced chairs are the work of Whitley Craftsman, Antique Restoration, Furniture Repair and Refinishing, in New Hope, Pennsylvania. In 1971, Robert Whitley's company was commissioned to make four reproductions to fill out the initial set of eight. The chair to the lower left is one of those reproductions. The four chairs now sit in the Governor's Council Chamber on the second floor of Independence Hall, Independence National Historical Park (U.S. National Park Service), Philadelphia, Pennsylvania.

Regarding historical reproduction, the Whitley Company has worked closely with Independence Hall and the U.S. National Park Service to restore and reproduce many important historical pieces throughout the nation. Robert Whitley says this about Savery's chair: "The straightforward dignity and simplicity of this chair is a desirable attribute to many collectors. The restrained design elements found in the serpentine crest, the splat, the cabriole legs and paneled slippered feet are indicative of much of Savery's work."[40] On the following page is a recent photograph of the Governor's Council Chamber and the original walnut Queen Anne chair dating from (1743–1750).

The chair on the right is an earlier Savery design, maple rush-seat chair (Figure 3.90). It is diminutive in size—H 36" × W 21" × D 18". This chair is located in the Met's American Wing.

Figure 3.89
William Savery side chair design for Independence Hall, Philadelphia (1743–1750) replica. A historical reproduction by craftsman Robert Whitely.

Source: Courtesy of Independence National Historic Park, Philadelphia, Pennsylvania.

Figure 3.90
Rush-seat chair, ca. 1745, William Savery. Medium, maple and rush.

Source: Metropolitan Museum of Art, New York, New York, Public Domain, OA [Open Access]. The American Wing. Purchase, Friends of the American Wing Fund and Vivian and Meyer P. Potamkin and Robert and Betty Hut Fifts, 1994.

An Illustrated Guide to Furniture History

Figure 3.91
The Governor's Chamber, Independence Hall, Philadelphia, Pennsylvania. View depicting William Savery's four original side chairs (1743–1750) and Robert Whitley's four replicas of the William Savery side chairs.
Source: Courtesy of Independence National Historical Park.

The Governor's Council Chamber is located on the second floor of Independence Hall, National Park Service, Philadelphia (Figure 3.91). The four Savery chairs co-exist with the four reproductions. All eight chairs surround the table.

The final piece of Savery's to discuss is this tilt-top mahogany tea table (Figure 3.92). This table is in the American collection at the Philadelphia Museum of Art. This type of tea table was ubiquitous in the homes of 18th-century upper- and middle-class Philadelphia families. It measures 29½" × 34⅝". Documentary sources and surviving tea tables suggest that the arrival and proliferation of this new form was inextricably linked to changes in the economy, such as increased Atlantic trade.[41] By the mid-1730s, middle-market tilt-top tables such as those made in London began appearing in well-to-do American homes and from the start were associated with genteel social interactions—especially tea drinking. Physically, these tea tables feature a single pillar supported by three legs. The tops tilted up and down on battens, and many had casters, making them easier to move and store. In addition, the table, with box mechanisms, could be oriented so the tripod feet fit either into the corner of a

Figure 3.92
William Savery tilt-top mahogany tea table, 1745–1750.

Source: Courtesy of Independence National Historical Park.

Piece categorically ■

room or along a wall. This table type is also referred to as a "tripod table" because of its three-leg base; later in the 18th century, it acquired the name "piecrust table" because the top was scalloped. Today, the tilt-top tea table is in virtually every major collection of 18th-century American furniture. In 1986, a Philadelphia tilt-top tea table was the first piece of American furniture to exceed $1,000,000 at auction.

To conclude this section, the next several pages feature a wide variety of furniture pieces unique to the Philadelphia furniture tradition, such as the tassel-back chair, high chest, marble slab table, and piecrust tea table. To begin this overview, the author has rendered a drawing from *Sutton Fine Furniture Glossary* to help explain the specific features that make the tassel-back chair uniquely

Fluted frame

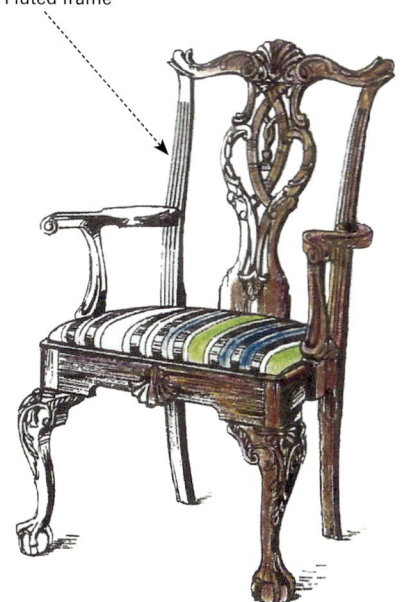

Typical is a carved cabriole leg and knee. The motif is acanthus leaf scrollwork that flows onto a prominent knuckle ball-and-claw foot

Scrollwork

Tassel

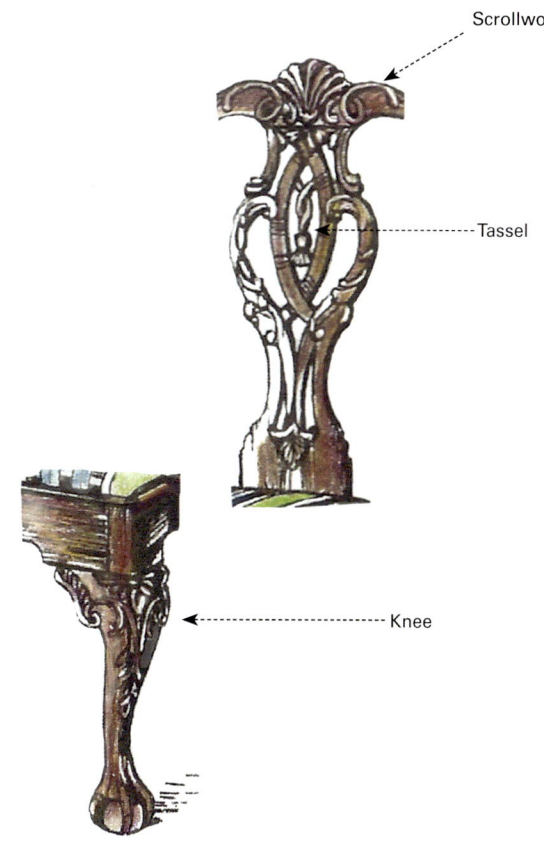

Knee

Typical is the splat detail reminiscent of the S- and C-shapes in French Rococo design. The acanthus leaf scrollwork is analogous to a ribbon, and note the tassel hanging freely in the central void.

Figure 3.93
Philadelphia tassel-back armchair and details. Author's rendition.
Source: Century Furniture Industries. *Sutton Fine Furniture Catalog,* Page 129, #22-562

Philadelphian: the yoke back with centralized scallop shell at the crest and seat apron, the fluted chair frame, the heavily carved cabriole leg and knee ending in a prominent knuckle claw-and-ball foot; the pieced splat design mimicking French Rococo *S*- and *C*-shapes; similar to Chippendale, the acanthus leaf scrollwork, analogous to a ribbon; and the tassel hanging freely in the central void. These exact details are present on all Philadelphia tassel-back chairs (Figure 3.93).

On the following page are Chippendale mahogany tassel-back side chairs, made in Philadelphia in 1765, auctioned at Freeman's Auction in Philadelphia, on April 19, 2016 (Figure 3.94). Justice Samuel Chase (1741–1811), a signer of the Declaration of Independence, originally owned the chairs. Chairs from the same set are in the collections of the Museum of Fine Arts, Boston, and the Diplomatic Reception Rooms in the U.S. Department of State.

Sometime during the mid-1760s, the Philadelphia chest form evolved into a second stage—lighter and more graceful. Over the next several pages you will see two high chests which superbly express Philadelphia Chippendale/Rococo styles (Figure 3.95 and Figure 3.96). The defining features included mahogany as the primary wood, and, for the upper case, use of a scroll pediment with intricate scrollwork and finials on urns, and crowned with a central sculptural element; for the lower case, features include cabriole legs with claw-and-ball feet, scalloped-edged bottom, and central shell motif with acanthus leaves. The drawers for the high chest usually descend in size with brass pulls and escutcheons. Lastly, the upper-case and lower-case corners are chamfered, or filled, with quarter round columns.

The third and final high-chest example is a famous piece, popularly called the "Pompadour Highboy" because of the supposed French character of the portrait bust in its pediment.[42]

The Pompadour embodies the influence of pattern books in an authentically creative manner (Figure 3.97). The choice of mahogany grain pattern communicates a tactile quality to otherwise unadorned drawer façades. In addition are the horizontal cornice surmounted by the portrait bust; the draped urn finials; the scroll pediment's volutes formed from acanthus leaves; at the bottom, the central panel with carved serpent and swans; and lastly, the unusual brass drawer pulls with star-shaped hardware; with these visual characteristics, it is obvious why this piece has gained its reputation.

The tripod tea table originated in 18th-century England with robust enthusiasm following suit in Philadelphia. The Philadelphia tea-table top became the celebratory feature with a pronounced profile—a ruffle-like edge referred to as a "piecrust." The tripod base was often fluted with sculptural cabriole legs (Figure 3.98). This table is an excellent example of its type.

John Cadwalader's home on Second Street, Philadelphia, has been mentioned in relation to Thomas Affleck and Benjamin Randolph. The Cadwalader slab table, ca. 1770, is not listed as part of the suite of furniture designed for the parlor by Affleck. However, it is so called because it descended in the family and was presumably part of the furnishings of the Second Street home.[43] It is a supreme example in American furniture of the fully developed French Rococo style. The fluid

Piece categorically ■

Figure 3.94
Philadelphia Chippendale-style mahogany tassel-back side chairs, 1765. Made for Justice Samuel Chase.
Image courtesy of Freeman's.

■ An Illustrated Guide to Furniture History

Figure 3.95
High chest 1760–1780, Philadelphia, Pennsylvania. Walnut and yellow poplar, 96¾" × 45½" × 23 11/16".

Source: Mabel Brady Garvan Collection, Yale University. Public Domain. High Chest of Drawers, American, 1760–1780, Accession 1930.2000.

Piece categorically

Figure 3.96
Philadelphia high chest, 1765–1780. Swietenia, tulip poplar, oak, yellow pine, and cedar, H 90¼".

Source: Winterthur Museum, Gardens & Library Chest of drawers, Unknown maker, Philadelphia, 1765–1780, Swietenia, tulip poplar, oak, yellow pine, and cedar, 1958.0592, Gift of Henry Francis du Pont, Courtesy of Winterthur Museum.

■ An Illustrated Guide to Furniture History

Figure 3.97
High chest, 1765–1775. Philadelphia. Mahogany, Mahogany veneer, tulip poplar, yellow pine, white cedar, 91¾" x 44⅝" x 24⅝".

Source: Metropolitan Museum of Art, The American Wing. Public Domain OA [Open Access]. John Stewart Kennedy Fund, 1918.

Figure 3.98
Tilt-top tea table, 1765–1775, Philadelphia. Medium mahogany, size H 29", Diam. 37".

Source: Metropolitan Museum of Art, American Wing. Public Domain OA [Open Access]. John Stewart Kennedy Fund, 1918.

Figure 3.99
(left) Slab table, ca. 1770, Philadelphia. Mahogany, marble, and yellow pine, L 48¼". *(right)* Slab table detail of cabriole leg and knee.
Source: Metropolitan Museum of Art, The American Wing Public Domain OA [Open Access]. The John Stewart Kennedy Fund, 1918.

carved scrollwork and *S*- and *C*-shape patterning moves from skirt to leg, allowing no separation between leg and skirt—in direct opposition to standard American designs (Figure 3.99).

Charleston, South Carolina
The Low Country of the North and South Carolina coast was dominated by the city of Charleston, a cultural rival to Philadelphia. Throughout the Colonial period, a steady mix of immigrant Dutch, French Huguenots, Swiss, German, Welsh, Scots, Scotch-Irish, and Sephardic Jews from Spain and Portugal added to the dominant British culture of the Low Country.[44] In the mid-18th century, "Charles Town" (Charleston) was an economically booming city, the average resident citizens being several times wealthier on the whole than those of New York or Philadelphia. Providing furniture to these wealthy Charlestonians was a lucrative business for the local wood craftsmen and cabinetmakers. The people of Charleston considered themselves English citizens who just happened to be living in the America colony of South Carolina and did everything possible to follow in the footsteps of London society, such as acquiring fine furniture.[45] The wealthy Charlestonians loved London-style furnishings and would purchase most anything of similar fashion that was hand-made by local woodworkers to furnish their plantations and homes in

town. Sadly, most examples from Charleston's furniture production heyday were lost to great fires in 1740, 1828, and 1861. For families who sent their valuable pieces to Columbia, South Carolina, the capital was torched in 1865 during the occupation of the Union forces under General William T. Sherman.[46]

Discussed in this section will be the furniture type that best epitomized Colonial Charleston, South Carolina: the double chest.[47] The double chest, of course, was found throughout British North America in the Late Colonial period and was not exclusive to Charleston. But what became unique was the Charleston cabinetmakers' design interpretation for the double chest—the impact of Charleston's customs, rituals, and traditions on the design aesthetic. It became a primary case piece for the homes of affluent Charlestonians. Its purpose was the storage and safekeeping of clothing, textiles, and valuables. This piece is referred to as a chest-on-chest in Charleston, and co-existed with the high chest of Massachusetts, Rhode Island, Pennsylvania, and New York, a form rarely made south of Maryland. Merchants responded to this demand for the Charleston double chest in the 1750s by importing double chests from Britain.[48]

Double chests were most popular in the city after the war. Several pre-Revolutionary cabinetmakers produced the double chest, such as Thomas Elfe, a Charleston cabinetmaker whose accounts show 20 double chests sold, and cabinetmaker Richard Magrath, who is recorded as having advertised in the *South Carolina Gazette* that he had a double chest of drawers for sale.

In research undertaken over the past 30 years, the Museum of Early Southern Decorative Arts (MESDA) has recorded the existence of 20 surviving double chests that represent the work of at least eight and possibly ten local shops.

The physiognomics of Charleston's double chest are as follows: the upper cases have a broad chamfer at the front edge, all have dust boards separating one drawer from another, the bottoms of all the large drawers have center muntins or battens, all have ogee feet, most have cypress as the secondary wood, and all feature mahogany as the primary wood. When fretwork is used on friezes, the pattern of a Late Colonial Charleston double chest is a figure eight.[49]

Thomas Elfe immigrated from England in the 1740s. He was an accomplished and prolific cabinetmaker, first living in Virginia and then moving to Charleston, whose booming economy made Elfe's woodworking shop successful and profitable. Thomas Elfe is perhaps the best known of Charleston's cabinetmakers—due in large part to the survival of an account book he kept, the only such document known to exist for a Colonial Charleston cabinetmaker.[50] Elfe's surviving account book of transactions is held by the Charleston Library Society. The book, covering several accounts, shows that between 1768 and 1775, Elfe, with several employees, hand-made more than 1,500 furniture pieces, including fine detailed cabinets. These records show that he sold about 17 pieces of furniture per month on average. Elfe was considered Charleston's best furniture craftsman of the 18th century. His working career spanned almost 30 years, from about 1746 to 1775. Ironically, despite his fame, no piece of furniture can be definitely attributed to his shop.[51]

Charleston records and surviving furniture suggest that there was minimal demand for the services of professional carvers during the first half of the 18th

Figure 3.100 *(left)* Historic image of Thomas Elfe house and shop, front façade, 54 Queen Street, Charleston, South Carolina. *(right)* Contemporary image of Thomas Elfe house, front façade.

Source: *(left)* Historic Charleston Foundation. *(right)* Wikimedia Commons, Creative Commons Attributions. Share Alike 3.0 Unported license, Public Domain.

century. Few pieces of Low Country furniture from this period are carved, and those that are carved have relatively simple ornament. But what is known is that Elfe worked closely with carver Thomas Watson, as documented in the 1740s. Watson left his entire estate to Elfe, a clear testimony to their close working relationship.

An intriguing fact is that Elfe's house and shop in Charleston still exist today and are open for tours (Figure 3.100). The house is located in Charleston's French Quarter at 54 Queen Street. Restoration of the Colonial Georgian–style house, built in 1760, has been done in order to conserve the house. It is the oldest restored historical residence in Charleston that is open to the public. There are older house structures in Charleston, but they are either private residences or businesses.

The property originally consisted of two buildings, one along the street front and the other on the back part of the property. It is believed the rear structure was Elfe's shop and that his home was the separate structure at the front.

Elfe was a contemporary of Thomas Chippendale (1718–1779) and was influenced by his work, not unlike other American cabinetmakers of the time. What is intriguing are the many parallels in their lives. Both were born in England about the same time. Both were apprenticed in the 1730s under family members—for Chippendale, this was his father, for Elfe, his uncle. Both men lived during tempestuous times leading to the American Revolution. Both had a son named Thomas who took over their furniture business.

Although no piece of furniture can be definitely attributed to his shop, on the next several pages are furniture pieces with design features and details associated with Thomas Elfe's workshop. Features include the figure-eight fret, which is the only fretwork pattern used on friezes of Late Colonial Charleston.[52] Other features include pediment head cut through—pierced pediment, fret round, and use of Doric dentil molding (Figure 3.101).

This double chest was owned by Charleston merchant and planter John Deas (1735–1790), a Scottish immigrant, and his wife, Elizabeth Allen Deas (1742–1802). This piece is probably the "double Chest Drawers" listed in the 1791 inventory of John Deas's estate, and is the finest known double chest of drawers from Colonial Charleston. It is clear evidence of the Deases' wealth.[53]

Visible are features typical of a Charleston double chest but far more complex. The cornice here is mesmerizing—enriched by a wall-of-Troy molding and sawn fretwork. Elfe referred to the sawn fretwork as a "fret around."[54] The top of the chest received a purely ornamental and labor-intensive broken pediment and carved finials. The Deases also chose to have the chest fitted with brass casters for ease of movement.[55] In Elfe's account books, these features increase the cost of the chest. Other features typical of Charleston are the chamfer at the front edge, the dustboard, and ogee feet. Two areas that also make this piece compelling are

■ An Illustrated Guide to Furniture History

Figure 3.101 Double chest, Charleston, 1765–1775. Not credited to Thomas Elfe but similar design elements as Elfe's work. Mahogany veneer, pierced work pediment with rosettes and globe.

Source: Colonial Williamsburg Foundation, Williamsburg, Virginia.

the flamed veneer wood grain and its patterning, texture, and tonal quality. Its secondary wood is cypress and tulip poplar. Notice the simple form of the drawer pulls. This form works well as it does not distract one from the grain patterning.

Another piece that has been attributed to Elfe is seen in the reproduction piece shown below (Figure 3.102). This drop-leaf mahogany table is similar in nature to the breakfast, or Pembroke, table of England. It seems to be a Charleston translation of the English piece. This table is seen in several of Charleston's historic house museums, such as Heyward-Washington House and Middle Place.

The form of the table is unique, the top and drop leaves have a serpentine shape, and the legs are straight and not with ornamental carving or piercing but are ribbed. One of the most visually striking elements of the table is the unusual flower-shaped X-stretcher. The sketches will help one become familiar with various components of table design (Figure 3.103).

The drawing to the right is a SketchUp drawing by Tim Killen. For *Fine Woodworking Magazine* he demonstrated making of a *rule joint* using this table design

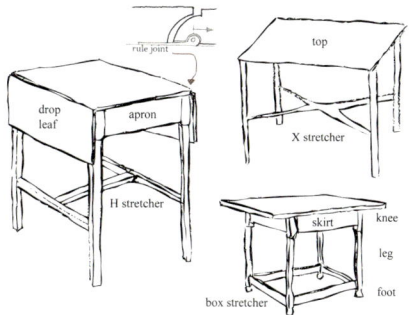

Figure 3.102
(left) Drop-leaf mahogany table. This replica is a table design attributed to Thomas Elfe. It is seen in various historic house museums, Heyward-Washington House, South Carolina, and Middleton Place House Museum, South Carolina. *(right)* Tim Killen, detailed SketchUp design 3D.

Source: *(left)* Century Furniture Industries. *Sutton Fine Home Furnishings* catalog, Elfe Pembroke table, Page 71, #22-731. *(right)* Detailed SketchUp design 3D, by Tim Killen, KillenWOOD.com.

Figure 3.103
Sketches of table examples showing a variety of stretcher conditions and thumbnail of rule joint.

Source: Table example sketches courtesy of Phil Hart. Thumbnail of rule joint, author's illustration.

as model. The rule joint is the construction joint used for the leaf portion of the table. It allows for the drop motion. Killen mentions: "The table has so many more interesting features that I decided to run a series of entries on its construction in SketchUp … I was able to see one of this table at Middleton Place and decided that it would be fun to re-construct."[56]

As mentioned previously, no piece of furniture can be definitely attributed to Thomas Elfe's shop, but this small yet elegant table has often been labeled as a Thomas Elfe piece by luxury furniture companies. In a Sutton Fine Furnishings catalog, the reproduction bears the label of the Elfe Pembroke table. Regardless of its provenance, it is a fine example of Chinese latticework visible in the fret design on the table's apron, and this feature is known to have been a motif incorporated in Elfe's designs. Overall, the decorative motifs of the table seem to pay homage to chinoiserie designs in Chippendale's pattern books.

Heyward-Washington was one of the signers of the Declaration of Independence. George Washington stayed at this house during his visit to Charleston in 1771. Thomas Heyward-Washington's townhouse is located at 87 Church Street (Figure 3.104). Shown here are a historical photograph and recent image as a house museum.

The mention of fretwork in Elfe's account book has led many to conclude that pieces that incorporate the figure-eight fret pattern are by Thomas Elfe. But such pieces have not been proven to be the work of Elfe. However, the Elfe account books document that he did apparently cut and sell fret to other local cabinetmakers. The chimneypiece ca. 1772–1773

Figure 3.104
(left) Historic image, Heyward-Washington House front elevation (façade), Charleston, South Carolina. *(right)* Contemporary, Heyward-Washington House Museum front elevation (façade), Charleston, South Carolina.

Source: *(left)* Historic Charleston Foundation Archives *(right)* The Charleston Museum.

■ An Illustrated Guide to Furniture History

Figure 3.105
Heyward-Washington House chimney piece.

Source: The Charleston Museum.

at the Heyward-Washington House features the same figure-eight fret found on furniture (Figure 3.105). Visible here is a historical photograph and a recent image from the house museum.

It was designed for the drawing room (Figure 3.106). The view of the room places the chimneypiece in context with upholstered furniture and other furnishings and accessories of the period. The house is now a historic house museum and was recognized as a National Historic Landmark in 1978. Again, shown here are both a historical photograph and a recent image of the house museum.

The three Charleston double chests discussed next exhibit the typical features for the piece, such as a flat cornice, chamfer edges, bracket feet, fret pattern under the cornice, and brass drawer pulls and escutcheons (Figure 3.107, Figure 3.108, and Figure 3.109).

Figure 3.106
(left) Historical image, Heyward-Washington House Museum Drawing Room with view of chimney piece.
(right) Heyward-Washington House Museum Drawing Room with view of chimney piece.

Source: *(left)* Gibbes Museum of Art/Carolina Art Association, Charleston, South Carolina *(right)* The Charleston Museum.

Figure 3.107
Double chest of drawers with desk drawer, 1765–1775, Charleston, South Carolina. Mahogany and mahogany veneer primary; cypress and mahogany secondary. H 78" x W 46½" x D 25 1/8". Courtesy of Museum of Early Southern Decorative Arts (MESDA) Acc. 946.

Source: Old Salem Museum and Gardens, Winston-Salem, North Carolina.

Figure 3.108
Double chest of drawers, 1765–1775, Charleston, South Carolina. Mahogany and mahogany veneer primary; cypress, tulip poplar, and mahogany secondary, H 76" x W 45¼" x D 24". Courtesy of Museum of Early Southern Decorative Arts MESDA, MRF 8018. Acc. HF 368.

Source: Old Salem Museum and Gardens, Winston-Salem, North Carolina.

Piece categorically ■

Figure 3.109
Chest-on-chest, ca. 1770, Charleston, South Carolina. Mahogany and cypress with brass hardware
74½" x 44¼" x 24 1/8".

Source: Chipstone Foundation, chest-on-chest, ca. 1770, #1997.14, Photo credit: Gavin Ashworth.

Below is a rendered drawing of a Charleston breakfront bookcase from *Sutton Fine Furniture Glossary*, by the author (Figure 3.111). The same breakfront bookcase is in the collection (MESDA) and will be discussed on the next several pages. This discussion will begin with the drawing below. There are numerous features of this breakfront bookcase that make scholars and experts believe it to be the work of Elfe. In *American Rococo, 1750–1775: Elegance in Ornament*, the authors, Morrison H. Heckscher and Leslie Greene Bowman, mention that in November 1772, Elfe billed John Dart £100 for a "Library Book Case with Chineas doors and Draws under them" [sic]. Heckscher and Bowman mention that this design is altered slightly from plate XCIII of Thomas Chippendale's *Gentleman and Cabinet-Maker's Director*. A photograph of the piece from their book is on the following page. Dating as far back as the 1860s, the piece was acquired by Captain Edward Willis (1835–1910), a Charleston rare-book collector, who lived at the Isaac Jenkins Mikell House at 94 Rutledge Street in Charleston.

On the next several pages, you will see photographic images of the breakfront bookcase taken at MESDA. The primary wood is mahogany, and cypress is the secondary wood. MESDA scholars explain that the source for design is influenced by Plate LXVII from Chippendale's first and second edition of *The Gentleman and Cabinet-Maker's Director* (1754 and 1755), which is seen on the next page, or third edition 1762, Plate XCIII (Figure 3.110). It is evident that the Charleston cabinetmaker changed the proportions (Figure 3.112). This was likely to accommodate the ceilings found in Charleston homes. Notice at the bottom of the bookcase that the four oval panels have been placed vertically and the plinth base has been replaced with bracket feet, and at the top of the base is a blind fret carved from

■ An Illustrated Guide to Furniture History

the hole. The central portion, which supports the pediment, is surmounted also by an applied blind fret.

The bookcase is in two sections. The upper contains adjustable shelves enclosed by double elongated hexagonal 13-light doors. It is crowned with a broken pediment originally with central finial. The upper mullions on the left and right arched doors are decorated with leaf motifs. The arches have Roman-key moldings and in the center an "Elfe" fret surmounted by the broken pediment (replaced).[57] The lower section containing compartments of shelves and drawers is enclosed by solid doors decorated with matched veneered panel outlined by a single band inlay, surmounted by a carved fret, the whole supported by straight bracket feet (partly replaced).[58]

The colored photograph and black and white images are of the breakfront bookcase as it is seen today at MESDA (Figure 3.112 and Figure 3.113). MESDA scholars explain that green baize has been placed behind the doors based on tack evidence found on the door. The use of tack was a typical treatment in the 18th century.[59] It provided privacy to the owner and protection for his or her books. During the period, the fabric would have been attached to the doors. The black and white photograph shows off the exquisite details, its decorative carved motifs at the pediment and semi-circular glass door, veneer patterning, as well as its back construction.

I cannot think of a better way to conclude this section than with the Port Royal parlor from the Winterthur Museum (Figure 3.114 and Figure 3.115). The first image provides a partial view of the parlor, while the thumbnail shows the majority of the space. Du Pont acquired this period room from Philadelphia and had it reassembled at Winterthur. Port Royal, the country home in which the parlor existed, was slated for demolition in 1920. Du Pont bought the Port Royal estate originally owned and built by Edward Stiles in 1762 on Frankford Creek, north of Philadelphia. Stiles, a planter and merchant from Port Royal, Bermuda, had prospered in the West Indies trade.[60] This

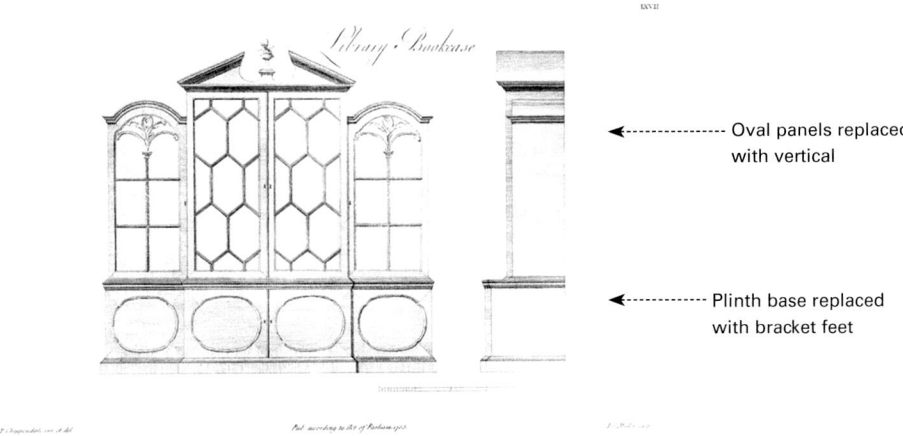

Figure 3.110
Thomas Chippendale book Plate LXVII, second edition of the *Gentleman and Cabinet-Maker's Director* (1754 and 1755), or third edition 1762, Plate XCIII.
Source: Old Salem Museums & Gardens, Winston-Salem, North Carolina.

Piece categorically ■

Figure 3.111
Breakfront bookcase, Charleston, South Carolina. Bookcase and details A–C.
Source: Century Furniture Industries. *Sutton Fine Furniture*, #22-425, page 128.

Key
A – Pediment portion
B – Arched portion of glass door
C – Breakfront portion

space, the interior envelope, and furnishings epitomize the 18th-century Philadelphia home of the affluent.

In conclusion, by selecting 18th-century furniture examples of France, England, and Late Colonial America, this chapter has demonstrated how to categorize a piece, enabling the student and adult learner to gain an understanding of the processes of categorization and classification of a furniture piece as to place of origin and within a timeline, and the importance of provenance.

Chapter 4—The Analysis of Form: Nine-Step Methodology—will explain the structure of the methodology to the student and adult learner, and how to navigate through the steps.

■ An Illustrated Guide to Furniture History

Figure 3.112 Breakfront bookcase, Charleston, South Carolina, color photograph.

Source: Old Salem Museums & Gardens, Winston-Salem, North Carolina.

Figure 3.113 Breakfront bookcase, Charleston, South Carolina, details, front and back, A–E. Black and white photographs.

Source: Old Salem Museums & Gardens, Winston-Salem, North Carolina.

Key
A – Back construction; B – Pediment opening; C – Pediment corner; D – Widow; E – Breakfront veneer

Figure 3.114 Port Royal Parlor. View in front of the fireplace. Winterthur Museum, Garden and Library.

Source: Winterthur Museum, Gardens & Library. View of Port Royal Parlor at Winterthur Delaware, Courtesy of Winterthur Museum.

Figure 3.115 Parlor Royal Parlor expanded view. Winterthur Museum, Garden and Library.

Source: Winterthur Museum, Gardens & Library. View of Port Royal Parlor at Winterthur Delaware, Courtesy of Winterthur Museum.

NOTES

1. www.thespruce.com.
2. Ibid.
3. https://en.wikipedia.org/wiki/Canapé (furniture).
4. Ken Johnson, "Gilding the Ancien Régime," *The New York Times*, November 9, 2007, E44.
5. James Parker … [et al.], *Period Rooms, in the Metropolitan Museum of Art Harry* (New York: Metropolitan Museum of Art, Harry N. Abrams, 1996), p.77.
6. Ibid.
7. Douglas Ash … [et al.], *World Furniture and Illustrated History* (London: Hamlyn Publishing Group, 1976), p.133.
8. Ibid.
9. https://en.wikipedia.org/wiki/Thomas_Chippendale.
10. Robbie G. Blakemore, *History of Interior Design and Furniture: From Ancient Egypt to Nineteenth-Century Europe* (New York: ITP International Thompson Publishing Company, Van Nostrand Reinhold, 1997), p.300.
11. https://en.wikipedia.org/wiki/George_Hepplewhite.
12. https://en.wikipedia.org/wiki/Thomas_Sheraton.
13. James Reginato, "Restoration Drama," *Architectural Digest*, February 2012: 58.
14. Ibid.
15. Ibid.: 63.
16. Jonathan L. Fairbanks and Elizabeth Bates, *American Furniture: 1620 to Present*, cited in Troy Segal, "How to Identify Sheraton Style Antique Furniture," www.thesprucecrafts.com/identifying-sheraton-style-furniture-148789.
17. Christie's, London, Furniture and Decorative Arts video, London, July 5, 2018, www.christies.com/features/How-to-spot-a-genuine-Thomas-Chippendale-9281-3.aspx.
18. Ibid.
19. www.EncyclopediaBritannica.com.
20. Judith Gura, *The Guide to Period Styles for Interiors* (New York: Fairchild Books, Bloomsbury, 2016), p.70.
21. www.furniturestyles.net/american/antique/early.html.
22. Judith Gura, *The Guide to Period Styles for Interiors* (New York: Fairchild Books, Bloomsbury, 2016), p.70.
23. Art Institute of Chicago, American Art before 1900, Gallery 166 descriptive panel text.
24. Nicholas C. Vincent, "American Furniture, 1730–1790: Queen Anne and Chippendale Styles," *Metropolitan Museum of Art*, New York, December 2009.
25. Judith Gura, *The Guide to Period Styles for Interiors* (New York: Fairchild Books, Bloomsbury, 2016), p.73.
26. Treena Crochet, *Designer's Guide to Furniture Styles* (New Jersey: Prentice Hall, 1999), p.163.
27. Morrison H. Heckscher and Leslie Greene Bowman, *American Rococo, 1750–1775: Elegance in Ornament* (New York: The Metropolitan Museum of Art and Los Angeles County Museum of Art, distributed by Harry N. Abrams, New York, 1991), p.4.
28. Ibid.
29. Art Institute of Chicago, Gallery 166, American Art before 1900, descriptive panel.
30. Margaretta Markle Lovell, "Boston Blockfront Furniture," *The Colonial Society of Massachusetts*, Vol 48 (1972).
31. Bernard & S. Dean Levy, Inc. Furniture listing description, New York, New York, 2020.
32. Ibid.
33. Morrison H. Heckscher and Leslie Greene Bowman, *American Rococo, 1750–1775: Elegance in Ornament* (New York: The Metropolitan Museum of Art and Los Angeles County Museum of Art, distributed by Harry N. Abrams, New York, 1991), p.182.

34. Ibid.
35. Ibid.
36. www.winterthur.org.
37. Morrison H. Heckscher and Leslie Greene Bowman, *American Rococo, 1750–1775: Elegance in Ornament* (New York: The Metropolitan Museum of Art and Los Angeles County Museum of Art, distributed by Harry N. Abrams, New York, 1991), p.182.
38. [[Missing Endnote Text]]
39. Ibid., p.206.
40. Quote taken from Robert Whitley's website, which is no longer live.
41. Sarah Neale Fayen, "Tilt-Top Tables and Eighteenth-Century Consumerism," America Furniture, *Chipstone*, 2003.
42. Morrison H. Heckscher and Leslie Greene Bowman, *American Rococo, 1750–1775: Elegance in Ornament* (New York: The Metropolitan Museum of Art and Los Angeles County Museum of Art, distributed by Harry N. Abrams, New York, 1991), p.202.
43. Ibid., p.191.
44. Mint Museum of Art/Mint Museum of Craft + Design, "Furniture of the American South 1680–1830: The Colonial Williamsburg Collection," *Resource Library Magazine* (November 23, 2002–January 26, 2003).
45. https://en.wikipedia.org/wiki/Thomas_Elfe.
46. https://en.wikipedia.org/wiki/Capture_of_Columbia.
47. Anne S. McPherson, "The Charleston Double Chest," *Antique & Fine Art Magazine*, third anniversary, January 2003.
48. Ibid.
49. Ibid.
50. Ibid.
51. Ibid.
52. Ibid.
53. http://emuseum.history.org/objects/27026/double-chest-of-drawers?ctx=8429e38f800ee5ab4407ce6f1909411077b4fae8&idx=3.
54. Ibid.
55. Ibid.
56. Tim Killen, "Challenging Features in Thomas Elfe Breakfast Table," *Fine Woodworking*, September 21, 2009, www.finewoodworking.com/2009/09/21/challenging-features-in-thomas-elfe-breakfast-table.
57. http://mesda.org/collections/mesda-collection.
58. Ibid.
59. Ibid.
60. www.winterthur.org/collections/museum/furniture.

PART II
Understanding the piece

4 The Analysis of Form
Nine-Step Methodology

For those who are captivated and interested in the visual world and the objects that define its richness, there isn't a more appropriate way to learn about furniture history than through visual means, using graphic communication as the primary tool for learning.

For university students seeking degrees in design-related disciplines, communicating through a graphic language and vocabulary is the norm. The Analysis of Form: Nine-Step Methodology intends to enhance that ability. It is the idea of interaction between brain and hand, memory and muscle memory, that will facilitate recall and recognition—creating an imprint in the student's memory. For others not in the midst of their university studies—those in adult education/continuing education and lifelong learners—using a graphic language and vocabulary will be a new skill developed. However difficult at first, this skill should prove to be an invaluable tool in learning about the visual world—decorative arts, architecture, interiors, design history, etc. At this point, I recommend that students or adult learners reaffirm their commitment to this methodological approach and finish the book. This affirmation will remind you of your decision to partake in this immersion-learning journey—gaining knowledge in several days instead of through a conventional semester course.

This chapter will explain the structure of the methodology and how to navigate through the nine steps. Structurally, the methodology is a process in which the nine steps are organized in a three-category structure: History, Aesthetics, and Visual Notes, with visual notes being the ninth step and a crucial part of the process. The two key aspects critical to the nine-step methodology are practice examples and visual notes exercises.

Let's discuss practice examples. The author will use practice examples to demonstrate how to work through the nine-step process. These examples will address each step by using visual notes, and written notes when appropriate. To demonstrate, the author has selected three furniture pieces as practice examples. What is important for the student or adult learner to be aware of is that he or she will also produce practice examples selected from the pictorial timeline for each chapter in Part III (Chapters 6 through 13). The practice examples and visual notes studies will communicate the student's or adult learner's process of analysis and investigation. Working through this process will imprint on one's mind the findings—the key features of the furniture piece chosen to investigate. The visual notes studies of the practice examples are an integral part for Step 9, and indelibly linked to the final drawing, or visual notes exercise. This final drawing (visual notes exercise) is testament that you have solidified your understanding about this piece, its timeframe, and context.

What exactly are visual notes? The concept of visual notes has roots in design disciplines such as architecture, interior architecture, interior design, product design, landscape architecture, and urban planning. With visual notes, analytical documentation is recorded graphically rather than with words, so sketching, drawing, diagramming, and rendering collectively becomes the analysis tool. When and how will the student or adult learner apply visual notes? As stated previously, the practice examples include the use of visual notes studies. As a series, these studies culminate in the final visual notes exercise in Part III (Chapters 6 through 13), where the nine-step methodology is brought to fruition. Imagine Part III as being analogous to a conventional survey course in which students take notes while the professor lectures: for this learning model, the notes are graphic—or visual. Crucial to the process, as mentioned in the Introduction, the student will need a sketchbook on hand to use for sketching—the recommended type and size for the book is a hardcover 8" × 11" or 9" × 12"—for students or adult learners to produce their practice examples and visual notes exercise. For the practice examples, the visual notes study should be numbered 1, 2, 3, etc. Most important: when the practice examples and visual notes exercises are completed, the student or adult learner will have a compendium deemed of interest to use for future reference.

What are the learning outcomes? Having completed the visual notes exercises in Part III, students or adult learners will have gained a certain breadth and depth of understanding of the particular pieces of furniture and historical periods they chose to analyze, they will have adapted to the immersion-learning model and nine-step methodology by completing the book, and they will have gained an awareness about theoretical findings regarding memory study—the interaction between brain and hand, memory and muscle memory, that will facilitate recall and recognition: an imprint in the learner's memory. This model demonstrates the intrinsic relationship between drawing and memory. In "The drawing effect: Evidence for reliable and robust memory benefits in free recall" in the February 2016 *Quarterly Journal of Experimental Psychology*, University of Waterloo researcher Jeffrey D. Wammes, PhD, and colleagues illustrate the ongoing scientific pursuit of this topic. The researchers have found that drawing pictures of information that needs to be remembered is a strong and reliable strategy to enhance memory. "We pitted drawing against a number of other known encoding strategies, but drawing always came out on top,"[1] said Wammes. "We believe that the benefit arises because drawing helps to create a more cohesive memory trace that better integrates visual, motor and semantic information."

Below is the structural diagram/chart of the nine-step methodology (Table 4.1). Notice the three categories, History, Aesthetics, and Visual Notes. Under each category are the specific steps to be taken with respect to the analysis. The practice examples incorporate these steps as visual notes studies. Once the student or adult learner has chosen a furniture piece he or she wants to investigate, he or she develops examples for that piece using the blank sheets provided at the end of each chapter.

The first several steps under the categories of History and Aesthetics will involve written/narrative documentation (Steps 1 to 3). By Steps 7 and 8, the student or adult learner will begin to use sketching, drawing, rendering, etc., for analysis. Notice all steps are incorporated with Step 9, which falls under the Visual Notes category. The practice examples culminate with the final drawing, or visual notes exercise. The visual notes exercise is the apex and formally treated, similar to a color plate in an art, architecture, or design history book. It is important to remember to number each practice example and visual notes exercise. When the practice examples and visual notes are completed, the student or adult learner will have a compendium of furniture examples to use for future reference.

Now that the reader has perused the Analysis of Form diagram, the author will explain the structure step by step using three furniture pieces, one furniture piece from the pictorial timeline, identified with a circle (Timeline 4.1). The two other furniture pieces selected are not from the pictorial timeline but are indicative of their respective periods—capturing the aesthetic spirit of the time. The three pieces are an 18th-century American Rococo high chest of drawers; an 18th-century French Rococo upholstered armchair; and a mid-20th-century American sofa.

Regarding missing criteria within the categories, any unavailable information should not prohibit one from being able to complete the other steps in the process.

Table 4.1
The Analysis of Form: Nine-Step Methodology.
Author

The Analysis of Form: Nine-Step Methodology		
Visual Notes Exercise		
History (identify – write)	**Aesthetics** (identify – write and delineate)	**Visual Notes** (delineate)
STEP	STEP	STEP
1. Period	4. Mass/Scale/Proportion	9. Delineation: sketching, drawing, rendering of the entire furniture piece, including Steps 7 and 8
2. Country/Place of origin	5. Construction method	
3. Cabinetmaker or Designer	6. Material	
	7. Constituent parts: back, seat, legs, arms	
	8. Decorative motifs	

Simply label the step as "missing information" or "unknown." Often under the History category, furniture pieces will not have the signature of the cabinetmaker/designer. The chapters in Part III will have the majority of the material needed for the exercises; however, this does not preclude one from looking at other material (books, websites, magazines, journals, etc.) for additional information to supplement missing information.

The sheet size for delineation will be approximately 8½" × 11". The orientation should be portrait for most examples. Compositionally, the title should be at the top, and the photographic image near the title. An image from the chapter is crucial because it is referenced for the investigation—Steps 1 through 9. This information is communicated via written notes and delineation. Also near the top should be a list of methodology steps being addressed with a brief description. The approach to delineation is up to the student. Chapter 5 will assist in this area. It is critical to remember that no matter the time frame in which a furniture piece exists, the nine-step methodology can be applied. For example, one can analyze a 20th-century piece and an 18th-century piece using the same nine-step process.

As mentioned, the three furniture pieces used to demonstrate how to apply the Analysis of Form: Nine-Step Methodology are as follows. The first—from the Art Institute of Chicago, Israel Sack Gallery of American Furniture—is an 18th-century high chest of drawers. The second is an 18th-century French piece from the Metropolitan Museum of Art, New York, Wrightsman Galleries—Hôtel de Varengeville, period room. The last piece is a mid-20th-century piece, designed by George Nelson for Herman Miller.

The format and graphic arrangement are the same for each of the three analysis examples that the author will use to demonstrate. Graphically, the organization is structured as follows. The title is placed at the top of the page in the left corner and a photograph of the piece to be analyzed resides below or beside (Figure 4.1, Figure 4.3, Figure 4.5, and Figure 4.7). The last photographic image is provided in preparation to interpret as acurately as possible Visual Notes Exercise 1 (Figure 4.9). Accompanying this photograph is the visual notes explanation in a narrative. At the top of the page is the information for the piece which applies to the three-category structure: History, Aesthetics, and Visual Notes. Next to this area there is a box with the visual notes study—sketch images/visual analysis of the piece (Figure 4.2, Figure 4.4, Figure 4.6, and Figure 4.8). The last image to be shown and a most crucial part is Step 9, the visual notes exercise—no longer a study but a final image of the completed analysis and depicted as a color plate with its own number (Plate 4.1). The format and graphic arrangement are repeated for all three examples. The visual pattern of this arrangement should quickly become familiar.

For the first example, the American 18th-century high chest of drawers, the author includes highlighted red text. This is used only on the first example of the three selections to help explain the format order. Remember, as the student or adult learner analyzes, he or she too should keep a consistent graphic arrangement for analysis. I recommend this one prescribed by the author, but the reader can certainly construct his or her own format and arrangement for the Analysis of Form: Nine-Step Methodology.

The Analysis of Form: Nine-Step Methodology ■

4.1
Furniture Pictorial timeline—18th century.

■ An Illustrated Guide to Furniture History

| TITLE | NUMBER FOR STUDY | LISTING OF STEPS AND DESCRIPTION |

Practice examples: Studies 1–4

High Chest of Drawers

History CATEGORY

Step 1—Period
American, Rococo, 1750–1760

Step 2—Country/Place of origin
USA, Philadephia, Pennsylvania

Step 3—Cabinetmaker/Designer
Unknown

Aesthetics CATEGORY

Step 4—Mass/Scale
Approximately H 108″ × W 52″ × D 24″ two-part mass—upper case and lower case

Step 5—Construction method
Dovetail joints for drawers, mortise and tenon joints.

Step 6—Material
Yellow pine, tulip, poplar, and mahogany

Step 7—Constituent parts: back, seat, legs, arms
Cabriole legs, claw-and-ball foot, and broken pediment

Step 8—Decorative motifs
Carved volutes and finials at pediment, carved acanthus leaves on cabriole leg/knee, claw-and-ball foot, shell motifs with carved acanthus leaves, and brass escutcheons at central top and base.

Figure 4.1
High chest of drawers. American, Philadelphia, 1750–1760. Mahogany, yellow pine, and tulip poplar, 256.7 × 113.1 × 59.1 cm.

Source: Art Institute of Chicago, The Israel Sack Gallery, American Furniture. Creative Common Zero, [CC0]. Gift of the Antiquarian Society.

The Analysis of Form: Nine-Step Methodology

Visual Notes STUDY 1

VISUAL NOTES EXPLANTION

For this high chest of drawers, the practice examples, Visual Notes STUDIES 1–4, cover the three categories culminating in the final and fifth drawing, Visual Notes Exercise 1, Step 9—Delineation: sketching, drawing, rendering, etc.

With respect to the History category, Visual Notes Study 1 has written notes for the analysis of Steps 1–3, identifying the period and country/place of origin. Notice the Cabinetmaker is marked unknown because this information could not be found.

Regarding the Aesthetics category, Study 1 has written notes to address Steps 5 and 6, plus a few visual notes for Step 5. For Steps 7 and 8, a quick sketch technique is used to analyze various parts and motifs, such as the broken pediment scrolls with finials, cabriole legs with claw-and-ball foot, carved shells, and brass escutcheons.

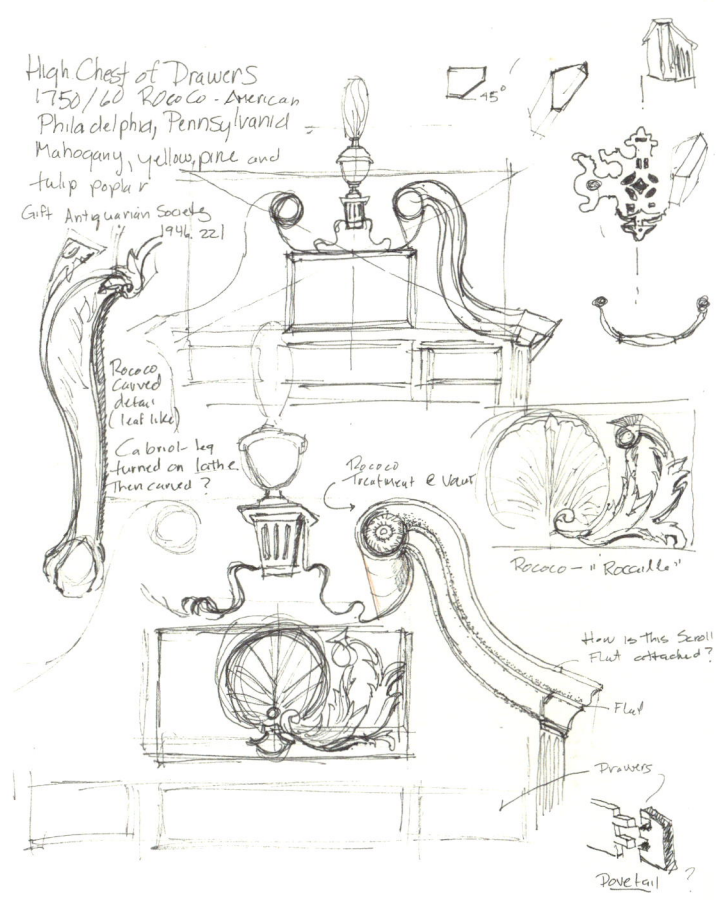

Figure 4.2
Author's drawing, for Visual Notes STUDY 1, High Chest of Drawers.
Author's illustration.

■ An Illustrated Guide to Furniture History

Practice examples: Studies 1–4

Aesthetics
Step 4—Mass/Scale

Approximately H 108″ × W 52″ × D24″
Two-part mass—upper case and lower case

Figure 4.3 High chest of drawers, American, Philadelphia, 1750–1760. Mahogany, yellow pine, and tulip poplar, 256.7 × 113.1 × 59.1 cm.

Source: Art Institute of Chicago, The Israel Sack Gallery, American Furniture. Creative Common Zero, [CC0]. Gift of the Antiquarian Society.

The Analysis of Form: Nine-Step Methodology ∎

Visual Notes STUDY 2

With respect to the Aesthetic category for Study 2, Step 4—Mass/Scale was a challenge since this piece was observed on-site at the Art Institute of Chicago.

It is not permissible at a museum to use a tape measure in the galleries. In such circumstances, the investigator must devise another system for measuring. A body part—hand or foot—can work. This will allow one to record an approximate size.

Depicted in Study 2 are diagrams investigating the relationship of the upper case and lower case, and their proportions—the golden mean/ratio is being considered. Lastly, the sketch of the entire piece summarizes the mass/scale studies.

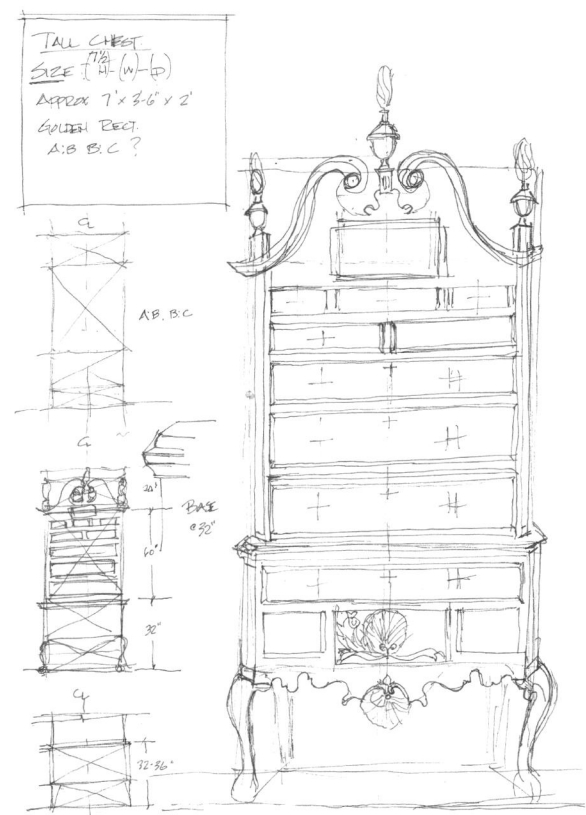

Figure 4.4
Author's drawing, for Visual Notes STUDY 2, High Chest of Drawers.
Author's illustration.

■ An Illustrated Guide to Furniture History

Practice examples: Studies 1–4

Aesthetics
Step 7—Constituent parts: back, seat, legs, arms
  Cabriole legs, claw-and-ball foot, and broken pediment
Step 8—Decorative motifs
  Carved volutes and finials at pediment, carved acanthus leaves on cabriole leg/knee, claw-and-ball foot, shell motifs with carved acanthus leaves, and brass escutcheons

Figure 4.5
High chest of drawers, American, Philadelphia, 1750–1760. Mahogany yellow pine, and tulip poplar, 256.7 × 113.1 × 59.1 cm.

Source: Art Institute of Chicago, The Israel Sack Gallery, American Furniture. Creative Common Zero, [CC0]. Gift of the Antiquarian Society.

The Analysis of Form: Nine-Step Methodology ■

Visual Notes STUDY 3

Study 3 revisits Steps 7–8. The visual notes examine the central portion of the pediment's volutes and finials. The relationship of the elements on the skirt/apron (scalloped-edge base with carved shell motif) in relation to the cabriole leg with claw-and-ball foot is also being analyzed.

These visual notes are similar in approach to Study 1—simple line sketches with some emphasis on tone, shadow, and texture. A red pencil is used to draw the set-up lines. The black sketching pen is used to communicate the final details.

Sketch study by the author

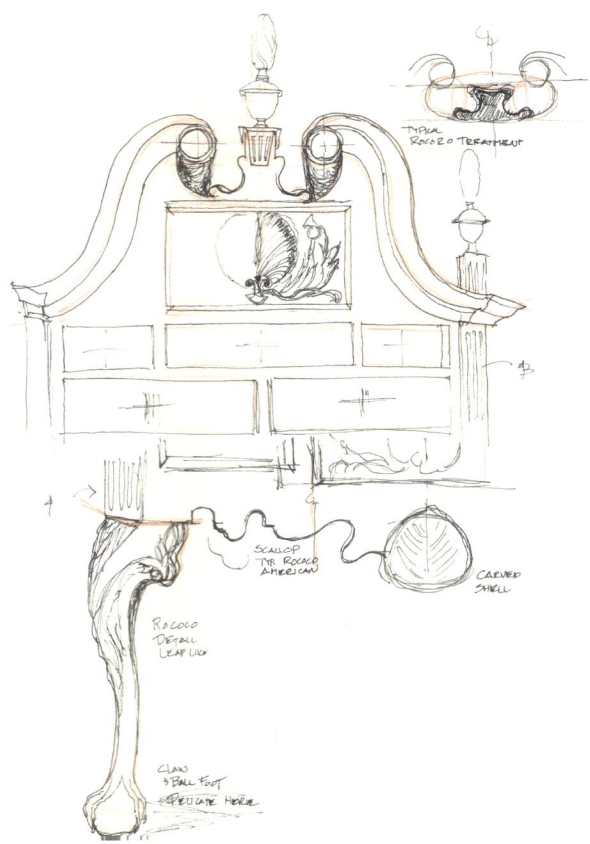

Figure 4.6
Author's drawing, for Visual Notes STUDY 3, High Chest of Drawers.
Author's illustration

■ An Illustrated Guide to Furniture History

Practice examples: Studies 1–4

Step 9—Delineation: sketching, drawing, rendering of the entire furniture piece, including Steps 7 and 8

Figure 4.7 High chest of drawers, American, Philadelphia, 1750–1760. Mahogany yellow pine, and tulip poplar, 256.7 × 113.1 × 59.1 cm.

Source: Art Institute of Chicago, The Israel Sack Gallery, American Furniture. Creative Common Zero, [CC0]. Gift of the Antiquarian Society.

The Analysis of Form: Nine-Step Methodology

Visual Notes STUDY 4

Study 4 is the last study and the set-up for the final drawing—Visual Notes Exercise 1, Step 9. With regard to the delineation set-up, it is a framework used as an underlay. It allows one to keep things accurate for the execution of the final version of a drawing.

The line work of a set-up is usually tightly constructed. For the guidelines, a straight edge is typically used. Also an architectural scale or graphic scale is used for the set-up. The set-up becomes a template and is closely followed for the final drawing.

Here the set-up was done to capture the accurate drawer size, which, for the upper portion, descends in scale from bottom to top. A straight edge was used for Study 4 in order to make the drawing read visually correct.

Sketch study by the author

Figure 4.8
Author's drawing, for Visual Notes STUDY 4, High Chest of Drawers.
Author's illustration.

■ An Illustrated Guide to Furniture History

Visual Note Exercise 1: High chest of drawers

**Visual notes
Step 9—Delineation: sketching, drawing, rendering of the entire furniture piece, including Steps 7 and 8**

As mentioned, the last photograph image of the piece is revisited at a larger scale prior to creating the visual notes exercise, Step 9, in preparation to interpret as acurately as possible the Visual Notes Exercise 1 seen above. On the following page is the Visual Notes Exercise 1 for the high chest of drawers (Plate 4.1). One can see how Study 4 has been meticulously developed into the final analysis—Visual Notes Exercise 1. This final drawing should convey visually all that is necessary for a student or adult learner to remember about this piece and the given period. All nine steps from the methodology are visible—noted and/or drawn.

This final drawing should feel similar to a color plate in a book. This drawing is articulate in its delineation—tight linework, rendering indicating texture, tone, and shadow. Every feature is treated as realistically as possible.

Visual Notes Exercise 1: High chest of drawers

That completes the Analysis of Form: Nine-Step Methodology for the first example piece. The analysis for the second piece begins on the next page, using the same format and graphic arrangement—photograph of the piece to the left (Figure 4.10, Figure 4.12, and Figure 4.14). As with the first example, the last photograph shown for the French armchair will be a larger-scale image in preparation to interpret as accurately as possible Visual Notes Exercise 2 (Figure 4.16). Residing below the photograph is the visual notes explanation in a narrative. At the top of the page on the right is the information for the piece which applies to the three-category structure, and below this area Visual Notes Study 1–3 consisting of the sketch images/visual analysis lower right (Figure 4.11, Figure 4.13, and Figure 4.15). The last image to be shown and a most crucial part is Step 9, the visual notes exercise, no longer a study but depicted as a color plate and with its own number (Plate 4.1).

Figure 4.9
High chest of drawers, American, Philadelphia, 1750–1760. Mahogany, yellow pine, and tulip poplar, 256.7 × 113.1 × 59.1 cm.

Source: Art Institute of Chicago, The Israel Sack Gallery, American Furniture. Creative Common Zero, [CC0]. Gift of the Antiquarian Society.

The Analysis of Form: Nine-Step Methodology ■

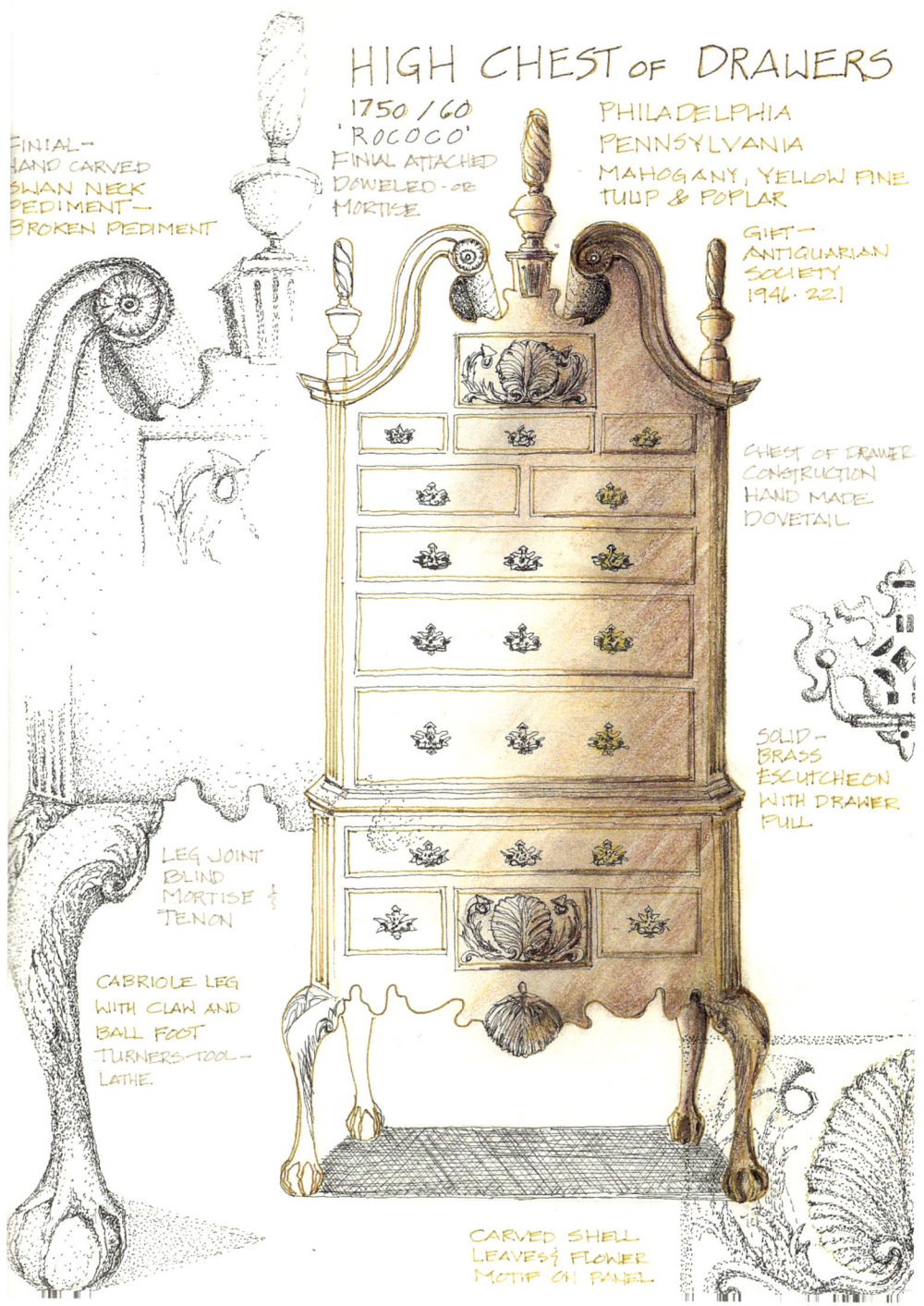

Plate 4.1
Author's drawing Visual Notes Exercise 1, High Chest of Drawers.

Source: Art Institute of Chicago, Chicago Illinois, Creative Common Zero, [CC0]. The Israel Sack Gallery, American Furniture.

■ An Illustrated Guide to Furniture History

Practice examples: Studies 1–3

French armchair

History

Step 1—Period
   18th-century Louis XV, Rococo

Step 2—Country of origin
   Paris, France, 1753
   One of two chairs made for Baron Johann Ernst Bernstorff, Dutch Ambassador to the Court of Versailles

Step 3—Cabinetmaker/Designer
   Unknown

Aesthetics

Step 4—Mass/Scale
   Approx. W 30″ × D 32″ × B 42″, seat H 17–18″

Step 5—Construction method
   Lathe turned (educated guess), mortise and tenon

Step 6—Material
   Beechwood, gilded gold frame, upholstery

Step 7—Constituent parts: back, seat, legs, arms
   Scroll arm and foot, cabriole leg, cartouche back

Step 8—Decorative motifs
   Carved *C*- and *S*-forms, cabriole leg, scroll foot, cartouche back

Figure 4.10 French armchair (Louis XV fauteuil), located in the Boiserie from the Hôtel de Varengeville, Period Room, French, Paris, ca. 1736–1752.

Source: Metropolitan Museum of Art, New York, New York Public Domain, [OA]—Open Access.

The Boiserie from the Hôtel de Varengeville, Period Room. French.

The Analysis of Form: Nine-Step Methodology

Visual notes STUDY 1

For this French armchair visual note, practice exercises Studies 1–3 cover the three categories, culminating in a final fourth drawing, which is the final visual notes exercise, Step 9—Delineation; sketching, drawing, rendering of the entire furniture piece, including Steps 7 and 8.

With respect to the History category, Study 1 contains written notes as seen for the tall chest example for Steps 1–3. The notes identify the period and country/place of origin. The designer is listed as unknown. However, information as to who the chair was first designed for was found.

In reference to the Aesthetics category, Study 1 explores Step 4—Mass/Scale, using loose sketches and perspective images to examine the scale and proportion of the shape of the back and its entire form. Written notes are used to address Step 6—Materials, including the upholstery (tapestry), and all information regarding the manufacturer and designer is recorded as notes. The sketch technique is quick and loose for both Step 7—Constituent parts and Step 8—Decorative motifs; the focus is not to be literal but to capture the spirit—idea.

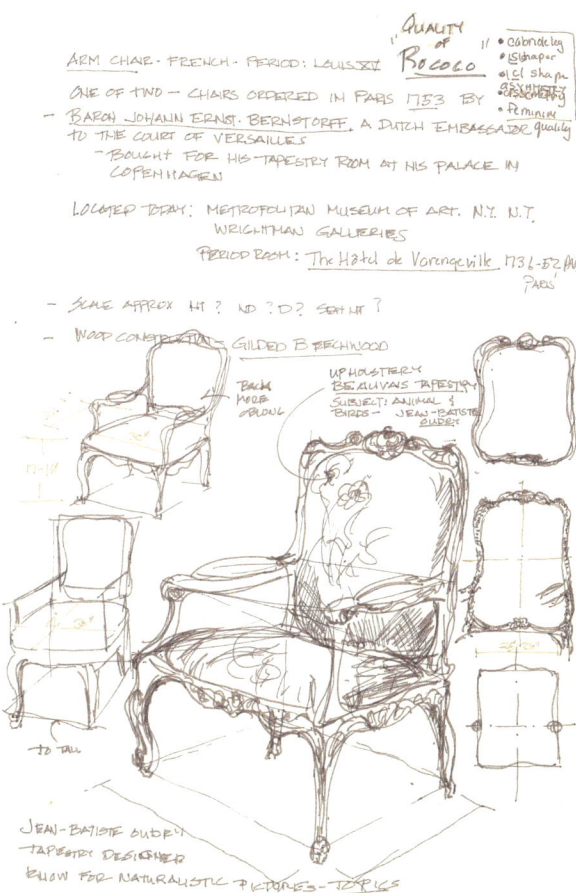

Figure 4.11
Author's drawing, for Visual Notes STUDY 1, French Armchair.
Author's illustration.

■ An Illustrated Guide to Furniture History

Practice examples: Studies 1–3

French armchair

Aesthetics

Step 4—Mass/Scale

W 30″ × D 32″ × B 42″, seat H 17–18″

Step 5—Construction method

Lathe turned (educated guess), mortise and tenon

Step 6—Material

Beechwood, gilded gold upholstery—Beauvais tapersty

Step 7—Constituent parts: back, seat, leg, arm

Scroll arm and foot, cabriole leg, cartouche back

Step 8—Decorative motifs

Carved C- and S-forms, cabriole leg, scroll foot, back at yoke arm, chair base

Figure 4.12 French armchair, (Louis XV fauteuil), located in the Boiserie from the Hôtel de Varengeville, Period Room, French, Paris, ca. 1736–1752.

Source: Metropolitan Museum of Art, New York, The Boiserie from the Hôtel de Varengeville, Period Room. French. Paris, ca. 1736–1752. Public Domain, [OA]—Open Access. Gift of John D. Rockefeller Jr., 1935.

The Analysis of Form: Nine-Step Methodology ■

Visual notes STUDY 2

Study 2, Step 4 is approached by investigating the entire form of the chair. The relationship between the cabriole legs, arms, seat frame, and the yoke area of the back is examined.

Looking closely at the front left cabriole leg, Step 5, e.g., joinery (educated guess), slotted mortise and tenon, the analysis of the construction information contains both written notes and sketches. For Step 6, both the wood-carved frame and upholstery are being observed. The upholstery color palette is studied, as seen in the sketch. The wood-carved motif, typical of Rococo style, use of asymmetrical sinuous curves, and leaf-like forms are also investigated. For Steps 7 and 8, the intent of the visual notes is not to be literal but to capture the essence, the spirit—idea.

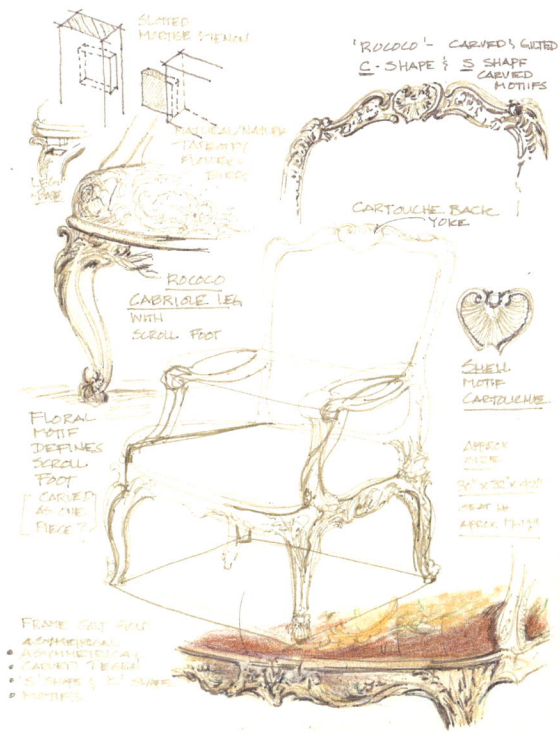

Figure 4.13
Author's drawing, for Visual Notes STUDY 2, French Armchair.
Author's illustration.

■ An Illustrated Guide to Furniture History

Practice examples: Studies 1–3

French armchair

Step 5—Construction method
Lathe turned (educated guess), mortise and tenon

Step 6—Material
Beechwood, gilded gold, upholstery—Beauvais tapestry

Step 7— Constituent parts: back, seat, legs, arms
Scroll arm and foot, cabriole leg, cartouche back

Step 8 —Decorative motifs
Carved C- and S-forms, cabriole leg, scroll foot, back at yoke arm, chair base

Figure 4.14 French armchair (Louis XV fauteuil), located in the Boiserie from the Hôtel de Varengeville, Period Room, French, Paris, ca. 1736–1752.

Source: Metropolitan Museum of Art, New York, The Boiserie from the Hôtel de Varengeville, Period Room. French. Paris, ca. 1736–1752. Public Domain, [OA]—Open Access. Gift of John D. Rockefeller Jr., 1935.

The Analysis of Form: Nine-Step Methodology

Visual notes STUDY 3

For Study 3, Step 5 is addressed in written notes for Step 6, the woven Beauvais tapestry—color palette, pattern, texture for the seat and back of the chair—is investigated. Attributed to Jean-Baptiste Oudry (1686–1755). His subjects are typically flora and fauna.

The visual notes for Steps 7 and Step 8 are examined through a series of thumbnail sketches. The thumbnails are exploring detail that is typical of carved Rococo designs: the ubiquitous *S-* and *C-*shape patterning.

Overall, Study 3 examines the chair's carved patterns, and textures—light and dark resulting from the gilded finish and relief of the carved elements.

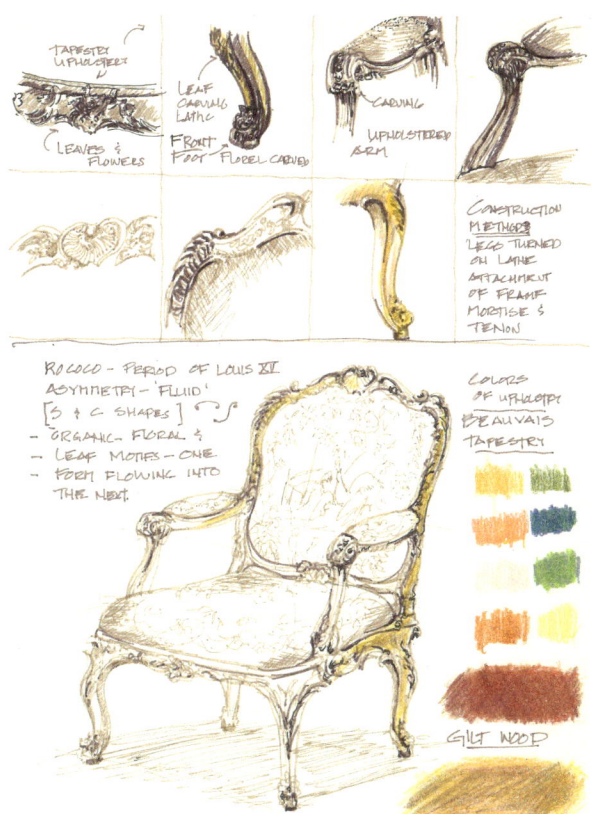

Figure 4.15
Author's drawing, for Visual Notes STUDY 3, French Armchair.
Author's illustration.

■ An Illustrated Guide to Furniture History

Visual Note Exercise 2: French armchair

Visual notes
Step 9—Delineation: sketching, drawing, rendering of the entire furniture piece, including Steps 7 and 8

For example two, the French armchair, as was the case with the first example, the American 18th-century high chest of drawers, the last photograph image of the piece is revisited prior to creating the Step 9, visual notes exercise in preparation to interpret as acurately as possibly the Visual Notes Exercise 2. Notice the number of the Visual Notes Exercise is 2 for the French armchair, corresponding with the example number.

Similar to the American 18th-century high chest of drawers, the Rococo armchair's Visual Notes Exercise 2 includes all nine steps of the methodology. As with the chest of drawers, these steps are represented in multiple ways—written notes, details, and perspectives. The rendering here also communicates the materiality as realistically as possible. Visually, this final drawing should convey all that is necessary for the student or adult learner to remember about the design of this furniture piece in the given time period. Like the high-chest drawing, this drawing is presented formally—resembling a color plate in a book (Plate 4.2). This completes the Analysis of Form: Nine-Step Methodology for example two, the French Rococo armchair. The third and last example piece, the Mid-Century Marshmallow sofa, will be analyzed next.

Figure 4.16
French armchair (Louis XV fauteuil), located in the Boiserie from the Hôtel de Varengeville, Period Room, French, Paris, ca. 1736–1752.

Source: Metropolitan Museum of Art, New York, The Boiserie from the Hôtel de Varengeville, Period Room. French. Paris, ca. 1736–1752. Public Domain, [OA]—Open Access. Gift of John D. Rockefeller Jr., 1935.

The Analysis of Form: Nine-Step Methodology

Visual Notes Exercise 2: French armchair

Plate 4.2
Author's drawing Visual Notes Exercise 2, French Armchair.

Author's illustration.

The Marshmallow sofa on the next page is the last example piece. It will be analyzed using the same format and graphic arrangement as the first and second examples, beginning with the photograph of the piece to the left (Figure 4.17, Figure 4.19, and Figure 4.21). The last photographic image will be larger scale in preparation to interpret as acurately as possible Visual Notes Exercise 3 (Figure 4.23). Residing below the photographs is the visual notes explanation in a narrative. As with the two previous examples, at the top of the page on the right resides Visual Notes Study 1–3 consisting of the sketch images/visual analysis on the lower right (Figure 4.18, Figure 4.20, and Figure 4.22). The last image shown is Visual Notes Exercise 3 depicted as a color plate with the number corresponding to the example (Plate 4.2).

■ An Illustrated Guide to Furniture History

Practice examples: Studies 1–3

Marshmallow sofa

History

Step 1—Period
20th Century, 1956

Step 2—Country of origin
USA, Zeeland, Michigan. Herman Miller

Step 3—Maker/Designer
Irving Harper, George Nelson

Step 4—Mass/Scale
Approx. W 52" × D 24" × B 31", seat H 15"

Aesthetics

Step 5—Construction method
Tubular steel and flat frame supports with metal connectors and screws, etc.

Step 6—Material
Tubular steel, flat steel, vinyl and foam

Step 7—Constituent parts: back, seat, legs, arms
Steel framing for back and legs

Step 8—Decorative motifs
N/A

Figure 4.17 Marshmallow Sofa, George Nelson. Designed for Herman Miller Furniture Company, 1956–1965. Painted tubular steel, with vinyl-covered latex foam circular pads.

Source: Charlotte Fiell and Peter Fiell, *1000 Chairs in the 20th Century* (Germany: Taschen Bibliotheca Unversalis, 1997), p.265.

The Analysis of Form: Nine-Step Methodology ■

Visual notes STUDY 1

As with the French armchair analysis, the Marshmallow sofa visual notes, practice, and examples, Studies 1–3, covers the three categories, culminating in a fourth and final drawing, Visual Notes Exercise 3, Step 9—Delineation: sketching, drawing, rendering of the entire furniture piece, including Steps 7 and 8.

The visual notes for Study 1, with respect to the History category, contain written notes and rough diagrams pertaining to Steps 1–7.

Regarding the Aesthetics category for Steps 5 and 6, the analysis is handled as written notes, while the analysis for Steps 6 and 7 consists of simple line drawings and diagrams to indicate seat and back configuration.

Step 8 is not applicable here. This mid-century sofa does not include decorative motifs in the design.

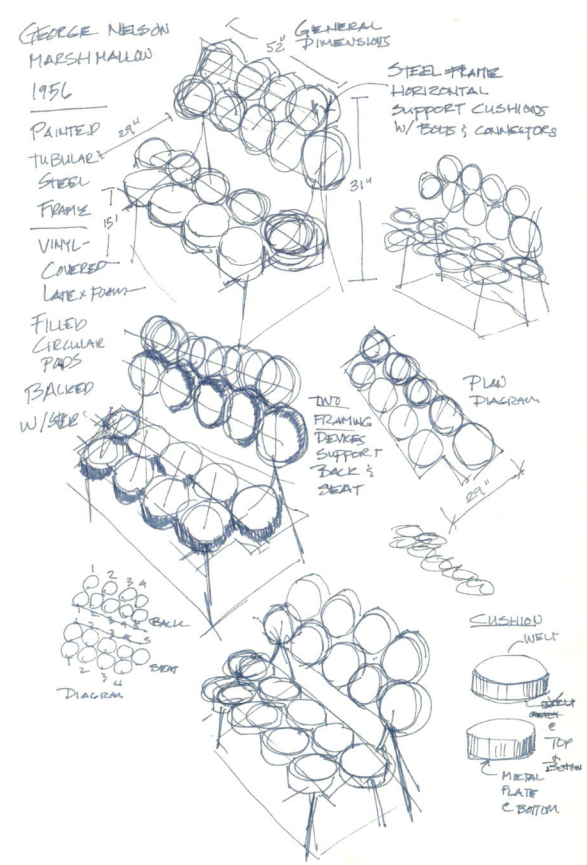

Figure 4.18
Author's illustration, Visual Notes STUDY 1, Marshmallow Sofa.
Author's illustration

147

■ An Illustrated Guide to Furniture History

Practice examples: Studies 1–3

Marshmallow sofa

Aesthetics

Step 4—Mass/Scale

Approx. W 52" × D 24" × B 31", seat H 15"

Step 5—Construction method

Tubular steel and flat frame support with metal connector and screws etc.

Step 6—Material

Tubular steel frame, flat steel, vinyl and foam

Step 7—Constituent parts: back, seat, legs, arms

Steel frame for back and legs

Step 8—Decorative motifs

N/A

Figure 4.19 Marshmallow Sofa, George Nelson. Designed for Herman Miller Furniture Company, 1956–1965. Painted tubular steel, with vinyl-covered latex foam circular pads.

Source: Charlotte Fiell and Peter Fiell, *1000 Chairs in the 20th Century* (Germany: Taschen Bibliotheca Unversalis, 1997), p.265

The Analysis of Form: Nine-Step Methodology ■

Visual notes STUDY 2

Study 2 continues to investigate the Aesthetics category. Step 5 is analyzed through investigation via an enlarged detail (upper right) showing the connecting components.

Pertaining to Steps 6 and 7, the analysis focuses on the entire sofa form. The frame and cushions are sketched using multiple views—right and left perspective views, as well as a view straight on, similar to an elevation.

The rendition of the sofa's upholstery color for the cushions is important here. The cushions—metaphor "marshmallow"—are crucial to the form and overall aesthetic quality of sofa design.

The sofa design has been manufactured to have one consistent color or several colors used together for the cushions. Keeping in mind mid-century pop art, the use of a bright color palette is still a choice for the piece today. As mentioned previously, Step 8 is not applicable. As is the case with most mid-century furniture, applied ornament does not exist.

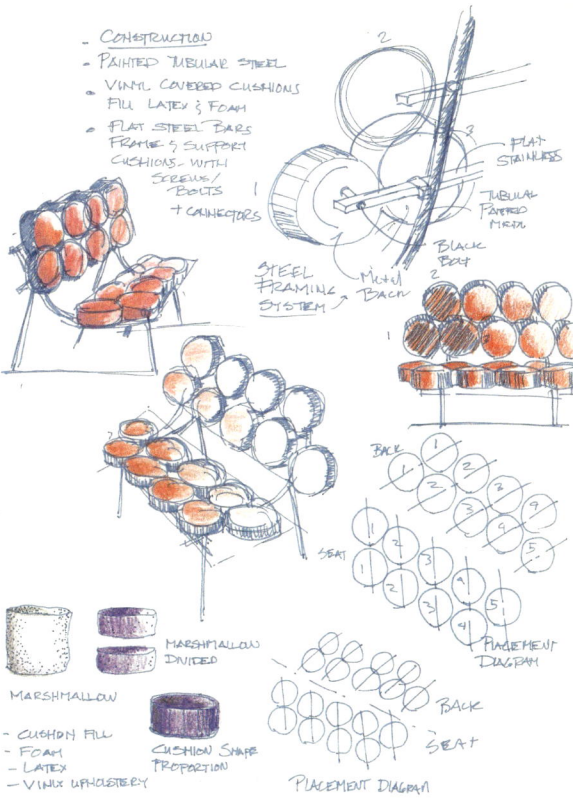

Figure 4.20
Author's drawing, Visual Notes STUDY 2, Marshmallow Sofa.
Author's illustration

■ An Illustrated Guide to Furniture History

Practice examples: Studies 1–3

Marshmallow sofa

Step 4—Mass/Scale
Approx. W 52″ × D 24″ × B 31″, seat H 15″

Step 5—Construction method
Tubular steel and flat frame supports with metal connector, screws, etc.

Step 6—Material
Tubular steel, flat steel, vinyl, and foam

Step 7—Constituent parts: back, seat, legs, arms
Painted tubular steel for back and steel for seat support-no paint

Step 8—Decorative motifs
N/A

Figure 4.21 Marshmallow Sofa, George Nelson. Designed for Herman Miller Furniture Company, 1956–1965. Painted tubular steel, with vinyl-covered latex foam circular pads.

Source: Charlotte Fiell and Peter Fiell, *1000 Chairs in the 20th Century* (Germany: Taschen Bibliotheca Unversalis, 1997), p.265

The Analysis of Form: Nine-Step Methodology ■

Visual Notes   STUDY 3

In Practice example Study 3, the visual notes touch lightly on analysis for Steps 4, 6, and 7. These drawings are primarily focused on 5. Unlike the loose sketch approach taken in Study 1 and Study 2, with Study 3, the delineation is tighter and more concise.

Investigation of the steel vertical and bent tubular frame/brace and the flat steel horizontal frame/brace is depicted as an enlarged detail, at the upper left. The center right study investigates the cushion and steel plate connection, attached to the horizontal steel frame with a vertical rod. This detail also looks at the "marshmallow"—foam and vinyl cushion with welting.

The rendering is important here for the investigative story. As mentioned previously, the cushion color is crucial to the form and overall aesthetics for the Marshmallow sofa design.

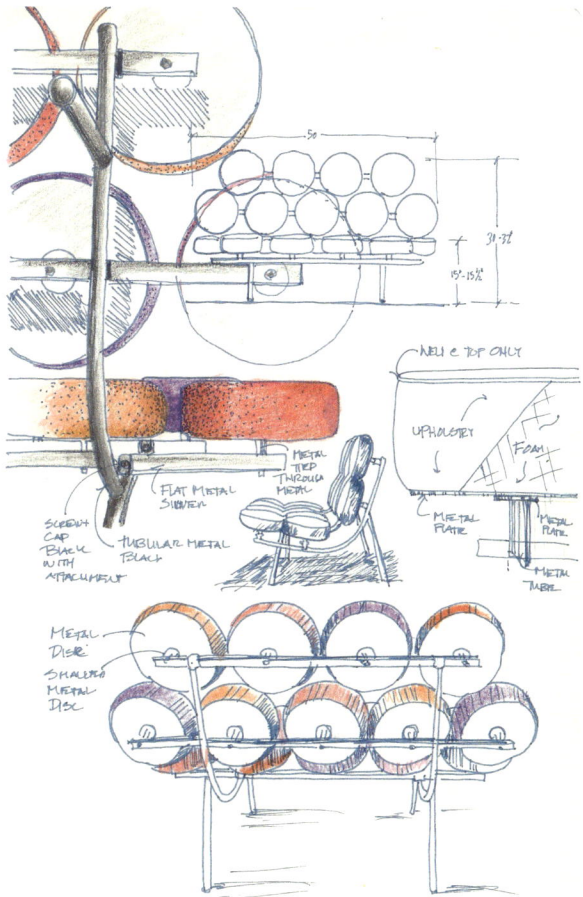

Figure 4.22
Author's drawing, Visual Notes STUDY 3, Marshmallow Sofa.
Author's illustration

151

■ An Illustrated Guide to Furniture History

Visual Notes Exercise 3: Marshmallow sofa

**Visual notes
Step 9—Delineation: sketching, drawing, rendering of the entire furniture piece, including Steps 7 and 8**

Figure 4.23 Marshmallow Sofa, George Nelson. Designed for Herman Miller Furniture Company, 1956–1965. Painted tubular steel, with vinyl-covered latex foam circular pads.

Source: Fiell, Charlotte and Peter. *1000 Chairs in the 20th Century*. Germany: Taschen Bibliotheca Unversalis, 1997, p 265.

As with the previous examples, the last photograph image for the Marshmallow sofa is revisited at a larger scale prior to creating Step 9, visual notes exercise, to interpret as accurately as possible the Visual Notes Exercise 3. On the following page is Visual Notes Exercise 3, as with the previous examples, depicted as a color plate with the number corresponding to the example (Plate 4.3). Visual Notes Exercise 3 demonstrates delineation using a concise line quality. A literal rendering technique is used to depict the metal frame and vinyl upholstery for the sofa. Although creative compositionally, this final exercise should convey visually all that is necessary for the student or adult learner to remember about the design of this furniture piece in the given period.

The Analysis of Form: Nine-Step Methodology

Visual Notes Exercise 3: Marshmallow sofa

Plate 4.3
Author's drawing
Visual Notes
Exercise 3,
Marshmallow
Sofa.

Author's illustration.

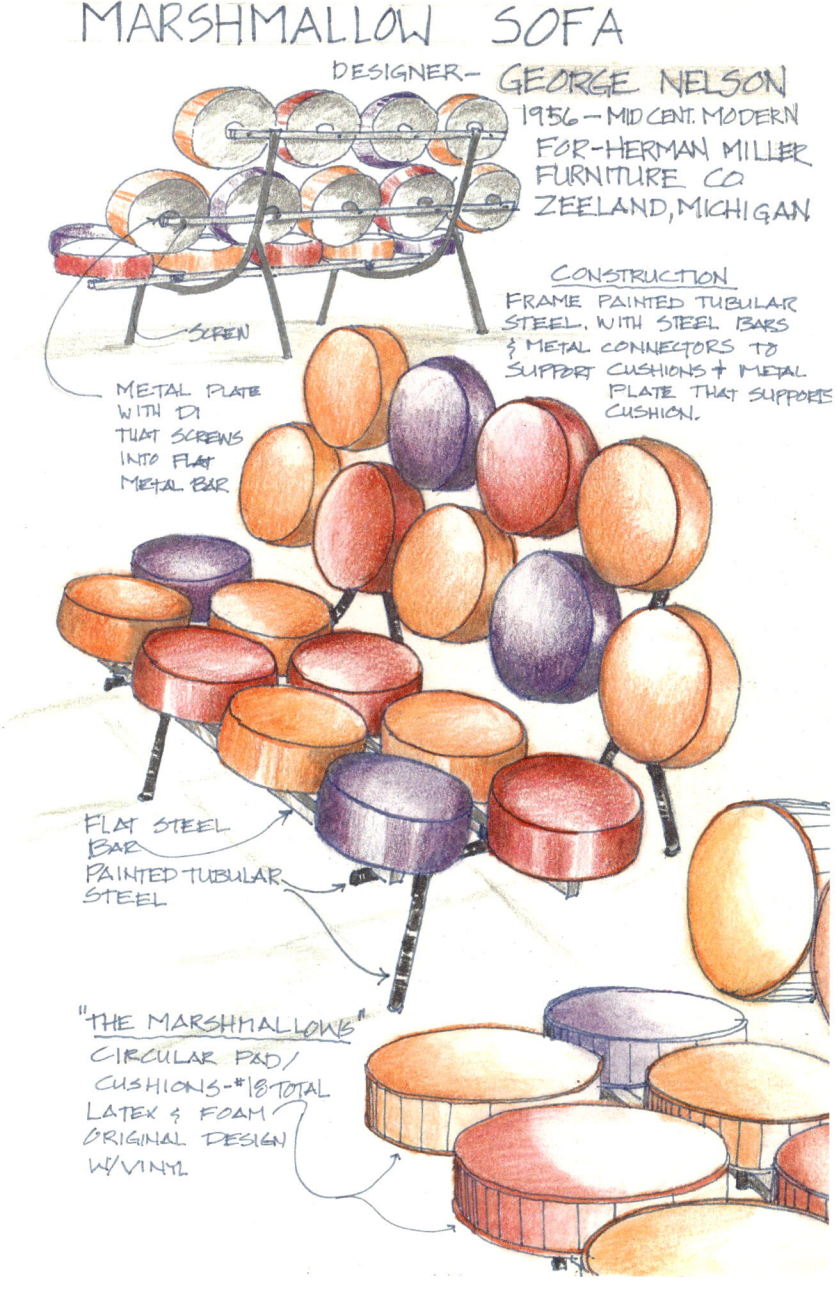

Thus concludes the explanation of the Analysis of Form: Nine-Step Methodology structure and how to navigate through each step within the three categories: History, Aesthetics, and Visual Notes. At the end of this explanation, the following question for the student or adult learner may arise: How many sheets are needed for each investigation?

Although I have demonstrated using three or four visual notes studies per practice examples, for the student or adult learner, I recommend two to three sheets for the visual notes studies and a third or fourth sheet dedicated to the final drawing—the visual notes exercise.

Regarding approach, the delineation method and technique is up to the student or adult learner. Chapter 5—Graphic narrative—will assist in this area.

NOTE

1   Jeffrey D. Wammes, Melissa E. Meade, and Myra A. Fernandes, "The drawing effect: Evidence for reliable and robust memory benefits in free recall," *Quarterly Journal of Experimental Psychology* (2016).

5   A graphic narrative

No different from a written narrative, the graphic narrative is an account of connected events, a story. It is a tool to communicate visual information. In this case, it is a visual story—a visual analysis of furniture using sketching as the analysis tool. As mentioned in Chapter 4, it is the idea of interaction between brain and hand, memory and muscle memory, that will facilitate recall and recognition—creating an imprint on one's memory. Using a graphic narrative encourages visual literacy.

The intent of Chapter 5 is to prepare the student and adult learner for Part III, Chapters 6–13. Part III could be considered analogous to a survey course. The student will survey the pictorial timeline, applying the Analysis of Form: Nine-Step Methodology, Steps 1–9. The student will need a sketchbook on hand to use for sketching—the recommended type and size is a hardcover, 8″ × 11″ or 9″ × 12″. On these pages the student will sketch practice examples and visual note studies. The preparation for Part III will occur in this chapter through reviewing sketch techniques and methods of design professionals. Design professionals use sketching as a tool for communicating their design process, research, investigation, and analysis. The author has selected furniture sketching examples from local Chicago practitioners—architects and designers—and other notable design professionals spanning the globe and decades. These examples will serve as a guide for your own practice examples and visual note studies you chose to investigate on the pictorial timeline. The end goal and apex of your analysis is the final *Visual Notes Exercise*, evidence of having grasped the essence of the piece from the pictorial timeline.

Design professionals use a graphic narrative for recording visual information that could not be as effectively recorded with words.[1] This is done for two purposes—*analysis* and *synthesis*. Beginning with the later synthesis—the design—bringing the design to fruition is comprised of a combination of steps or design phases culminating in the finished project. Beginning with the conceptual phase, professionals use the graphic narrative to express a design idea translated graphically as a basic element of thought, focusing conceptually, not necessarily on details. This process is often referred to as *ideation*. Ideation is typically demonstrated as a rapid creation of free-hand drawings. For design professionals, ideation is a creative process of generating, developing, and communicating new ideas. Designers ideate, no matter how large or small the project—an urban plan, building, house, furniture or decorative arts object.

The sketch as a graphic analysis tool is a conversation between the sketcher and the designed piece or artifact. The critical piece of the concept is that the sketcher selects the information to sketch, keeping in mind that, as an analytical tool, sketching is used to organize and give order to the sketcher's thoughts and to visually record those thoughts—"getting the information down" in order to use as reference.[2]

For Part III, Chapters 6–13, after reading a chapter the reader's role will be to analyze by using practice examples and visual note studies. It is important to understand that for this purpose the author's concept of sketching is speaking to the utility of sketching—sketching as a tool. This concept is not focused on a notion of being endowed with appropriate artistic talent.[3] The reader should note that sketches are not an unsuccessful attempt to create a visual reality but can be used as notes to record visual features.[4] For the sake of learning furniture history, Chapter 5 will focus on the latter to help facilitate success for when one arrives at Part III.

In their publication *Visual Notes for Architects and Designers*, Norman Crowe and Paul Laseau addressed the notion of visual literacy as being comprised of two skills: *visual acuity*, an ability to see information in one's environment with clarity, and *visual expression*, the ability to initiate visual messages.[5] People such as artists, designers, choreographers, photographers, and architects initiate visual messages. Pertaining to understanding the Analysis of Form: Nine-Step Methodology, this book's focus is *visual acuity*. The education goal is for the student to see with clarity the constituent parts of a furniture piece, in order to understand the whole—the entire piece—and, ultimately, to be able to place it within its appropriate period. Since this book's framework is an immersion-learning model, a reader might have some anxiety about time. However, please remember there is no time limit to learning and one can continue to sketch the furniture piece beyond completion of the book.

The rest of this chapter is dedicated to looking at the sketch examples of Chicago architects and designers, and other notable design professionals spanning the globe and decades. The design professionals are listed in alphabetical order. The generosity and courtesy of these architecture and design professionals for allowing the use of their sketches in this publication is greatly appreciated; it is fortunate for both the publication and reader.

RON ARAD ASSOCIATES LTD., LONDON, ENGLAND

Ron Arad was born in Tel Aviv, studied at the Bezalel Academy of Art and Design in Jerusalem, and at the Architectural Association in London. His practice includes architecture, industrial design, and art. His work is exhibited in prestigious public collections including the Centre Pompidou (Paris), Victoria and Albert Museum (V&A) (London), and Museum of Modern Art (MoMA) (New York).[6]

A graphic narrative

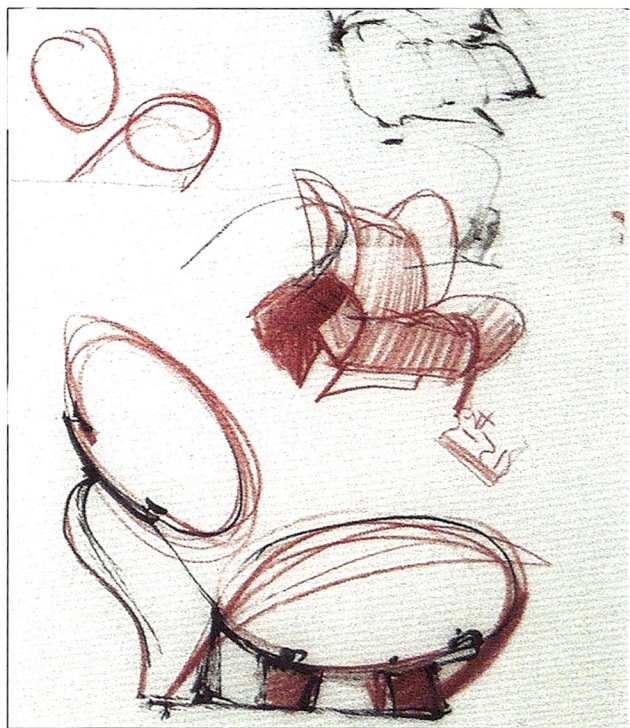

Figure 5.1
Ron Arad, sketch studies for "Well Tempered Chair".
Source: Ron Arad and Associates Limited.

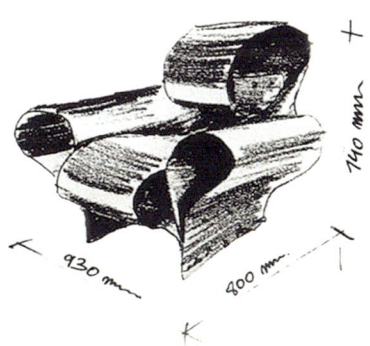

Figure 5.2
Ron Arad, Sketch study for "Well Tempered Chair".
Source: Ron Arad and Associates Limited.

First notice the paper for Ron Arad's sheet of sketches for "Well Tempered Chair," 1986 (Figure 5.1). When it comes to sketching, the paper medium/type as well as drawing medium—pen, pencil, charcoal, oil pastel, marker, etc.—matters greatly to the design professional. There will be a preference, and individuals takes pride in these preferences. Looking at Ron Arad's sketches, the energetic and spirited nature comes forward. He uses textured and toned paper, with pen and pencil, and his application of red is indicative of his energetic linework.

The lone sketch illustrates an arch-like bulbous shape that forms the chairs seat, back. and arms. This sketch visually is very close to the final design manufactured by Vitra (Figure 5.2). "Well Tempered Chair" was designed for Vitra Editions, which presents limited editions of experimental prototypes. The final design of "Well Tempered Chair" is comprised of steel screwed into arches to form its body. The steel sheets that comprise its form have flexibility and can spring and bounce back into its original shape.[7] As stated by Vitra, "a completely new feeling for sitting."

KAREN HEROLD, STUDIO K CREATIVE, CHICAGO, ILLINOIS

With her recent degree in fashion design, Karen Herold arrived in Chicago 20 years ago from Amsterdam. Not unusually, the attraction was Chicago's publicized architecture and design pedigree. Yet Karen had no idea she would fall in love with Chicago and make it her home.[8] Karen shifted her career path from fashion design to interior design. She began working with the established Chicago firm

■ An Illustrated Guide to Furniture History

555 International, an award-winning global design, development, and fabrication firm with specialization in commercial, retail, and hospitality industries. Her collaboration with 555 International lasted for 13 years.[9] At 555 International, she was able to quickly evolve its retail-focused interiors work into the popular hospitality design department it is recognized for today.[10] Her design success at 555 attracted an impressive client list, including Hugh Hefner, restaurateur Michael Morton, and Steve Wynn of Wynn Resorts.[11]

As a prolific designer, she was looking to expand her design versatility, and in early 2014 Karen started her own multidisciplinary creative house, Studio K. Because of Karen's business and design acumen, Studio K has delivered many of Chicago's most popular restaurants and bars. These timeless and eclectic projects include Maple & Ash, Monteverde, BLVD, GT Prime, Bellemore, the Aurelien, and, most recently, Hayden Hall, a new food hall in the Chicago Loop.

Never trend-driven, Karen continues to develop Studio K into a firm focused on authentic design, personal relationships, and a relentless desire to learn and grow.[12] The sketches featured were completed by Michael Regan, a 3D Modeler at Studio K. The studies are pieces for three restaurants. The first sketch, for Bellemore, is a loose pen study for a custom round banquet seen in plan and elevation (Figure 5.3). The linework for the plan is quick yet purposeful. The companion sketch is more concise and controlled and gives a three-dimensional idea of what the round banquet looks like (Figure 5.4). Notice on this sketch the notes about specific details and materials. The last several sketches are for custom light fixtures. For hospitality design, light fixtures are classified as furniture. Shown for GT Fish & Oyster are two variations of rope chandeliers. These sketches are exquisitely detailed, and illustrate a strong command of line weight manipulation, the use of shadow, tone, and texture. There is a looseness to the sketches, but there is clarity—they

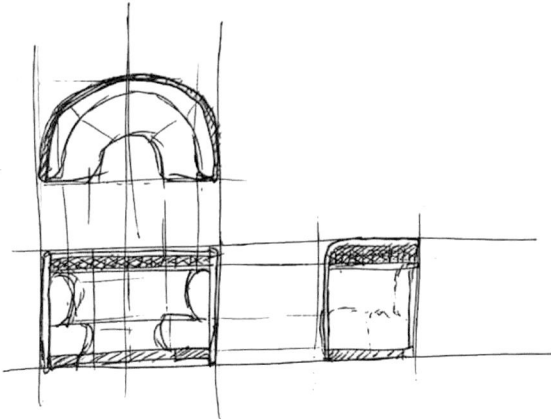

Figure 5.3
Studio K Creative, Bellemore custom Round banquet, plan and elevations. Sketch by Michael Regan.

Source: Studio K Creative, Project: Bellemore, Custom Furniture: Round banquet.

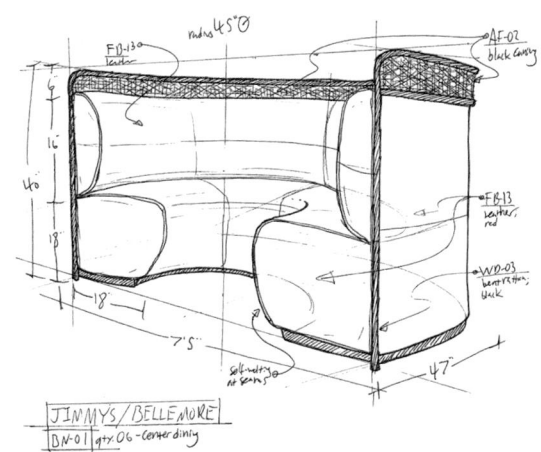

Figure 5.4
Studio K Creative, Bellemore, custom Round banquet three-dimension. Sketch by Michael.

Source: Studio K Creative, Project: Bellemore, Custom Furniture: Round banquet.

A graphic narrative

Figure 5.5
Studio K Creative, GT Fish & Oyster custom Rope chandelier (Concept 1). Sketch by Michael Regan, 3D modeler.

Source: Studio K Creative, Project: GT Fish & Project: GT Fish & chandelier.

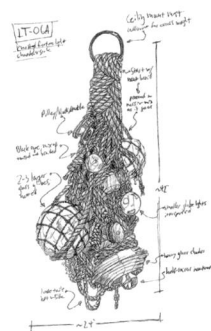

Figure 5.6
Studio K Creative, GT Fish & Oyster custom Rope chandelier (Concept 2). Sketch by Michael Regan, 3D modeler.

Source: Studio K Creative, Project: GT Fish & Project: GT Fish & chandelier.

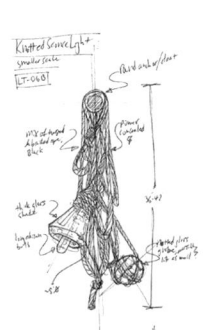

Figure 5.7
Studio K Creative, Maple & Ash custom Necklace chandelier. Sketch by Michael Regan, 3D.

Source: Studio K Creative, Project: Maple & Ash, Custom Furniture: Necklace chandelier.

are legible (Figure 5.5 and Figure 5.6). The last sketch for Maple and Ash restaurant is a necklace chandelier. There is a delicateness in the linework of this sketch which duplicates the light, airy quality of the necklace chandelier (Figure 5.7).

FLORENCE KNOLL BASSETT, KNOLL ASSOCIATES, INC.

Florence Marguerite Knoll Bassett (née Schust, 1917–2019), was an American architect, interior designer, furniture designer, and entrepreneur. Florence Schust married German-born Hans Knoll (1914–1955) in 1946. However, prior to meeting Hans Knoll, she already had a distinctive life. She was educated under the Cranbrook Educational Community in Bloomfield Hills, Michigan, having a close relationship with Eliel Saarinen, the Cranbrook Academy of Art President and his family, and through various advanced education experiences at Columbia University, New York, Architectural Association, UK, and the Armour Institute, Chicago, where she received her bachelor's degree in architecture.

After marrying Hans Knoll, she became his collaborator and business partner, and together they built Knoll Associates, Inc., where she worked from 1940s until her resignation in 1965. Her unique concept at Knoll—the Planning Unit—revolutionized office design. The Planning Unit consisted of a team of Knoll designers who collectively designed the corporate office project, offering a comprehensive design expressing mid-century "modernity." The projects incorporated a rational space plan, modern furniture selection, and color, finish, and material selection. Overall, the aesthetic was minimalist. Under Florence Knoll's entrepreneurial vision, the Knoll mission for designing interior space was that of a synthesized space, furniture, and design by creating interiors based on practical use, comfort, and aesthetics. She was instrumental in Knoll's international reputation for its modern furnishings and interiors, and the impact of a business philosophy that encompassed design excellence, technological innovation, and mass production.

The four interior sketches are fascinating to behold. The selection of images does not represent the signature Florence Knoll furniture pieces that she designed but demonstrates her ability to translate her interior design concept succinctly using a quick loose sketching approach (Figure 5.8 and Figure 5.9). The sketches were composed as a guide for a photographer for a photo shoot. Although quick and loose, the sketches are articulate, including the furniture layout, the specific furniture pieces, the envelope; wall, ceiling, and floor planes and accessory items placed on

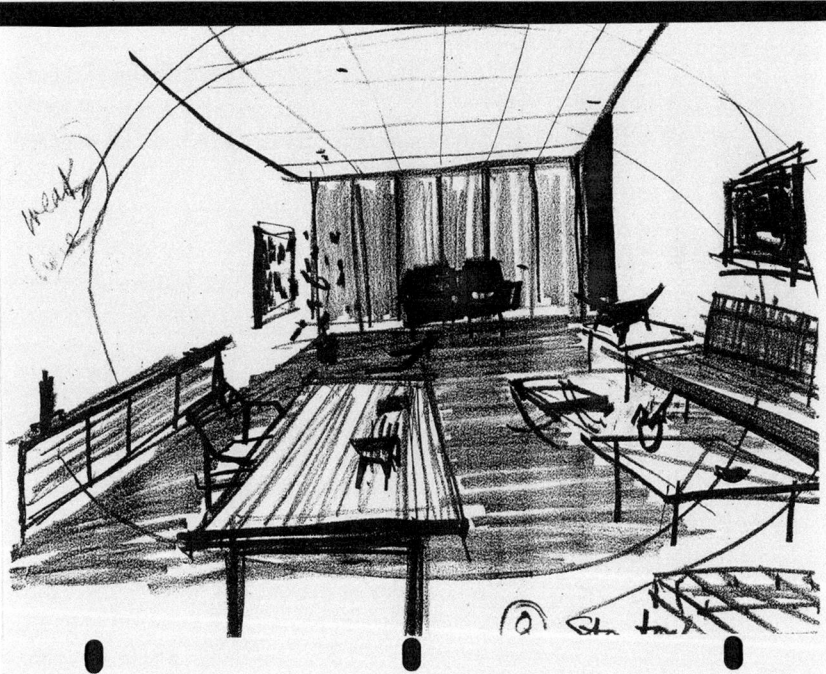

Figure 5.8 Florence Knoll office sketches. *(above)* Desk with Barcelona chairs and table, *(below)* desk and credenza, sofa, and Barcelona table and stool.

Source: Archives of American Art, the Smithsonian. Florence Knoll Basset Papers, 1932–2000.

Figure 5.9
Florence Knoll office sketches. *(above)* Seating area chairs and table, *(below)* open office view with work surface, return, storage bins above, and two-drawer pedestal.

Source: Archives of American Art, the Smithsonian. Florence Knoll Basset Papers, 1932–2000.

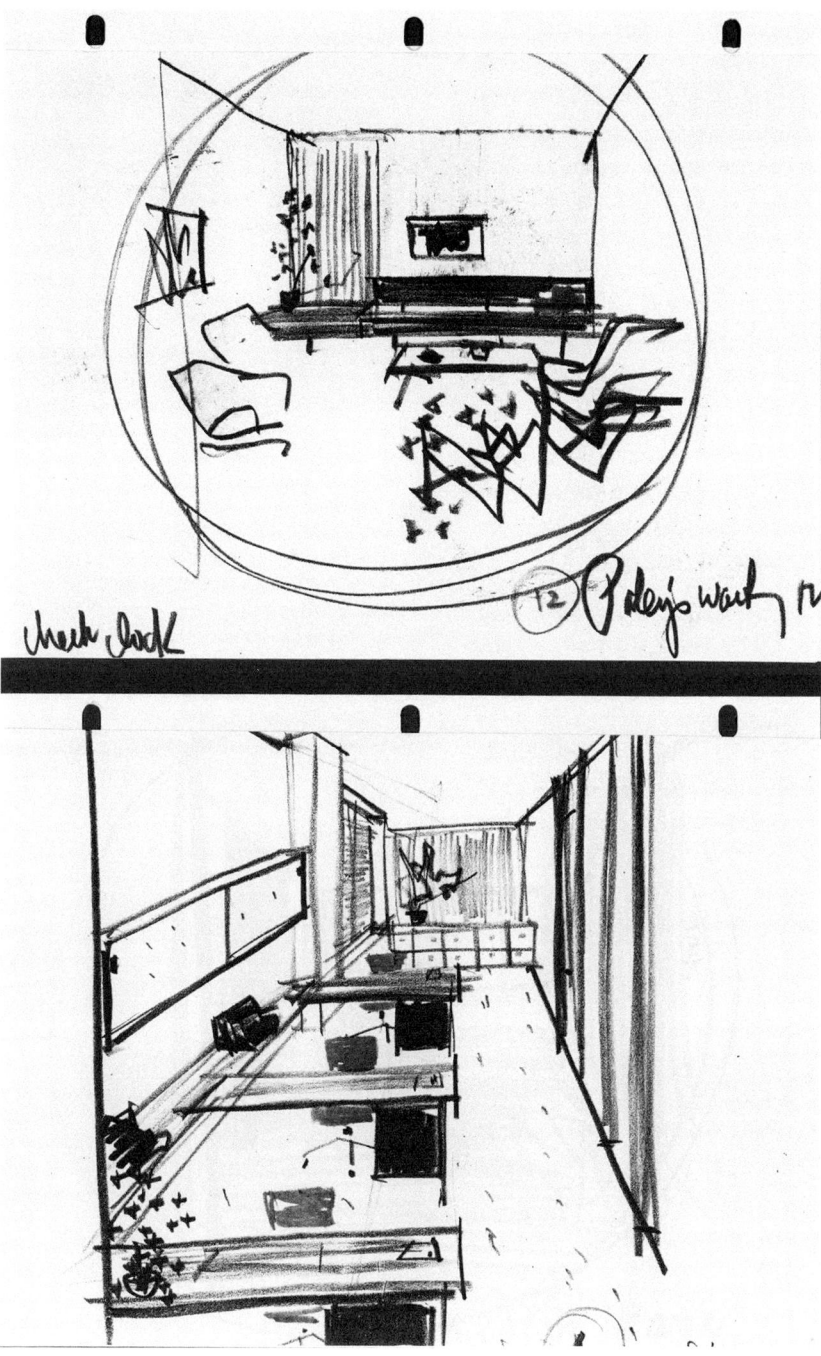

■ An Illustrated Guide to Furniture History

the desk, tables, and artwork. What is intriguing is that this succinct sketching quality visually communicates explicitly a comprehensive design concept for the office. The medium appears to be a soft pencil instead of a preferred sketching pen. Yet this choice is effective for the approach and technique. The variation of line quality—sharp, fuzzy, thick, thin, tonal—produces visually powerful imagery.

CHRIS KOULES, CJK DESIGN CUSTOM WOODWORKING, CHICAGO, ILLINOIS

Woodworking has been a life passion for Chris Koules. He has been working with wood since he was a youngster. When it became time to head for university, Chris chose graphic design as a major and to pursue professionally. Chris also has pursued academia as a professional path and is a tenured professor of graphic design at Columbia College Chicago where he has taught for more than 25 years. Chris realized he could continue his woodworking passion in conjunction with working professionally as a graphic designer and college professor; he founded CJK Design Custom Woodworking several decades ago, and the workshop continues to thrive today.

The wonderful quality about CJK custom furniture is the attention to handcrafting and being well made, as well as the thoughtful attention to a functional form and proportion (Figure 5.10 and Figure 5.11). These furniture designs are classic examples of clean lines and good craftsmanship. They have a timeless simplicity—as

Figure 5.10
Chris Koules, CJK Design Custom Woodworking. *(above)* Sketch and photo Oak Reading Side Table designed to accommodate a book or laptop in a lift up compartment. Lower shelf is designed to vertically store books. *(below)* Sketch and photo of Chair Round Side Table (pair). These tables are designed curved as an alternative to the traditional rectangular side table. The table provides hidden lower storage. The medium is oak bead board which was a popular decorative material used in early 20th-century architecture.

Source: Courtesy of Chris Koules, CJK Design Custom Woodworking. Photography, Chris Koules.

Figure 5.11
Chris Koules, CJK Design Custom Woodworking, Red Oak Radiator Cover and photo. This piece is in the American Arts and Crafts tradition. The two-part piece is designed to allow air flow through all sides of the slatted base. The top portion provides shelving for books and or decorative art pieces.

Source: Courtesy of Chris Koules, CJK Design Custom Woodworking. Photography, Chris Koules.

do the sketch studies done in graphite. The sketching approach is straightforward. Instead of using a sharp, crisp line quality, a soft edge is used for the ideation. The lines are exact in some regards and less so in others. However, the use of the graph paper is an indication that even if the study seems loose, scale is being considered. Additionally, the ideation for all three pieces includes multiple views of the designed piece—plan or top view, elevation, three-dimensional, etc. This approach to ideation, humble use of graphite, and depiction of multiple views reinforces the attention to handcrafting and being well made.

KRUECK + SEXTON ARCHITECTS, CHICAGO, ILLINOIS

Ron Krueck and Mark Sexton have practiced architecture in Chicago for more than 25 years. The partners received their architecture degrees from Illinois Institute of Technology (IIT). Krueck + Sexton Architects projects have received US national and regional awards. The firm exercises an interdisciplinary ideology and has completed a variety of projects including commercial, institutional, and residential design, modern preservation, and object and exhibit design.[13]

In looking at the K + S positive and negative sketches for a seating piece, one can see that the same sketch using reverse imagery can communicate a different essence in form and visual quality. This sketch is a type of composite drawing, simultaneously showing the side of the seating piece and back of the piece. Architects and designers often use composite imagery (Figure 5.12 and Figure 5.13). Yet as one views the sketches, it becomes apparent that each exudes a different quality and character. The sketch on the white ground illustrates the back and side softly folding into one another, and the form seems somewhat malleable and gentle. In the negative image of the same seating piece, however, white lines on the black background make the chair appear edgy and dramatic. Same linework, but in the image delivery, a very different visual quality.

The last K + S sketch is on tracing paper. Without hesitation, one can declare that tracing paper is the medium that is used by all design professional for ideation. The color of the tracing paper matters. It comes in yellow, canary yellow, and white. This third K + S sketch is a rather loose sketch for a table study. The color rendition communicates multitudes about the piece's materiality—wood, glass, and metal

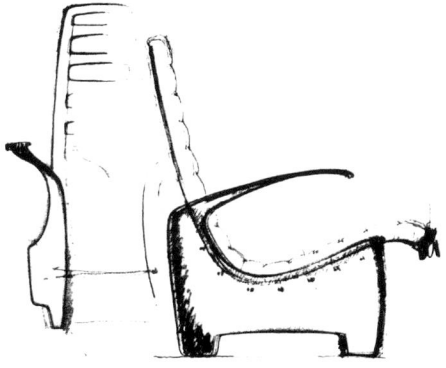

Figure 5.12
Krueck and Sexton Architects, sketch of seating piece black in on white paper.

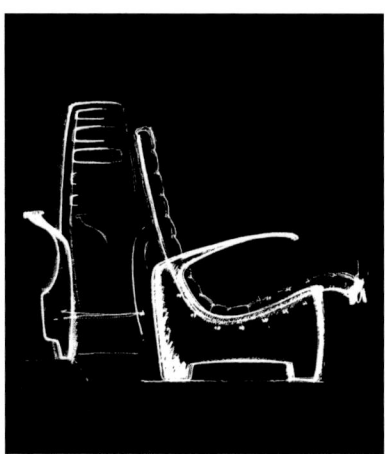

Figure 5.13
Krueck and Sexton Architects, sketch of seating piece, reverse reading, white on black.

(Figure 5.14). When sketching furniture, it prevails that when color is added, allowing one to visualize the materiality, a completed sense of the design and aesthetics is formed—a comprehended visual narrative.

GARY LEE PARTNERS, CHICAGO, ILLINOIS

In the industry, Gary Lee is referred to as being a natural designer. Not that one precludes the other, but his academic training was at the University of Michigan, in Ann Arbor, a national and internationally renowned university where Gary earned a Bachelor of Fine Arts with a focus on interior and graphic design.[14]

Figure 5.14
Krueck and Sexton Architects, rendered sketch of table on yellow tracing paper.

Source: Courtesy of Krueck and Sexton Architects.

Gary Lee is a designer, entrepreneur, and businessman. In 1993, he established Gary Lee Partners, an interior design collective that harnesses the power of space to elevate how people think, work, and live in the physical environment.[15] From its inception, the award-winning firm has received numerous awards from architecture and design organizations, AIA, ASID, IIDA, and Best of NeoCon honors. Gary's personal accolades and awards include the prestigious Interiors Designer of the Year and membership in the highly selective Interior Design Hall of Fame.[16]

In 2011, Gary Lee opened Chai Ming Studios, which offer refined, bespoke furniture pieces.[17] Other than Chicago, Chia Ming Studios has locations in Denver, Los Angeles, and New York. Gary's vision was to create a studio that values transcendent design, impeccable craftsmanship, and quality service in every detail of every piece.[18] The design emphasis for the furniture by Gary Lee for Chai Ming Studios is modern and detailed, and honors classic design. The pieces embrace juxtapositions and the unexpected, and are designed to celebrate textures and finishes.[19] The inspiration—international community—is extraordinarily executed by hand using traditional methods.[20] Lee mentions about the pieces: "We honor the smallest detail and the elegant whole—to us, they are equally essential."

Gary Lee's graphite sketch is of the Campbell Bench. He explains the bench's origin in this

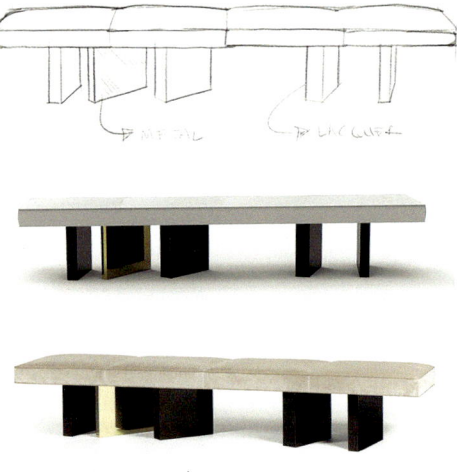

Figure 5.15
Gary Lee, *(top)* graphite sketch of the Campbell Bench, from the Chai Mingcollection, *(center)* Campbell Bench rendering, *(bottom)* Campbell Bench photograph, Chai Ming Studios.

Source: Courtesy of Gary Lee, Chai Ming Studios.

way: "This piece began as a custom design for an extraordinary residence and we have enjoyed its subsequent success as a part of our collection" (Figure 5.15). The top sketch depicts five rectangular blocks; four are of a lacquer finish as noted and one metal. The top horizontal portion is the seat area. Its size is W 84" × D 18" × H 15". The simple lines crossing the bench seat enable the viewer to discern that this portion is designed to be upholstered and divided into four equal segments. The center image is a rendition of the Campbell Bench. This rendition epitomizes Chair Ming Studios' emphasis—honoring classic design and embracing juxtapositions and the unexpected, simultaneously celebrating textures and finishes. As mentioned with the K & S rendered sketch on yellow trace, a rendition communicates multitudes. Here, the materiality is lacquer, metal, and upholstery. The bottom image of the Campbell Bench is a photograph of the actual bench; clearly visible is the lacquer and metal base pieces and upholstered seat supporting the statement of honoring the smallest detail and the elegant whole.

THOMAS PHEASANT, THOMAS PHEASANT INTERIOR DESIGN & STUDIO, WASHINGTON, DC

For approximately 30 years, Thomas Pheasant has created internationally recognized interiors in the United States, Europe, and Asia. His projects have been featured in the most prestigious architectural and interior design publications around the world. Thomas Pheasant has received numerous honors. In 2005, he was honored with the distinction "Dean of American Design" by *Architectural Digest* (US). Other notable awards include the Institute of Classical Architecture & Art's John Russell Pope Award in 2015, the Hall of Fame Award, and Designers' Choice Award, Home and Garden, 2012.[21]

Thomas Pheasant explains his work to be a Neoclassical-influenced design vocabulary. His aesthetic is guided by symmetry, restraint, and geometric forms.[22] This aesthetic is visible in Pheasant's Athens Lounge Chair, 2017, for the Baker Furniture Thomas Pheasant Collection (Figure 5.16). This elegant minimalist ink sketch employs very few lines to communicate the form of the lounge chair. The pen strokes for the splayed legs, back, and arms terminate as a wisp of a line. The form is derivative of the Greek Classical Klismos chair, ca. 5th–4th B.C., which is considered the signature of Greek furniture.[23] The Greek Klismos chair possessed

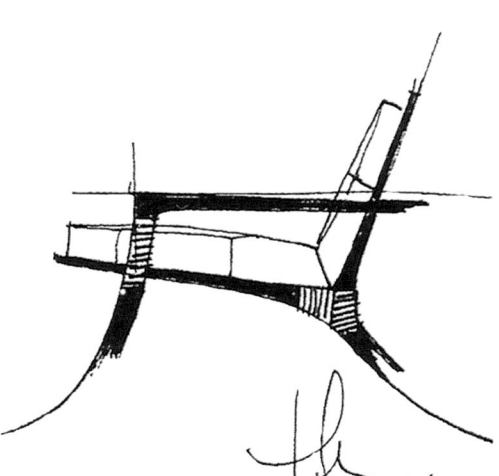

Figure 5.16
Thomas Pheasant, ink sketch of Athens Lounge Chair, for Baker Furniture Thomas Pheasant. Collection.
Source: Courtesy of Thomas Pheasant.

elegance and grace, with curved splayed legs front and back, and a slightly angled splat-back. Pheasant's contemporary design and ink sketch encapsulate the same qualities. The Athens Lounge is light, graceful, and elegant.

About the collection Thomas Pheasant designed for the company, Baker Furniture states: "Pheasant focuses on bringing a contemporary dimension to classic design principles, bridging past and present with beautiful silhouettes and distinctive fabrics."

PIRETTI DESIGN, BOLOGNA, ITALY

Giancarlo Piretti is an interior designer, industrial designer, and teacher. Through four decades of invention and recognition, he has some of the best-known chair designs of contemporary furniture history. Today he lives in Bologna and is in design practice with his son, Alessandro Piretti.

Giancarlo Piretti studied at the Istituto Statale d'Arte of Bologna and later attended the Accademia di Belle Arti of Bologna.[24] In the late 1960s he taught interior design at the Art Institute of Bologna and around this time he joined the renowned Italian design company of Anonima Castelli as an interior designer. In the late 1970s, he collaborated with Argentine architect-designer Emilio Ambasz and designed the Vertebra Operational chair, 1976.[25] This chair was the first automatically adjustable office chair. It won the ID Award for Excellence in Design in 1977. He has been the recipient of many honors and awards including the Compasso d'Oro (Golden Compass) industrial design award, the Bio 5 award, at the Ljubljana Biennial in 1971, and the German Gute Prize (the Good Form), a German craftmanship competition, distinguishing creativity and skill. Giancarlo Piretti's chairs can be found in permanent collections in various museums worldwide. Both the Vertebra Operational chair and the well-known Plia chair, 1968, can be found at MoMA, New York.

In 1988, Piretti revealed *The Piretti Collection* in Chicago, which included more than 50 different office chairs and seating styles.[26] The collection is currently manufactured by various licensees around the world. At the Chicago NeoCon convention 2008, KI, Krueger International, Inc., unveiled the apparatus-free Strive chair designed by Giancarlo Piretti. This simple polypropylene chair comes in six styles based on arm, tablet, color, and upholstery options. The multiple sketch images of the Strive chair demonstrate how Piretti thinks visually on paper (Figure 5.17). Notice how he clearly illustrates the chair's achieved motion with the polypropylene back. He uses angled lines adjacent to the chair back, arched lines to indicate motion, and even at times an arrow showing direction. The sheet is a rich composite of loosely drawn ideas for the Strive chair, exercising various line weights, tones, and textures, allowing one to clearly see Piretti's ideation process and visual thoughts.

Figure 5.17
Giancarlo Piretti, ideation sketches for the Strive chair, Krueger International, KI.
Source: Courtesy of Giancarlo Piretti.

■ An Illustrated Guide to Furniture History

JEAN PROUVÉ (1901–1984), NANCY FRANCE

Jean Prouvé's oeuvre is complex and diverse, consisting of architecture, industrial design, engineering, and furniture design. Certain contemporaries referred to him as "constructeur"—one who blends architecture and engineering. He began his training in visual arts, then the art of blacksmithery where he apprenticed with the well-known Parisian metal workshop of Adalbert Szabo. He returned to Nancy where he grew up and open his studio/workshop. By the 1930s, his studio created essentially anything that suited industrial production methods—furniture and architectural components for schools, factories, and other buildings. It is his furnishings designed for academic institutions that are deemed icons of the Modern movement.

For a long period of time, the lifework of this creative man seemed nearly forgotten. However, in recent years his work again attracted the interest of both the architectural world and broader public.[27] It is fortunate for the architecture and design community, and the public sector, that in 2002, Vitra International, in close cooperation with the Prouvé family, began to issue re-editions of his furniture designs.

The sketch of the Cité armchair, 1930, was done by Jean Prouvé for his classes at the Conservatoire National des Arts et Métiers (CNAM), Paris (Figure 5.18). Prouvé taught at the higher education institution from 1957 to 1971. The image is from the collection of the Bibliothèque Kandinsky, Musée National d'Art Moderne, Centre Pompidou, Paris, France.

Similar to the Krueck + Sexton sketch, it is a composite drawing, showing the chair's form through the integration of the side elevation—powder-coated steel runners and top view/plan—seat, and leather belt armrest. The quality of the sketch appears loose at first glance, but with continued observation, the control and articulation of the line quality is obvious. Adding the color rendition allows one to fully comprehend the design. The relationship of the images is encapsulating visually one image moving fluidly into another. Lastly, the bottom sketch of the enlarge detail successfully anchors the composition. This detail appears to be the connection for the leather belt armrest. It is good to keep in mind how one can take three individual sketches, yet arrange them so as to visually appear as one balanced composition.

KARIM RASHID, KARIM RASHID INC., NEW YORK

Karim Rashid is an industrial designer, Canadian-raised, practicing in New York City. He opened his private studio in New York City in the early 1990s. His design work crosses discipline boundaries into interior design, luxury goods, lighting design, and brand identity. Karim Rashid's pieces are exhibited in museums worldwide, including the Centre Pompidou (Paris), MoMA (New York), and San Francisco Museum of Modern Art. Karim has created award-winning designs for companies such as Asus, Samsung, Christofle, Veuve Clicquot, Umbra, Bobble, Citibank,

A graphic narrative

Figure 5.18
Jean Prouvé sketch, ink and colored pencil, Cité Chair, 1930, Paris. Sketched for his class at The Conservatoire National des Arts et Métiers (CNAM), Paris, France.
Source: Art Resource, Inc. New York, N.Y. © CNAC/MNAM/Dist. RMN-Grand Palais / Art Resource, NY.

■ An Illustrated Guide to Furniture History

Alessi, 3M, and Sony Ericsson.[28] He is the winner of many awards, including the Red Dot award, the I.D. Magazine Annual Design Review, the IDSA Industrial Design Excellence award, and the Chicago Athenaeum Good Design award.

Featured in the vignette sketch is his Oh Chair, 1999 (Figure 5.19). In this vignette the Oh Chair is accompanied by its complementary table and stool. This sketch is a wonderful example of how a designer uses a simple line drawing to fully communicate the essence of the piece—the Oh Chair's curvy and airy form. Notice how the lines of each piece in the composition communicate their individual form with a particular character—straight line, curved line, oval line—yet the lines clearly work in tandem begetting a harmonious whole and enchanting vignette.

The Oh Chair is made of polypropylene and metal with nylon feet.[29] The size is H 34″ × W 24″ × D 24″, and it is designed to be used indoor and outdoor, comes in multiple colors, has an ultraviolet stabilizer built into it so it won't become faded in sunlight, and is stackable.[30]

Deborah Rogers, DRD, Deborah Rogers Design, Inc., Chicago, Illinois
Deborah came to pursue her interior design career in Chicago after taking studio classes in interior design at the University of Michigan in Ann Arbor and doing a stint as a painter.[31] Early in her career, she worked for recognized Chicago architecture and design firms such as Holabird & Root and the design firm Larson Associates. After 11 years she left Larson Associates to open DRD, Deborah Rogers Design in 1998.[32] The firm's portfolio is primarily residential design. The design direction is that of a contemporary aesthetic. However, DRD does not preclude projects with a tradition genre, and the opportunity of using fine fabrics and trims, handcrafted furniture, and lighting associated with traditional interiors is welcome.[33]

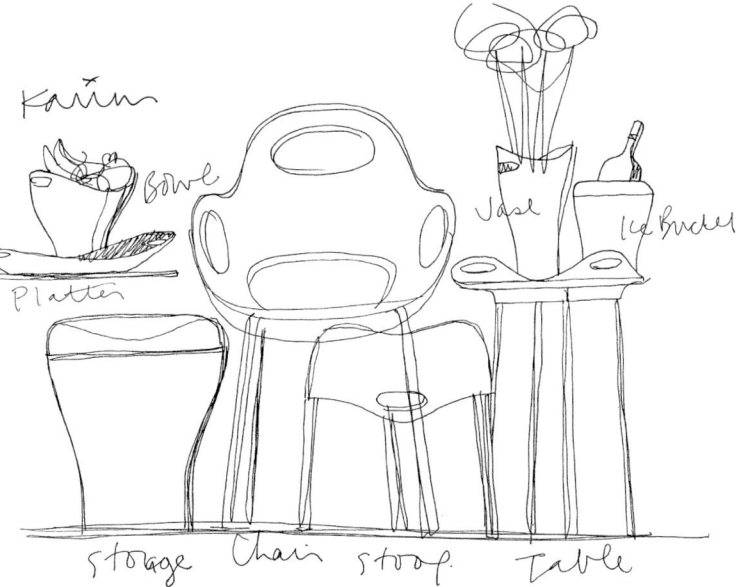

Figure 5.19
Karim Rashid, vignette sketch of the Oh Chair with table and stool.

Source: Courtesy of Karim Rashid.

A graphic narrative

Deborah has spent years building relationships with sources and vendors in order to realize designs for each client. She states: "I love being able to realize my client' dreams, or solve a design problem that makes their lives better … I am not so interested in the latest trends and what other designers are doing; good design goes beyond this exact moment."

The drawings seen here for DRD are not quick sketches, yet not a diversion either. They are important because they demonstrate the step after ideation. The step that moves the furniture piece closer to being made for use—the scaled drawing. A scaled drawing is needed in order to build anything, in this case furniture. These graphite drawings are for a millwork piece, a custom bookcase for the Goodgold family room. The plan is drawn to scale in a straightforward way. The plan is crucial in the narrative for this millwork piece indicating that it is built-in, perpendicular, and permanent (Figure 5.20). The next two drawings are elevations of the bookcase, right and left sides. The last image is the photograph of the installed piece with a sofa in front, just as shown in the floorplan. The manifestation of the drawings translated into a visually pleasing contemporary custom furniture piece.

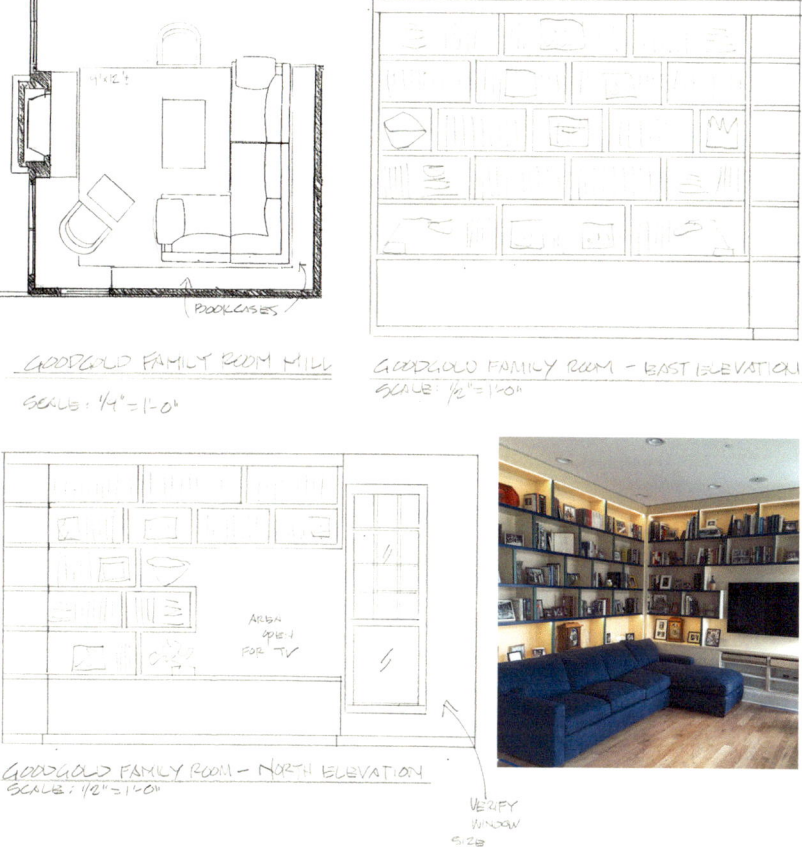

Figure 5.20
Deborah Rogers, graphite drawing, floor plan for the Goodgold family room built-in bookcase,
(right) graphite drawing of the west elevation of built-in bookcase,
(below left) graphite drawing, north elevation of Built-in bookcase,
(below right) Goodgold family room photograph of the built-in bookcase installed

Source: Courtesy of Deborah Rogers Design Inc.

171

HJÖRDÍS SIGURGÍSLADÓTTIR AND DENNIS DAVID JÓHANNESSON, ARKITEKTAR HJÖRDÍS & DENNIS, ARK|HD, REYKJAVÍK, ICELAND

Hjördís Sigurgísladóttir and Dennis Jóhannesson practice architecture in Reykjavík, Iceland. They have built a successful practice over more than 20 years and share a unique relationship as married and business partners. Although they hold conventional degrees in architecture, ARK|HD ideologically defines architecture less conventionally. Their approach is interdisciplinary welcoming all forms of design challenges and collaborations, such as research, writing, publishing, and designing products. ARK|HD's portfolio has a variety of project types—residential, retail, hospitality, municipal, and low-cost housing.

Hjördís and Dennis have received plenty of recognition through the years. They have been awarded competition prizes, grants, and institutional awards. One most recognizable awards was the Berlin competition to design and build the residence of the Icelandic Ambassador. The project was completed in 2006 at Trabener Strasse 68, Berlin, Germany. The Icelandic architects mainly used materials that are typical of the country, such as blue-black stone, oak, and corrugated zinc. This project reverberated throughout Europe and was featured in multiple architecture and design publications such as *Disenart Magazine*.[34] In 2012, ARK|HD received a grant from the National Architectural Heritage Board of Iceland, to support ARK|HD's research project "Icelandic Architectural History—Influences from the British Isles."[35] In December 2014, they received a grant from the Design Fund for the project House of the Seasons—Sustainable Homes. One last mention: in December 2017, their low-cost prefabricated housing system was recognized and an interview of Hjördís and Dennis was published by *Bændablaðið* (The Farmers' Newspaper) about these prefabricated houses.[36]

Figure 5.21 Hjördís Sigurgísladóttir & Dennis Jóhannesson, ARK|HD, Reykjavík, Iceland, Hjördís' sketch of the "Swing" chair, front view, 100% recyclable steel.

Seen here is the front and back view of the "Swing" chair Hjördís and Dennis designed for a competition (Figure 5.21 and Figure 5.22). It was chosen as one of the finalists of the "Nordic Design Competition—Sustainable Chairs" and later shown at the UN Conference on Climate Change in Katowice, Poland, in December 2018. The structure is made of steel which is 100% recyclable and covered with fish leather which is tanned in an ecofriendly way at the workshop of Atlantic Leather in northern Iceland. There is nothing complicated about

Figure 5.22 Hjördís Sigurgísladóttir & Dennis Jóhannesson, ARK|HD, Hjördís' sketch of the "Swing" chair back view, 100% recyclable steel.

Source: Courtesy of Hjördís Sigurgísladóttir & Dennis Jóhannesson, ARKITEKTAR Hjördís & Dennis, ARK|HD, Reykjavík, Iceland.

the drawing approach here. The two drawings visually allow the observer to comprehend the form with the first glance. Applying this minimalist approach allows nothing to distract the observer's eye from the chair's form—no shade, shadow, texture, or line hierarchy. Hjördís's approach and drawing technique complements the design idea for the chair. The delicate line weight appears to match the lightness of the chair's frame down to the finest detail. Notice on the back support the thin simple line that loops around forming the opening where the back rest can slide up or down. The delicate impression conveyed by the line drawings matches the chair's slight steel structure perfectly. The curved configuration of the steel back, base support, cantilever back rest, and seat appear as weightless as the line quality—simple, clean, and visually legible.

MORLEN SINOWAY, MORLEN SINOWAY ATELIER, CHICAGO, ILLINOIS

For over 30 years, Morlen Sinoway has been a part of the Chicago design community. He is a recognized designer, furniture maker, and artist. The scope of his work ranges from the micro to the macro, and his designs are highly valued and ubiquitous among interior designers and architects.

Morlen Sinoway Atelier is a multi-discipline design studio.[37] The business includes interior design service for contract and residential design projects. As a showroom, the Atelier represents more than 60 brands including furniture, lighting, and jewelry.[38] His interdisciplinary ideology in 2004 beget his founding of the Guerilla Truck Show. The event allowed seasoned and up-and-coming artists, designers, furniture makers, fabricators, industrial designers, and jewelry designers to showcase and market their work literally in a truck. These trucks were mini exhibition halls lined outside his atelier.[39] The show coincided every June with Neo-Con, the nation's largest trade show for the built environment industry. A perfect pairing. The Guerilla Truck Show lasted a decade and its memory is a highlight for Chicago's design community.

Morlen's sketches communicate multitudes using few lines. Looking at the sketches for Bob Messerly's desk, the designer succinctly narrates its essence. This is communicated with minimum lines and without implementing the use of texture, shade, or shadow (Figure 5.23). Yet these lines communicate its form completely; the leg type with cross bracing, and the repetitive vertical detail at the apron wrapping the writing surface visually communicate an elegant piece. The placement of the file pedestal in its delicate line quality informs the viewer about the function for the workplace.

The next sketch examples are from the Morlen's opened sketchbook, right and left pages. Being able to see a designer's sketchbook is like finding a treasure (Figure 5.24). The two pages wonderfully illustrate the use of the graphic narrative to explore (ideate) an idea. The idea is for the design of a jewelry dresser. On the left page, the sketches depict a rather minimalist approach for the jewelry

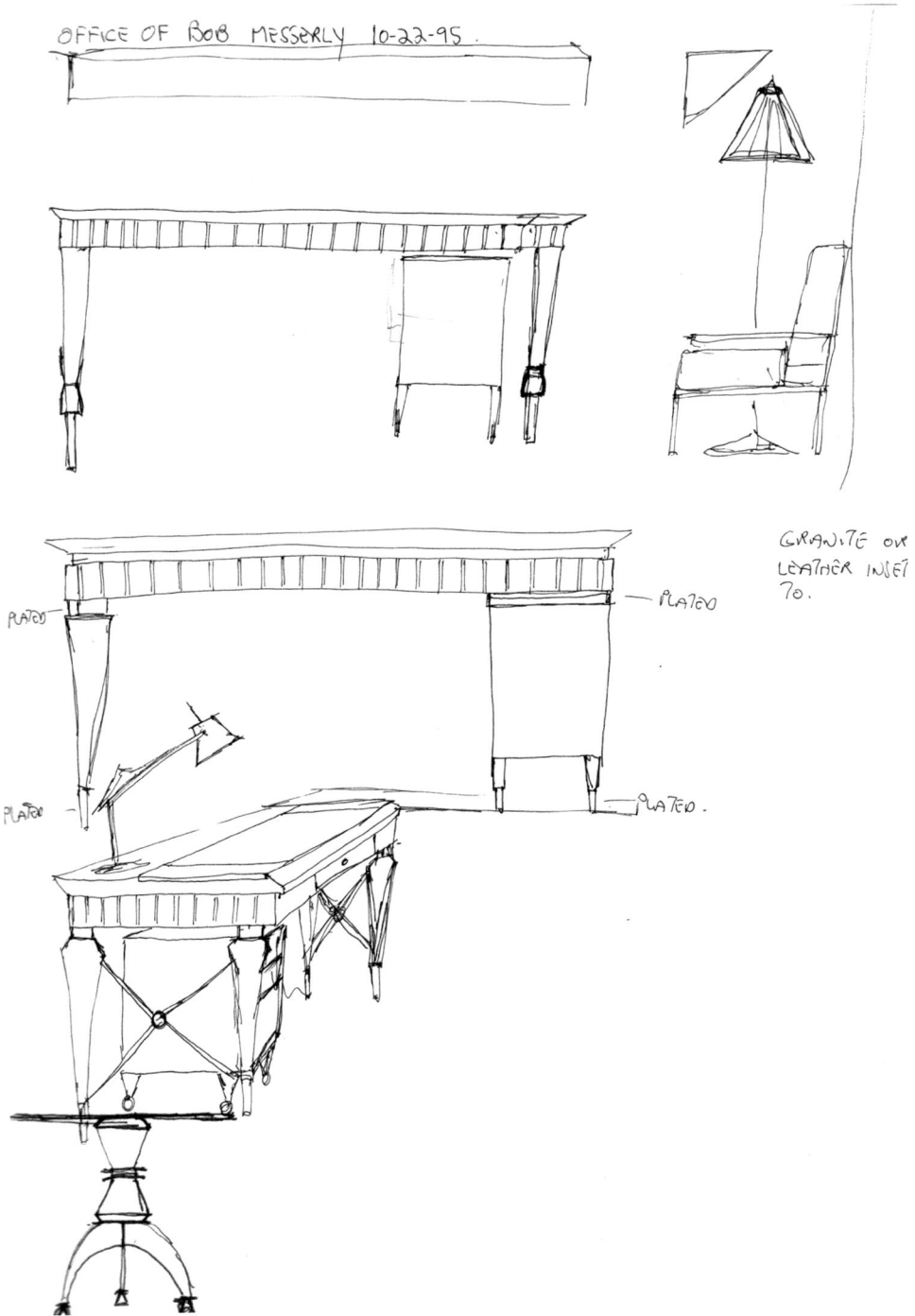

Figure 5.23
Morlen Sinoway, sketch studies for Bob Messerly's desk.

Courtesy of Morlen Sinoway.

A graphic narrative

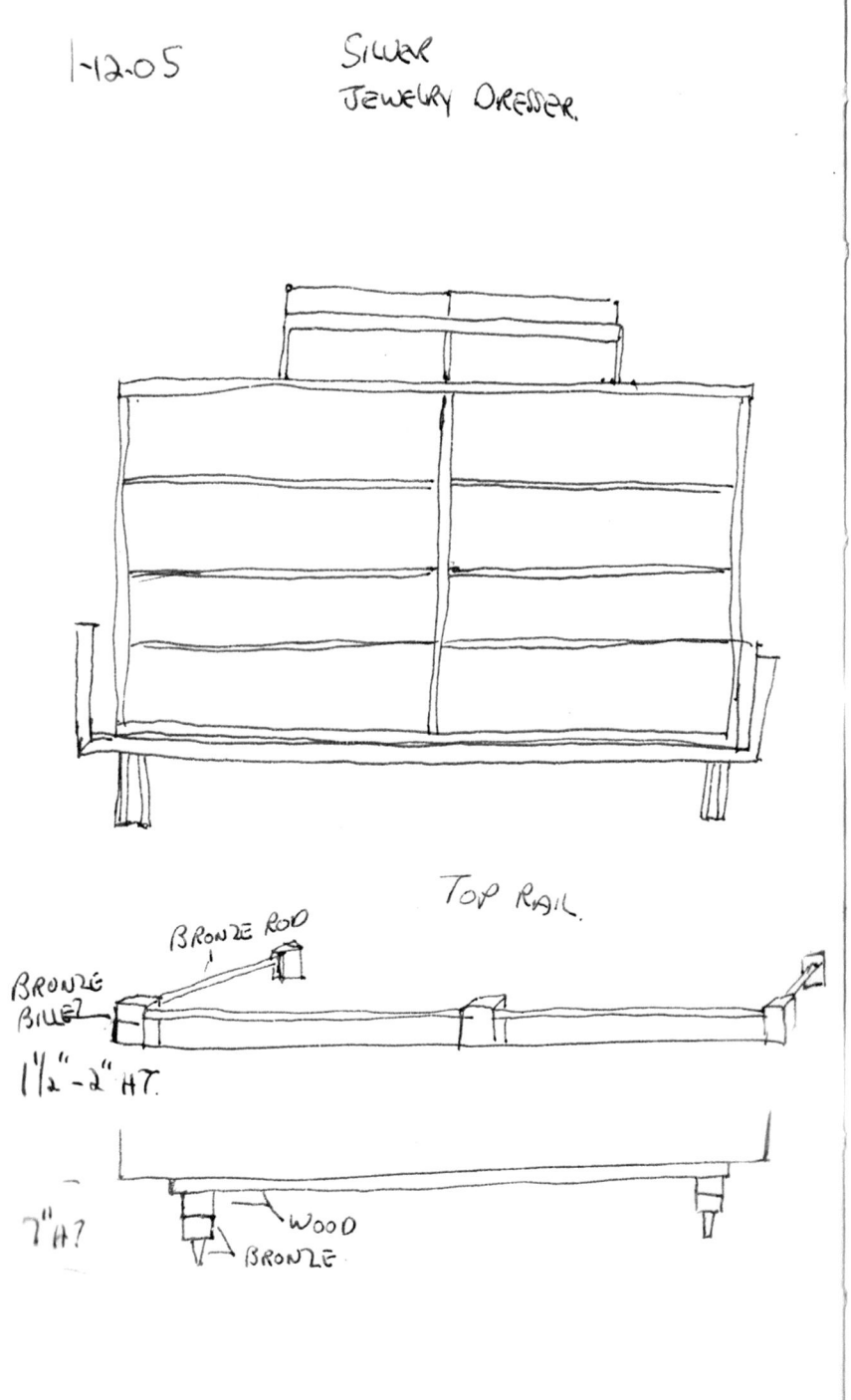

Figure 5.24
Morlen Sinoway, sketchbook, two-page study for a jewelry dresser.
Courtesy of Morlen Sinoway.

An Illustrated Guide to Furniture History

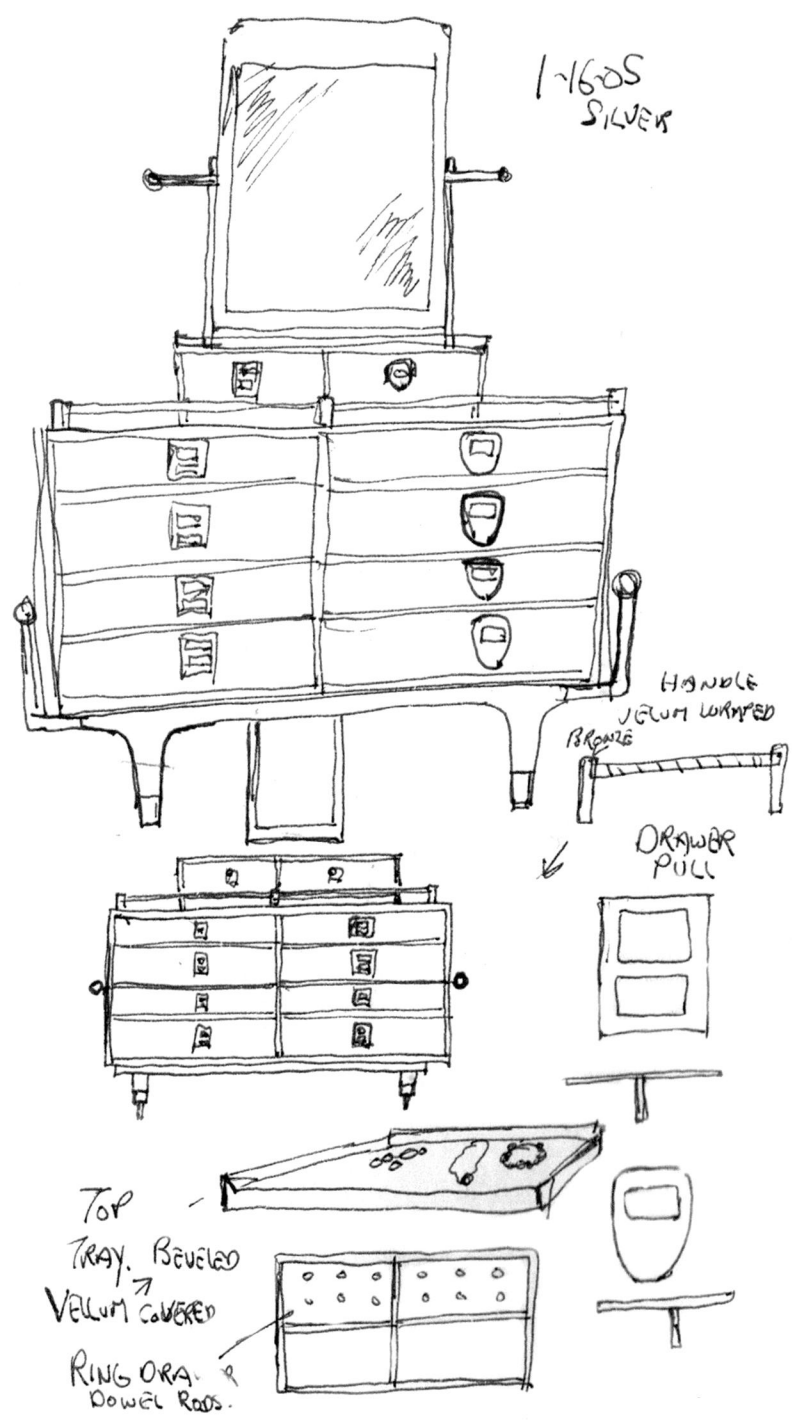

Figure 5.24
(Continued)

dresser. The line quality is straightforward and communicates the minimalist intent well. On the right page is a series of sketches that reveal a very different idea about the jewelry dresser's character. A definite move away from minimalism. The many sketches narrate the designer's thoughts—thoughts about the drawer pulls' shape and size, the use of a mirror that could be mounted two ways, and so on. However, both pages have equally achieved their purpose in communicating the design ideas.

This concludes Chapter 5. The final portion of the book, Part III—Object of desire: Furniture periods, movements and styles from Antiquity to the twentieth century—will be next. There is a brief introduction and instruction at the beginning to help facilitate a successful completion of the book.

NOTES

1. Norman Crowe and Paul Laseau, *Visual Notes for Architects and Designers* (New York: John Wiley and Sons, 1984), 1.
2. Ibid., 2.
3. Ibid., V.
4. Ibid.
5. Ibid., 2.
6. https://en.wikipedia.org/wiki/Ron_Arad_(industrial_designer).
7. www.vitra.com/en-us/living/product/minature-collection-wll-tempered-chair.
8. www.studiokcreative.com.
9. Ibid.
10. www.555.com.
11. Ibid.
12. Ibid.
13. https://ks.partners/projects.
14. www.ateliergarylee.com/chai-ming-studios-1.
15. www.linkedin.com/company/gary-lee-partners.
16. www.garyleepartners.com/firm/people.html.
17. www.ateliergarylee.com/chai-ming-studios-1.
18. Ibid.
19. Ibid.
20. Ibid.
21. www.thomaspheasant.com.
22. www.bakerfurniture.com/design-story/designers-and-collections/thomas-pheasant.
23. Mark Hinchman, *History of Furniture a Global View* (New York, Fairchild Books, A Division of Condé Nash Publications), 44.
24. www.pamono.com/designers/giancarlo-piretti.
25. www.metmuseum.org/art/collection.
26. www/pamona.com/designers/giancarlo-piretti.
27. Nils Peters, *Prouvé 1901–1984: The Dynamics of Creation* (Köln: Taschen, 2006), 7.
28. www.artnet.com/artists/karim-rashid/biography.
29. www.wayfair.com/furniture/pdp/umbra-oh-armchair-umb2467.html.
30. Ibid.
31. Lisa Skolnik, *Chicago Tribune* Article, Interior Motives, January 10, 1999.
32. Ibid.
33. www.deborahrogersdesigninc.com.

■ **An Illustrated Guide to Furniture History**

34 www.arkhd.is/e_news.htm.
35 Ibid.
36 www.arkhd.is/e_news.htm.
37 www.morlensinoway.com.
38 Ibid.
39 www.chicagoreader.com/Bleader/archives/2016/06/15/the-guerrilla-truck-show-returns-after-a-brief-hiatus.

PART III

Object of desire

Furniture periods, movements, and styles, from Antiquity to the 20th century

INTRODUCTION

As discussed in Chapter 4, Part III (Chapters 6 through 13) is analogous to a series of lectures in a conventional survey course. At the end of each chapter, the reader will select from the pictorial timeline the furniture piece(s) of interest that has been discussed in the chapter to graphically analyze using the sketchbook. To reiterate, the recommended type and size for the sketchbook is a hardcover, 8″ × 11″ or 9″ × 12″. Part III is where the nine-step methodology is brought to fruition, implemented by using practice examples and visual notes studies for analysis and investigation. Chapter 5 should have provided ample professional examples as models to assist with your own visual analysis. This visual investigation will culminate with the ninth step and final drawing—the visual notes exercise—a testament that the reader has solidified his or her understanding about the piece, its timeframe, and context.

Chapters 6 through 13 correspond with the pictorial timeline seen at the beginning of the book. However, the timeline is divided into small sections corresponding to a certain time period. The timeline section is placed at the beginning of each chapter. The furniture from the timeline portion is discussed in the chapter.

Each chapter in Part III is structured the same. At the top is the **pictorial timeline**, underneath the **time period overview** for that pictorial timeline. Next, three specific areas will be discussed for each furniture piece in this sequence: **history**, **aesthetics**, and **furniture** (the description for that specific piece). The sequential section will end with the answered question: **What makes the piece a ____ piece?** The chapter will conclude with an image of an interior space that corresponds to a period, movement, or style from the pictorial timeline. The interior example will provide context and an opportunity for the reader to visually enter a total environment.

Before beginning Part III, the author recommends the student/reader take a few minutes to revisit Chapter 4 as a memory refresher of the Analysis of Form: Nine-Step Methodology and to review the author's explanation of the methodology structure.

6   Antiquity

Egypt, Greece, and Rome

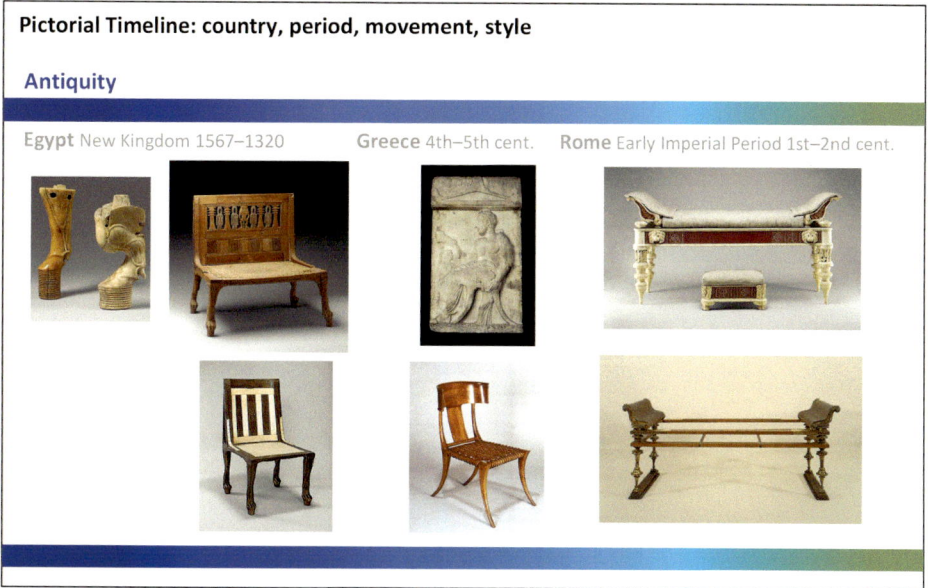

6.1
Pictorial timeline—Antiquity: Egypt, Greece, and Rome.

TIME PERIOD OVERVIEW

The term *Antiquity* refers to the ancient past, "the great civilizations," the periods before the Middle Ages, ca. 5th–15th centuries. Pertaining to this book, the great civilizations denote Egypt, Greece, and Rome. Chapter 6 will cover these periods briefly. Provided on the pictorial timeline are specific furniture examples that the author believes exemplify furniture design and construction of the time periods (Timeline 6.1). The selections will hopefully stimulate your visual acuity as discussed in Chapter 5.

The furniture pieces on the pictorial timeline pertaining to Egypt focus on the last Dynasty, the New Kingdom, except for the two animal legs from a bed or chair carved from ivory, which belong to the First Dynasty. The discussion surrounding

■ An Illustrated Guide to Furniture History

this selection will pertain to three areas **history**, **aesthetic**, and **furniture**, as explained in the Introduction to Section III. For Greece, the timeline pieces are representative of Classical Greece, 4th–5th centuries. The discussion will briefly touch on the influence of Greek Classicism in the 21st century, already brought to your attention with Thomas Pheasant's sketch of the Athens Lounge chair for Baker Furniture in Chapter 5. We will look at the Baker Furniture piece in this section as a comparison to its inspiration, the Greek Klismos chair. This portion of the pictorial timeline will conclude with discussing furniture from Rome's Early Imperial Period, A.D. 1st–2nd century. Renown works of architecture during this period are the Colosseum, Pantheon, the Column of Trajan, etc.

EGYPT—EIGHTEENTH DYNASTY: CA. 1567–1320 B.C.

History

In 3000 B.C., King Namar of Upper Egypt defeated the ruler of Lower Egypt and established the first political dynasty to rule one unified country. Its location on the Nile River, which flowed into the Mediterranian Sea, supported economic growth and devlopment along its banks.[1] Egypt became a powerful nation and many Egyptians prospered throughout its lengthy history that survived through 30 dynasties.[2] The Egyptian chronology ca. 3100–1085 B.C. is divided into three dynastic periods—the Old Kingdom, Middle Kingdom, and New Kingdom.

The survival of early Egyptian furniture is mainly due to the Egyptian's firm belief in life after death, which resulted in the taking of worldly goods, suitable to his status in life, into his tomb for use in the afterlife.[3] However, furniture in Antiquity, no different from today, was used in a home. Residential structures of this time clearly indicate a distinction between rank and social class. Wealthy priests and noblemen lived in large compounds, the merchant class in row houses, whereas the lower classes resided in less sizeable dwellings. Both the lower and upper classes had only basic pieces such as stools, chairs, chest, and tables.[4]

The furniture pieces on the pictorial timeline for Egypt are from the New Kindom, Eighteenth Dynasty (ca. 1567–1320 B.C.). The furniture and other artifacts seen in museums, original and reconstructed, are typically from this period. These items yield from the 19th-century Egyptian excavations marking the beginning of Egyptology. This new area of study was facilitated by scholars and artists who acompanied Napolean Bonaparte in the invasion of Egypt. The scholars and artist made the first systematic survey of the paintings in temples and tombs, and found many scenes in which elaborate chairs and beds were represented.[5]

However, ancient sculptures showed that furniture was already in use long before the New Kindom. By the beginning of the First Dynasty, the basic principles of woodworking were already well established, and the mortise-and-tenon joint—one of the most practical inventions of the ancient woodworkers—was in common use.[6] Tangible evidence of earliest carved examples are ivory legs found at Abydos, ca. 3100 B.C., shown on the pictorial timeline. These pieces are evidence of early Egyptian craftsmen's skills—crisp carving and design, combining realism with a highly stylized sense of form.[7] Such works served as a model for furntiure makers in Egypt for the the next 3,000 years.

This concludes the abreviated history of Egypt. This brief background, however, should be a foundation for understanding the furniture pieces on the timeline. Lastly, to reiterate, when going through this section, do not get ahead of yourself and decide which furniture piece to analyze prior to finishing the entire chapter. Afterward, make your decision regarding which pieces you will document using the Analysis of Form: Nine-Step Methodology.

Bull's legs, ca. 2960–2770 B.C. and ca. 3100–2650 B.C., First Dynasty

Aesthetics

Furniture legs and frame were usually carved of wood, but the legs could also be carved from ivory. Because Egyptian tree species were not suitable for construction, the wood was imported form Phoenicia. From the First Dynasty to the last, the aesthetics expression for these carvings were both literal and stylized. This is demonstrated on the carving seen on both leg examples from the pictorial timeline. When one looks at the depiction of the leg, hoof angle, and claw set, and the exactness in the manner the vein is carved, the realistic nature is obvious. Yet Egyptian furniture is duplicitous, expressing both realism and stylization. The deviation from realism is visible with these examples at the bottom of the hoof. Here one sees the stylization—a beaded cylinder that rests on the floor instead of the animal hooves resting on the floor. The cylinder is a typical furniture feature of the Early Dynastic period. It has been recorded that sometimes these cylinders would be sheathed in metal. The beaded cylinder continues as a design feature throughout the Dynastic periods.

Furniture

Figure 6.1 Egyptian bed or chair legs. *(left)* Bull leg, ca. 2960–2770 B.C. *(right)* Animal leg, ca. 3100–2650 B.C.

Source: Metropolitan Museum of Art, New York, Egyptian Art. Public Domain OA [Open Access]. Edward S. Harkness Gift, 1926

The left **bull's leg**, ca. 2960–2770 B.C., and the right **animal leg**, ca. 3100–2650 B.C. are furniture legs believed to have been carved for a bed or chair. Both were designed to emulate an animal leg. The bull's leg is carved from hippopotamus ivory; the height is 17".[8] The leg to the right is also carved from ivory but it is elephant ivory; the height is 6⅛".[9] The pieces were discovered in Northern Upper Egypt, Abydos, Amélineau Excavations (Figure 6.1). Currently, these artifacts reside at the Metropolitan Museum of Art, New York City.

Starting the pictorial timeline with furniture legs might seem an odd way to begin. However, this is an ideal place to start because they incapsulate the essence of Egyptian design—the Egyptian furniture maker's exactness and clarity of form. This approach no doubt stems from the woodworker's invention and application of various methods of joint construction such as the mortise-and-tenon joint and scarf joint as well as others—this, coupled with the woodworker's ability to combine realism and stylization in one piece, begetting exactness and clarity of form. This approach served as a model from the Early Dynastic Period through the New Kingdom—the next 3,000 years.

■ An Illustrated Guide to Furniture History

Hatnefer's chair, ca. 1492–1473 B.C., New Kingdom, 18th Dynasty

Aesthetics

Although not visible with Hatnefer's chair, it is helpful to keep in mind that Egyptian ornament included a variety of ubiquitous motifs. The use of ornament in Ancient Egyptian furniture and other decorative arts was intertwined with religious and cultural beliefs. The symbols and motifs are vast. The recurring motif was the lotus bud and flower, the dung beetle or scarab, the sun disk or globe, the vulture with outspread wings. Also recurring was the depiction of deities; Amun, a creator god and patron deity of the city of Thebes; Ra, the sun god; Bes, protector of the home; Osiris, god of death and resurrection, and the goddess Isis, sister and wife of Osiris, a goddess of life and magic, and Horus their son, known as the sky god. Other decorative ornament included the use of glass beads, gold and silver, lapis, turquoise, malachite, etc. The color palette lends itself to blues and green but can include a polychrome palette.

Specifically looking at Hatnefer's chair, the major decoration is on the upper back of the chair. The decoration includes a row of protective symbols (Figure 6.2a). Featured in the center of the symbols is the deity Bes, god and protector of households, mothers, and children.[10] On either side of Bes is the tit-amulet.[11] The tit-amulet form is somewhat humanoid, with a loop head connecting arm- and leg-like elements. The tit-amulet is closely associated with the Isis, goddess of life and magic; it is also referred to as Isis knot. Next to the tit amulet is the columnar djed-pillar.[12] This symbol typically has a broad base and will narrow as it rises. This column like form will be crossed with four parallel lines perpendicular. The djed-pillar symbolizes stability, endurance, and immutability. The seat is made of linen cord and is original.[13] When examining the Ancient Egyptian chair, it is apparent that seats are not made of wood, but most often constructed of fiber that is woven.

Figure 6.2a Hatnefer's chair back detail of deity Bess in the center, tit-amulet on either side and djed-pillar at the ends.

Source: Metropolitan Museum of Art, New York, Egyptian Art. Public Domain OA [Open Access].

The Rogers Fund, 1936.

Furniture

Hatnefer's chair, ca. 1492 1473 B.C., New Kingdom, 18th Dynasty. The chair is a royal piece and belonged to the mother of Senenmut, one of Hatshepsut's best-known officials. Her undisturbed tomb was discovered by the Museum's Egyptian expedition in 1936 on the hillside below Senenmut's tomb chapel (Upper Egypt, Thebes, Sheikh Abd el-Qurna, Tomb of Hatnefer and Ramose). This chair was found in front of the tomb's entrance and was given to the Museum in the division of finds by the Egyptian government (Figure 6.2).

Hatnefer's Chair is a fine example of Egyptian woodworking. The various elements were assembled with mortise-and-tenon joinery, and pegs were used to hold the tenons in place. Pegs also fastened the

Figure 6.2 Hatnefer's chair, New Kingdom, ca. 1492–1473 B.C., 18th Dynasty, Egypt.

184

Antiquity

braces to the back and seat.[14] The joints were reinforced with resinous glue. The material is boxwood, cypress, ebony, and linen cord.[15] The chair is low. The overall size, H 20⅞" × W 19 11/16" × D 16 9/16", and the seat H 9⅝". In banquet scenes found on the walls of elite tombs, the tomb owner and his wife are shown seated, side by side, on full-size chairs; however, women are often shown sitting on low chairs like Hatnefer's.[16]

Chair of Reniseneb, New Kingdom, 18th Dynasty, ca. 1450 B.C.

Aesthetics

The next piece on the timeline is the chair of Reniseneb. The medium is wood, the species ebony. This handsomely veneered chair has vertical and horizontal inlays of ivory that accentuate the form of the chair back (Figure 6.3a). The chair back's center area has incised decoration depicting the owner seated on a chair of identical form, with accompanying text with funerary import, which may have been added following Reniseneb's death to make the chair a more suitable funerary object.[17] It is the earliest surviving chair with such a representation, and it is the only non-royal example known.[18] The contrasting tone of the dark wood and lightness of the ivory complement each other in a visually attractive manner. The height is generous, from the ground to the top of back is 33 15/16". The seat is mesh and has been restored following ancient models.[19] Like Hatnefer's chair, the seat is not constructed of wood but fiber.

Figure 6.3a Reniseneb's chair back detail incised decoration depicting owner seated on a chair of identical form with accompanying text.

Source: Metropolitan Museum of Art, New York, Egyptian Art Public Domain OA [Open Access]. Patricia R. Lassalle Gift, 1968.

Furniture

Chair of Reniseneb, New Kingdom, 18th Dynasty, ca. 1450 B.C. Reniseneb was a scribe living in Upper Egypt, Thebes, during the New Kingdom, 18th Dynasty. Scribes were important people in Ancient Egypt who carried out both administrative and religious functions, and were highly prized for their skills.[20] A scribe's training to become literate took many years. Common to most civilizations, literacy is a key to a successful life. This ideal can be applied to scribes in ancient Egypt. They were able to live a wealthy lifestyle and were highly respected in everyday life.[21] They were part of a large task force which helped keep track of taxes, censuses, and building projects. A scribe's training to learn to read and write happened over many years. There were hundreds of hieroglyphs; therefore, one can assume the scribe possessed a significant depth and breadth of knowledge. Almost all knowledge of Ancient Egyptian life comes from the written work the Egyptian scribe provided.

Reniseneb's chair is harmoniously proportioned and exhibits a superb quality of joinery (Figure 6.3). Its four legs are meticulously carved to look like four animal legs with the paws resting on the cylinders—very realistic in their detail. Again, however, the duplicitous nature reveals itself at the base with realistic paws and stylized cylinders, like the First Dynasty legs. Notice the smooth joinery transition between the chair seat and chair legs. The sense of anthropomorphism is omnipotent with the slight slant of the chair's back, which accommodates the human contour. The height of the back is accentuated with the leg rising into a vertical brace tangent near the top of the rectangular ivory and ebony chair back, supporting it functionally and visually. The author's sketch illustrates this back tangent condition from the rear (Figure 6.3b). This chair's carving and attention to detail is a testament to the Egyptian craftsman's woodworking skill and artistry. Lastly, the mesh seat has been restored following ancient models.[22]

Figure 6.3 Chair of Reniseneb, New Kingdom, ca. 1450 B.C., Egypt.

What makes these pieces Ancient Egyptian?

Succinctly, the key indicators for identifying Ancient Egyptian chairs begins with recognizing the exactness of the carved animal legs—the realistic portrayal of the leg, paw, or hoof, etc., coupled with a stylized cylinder as the base. Another indicator is the use of the medium wood, and implementation of construction joints such as the mortise-and-tenon joint. Regarding the mass/form, the back will be rectilinear with an emphasis on the vertical or horizontal. The back will display carving, and in royal furniture will incorporate metal—gold, silver—and precious stones, such as lapis, turquoise, malachite. Ubiquitous decorative motifs are the lotus bud and flower, scarab, the sun disk, the vulture. The carved symbols include various deities. The color palette lends itself to blue and green, but also can include polychrome incorporating lapis, turquoise, and malachite.

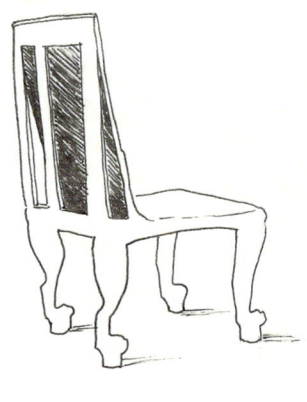

Figure 6.3b Author's illustration of back chair back detail similar to Renisenbe's chair.

Author's illustration.

GREECE—CLASSICAL GREECE, 4TH AND 5TH CENTURY

Klismos chair, Gravestone of Xanthippuos, ca. 420 B.C., Athens, Greece, and Klismos chair replica, 1961, Athens, Greece, Terence Harold Robjohn-Gibbings

Aesthetics

This aesthetic description will account for both examples on the pictorial timeline. The Greek Klismos Chair is considered the signature piece of Greek furniture.[23] There are no known examples to have survived which is understandable since very few furniture pieces survive from this period. The two examples on the pictorial timeline include the sculpted gravestone of Xanthippus, from Athens, Greece, ca. 450 B.C., and a 20th-century Klismos replica, 1961 designed by Terence Harold Robjohn-Gibbings, British, 1905–1976.

What we know of Classical Greek furniture comes from its depiction in works of art—painted pottery (e.g. black figure ware and red figure ware), low reliefs, and sculpture. Wood was used extensively by the Greeks for furniture construction.[24] A variety of species were used—oak, maple, cedar, boxwood, olive, citron, and beech.[25] Thought to be imported were maple, citron, and ebony. There is evidence of metal being used. Some pieces of furniture or parts of furniture that have survived are constructed of copper, bronze, or iron. Evidence has shown that, for the affluent, the wood furniture pieces were fitted with metalwork.

In examining the Greek Klismos chair, what seems unusual by today's standard for chair construction is the missing stretcher(s) at the chair legs. The stretcher is a key feature for horizontal support and stability seen in contemporary chair design and throughout other historical periods. This missing detail is curious. In his book *History of Furniture a Global View*, Mark Hinchman suggests: "One possibility is that the mode of representing the furniture departed from actual construction techniques; perhaps the chairs had stretchers, and for whatever reason, the vase painters eliminated them from their paintings."[26]

Furniture

Figure 6.4 Gravestone of Xanthippos, Athens, Greece, ca. 420 B.C.

Source: British Museum, London England, Egypt Gallery, Creative Common Zero [CC0].

The **Gravestone of Xanthippuos**, ca. 420 B.C., Athens, Greece. This piece can be found in the British Museum, Egypt Gallery Room. It is considered a paramount 5th-century example (Figure 6.4). Xanthippus sits on a Klismos chair holding out a shoemaker's list; beside him are two girls, perhaps his daughters.[27] The relief clearly shows the graceful quality of the chair—the splayed front and back legs—and although the chair back is not visible, the contour of Xanthippus's body indicates a curved splat conforming to the human shape.

This **Klismos chair replica**, 1961, Athens, Greece, is designed by Terence Harold Robjohn-Gibbings. This replica was manufactured by Eleftherios Saridis, "the House of Saridis," established in 1867 in Athens, Greece.[28] In the early 1960s, Robjohn-Gibbings worked with the House of Saridis to design a complete line of furniture—Klismos line of furniture.[29] These pieces are highly valued and collected today. Saridis reproduced authentic furniture from all styles and periods, although his fame came from the remakes of the Classical Ancient Greek furniture.[30] The Robjohn-Gibbings design is in the collection at Brooklyn Museum of Art, Brooklyn, New York (Figure 6.5).

Looking at the Robjohn-Gibbings Klismos design, we can see why furniture historians refer to the Classical Greek Klismos chair as possessing both elegance and grace. Furniture scholars often deem the Klismos an ideal Classical form. The essence of the Robjohn-Gibbings chair is its lightness in form, which epitomizes the attributes given the piece by furniture historians. The medium—walnut frame and leather seat. The chair is not large in scale. The size is H 35 3/8" × W 20⅞" × D 28¼".

Starting at the top of the chair back, notice a rectangular crest rail bent forward at the sides, indicating the ability to wrap around the sitter's shoulder. This back piece is supported by a center splat, slightly concaved with two stiles flanking it left and right. The stiles are squared at top and become columnar forms widening toward the seat. Here they continue into back legs and terminate in tapered, flat-cut feet. At the seat, the legs splay out, backward and frontward (saber legs). The back and front legs have pointed top corners at seat level, and a seat rail joins the leg along all four sides forming a trapezoidal frame (wider at front). The seat is made of strips of leather rope woven loosely between the frame. Each rope wraps around the bottom of the seat rail and is secured at the end with nails.[31]

Figure 6.5 Klismos chair replica. Designer, Terrance Harold Robjohn-Gibbings. Manufacturer, Eleftherios Saridis, Athens, Greece, 1961.

Source: Brooklyn Museum of Art, Brooklyn, New York, Decorative Arts. Creative Commons, Commons-BY (Photo: Brooklyn Museum, CUR.1991.197_view1.jpg) H. Randolph Lever Fund.

Mentioned briefly in the **time period overview** was the influence of Greek Classicism in the 21st century. The photograph of the Athens Lounge Chair from the Baker Furniture collection next to Pheasant's sketch of his design is a testament of bridging past and present as stated by Baker Furniture. This chair design gives one a clear idea how precedent can have an impact on contemporary design.

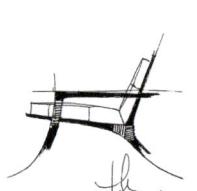 

Figure 6.6 *(left)* Ink sketch by designer Thomas Pheasant, Athens Lounge Chair, *(right)* Lounge chair, Baker Furniture Thomas Pheasant Collection.

Source: Courtesy of Thomas Pheasant.

What makes these pieces Classical Greek?

Keep in mind that since few actual pieces of Greek furniture remain, scholars have referred to sources such as vase painting to learn about the form. What is evident is that Greek furniture tends to combine simplicity and elegance, as seen in the Klismos piece. The furniture pieces most commonly depicted were the stool, chair, and couch (kline). The Roman couch design is derivative of the Greek Kline. Greek leg construction is depicted as a slim or slight form, not broad, abetting that sense of elegance. The construction method and joint type did not very from what was used for Egyptian furniture. Wood was the primary medium used. The furniture tended to be void of applied decoration, relying upon simple lines for its beauty.

ROME—1ST CENTURY B.C. (LATE HELLENISTIC–EARLY IMPERIAL) AND EARLY IMPERIAL PERIOD, A.D. 1ST–2ND CENTURY

History

The grandiose imperial designs of the early Roman Empire are reflected perhaps most conspicuously in its architecture.[32] The primary examples of Roman architecture date from the period between 100 B.C. and A.D. 300.[33] At the beginning of the Early Empire, all land surrounding the Mediterranean was at peace because everyone was under Roman Law—Pax Romana (Roman Peace). This was a long period of peace and minimal military expansion, ca. 27 B.C.–A.D. 180. Economic stability facilitated urbanism—the planning and building of cities.[34] In Rome, a population of close to one million people had to be housed in multistory apartment blocks.[35] The shape of urban Rome was influenced by Roman jurisdiction over Greek cities and the Roman ability to examine Greek temples, theatres, and walls, and thus began their assimilation.[36] Furthermore because of Roman admiration of Hellenistic Greek art (ca. 323–30 B.C.), Greek scholars and craftsman were imported to Rome.

Romans gave more attention to the interior than did the Greeks, whose architectural focus was the exterior. Ornament and decorative exuberance characterized Roman interiors as they drew upon the repertoire of Hellenistic design elements. As an integral part of the interior, furniture also relied on Greek prototypes of the Hellenistic Period.[37] Although there are very few furniture examples left from this period, documentary evidence assists in the understanding of the furniture characteristics. The findings—reliefs, wall painting, decorative objects, sarcophagi—displayed an intense interest in the opulent and costly and exuberant taste. The couches and stool featured on the pictorial timeline are excellent indicators of this exuberance.

Roman banquet couch, 1st century B.C. (Late Hellenistic–early Imperial)

Aesthetics

Typical materials used by the Romans for furniture design and construction were wood, metal, and stone. However, documentary evidence indicates that a characteristic feature of Roman furniture included the use of metals such as bronze, gold, and silver. Bronze was the most widely use metal.[38] What was commonly used for inlay decoration on Roman furniture included bronze, gold, silver, ivory, glass, tortoiseshell, and ebony. The form of the Roman couch was simple, consisting of a horizontal plane for reclining, supported by four vertical piers or legs. The head and foot areas were decorated with end supports referred to as *fulcra*. The *fulcra* rest above the legs. These supports were typically adorned.

Furniture

The first timeline piece is a **Roman banquet couch**, 1st century b.c. (Late Hellenistic–early Imperial). The Roman banquet couch was discovered at Canosa di Puglia. The piece can be found at the Walters Art Museum in Baltimore, Maryland (Figure 6.7). Couches were highly valued pieces of furniture that were often

■ An Illustrated Guide to Furniture History

buried with honored family members. Its opulent character is not uncommon for a piece found in a wealthy Roman's home. What is interesting is the fact that wealthy citizens did not eat sitting upright at a table but while reclining on couches such as this one. The dining room, or "triclinium," of a Roman house derived its name from the triple arrangement of three couches grouped at right angles to one another in a U-shape. The couches were arranged around a central table or tables. The length of the couch was not actually long by today's standard.

The frame of the banquet couch is wood (restored); the size is H 31 15/16" × W 76¾" × D 28¾".[39] The featured material is bronze, however; it is decorated with bronze fitting.[40] The exuberant turnings are like the English Baroque trumpet form and bell turnings or inverted cups seen centuries later during the Late Jacobean and William and Mary periods. Straps originally would have supported a mattress covered with luxurious textiles.[41] The ends of the couch are decorated with bronze fulcra (supports) which rest above the legs (Figure 6.7a). The fulcra are S-shape and resemble an armrest and footrest. The fulcra on this couch terminate in lion's heads in the front and duck heads in the back.[42]

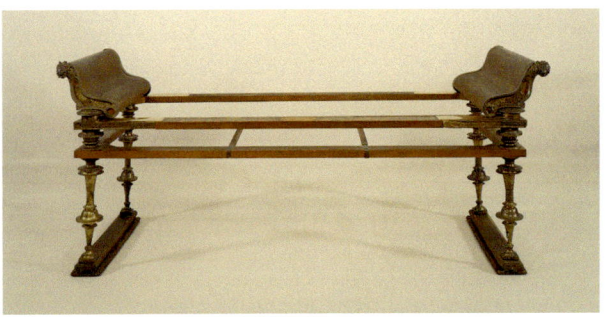

Figure 6.7
Roman banquet couch, 1st century B.C. (Late Hellenistic–Early Imperial), wood and brass.

Figure 6.7a Roman banquet couch detail showing the leg with brass fittings and fulcra.

Source: Walters Art Museum, Baltimore, Maryland, Collection: Roman Art. Museum purchase 1949.

Roman couch and footstool, A.D. 1st–2nd century

Aesthetics

The last timeline example is a Roman couch and footstool, A.D. 1st–2nd century. The frame, as mentioned with the previous example, is a simple a horizontal plane and four verticals. This couch's frame has no metal fittings as did the previous. It is constructed of the most typical medium, wood, yet the carving on the legs and other decorative motifs are as impressive, carved from bone instead of metal. For Roman furniture construction, the wood species most highly valued were maple and citron, and among the rare woods used for decorative purposes were primarily ebony and satinwood.[43] However, the extravagance and opulent nature of this couch and footstool do not reside with the use of wood but comes from the intricate and exquisitely carved bone and use of glass inlay throughout.

Antiquity

Figure 6.8
Roman couch and footstool, A.D. 1st–2nd century, wood and bone reassembled from fragments.

Furniture

This **Roman couch**, A.D. 1st–2nd century is from the Metropolitan Museum of Art, New York, and has been reassembled from fragments.[44] It is believed that some of the fragments may have come from the imperial villa of Lucius Verus (co-emperor, A.D. 161–169), on the Via Cassia outside Rome.[45] What is uncertain is if the square glass panels seen on the side of both pieces are original to the bed frame and stool, but the carved bone inlays are paralleled on other Roman couches (Figure 6.8).[46]

Figure 6.8a
Roman couch detail of the corner showing carved bone leg and crescent shape fulcra, carved head above lion pantome (animal head).

Figure 6.8b
Footstool detail of wing cupids and leopards.

Source: Metropolitan Museum of Art, New York, Roman Art. Public Domain OA [Open Access]. Gift of J. Pierpont Morgan, 1917.

Although the ornament and carving are opulent on the couch and footstool, the construction is straightforward. The Roman couch, like its Greek prototype, is a rectangle supported by four vertical post/legs, usually turned with a lathe and carved. Like the previous banquet couch, both ends contain fulcra. However, here the fulcra are formed from a crescent shape instead of an S-shape. A fascinating detail is at the base: where the fulcra touch the frame, they are terminated by a carved head (Figure 6.8a). This figure is placed above the side of the bed frame where the striking lion protome (animal head) rests with eyes made of inlaid glass.[47] Below the fulcra are the exquisitely carved legs with friezes of huntsmen, horses, and hounds flanking Ganymede, the handsome Trojan youth who was abducted by Zeus in the guise of an eagle to serve as his wine steward, and on the footstool are scenes of winged cupids and leopards (Figure 6.8b). The dimension of the couch is 41½″ × 30″ × 84½″ and the footstool size is 9½″ × 17½″ × 25½″.[48]

What makes these Roman (1st century B.C.–A.D. 1st–2nd century)?

What one should identify easily is the basic structure of the Roman couch. It is a horizontal frame held erect by four legs. The horizontal frame is terminated at

191

Plate 6.1
Cubiculum (bedroom) from the Villa of P. Fannius Synistor at Boscorealeca. 50–40 B.C.

Source: Metropolitan Museum of Art, New York, Greek & Roman Art. Public Domain OA [Open Access]. Rogers Fund, 1903.

each end with fulcra which resemble a headrest or both headrest and footrest. The fulcra are typically an *S*-shape or can be crescent-like. The fulcra give an extended quality to the legs, making the entire piece appear higher. The legs will be turned and carved or fitted with metal. The ornament and use of materials are luxurious and opulent. The overall characteristic of the piece is decoratively more exuberant than its Hellenistic Greek predecessor.

To conclude this chapter and provide for the reader a total environment and context, the author has selected a Roman bedroom, a period room from the Metropolitan Museum of Art (Plate 6.1). The Cubiculum (bedroom) is from the villa of P. Fannius Synistor at Boscoreale, 50–40 B.C. Greek and Roman collection, Gallery 165.[49] The villa was discovered in 1900.[50] It had been buried by the eruption of Vesuvius in A.D. 79.

The bedroom was located on the northwest of the villa of P. Fannius Synistor, preceded by a vestibule.[51] Typical for architecture planning of the time, the villa was organized around a central atrium—columned courtyard—open to the sky. The room is diminutive—approximately 8′ × 10′ × 19′—with walls covered in frescos, also typical at the time. The owner responsible for the wall painting has not been identified; the name of one of his successors in the 1st century A.D., Publius Fannius Synistor, is used to identify the villa.[52] The frescos are a visual feast of architecture and create an extraordinary illusion of space. The side walls are symmetrical and the frescos depict a continuous classical urban scape. The visible Classical architecture vocabulary are Ionic and Corinthian columns and pilasters, pediments, porticoes, entablatures, and dental work. Urban clusters of houses with these Classical features fill out the scenes. The ceiling is a modern structure based on similar cubicula.[53] However, also indicative of Classical Roman architecture is the barrel-vaulted ceiling near the end of the room. The Roman house bedroom is small in stature but gigantic in visual presence.

This concludes Chapter 6. The period discussed in Chapter 7 is the Renaissance. As a reminder, the pictorial timeline is dedicated to periods that frame the cannons the author deems as having the strongest impact on furniture history—movements, stylistic era, and historical periods.

NOTES

1. Treena Crochet, *Designer's Guide to Furniture Styles* (New Jersey, Prentice Hall, 1999), p.5.
2. Ibid.
3. Hollis S. Baker, *Furniture in The Ancient World: Origins & Evolutions 3100–475 B.C.* (New York, A Giniger Book, in association with The Macmillan Company), p.19.
4. Treena Crochet, *Designer's Guide to Furniture Styles* (New Jersey, Prentice Hall, 1999), pp.8, 10.
5. Hollis S. Baker, *Furniture in The Ancient World: Origins & Evolutions 3100–475 B.C.* (New York, A Giniger Book, in association with The Macmillan Company), p.61.
6. Hollis S. Baker, *Furniture in The Ancient World: Origins & Evolutions 3100–475 B.C.* (New York, A Giniger Book, in association with The Macmillan Company), p.19.
7. Ibid., p.21.
8. On-line Collection, Object Label, Metropolitan Museum of Art, New York, New York, 2020.

9. Ibid.
10. Ibid.
11. Ibid.
12. Ibid.
13. Ibid.
14. Ibid.
15. Ibid.
16. Ibid.
17. Ibid.
18. Ibid.
19. Ibid.
20. "Scribes in Ancient Egypt," World History, https://worldhistory.us/ancient-history/ancient-egypt/scribes-in-ancient-egypt.php.
21. Ibid.
22. On-line Collection, Object Label, Metropolitan Museum of Art, New York, New York, 2020.
23. Mark Hinchman, *History of Furniture: A Global View* (New York, Fairchild Books, A Division of Condé Nash Publications), p.44.
24. Robbie G. Blakemore, *History of Interior Design and Furniture: From Ancient Egypt to Nineteenth-Century Europe* (New Jersey, John Wiley & Sons, 2006), p.39.
25. Ibid.
26. Mark Hinchman, *History of Furniture: A Global View* (New York, Fairchild Books, A Division of Condé Nash Publications), p.45.
27. On-line Collection, Object Label, British Museum, London, England, 2020.
28. www.saridisofathens.com/about.
29. Ibid.
30. Ibid.
31. On-line Collection, Object Label, Brooklyn Museum of Art, Brooklyn, New York, 2020.
32. Horst de la Croix … [et al.], *Garner's Art Through the Ages* (New York, Harcourt Brace College Publishers, 1991), p.217.
33. Robbie G. Blakemore, *History of Interior Design & Furniture: From Ancient Egypt to Nineteenth-Century Europe* (New Jersey, John Wiley & Sons), p.53.
34. Horst de la Croix … [et al.], *Garner's Art Through the Ages* (New York, Harcourt Brace College Publishers, 1991), p.217.
35. Ibid.
36. Robbie G. Blakemore, *History of Interior Design & Furniture: From Ancient Egypt to Nineteenth-Century Europe* (New Jersey, John Wiley & Sons), p.46.
37. Ibid., p.61.
38. Ibid.
39. On-line Collection, Object Label, Walters Museum of Art, Baltimore Maryland, 2020.
40. Ibid.
41. Ibid.
42. Ibid.
43. Robbie G. Blakemore, *History of Interior Design & Furniture, From Ancient Egypt to Nineteenth-Century Europe* (New Jersey, John Wiley & Sons), p.61.
44. On-line Collection, Object Label, Metropolitan Museum of Art, New York, New York, 2020.
45. Ibid.
46. Ibid.
47. On-line Collection, Object Label, Walters Museum of Art, Baltimore, Maryland, 2020.
48. Ibid.

49 On-line Collection, Object Label, Metropolitan Museum of Art, New York, New York, 2020.
50 Joan R. Mertens … [et al.], *Period Rooms in the Metropolitan Museum of Art* (The Metropolitan Museum of Art, New York, and Harry N. Abrams, New York), p.18.
51 Ibid., p.17.
52 Ibid.
53 Ibid., p.18.

7 Renaissance

Italy, France, and England

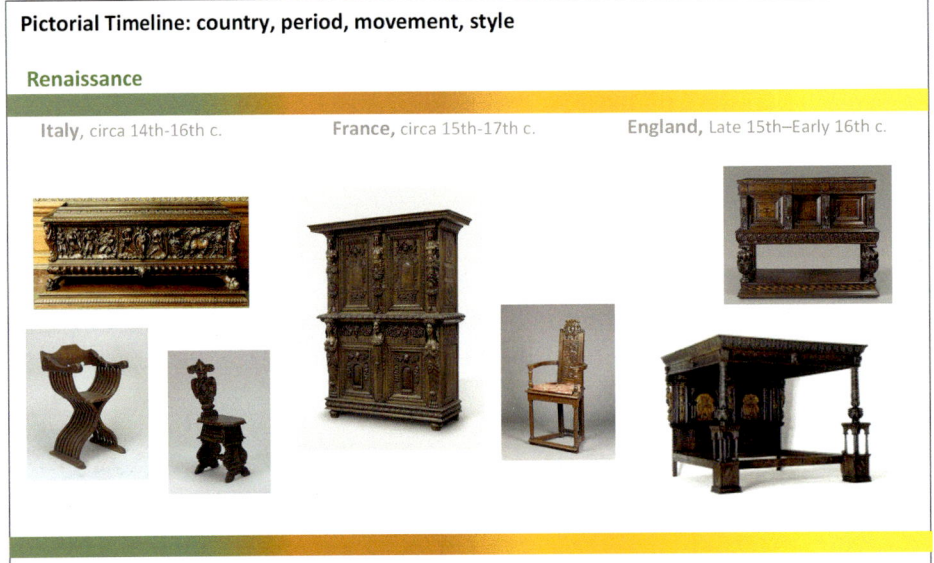

7.1
Pictorial timeline—Renaissance: Italy, France, and England

TIME PERIOD OVERVIEW

The Renaissance refers to a historical period in European history roughly between the 14th and 17th centuries. As a historical period, the Renaissance was preceded by the Middle Ages and succeeded by the Early Modern period. Sometimes this period is categorized as the Early Renaissance, High Renaissance, and Late Renaissance periods. This chapter will not use these specific categories. The furniture featured on the pictorial timeline above for Chapter 7 will concentrate on the Renaissance beginning with its origins in Italy, spreading across Europe to France and England (Timeline 7.1). Following the same format as Chapter 6, the discussion surrounding the selections will pertain to the three areas—**history**, **aesthetic**, and **furniture**.

Italy was the springboard for the Renaissance in architecture and the visual arts, beginning in 15th-century Florence.[1] The Italian peninsula during the Gothic period (Late Middle Ages) involve a number of autonomous states of varying size and character. They shared one noteworthy feature: a fairly large and rather wealthy fortified city.[2] Another commonality for the states is that the essential Northern qualities of the Gothic style had never been sympathetic to the Italians, and they abandoned its alien tenets as quickly as they could (except for Venice).[3] The typical architect of the Renaissance in Italy was exceptionally versatile in that he performed services not only in architecture but also in painting, sculpture, furniture design, etc.[4] In these private palaces designed by the Italian Renaissance architect, furniture was included in the overall design and was made as much for decoration as for practical use.

The reader might wonder why the term Renaissance is used instead of the Italian word *Rinascimento*. Renaissance is a French word meaning "rebirth."[5] The 19th-century French historian Jules Michelet was the first to use and define the term Renaissance as a period in Europe's cultural history that represented a drastic break from the Middle Ages.[6] Intellectuals believed this time signified the modern understanding of humanity and its place in the world. From the 19th century onwards, the term has been used globally to reference this period in history.

To conclude, it is good to keep in mind that the ideas and ideals of the Italian Renaissance spread into the rest of Europe, setting off the Northern Renaissance. Regardless of the region, the Renaissance period was defined as the period of cultural revival and renewed interest in Classical Antiquity after the centuries labeled the Dark Ages. For southern regions and northern regions, the Renaissance is best known for its achievements in painting, architecture, sculpture, literature, music, philosophy, science and technology, and even exploration.

ITALIAN RENAISSANCE—CA. 14TH–16TH CENTURY

History

Italy is recognized as the birthplace of the Italian Renaissance (*Rinascimento* in Italian). The Italian Renaissance lasted approximately from the 14th century to the 16th century. The origins can be traced to the city of Florence, in the region of Tuscany. Florence was economically powerful and had political prominence at this time. This powerful position was the result of the city providing credit for European monarchs. Florence is also recognized as laying down the groundwork for capitalism and banking. The Italian Renaissance is known for its achievements in painting, sculpture, architecture, literature, science, etc. Notable Renaissance artists include Botticelli, Titian, Leonardo da Vinci, Michelangelo, and architects such as Andrea Palladio, Leon Battista Alberti, Brunelleschi, and Bramante. By the late 15th century, Italy became recognized as the European leader in these areas. The Renaissance in Italy peaked in the mid-16th century as domestic disputes and foreign invasions plunged the region into turmoil (Italian Wars 1494–1559).

■ An Illustrated Guide to Furniture History

Cassone, 16th century, Italy

Aesthetics

The first timeline piece discussed will be the Italian *cassone*, a low chest. Its development, as with all Italian Renaissance furniture, is intrinsically linked to the architectural design and interior of the private palace. Architects influenced their patron in all areas: decorative arts, furniture design, painting, sculpture, and even dishes and cutlery. Architects such as Leon Battista Alberti (1404–1472) and Michelozzo di Bartolommeo (1396–1472) were especially influential in encouraging and fostering the Renaissance style for they studied ancient architectural design and published their findings in such works as Alberti's *Ten Books of Architecture*.[7] Alberti and Michelozzo executed great private palaces that mirrored the design of sumptuous civil and religious buildings of early Rome.[8] Because of the architect's renewed interest in Classicism, early on during the period furniture was endowed with architectonic features and profile. Italian Renaissance furniture possessed qualities found in buildings, and therefore would contain a base, mid-section, and top.

There are several furniture pieces whose origins are distinguishably early Italian Renaissance designs, such as the timeline *cassone* which was frequently used at the foot and side of beds. Other such pieces are the *cassapanca*, similar to the cassone but with a back, *credenza*, used as a sideboard for display of opulent gold and silver vessels and dishes, *X*-shape folding chairs such as the *dante* and *savonarola*, and later fixed and or hinged *sgabello*. Discussed later will be the savonarola, and sgabello. The medium of choice for furniture was walnut. The *cassone* as well as the other furniture mentioned was embellished with relief ornament, light to more heavily carved, and intarsia with inlayed woods was used to create a design and patterning similar to marquetry. The relief referenced details from Roman Antiquity like that of the timeline *cassone*. Color embellishment for furniture was painted or rendered by gilding.

Furniture

This **cassone**, 16th century, Italy, is one of a pair at the Frick Collection in New York City and dates to the third quarter of the 16th century. In essence, the *cassone* is an archaic form, a type of chest or coffer—a storage piece (Figure 7.1). The earliest form of the coffer was iron and was intended to be portable.[9] The Italian Renaissance *cassone* design is based on the sarcophagi of Ancient Rome.[10] This is not surprising since architecture, interiors, and furnishings inspiration came from the sumptuous civil and religious buildings of early Rome. *Cassoni*, or chests, were frequently used at the foot and sides of the bed, which was often inordinately high.[11] During the Italian Renaissance, the *cassone* developed into an elaborate, carved, painted, and decorated piece of furniture which sometimes included applied stucco motifs, rich gilding, complex moldings, and painted panels. Throughout the Italian Renaissance, the *cassoni* created an unprecedented sense of luxury. This *cassone* from the Frick Collection is a fine example of such luxury. The *cassone*'s maker is unknown. The medium is walnut on pine and displays a wonderfully rich patina and exuberant carvings. The carving is exquisitely detailed.

Renaissance

Figure 7.1
Cassone with reliefs of Caesar, the Slaying of Niobe's sons. Italy, third quarter of the 16th century, walnut on pine.

Source: Frick Collection, New York, Henty Clay Frick Bequest.

The exuberant moldings at the top and bottom are unmistakably Classically derivative, as are the lion's feet and winged griffin corner brackets. The relief subjects on this *cassone* are Caesar and the slaying of Niobe's sons. The human form is depicted rather realistically. Niobe from Greek mythology becomes the prototype of the bereaved mother weeping for the loss of her children.[12] The *cassone*'s dimension is 29¼" × 74½".[13] It is a visually powerful Classical interpretation and excellent example of this Renaissance furniture type.

Savonarola chair, 16th century, Italy

Aesthetics

The next Italian Renaissance piece to discuss from the pictorial timeline is a style of chair known as a *savonarola*. The design and form of the *savonarola* chair is *X*-shape (curule) legs. This chair's form is always the same, its parts formulaic. Its form has interlacing curved slats that define the base/legs of the chair. As the slats cross and interlock, they form an enclosure around the seat and terminate with the arms of the chair. The arms attach to the rail that form the back. At times, there might be relief on the back rail or certosina applied; a geometric pattern is created using wood, bone, metal or mother of pearl.

Figure 7.2
Savonarola chair, Italy, 16th century, 38⅛" × 25" × 21".

Source: Copper-Hewitt Museum, New York, Creative Common Zero, [CC0]. Gift of Harvey Smith.

Furniture

This **Savonarola chair**, 16th century, Italian Renaissance, is in the Cooper-Hewitt Museum collection, New York City (Figure 7.2). The *savonarola* chair, was named after martyr Girolamo Savonarola.[14] Savonarola was an Italian Dominican friar and preacher active in Renaissance Florence, known for his prophecies and calls for Christian renewal.[15] The names of famous Renaissance Italians are used today to describe several different types of furniture from the 16th-century Italian Renaissance.

■ An Illustrated Guide to Furniture History

The chair's medium is walnut, which is the most commonly used wood for furniture at this time. The size of the *savonarola* is normative, 38⅜" × 25" × 21".[16] The maker is unknown. The chair depicts the features discussed under **Aesthetics** that are commonly associated with the *savonarola* design. Evident are the X-shape interlacing curved slats that define the legs (curule legs) and area for the horizontal seat at the arms. The arms attach to the back horizontal rail. It is unusual that there is no applied ornament on the crest rail. However, the cut pattern on the top and bottom of the crest rail could be considered ornamental and makes the rail visually attractive.

Sgabello chair, 16th century, Italy

Aesthetics

The next Italian Renaissance chair on the timeline is the *sgabello* chair which is a comparatively small chair. Its origins are from 15th-century Italy. The design and form of *sgabello* remains virtually the same throughout the Italian Renaissance. Its typical features are an octagonal seat that rests on solid trestle supports, one in the front and one in the back. Also typical is the fan-shaped back that is narrow at the seat level but strongly flared at the crest of the back.[17] This form of chair became more ornate later during Renaissance period often with elaborately outlined trestles and ornately carved embellishments.

Figure 7.3 Sgabello chair, Italy, 16th Century, 41 5/16" × 11⅞" × 16¾".

Furniture

This **sgabello chair**, 16th century, Italian Renaissance, like the *Savonarola*, is from the Cooper-Hewitt Museum collection (Figure 7.3). The medium is walnut and the size of the chair is normal for a 16th-century Italian Renaissance *sgabello*, 41 5/16" × 11⅞" × 16¾".[18]

The maker is unknown. Typical of the *sgabello*, as mentioned under **Aesthetics**, are elaborately carved back trestle supports. The back crest has a fleur-de-lis-like design flanked right and left with rosettes. As one's eyes move down the back to the central portion, the carving recalls the motifs of Classical Rome. There are volutes that define the edge with acanthus-like leaf patterning (Figure 7.3a). Another interesting feature of the chair is in the back: there exists a carved monogram "A.D." in cartouche (Figure 7.3b).

Figure 7.3a Sgabello chair detail back crest area with a fleur-de-lis-like design flanked right and left with rosettes.

200 □

Figure 7.3b
Sgabello chair detail view of the back of the chair showing a carved monogram "A.D."

Source: Cooper-Hewitt Museum, New York, Creative Common Zero, [CC0]. Gift of Charles W. Gould.

What makes these pieces Italian Renaissance?

Beginning with the repetitive form and stylistic features of the three ubiquitous pieces—*cassone*, *savonarola*, and *sgabello*—their forms epitomize Italian Renaissance furniture. The design and form of the pieces are fixed—sarcophagus-shaped *cassone*, interlocking X-shape (curule) *savonarola*, and trestle support and octagonal base *sgabello*. Because of renewed interest in Antiquity at this time, the Greco-Roman decorative details will reflect Classical architectural features such as the plinth base, pilaster, column, and pediment. The furniture, as seen with the *cassone* and *sgabello* from the timeline, were highly decorative pieces. Light to heavy relief was used for embellishment. The primary wood was walnut; however, it was usually embellished with some type of inlaying process such as intarsia (multicolored wood) and certosina (bone or ivory). Veneer could be used to enhance the walnut, as was gesso to establish relief. The design and decoration of the furniture required a high level of technical skill and craftsmanship. The result was a high-quality, expensive, regal furniture piece, which would be in keeping with the wealthy owner who commissioned the piece and the sumptuous palace in which the piece would reside.

French Renaissance—ca. 15th–17th century

History

The second group of furniture pieces on the pictorial timeline are from the French Renaissance. The French Renaissance occurs between the 15th and early 17th centuries. The time period begins roughly with the French invasion of Italy in the reign of Charles VIII until the death of Henry IV in 1610. A notable period for the French Renaissance centers on the reigns of Francis I (1515–1547) and his son Henry II (1547–1559). As in Italy, the Renaissance in France is regarded as a cultural and artistic movement.[19]

The French association with the Italian Renaissance began in the late 15th century. Charles VIII invaded Naples and held it for two years (1494–1496).[20] During the invasions, the French were exposed to the Renaissance spirit, its art, architecture, literature, and Italian goods. Art, which had been in a feeble, languishing state in France, began to revive.[21] These invasions influenced the creative direction of France.

Francis I took the lead in one of the most ambitious Renaissance architecture commissions for one of the largest French royal palaces, Château de Fontainebleau. He employed Italians to work on Château de Fontainebleau, an old-fashioned hunting lodge from the Middle Ages, surrounded by forest. He first hired French architect Gilles Le Breton to rebuild the lodge in the new Renaissance style. Le

Breton designed for Fontainebleau a *Court Ovalle*, or oval courtyard, a monumental *Porte Dorée*, as its southern entrance, and a monumental Renaissance stair, *Portique de Serlio*. Francis I later brought Leonardo da Vinci and Andrea del Sarto to France to decorate the interior. In 1528, he had built the *Galerie François I* and for this new construction he brought to France the Italian architect Sebastiano Serlio and Florentine painter Giovanni Battista de Jacopo (Rosso Florentino) and later Francesco Primaticcio. Together, their style of decoration became known as the first School of Fontainebleau. Besides Fontainebleau, Francis I built several more renowned Renaissance châteaux—Château de Chambord, Château de Chenonceau on the Loire, the Château de Madrid, and others—and commenced the Louvre.[22] These great palaces remain great cultural attractions today.

Cabinet (meuble à deux corps) or cupboard, ca. 16th century, France, and armchair (caquetoire), ca. 16th century, France

Aesthetics

The following explanation in respect to aesthetics applies to both French Renaissance furniture pieces on the pictorial timeline—the cabinet/cupboard (*meuble à deux corps*) and armchair *caquetoire*. During the French Renaissance, the wealthy subjects of Francis I followed the king's example and rebuilt or altered their chateaux and hotels, decorated them in the Italian style, and furnished them with cabinets, chairs, coffers, armoires, tables, and various other articles, designed after the Italian models.[23] However, furniture of the French Renaissance can be divided into two phases: Francis I and Henry II.

Under Francis I, the Italian influence was instrumental for architecture and interiors. Furniture design followed that of both exterior and interior Italian architecture in proportionate relationship between form and decorative detail.[24] Medieval construction techniques and joints where still used, such as mortise and tenon, dovetail, and tongue and groove. The stylistic character of French Renaissance furniture began by applying Gothic and Renaissance motifs to Medieval forms. Popular Renaissance motifs such as arabesque or rounded arch were used with Gothic features such as linen fold, crockets, and pinnacles.[25]

Through the Medieval period, oak was the medium of choice, but it was gradually superseded by walnut. Decorative processes for furniture included inlay, carving, and polychrome enhancement. The Italian influence was instrumental in introducing marquetry, applying pieces of veneer to wood to form a pattern, as already mentioned in regard to Italian Renaissance furniture. Other inlay materials besides wood were marble, gold, ivory, soft colored paste, and expensive wood such as ebony.

During the reign of Henry II, a Renaissance stylistic transformation occurred. There was an emancipation from the Italian Renaissance style. Structural form and decorative detail were developed by the French architect, artist, sculptor, and craftsman according to their own taste. This was the result of two schools, the school of du Cerceau in Île de France, and that of Hugues Sambin in Burgundy, the Burgundian school. The school of du Cerceau shows grace of line and fine details, while the Burgundian style suggested richness through lavish carving.[26]

Regarding specific furniture pieces, throughout the period the chair maintained the Gothic form—rectilinear high-panel back, with or without arms; however, Classical motifs prevalent during the Renaissance were added—decorative motifs such as pilasters, columns, arabesque, palmettes, anthemion, acanthus leaves, etc. These motifs took the form of stiles and rails for chairs, and light relief or heavy relief on furniture panels. The cabinet form was made with an upper and lower parts throughout the French Renaissance; however, the style of ornamentation depended on who reigned—Francis I or

Henry II. But both incorporated carved panels, with floral designs, and caryatid-figured columns. Cabinet doors were generally decorated with richly carved panels that could include flora and fauna, and Classical elements such as caryatids, pilasters, and columns. Behind the panels were drawers with fronts that were usually minutely carved.

Furniture

The **cabinet** (*meuble à deux corps*), ca. 1570, with 19th-century additions, is the first French Renaissance piece on the pictorial timeline.[27] It is a two-part piece, synonymous with a cupboard, and is typical for the furniture type. The medium is walnut; overall size top and bottom portion is approximately H 6″ × W 5″ × D 2″. The piece is from the Philadelphia Museum of Art collection (Figure 7.4). The maker is unknown; however, its geographic location is Burgundy, which is possibly why the authors of *Furniture I, Smithsonian Illustrated Library of Antiques* associate the piece with the Burgundian school. The cupboard is a testament of the Renaissance stylistic transformation that happened from the reign of Francis I to the reign of Henry II, his son. The cupboard's design defines the style of French Renaissance furniture associated with the reign of Henry II—the emancipation from the Italian Renaissance style. In the publication *Furniture I, Smithsonian Illustrated Library of Antiques*, the authors make mention of the cupboard: "The designs of both Du Cerceau and Sambin were the inspiration for the decorative carving." They further credit the French Burgundian of Hugues Sambin in Burgundy.

Figure 7.4 Walnut cupboard, two-part, French cabinet (*meuble à deux corps*), ca. 1570, with 19th-century additions, walnut, approximate size, top and bottom, 6″ × 5″ × 2″.

Source: Philadelphia Museum of Art, Philadelphia, Pennsylvania Public Domain OA [Open Access] European Decorative Arts and Sculpture.

The association of this cabinet to the two schools is attributed to the extravagantly fanciful carving and sculptural quality—the grace of line and fine detail of the carved festoons on the center drawer fronts, and fanciful garland and moldings on the panel doors (school of du Cerceau); and the expressively three-dimensional sculptural quality seen in the

■ An Illustrated Guide to Furniture History

precisely carved figures accentuating the ends and center, reminiscent of caryatids seen on Classical buildings (Sambin's Burgundian School). The exaggerated Classical cornice and center molding, distinguishing the top piece from its bottom, add to its three-dimensional expression. Lastly, this fanciful treatment of architectural features is the hallmark of the French creative genius and defines stylistically the French Renaissance of Henry II.

The second French Renaissance piece, the **caquetoire**, ca. 16th century, is a type of armchair. It is from the collection of the Metropolitan Museum of Art (Figure 7.5). The design was popular during the second half of the 16th century. The chair dates from this period but contains 19th-century restoration work.[28] The medium is walnut, which is typical of the time, and the cushion on the chair is cut silk velvet.[29]

Figure 7.5 Caquetoire armchair, France, second half of 16th century and 19th century, walnut, cut silk cushion.

Source: Metropolitan Museum of Art, New York, Public Domain OA [Open Access] Robert Lehman Collection, 1975.

Since the 19th century, the chair type has been associated with the word *caquetoire*, derivative of the French *caqueter*, meaning "cackle."[30] A translation in English means "gossip." The term appears in contemporary inventories: a document of 1583 lists "4 chaires faictes en façon de caquetoire," The design and form of the chair remained the same throughout the period. The common characteristics of the chair are its lightness in scale and tall, narrow paneled back attached to a trapezoidal seat. The chair's form always has arms which flair or curve outward, and the leg placement is designed to be spaced closely at the back and wider at the front. The legs are supported with a perimeter stretcher. Remember from Chapter 3 that the purpose of stretchers for tables and chairs is structural support. The wide front of this chair appears to welcome a potential user.

What makes these pieces French Renaissance?

The two-part walnut cabinet and *caquetoire* epitomize French Renaissance furniture. The same can be said for the *caquetoire* as for the Italian Renaissance selection: the form and stylistic features do not change— tall narrow back, trapezoid seat, etc. The French Renaissance cupboard/cabinet will have a top piece and bottom piece. The Classical architecture features are addressed in a visually creative way and are typically overwhelmingly ornate. The ornament on French Renaissance furniture is sculptural in appearance, moving beyond relief. The timeline cabinet demonstrates this brilliantly with its two-part details of carved ornament on the four boldly raised convex panels and the precisely carved caryatid-like figures. The Classical elements are the subject, just as for Italian Renaissance furniture, but orchestrated with much more exuberance and three-dimensional quality.

English Renaissance—ca. late 15th–early 17th century

History

The English Renaissance from late 15th century to early 17th century, as in Italy and France, is considered to be a cultural and artistic movement. The beginning of the English Renaissance is often taken, as a convenience, to be 1485, when the Battle of Bosworth Field ended the War of the Roses and inaugurated the Tudor Dynasty.[31] The ruling monarchs during this period are Henry VIII (1509–1547) and Elizabeth I (1558–1603), the last monarch of the House of Tudor. The reign of Henry VIII can be considered a transition in which there is evidence of Italian Renaissance influence on design but not fully absorbed.[32] Therefore, the Renaissance style and ideas were slow to penetrate England, and the Elizabethan era in the second half of the 16th century is usually regarded as the height of the English Renaissance.[33] Highly influential in the progression of the English Renaissance during Elizabeth's reign was Somerset House (1547–1552) for the Duke of Somerset, Edward Seymour; since 1989, its North Wing has been the home of The Courtauld Institute of Art, one of London's world-famous collections.

The English Renaissance was different from the Italian Renaissance and French Renaissance in that the dominant art forms of the English Renaissance were literature and music. Visual arts were much less significant for the Renaissance in England, and England was slow to produce visual arts in the Renaissance style. The artists of the Tudor court were imported foreigners.[34] John of Padua, Holbein, Havernius of Cleves, and other artists were induced to come to England and to introduce the new style.[35] It was of slow growth, however, and a mixture of Gothic, Italian, and Flemish ornament forms the style known as "Tudor."[36] For architecture projects, Henry VIII employed foreigners from Italy—two Italian sculptors, Pietro Torrigiano and Giovanni de Maio—and later the Florentine Torrigiano. Henry VIII was a benefactor of the arts, which provided stimulus for the adaptation of the Renaissance style. The reign of Henry VIII was a peaceful and prosperous time, and he used the proceeds from the dissolution of monasteries and converted money that was formerly paid to Rome into revenue.[37] Despite the money from these sources, he was continually on the verge of financial ruin due to his personal extravagance.

There was ample competition between the Renaissance Kings, Henry VIII and Francis I of France. This became obvious in June 1520 during the Field of Cloth and Gold (*Camp du Drap d'Or*), a field tournament and summit site which was arranged by Cardinal Thomas Wolsey to increase the bond of friendship between the two monarchs. Instead, this event had an adverse effect.[38] Each king, English and French, tried to outshine the other with dazzling tents, clothes, huge feast, music, jousting, and games.

■ An Illustrated Guide to Furniture History

As the Renaissance progressed, Henry VIII was ambitious to outdo his French contemporary, Francis I, in the sumptuousness of his palaces.[39] However, despite his ambitions, it is difficult to find an English royal palace that rivals the Renaissance update to Fontainebleau. Visible in Hampton Court Palace this very day, however, there exist Italian Renaissance details from a Henry VIII commission—the decorative sculpture of Roman emperors in roundels of terracotta are a fine example. However, many of Henry VIII's Renaissance commissions have vanished. Two such works with Renaissance features are Nonsuch Palace and Sutton Place.[40] As mentioned previously, it was not until the end of the century, when Elizabethan architecture emerged, that there was an expression of a mature Renaissance style, as evident with Somerset House. Some would argue that this style was influenced more by Northern Europe than Italy. Regardless, still visible today are spectacular examples of English Renaissance *prodigy* houses—Longleat House, Hardwick Hall, and Hatfield house are a few. The term *prodigy* originates with the architectural historian Sir John Summerson and has been generally adapted.[41] The prodigy house was a large English country house built by courtiers and other wealthy families. These houses epitomize the English Renaissance style of building with an abundant use of glass, in which the facades become heavily fenestrated and brilliantly articulated with glazed windows—a visual spectacle of natural daylight.

Court cupboard (standing livery cupboard), 16th century, England

Aesthetics

The first piece from the English Renaissance pictorial timeline represents one of two types of cupboard design that predominated during this period. The first, the *court cupboard* (timeline piece), was primarily used for display. The term *court* derives from the French vocabulary and means short. In respect to this English Renaissance furniture piece, the *court cupboard* is a low cupboard mounted on legs. The second type, the *press cupboard*, was used for storage. The form of the *court cupboard* is low, two-part, either closed for storage at the top half with panel doors and an open shelf at the bottom, or alternately three levels of shelves at the upper portion and closed storage below.

The stylistic features were from Antiquity as was Italian and French Renaissance furniture. However, the aesthetic was also influenced by Flanders and Germany, due to the friendly alliance and proximity the foreign craftsman was employed in England. The subject of the ornamentation was still from Antiquity and Classically referenced, so incorporated in the design was the cornice, frieze, figures both carved and inlayed, however also incorporated was regional influences by the Dutch and Flemish craftsman. Regarding the form, the door panel could be raised or recessed with carved details. The legs on the cupboard were typically a bulbous, cup-and-cover, and carved in relief. Wood species used was typically walnut and oak.

Furniture

The first English Renaissance piece **court cupboard (standing livery cupboard), ca. 1585**, is from the Philadelphia Museum of Art collection (Figure 7.6). This type of furniture piece officially has another name which depends on use—"standing livery cupboard." Standing livery cupboards have an interesting history and function. The top portion was use by the owner to display valuable objects as mentioned, but the bottom part was usually a receptacle for food.[42] "Livery" is an old form of delivery and referred to the taking of food during the night, and therefore the livery cupboard was often found in the bedchamber.[43] The maker of this court cupboard is unknown.

Figure 7.6 Standing livery cupboard, England, ca. 1585, walnut with ebony, cedar, and holly inlays, oak interior and back panels.

Source: Philadelphia Museum of Art, Philadelphia, Pennsylvania Public Domain OA [Open Access] European Decorative Arts and Sculpture.

Figure 7.6(a)

Figure 7.6(b)

The Renaissance English cupboard differs from the French Renaissance cupboard discussed earlier in that its use was to specifically display some of the family's most valuable objects—objects such as metal plates, gold or silver, or other decorative art objects the family held in high esteem.

This piece is a splendid example of English Renaissance furniture—its form, decorative detail, and overall aesthetic character. There is an abundance of wood species used for this furniture piece which contribute to its richness in appearance. The wood varieties include walnut, ebony, cedar, and inlays of holly, with an oak interior and back panel.[44] Its size is 46" × 52" × 19".[45]

The piece has an array of rich details beginning with the upper-section storage area. This section is divided into three areas covered by recessed panel inlayed doors. The doors are a spectacular geometric pattern of various wood species (Figure 7.6a). The doors are separated by four leaf-work brackets that are capped off at the top by raised blocks. Above the three storage section doors is an interlocking pattern of light and dark wood. Above this section is the cornice with a frieze of wonderful annular carvings. The top section is supported by two globular turned melon-like legs (Figure 7.6b). The leg turning is referred to as the cup-and-cover and resembles a cup topped with a lid. This was a popular turning during the Elizabethan and Jacobean period. The bulbous legs are terminated at the bottom by a base molding and checker-board lozenge pattern of dark and light wood, an ideal way to visually solidify the base and complete the form.

Great Bed of Ware, 1590–1600, England

Aesthetics

From the mid-16th century, English Renaissance beds were large, luxurious, and extravagant.[46] They were elaborately carved. Noticeable about these beds is that the frame was architecturally conceived.[47] The frame typically consisted of columnar posts engaged at the headboard and freestanding at the foot. The pictorial timeline bed's headboard is designed somewhat differently. The English Renaissance bed had freestanding columnar posts which were intricately carved using Classical details such as fluting and leaf-work. An integral part of the columnar post was a globular bulbous turning—cup-and-cover, a common design, as seen previously with the standing livery cupboard. The headboard was a framed rectangular shape. These headboards typically were a feast to the eyes, intricately carved, using varied woods and inlay; panels could be raised or recessed, and the ornamentation was Classically derivative, using dentils, lozenge design, and molding—notched molding, nail head molding, etc. The timeline bed is an exquisite display in this regard. Also typical of the English Renaissance bed is that both ends support a canopy or tester at the top, as seen with the timeline piece. The canopy or tester was comprised of an entablature and cornice with elaborately carved and inlay designs. Even the roof of the tester was decorated, carved, and/or painted moldings, coffering, recessed or raised panels, decorated with motifs typical of the period.

Lastly, regarding the dressing of the Renaissance bed, its framework would be heavily draped and swathed with valances.[48] The draped textile was functional as well as aesthetically pleasing. When closed, it could shield the sleeper from the cold air and drafts. Bed linens and draperies were expensive, and often finer than many pieces of furniture.[49] These extravagant textiles were hung from a rod inside the canopy; these hangings were referred to as furniture.[50]

Furniture

The **Great Bed of Ware**, ca. 1590–1600, probably made in Ware, England,[51] is a magnificent example of an English Renaissance bed (Figure 7.7). It is one of the best-known pieces of English furniture.[52] It is in the Victoria and Albert Museum collection, London, England. Fortunately, its provenance can be identified. The design is attributed to the Dutch architect and painter Hans Vredeman de Vries (1527–1604).[53] He is known to have published pattern books so that designs could be copied,[54] Italian Renaissance being his inspiration of the time.

The Great Bed of Ware like other Elizabethan beds copies architectural details. These architectural details are incorporated into the frame design, such as columns, arches, friezes, and canopy/tester that looks like a Classical cornice. This bed is of an unusually large size—no other beds from this period on this scale are known.[55] The height was slightly reduced in the 19th century.[56] Its style is typical of carved wooden beds of the 1590s.[57] The medium is oak, carved, inlaid, and painted. The headboard is inlaid with two marquetry panels within arched frames, and is divided vertically by three carved figures, two male and one female.[58]

Figure 7.7
Bed—Great Bed of Ware, Ware, England, 1590–1600, oak, carved and originally painted, with panels of marquetry.

On each side of the headboard is a figure of a satyr. The woodwork shows traces of paint. The top of this Elizabethan bed's wood canopy is flat; however, at times canopies on these beds could also be paneled and carved.

The bed was probably made as a curiosity to attract customers to one of the inns at Ware, Hertfordshire. Ware is 22 miles from London, which was then a day's journey on horseback or by coach. The town had many inns in the 1590s. The bed has been famous since it was made and its historical associates are interesting. William Shakespeare mentioned it in his play *Twelfth Night*, first performed in 1601.[59] The contemporary playwright Ben Jonson called it "the great bed of Ware" in a play in 1609.[60] Visitors often carved their initials on the bed or applied red wax seals, which are still visible on the bedposts and headboard today.

Figure 7.7a
Bed—Great Bed of Ware, dressed with bedlinens.

Source: Victoria and Albert Museum, London England, Public Domain OA [Open Access], British Galleries, Room 57. Case 2.

The Victoria and Albert Museum has re-hung the bed (Figure 7.7a). Notes about this process can be found at the V&A.[61]

What makes these pieces English Renaissance?

These pieces are large in scale, heavily ornamental, and an amalgamation of the Northern decorative traditions of Flanders and Germany and the use of Roman Classicism of the Italian Renaissance architects, artist and craftsmen. This merging of styles resulted from the use of pattern books created by the Flemish architects and artists. English designs that derived from the books are elements such as floral and checkered inlays, scrapwork, and low-relief arabesques. Such motifs were combined with those of the Roman Classicism driving Italian Renaissance design. The English Renaissance piece is the combination of Medieval forms with Renaissance ornamental application. This mixture of motifs and ornamental emphasis is seen with both pictorial timeline pieces—the standing livery cupboard and the Great Bed of Ware.

■ An Illustrated Guide to Furniture History

To conclude Chapter 7 and provide for the reader context and a total environment, a well-known room has been selected form the Metropolitan Museum of Art, the Studiolo from the Ducal Palace in Gubbio, ca. 1478–1482. The Metropolitan Museum of Art acquired the work in 1939. The studio was reinstalled at the Met in 1996. The room was commissioned by Duke Federico da Montefeltro, a major geopolitical force in North-Central Italy during his lifetime.[62] The small room was intended for meditation and study, its size roughly 15′ × 12′ (Plate 7.1).[63] The Studiolo remained in the Palazzo at Gubbio until 1874, when it was disassembled and moved to a villa in Frascati.[64] If interested in knowing more about the room and re-installation, an excellent resource by Olga Raggio provides an in-depth presentation of the process, *The Gubbio Studiolo and Its Conservation Vol 1, Federico da Montefeltro's Palace at Gubbio and Its Studiolo*.[65]

The studio walls are carried out in the wood-inlay technique known as intarsia. This technique was mentioned at the beginning of this chapter pertaining to the Italian Renaissance aesthetic. For this studio's walls, a variety of woods were used—walnut, beech, rosewood, oak, and fruitwoods in a walnut base. The intarsia cabinets display objects reflecting Duke Federico's wide-ranging artistic and scientific interests, and the depiction of books recall his extensive library.[66] This room may have been designed by Francesco di Giorgio (1439–1502) and was executed by Giuliano da Maiano (1435–1490).[67]

This concludes Chapter 7 and a look at Renaissance Italy, France, and England. As mentioned, the Renaissance is succeeded by the Early Modern period. Chapter 8 begins at this point in the 18th century. The pictorial timeline pieces will be dedicated to 18th-century, Italy, France, and England, and Late Colonial America. Several of the furniture pieces in Chapter 8 will be familiar because they were introduced in Chapter 3.

Renaissance

Plate 7.1
(above) The Gubbio Studiolo, ca. 1478–1482. From Ducal Palace in Gubbio. Entrance of the studiolo with walls using illusionistic intarsia panels depicting latticed cupboards holding a variety of books, scientific and musical instruments, and other objects. *(below)* Room view with visible window.

Source: Metropolitan Museum of Art, New York. Studiolo from the Ducal Palace in Gubbioca. Public Domain OA [Open Access]. Rogers Fund, 1939.

NOTES

1. Robbie G. Blakemore, *History of Interior Design & Furniture: From Ancient Egypt to Nineteenth-Century Europe* (New Jersey: John Wiley & Sons, 2006), p.91.
2. H.D. Molesworth and John Kenworthy-Browne, *Three Centuries of Furniture in Color* (New York: A Studio Book, The Viking Press), p.11.
3. Ibid.
4. Robbie G. Blakemore, *History of Interior Design & Furniture: From Ancient Egypt to Nineteenth-Century Europe* (New Jersey: John Wiley & Sons), p.91.
5. https://en.wikipedia.org/wiki/Italian_Renaissance.
6. Ibid.
7. Robert Bishop and Patricia Coblentz, *The Smithsonian Illustrated Library of Antiques. Furniture I: Prehistoric Through Rococo* (New York: Cooper-Hewitt Museum, The Smithsonian Institution's National Design Museum, 1979), p.35.
8. Ibid.
9. Tim Forrest ... [et al.]. *The Bulfinch Anatomy of Antique Furniture: An Illustrated Guide to Identifying Period, Detail, and Design* (New York: A Bulfinch Press Book, Little, Brown and Company, 1996), p.68.
10. Robert Bishop and Patricia Coblentz, *The Smithsonian Illustrated Library of Antiques. Furniture I: Prehistoric Through Rococo* (New York: Cooper-Hewitt Museum, The Smithsonian Institution's National Design Museum, 1970), p.35.
11. Ibid.
12. On-line Collection, Object Label, The Frick Collection, New York, 2020.
13. Ibid.
14. Robert Bishop and Patricia Coblentz, *The Smithsonian Illustrated Library of Antiques. Furniture I: Prehistoric Through Rococo* (New York: Cooper-Hewitt Museum, The Smithsonian Institution's National Design Museum, 1979), p.41.
15. https://en.wikipedia.org/wiki/Girolamo_Savonarola.
16. On-line Collection, Object Label, Cooper-Hewitt, Smithsonian Design Museum, New York, 2020.
17. Robbie G. Blakemore, *History of Interior Design & Furniture: From Ancient Egypt to Nineteenth-Century Europe* (New Jersey: John Wiley & Sons, 2006), p.109.
18. On-line Collection, Object Label, Cooper-Hewitt, Smithsonian Design Museum, New York, 2020.
19. https://en.wikipedia.org/wiki/French_Renaissance.
20. Frederick Litchfield, *Illustrated History of Furniture: From the Earliest to the Present Time*, fifth ed. (www.gutenberg.org/files/60369/60369-h/60369-h.htm), p.58.
21. Ibid.
22. Ibid.
23. Ibid.
24. Robbie G. Blakemore, *History of Interior Design & Furniture: From Ancient Egypt to Nineteenth-Century Europe* (New Jersey: John Wiley & Sons, 2006), p.121.
25. Ibid., p.122.
26. www.European-furniture-styles.com/French-Renaissance-Furniture.html.
27. On-Line Collection, Object Label, Philadelphia Museum of Art, Philadelphia, Pennsylvania, 2020.
28. On-line Collection, Object Label, Metropolitan Museum of Art, New York, New York, 2020
29. Ibid.
30. Ibid.
31. https://en.wikipedia.org/wiki/English_Renaissance.
32. Robbie G. Blakemore, *History of Interior Design & Furniture: From Ancient Egypt to Nineteenth-Century Europe* (New Jersey: John Wiley & Sons, 2006), p.128.

33 Ibid.
34 Ibid.
35 Frederick Litchfield, *Illustrated History of Furniture: From the Earliest to the Present Time*, fifth ed. (www.gutenberg.org/files/60369/60369-h/60369-h.htm), p.72.
36 Ibid.
37 https://en.wikipedia.org/wiki/English_Renaissance.
38 https://en.wikipedia.org/wiki/Field_of_the_Cloth_of_Gold.
39 Frederick Litchfield, *Illustrated History of Furniture: From the Earliest to the Present Time*, fifth ed. (www.gutenberg.org/files/60369/60369-h/60369-h.htm), p.72.
40 https://en.wikipedia.org/wiki/English_Renaissance.
41 Robbie G. Blakemore, *History of Interior Design & Furniture: From Ancient Egypt to Nineteenth-Century Europe* (New Jersey: John Wiley & Sons, 2006), p.129.
42 Martin M. Pegler, *Dictionary of Interior Design* (New York: Fairchild Publication, 2006), p.159.
43 Ibid.
44 On-line, Collection, Object label, Philadelphia Museum of Art, Philadelphia, Pennsylvania, 2020.
45 Ibid.
46 Mark Hinchman, *History of Furniture: A Global View* (New York: Fairchild Books, 2009), p.270.
47 Robbie G. Blakemore, *History of Interior Design & Furniture: From Ancient Egypt to Nineteenth-Century Europe* (New Jersey: John Wiley & Sons, 2006), p.149.
48 Martin M. Pegler, *Dictionary of Interior Design* (New York: Fairchild Publication, 2006), p.260.
49 Mark Hinchman, *History of Furniture a Global View* (New York: Fairchild Books, 2009), p.270.
50 Robbie G. Blakemore, *History of Interior Design & Furniture: From Ancient Egypt to Nineteenth-Century Europe* (New Jersey: John Wiley & Sons, 2006), p.151.
51 On-line Open Image Collection, Object Label, Victoria and Albert Museum, London, England, 2020.
52 Ibid.
53 Ibid.
54 Mark Hinchman, *History of Furniture: A Global View* (New York: Fairchild Books, 2009), p.270.
55 On-line Open Image Collection, Object Label, Victoria and Albert Museum, London, England, 2020.
56 Ibid.
57 Ibid.
58 Ibid.
59 Ibid.
60 Ibid.
61 www.vam.ac.uk/articles/great-bed-of-ware.
62 https://en.wikipedia.org/wiki/Studiolo_from_the_Ducal_Palace_in_Gubbio.
63 On-line Open Image Collection, Object Label, Metropolitan Museum of Art, New York, 2020.
64 https://en.wikipedia.org/wiki/Studiolo_from_the_Ducal_Palace_in_Gubbio.
65 Olga Raggio, *The Gubbio Studiolo and Its Conservation Vol 1, Federico da Montefeltro's Palace at Gubbio and Its Studiolo* (Metropolitan Museum of Art/Yale University Press, 2000).
66 On-line Open Image Collection, Object Label, Metropolitan Museum of Art, New York, 2020.
67 Ibid.

8 18th century

Italy, France, England, and America—Late Colonial

8.1
Pictorial timeline—18th century: Italy, France, England, and America—Late Colonial

TIME PERIOD OVERVIEW

To begin the discussion of the pictorial timeline above depicting 18th-century European furniture for Italy, France, and England, the preceding historical period must be touched upon (Timeline 8.1). This is particularly important in respect to Italy and its impact on 18th-century Italian furniture and interiors. The Baroque period follows the Renaissance and precedes the 18th-century Rococo style in France, and Queen Anne and Georgian in England. The origins of Baroque formal and aesthetic direction are associated with the Counter-Reformation when the Catholic Church launched an overtly emotional sensory appeal to the faithful through architecture in response to the Protestant Reformation.[1] Keeping this in mind, the vocabulary of Antiquity prevalent in Renaissance architecture and interiors during the Baroque was used in a new rhetorical fashion, highly decorative and theatrical. It was characterized by new explorations of form, light, and shadow. This plasticity of form possessed a dramatic intensity.

The Baroque style remained in Italy longer than elsewhere.[2] This can possibly be attributed to the first half of the 18th century when most of the Italian state came under the control of Spain and Austria. Only Venice, Genoa, and Lucca remained independent. The Italian noble landowners were conservative, and the Baroque style was favored.[3] There is no dividing line between the late 17th century and the early 18th century in the history of Italian furniture.[4] The grandiose palace furniture, especially console tables, made in the first three decades of the new century seem to have differed little from those that had become popular in the 1600s.

However, the desire for splendor continued unabated in the 18th century.[5] This can be said for Genoa, Lucca, and Venice, the regions that remained independent from Spain and Austria. This idea of splendor can be clearly seen in Venetian Rococo furniture. Venice produced especially unusual Rococo furniture.[6] Venetian Rococo was well known for being rich and luxurious, with usually very extravagant designs.

The timeline secretary is an example of the indelible Venetian Rococo style. Venetian design was the embodiment of the effusive Rococo style, which remained fashionable in Venice after its popularity had waned elsewhere.[7]

The aesthetic direction of decorative arts—interiors and furniture design in 18th-century France is influenced by the Capetian Dynasty, the House of Bourbon's three monarchs Louis XIV (1643–1715), Louis XV (1715–1774), and Louis XVI (1774–1792). Louis XIV is the French monarch associated with Baroque, making it the style of the court—a staunch style with pageantry, pomp, and formality. Furniture and interiors were bold, big, and ornate, the palette colorful and rich. Under Philippe II, Duke of Orléans, who served as regent until Louis XV was crowned in 1723, the Baroque gave way to the transitional Régence. The Régence styling reflects the heaviness of Louis XIV furniture but anticipates the more delicate style of Louis XV evolving into the Rococo style.[8]

The transition to Rococo can be attributed to Philippe II not favoring the restrictive lifestyle of Versailles and moving the court back to Paris. In Paris, the aristocrats enjoyed a less restrictive lifestyle in the *hôtels particuliers*, the elegant townhouses that were the centers of life away from court.[9] The Parisian *hôtel particulier* was on a smaller scale than a palace, the rooms were less formal, the furniture was scaled down to proportionally work within the room, both in terms of form and robustness in decorative detail. Thus, the transition to Rococo is associated with Louis XV.

Rococo-style furniture was designed for the human body, not for pageantry, and was therefore delicate and diminutive in scale. Lighter colors were used for walls and upholstery. The ornamentation included the use of sinuous lines enlacing

C-shape and *S*-shape minute decorative details, and gild-bronze (ormolu) became a metal of choice for fittings. The use of straight lines, Classical orders, and symmetry were replaced with the fanciful and exotic ornamentation, yet these were light and elegant. Toward the end of Louis XV's reign, during the last 15 years or so, there was a dramatic change in style.[10] The Rococo style was replaced by a new sobriety and an even more rigorous respect for Classical principles.[11] A large contributor to the return to Classicism was the excitement over the discoveries and excavations of Herculaneum and Pompeii. The excavation of Pompeii began properly in the 1750s. Louis XVI is the French monarch associated with moving the decorative style in architecture and decorative arts back to Greco-Roman Classicism. Furniture and rooms were designed with Classical orders, and curved forms and sinuous lines were replaced by straight and rectangular shapes. The one area that remained similar was the scale and proportion of rooms and furniture, which remained the same in scale as Rococo.

In England, the same could be said about the 18th-century aesthetic direction of decorative arts—interiors and furniture—as for France. The English monarchs had impact on its outcome. Eighteenth-century England is influenced by the House of Hanover, the reigns of George I (1714–1727), George II (1727–1760), and George III (1760–1820). This period 1714–1830 is historically called the Georgian era or period. This eponymous label reflects various stylistic phases including Rococo, Palladian, and Neoclassical.

The first true style of the English Rococo period is named after Queen Anne (1702–1714). The Queen Anne style was the first to emphasize the curving forms of the French Rococo, yet subdued, as well as modifying the shapely French Rococo silhouette. But it was during the reigns of George I and George II that Rococo reigned supreme.[12] Early–mid-Georgian interiors and furnishing reflected the accomplished French Rococo furniture designs, yet translated with characteristic British restraint. English designs modified the fanciful, exotic style and shapely silhouettes of French Rococo into more subdued curves and minimal decoration. In England, proportions were broader, visible in wider chair backs and seats, and the less delicate cabriole leg terminating with claw-and-ball foot.

Seminal to English design throughout the 18th century was the omnipotent pattern book which was discussed in depth in Chapter 3. These publications guided popular taste in furniture design and influenced interiors. As a result of such books and the rise of influential architects, cabinetmakers, and their workshops, these decades were considered the "Golden Age of English design."[13] Witnessed during this period was the country's most exceptional design achievements in architecture, interiors, furniture design, and construction.

By the reign of George III, around the 1770s, England would see the revival of Classicism—the Neoclassical movement. The English had a reaction to the Rococo like the French. There came to be a predilection for the linear, the symmetrical, and low relief as opposed to the plasticity. The Rococo style was becoming replaced with ordered arrangements, simplicity, and quiet distinction.

To conclude the **Time period overview** of 18th-century Italy, France, and England, it would be helpful to keep in mind that the close proximity of European countries including across the English Channel greatly influenced the development of architecture, furniture, and decorative arts among regions and nations. For the pictorial timeline, 18th-century America—Late Colonial pieces, the **Time period overview** will be combined with its **History** section.

18th-century Italy

History

As mentioned earlier, the Baroque style suited the tastes and conservative attitude of Italian noblemen and landowners, and consequently cabinetmakers in Italy used the concepts of Baroque design long after they had fallen out of favor in France. The new Rococo style was acknowledged by 1730–1750, and 18th-century Italian Rococo reflected the opulent lifestyles enjoyed by the country's leading citizens. Dazzling furnishing, capricious beyond description, were created for their magnificent palazzos.

Furniture was embellished with decorative lacquerwork, colorful paintwork, and extravagant carved details. These features are visible on the pictorial timeline pieces. The styles of furniture varied considerably from one region to another. Craftsmen in Piedmont were strongly influenced by neighboring France, and Genoese furniture was renowned for its skillful construction.[14] Furniture form Lombardy was more sober and severe, whereas Venetian furniture was theatrical and colorful.[15]

Italian Rococo furniture was usually upholstered with rich and colorful fabrics, such as velvet and silk, and furniture was often lacquered. Console and side tables, however, remained very similar to the Baroque ones, often very rich in decoration, with caryatids and putti, and carvings gilded in gold and bronze. The furniture would be placed against the wall in the halls and galleries of the palazzos. Walls, ceilings, and floors were treated as opulently as the furnishing. The Venetian bedroom was held in high esteem and usually was sumptuous and grand, with rich damask, velvet and silk drapery and curtains, and, most important, a beautifully carved Rococo bed with statues of putti, flowers, and angels.

Console table, ca. 1700–1725, Rome, Italy

Aesthetics

The 18th-century Italian furniture style varied considerably from one region to another. The first pictorial timeline piece is a late Baroque console table—at times referred to as a pier table if used in conjunction with a pier mirror. The table's exuberant quality is the epitome of late Baroque table design. Late Baroque furniture took on a sculptural appearance—extremely plastic. As mentioned earlier, this plasticity of form possessed a dramatic visual intensity. This quality is evident in the table's robust carved legs, stretcher, and central demon mask. The motifs are exaggerated. Larger-than-life carvings, such as busts and masks, scrolls, floral

■ An Illustrated Guide to Furniture History

sprays, and wood-carved lambrequins, embellished tables. The boldly carved pieces were often gilded, lacquered, or painted, such as this console table. The gilding was often used to create an illusion that a piece was entirely made of precious metal.

Furniture

This **console table**, ca. 1700–1725, Rome, Italy, resides at the Metropolitan Museum of Art (Figure 8.1). Large console tables were an obligatory feature of the parade of rooms in aristocratic Italian palaces throughout the 18th century.[16] They were typically ordered in pairs or sometimes even a set of four, often with mirrors above (pier table). The concept of pairing tables was to achieve a perfect symmetry for the room.[17] The Italian console table was placed against a wall, unlike the French console table which is often attached to the wall.

Figure 8.1
Console table, Italian, Rome, ca. 1700–1725. Gilded linden and poplar, green porphyry, gilt-bronze, 38½" × 69¼" × 27¾".

Source: Metropolitan Museum of Art, New York, Public Domain OA [Open Access] Department of European Sculpture and Decorative Arts (43.0840).

Noticeable on this console table are boldly scrolled legs carved with female busts wearing light-catching tiaras contrast with the almost weightless look of the fanciful stretchers and pierced apron friezes.[18] The latter incorporates wing-shaped lambrequins and floral sprays over elongated scrolls with a central theatrical demon mask.[19] The gilding of the legs, stretcher, and apron give the illusion that the entire piece is a precious metal. Lastly, a textural gilt-bronze border brilliantly frames the colorful green porphyry stone, perfectly completing the bold and plastic form.

Armchair, ca. 1730–1740, Venice, Italy

Aesthetics

Next, the discussion focuses on the second piece on the pictorial timeline—a gilt armchair, one of four. Although the maker is unknown, the set of armchairs is believed to be Venetian. This timeline piece has strong stylistic Venetian Rococo features which by mid-century transitioned from a heavier Baroque style toward the more graceful and voluptuous form of the Rococo.[20] Furniture design became a combination of exuberant and delicate forms. The French Rococo style served as model, and the French forms and motifs were thus interpreted Venetian style—most notably, the French Rococo cartouche chair back and cabriole leg and other such motifs such as the formed *C*-scroll and *S*-scroll that interlace sinuously with the carved flowers, scallop shells, and garlands as stylized leaves. The use of gold leaf on furniture was more prevalent in Italy than France, but, like the French gilt-bronze (ormolu), was the metal of choice for fittings.

Furniture

The **armchair**, ca. 1730–1740, Venice, Italy, is from the J. Paul Getty Museum collection (Figure 8.2). It is believed to be the work of sculptor Antonio Corradini

218

18th century

Figure 8.2 Armchair, Italian, ca. 1730–1740. A set of four. Carved, gessoed, and gilt walnut with upholstery, 55¼″ × 33½″ × 34¾″.

Source: J. Paul Getty Museum, Los Angeles, California. Open Content Program. Alexander & Berendt Ltd. (London, England), sold to the J. Paul Getty Museum, 1987.

because scholars have been able to attribute to this artist a number of side chairs, consoles, tales, and a throne.[21] The medium is carved gesso and gilt walnut, with upholstery in modern Genoese velvet. The scale of furniture for Venetian palaces and or palazzos was large, no different from palatial estates and or palaces in France and England. The size of the armchair is evidence of this, its back nearly five feet tall—the overall size is H 55¼″ × L 33½″ × D 34¾″.

One of the most striking features of the armchair is its cartouche back and its duplicitous nature, both exuberant and delicate. This armchair's silhouette has a distinctive serpentine outline, a perfect example of mid-18th-century Venetian furniture.

Visible are the splendid carvings with no distinction as to where the curvilinear carving begins or ends, all seamlessly moving into *S*-shapes and *C*-shapes at the crest of the back, the arms, and cabriole legs. The result is sinuous harmony and a remarkable chair.

Desk (secretary), ca. 1730–1735, Venice, Italy

Aesthetics

The last timeline piece for Italy is a Venetian desk (secretary), ca. 1730–1750. The Venetian secretary shape was influenced by English and Dutch examples.[22] What became unique in respect to the Venetian aesthetic was the use of polychrome furniture surfaces—meaning they were painted, printed, or decorated in several colors. The decoration could be painted, lacquered, or découpage known as *lacca povera or lacca contrafatta* in Italian.[23] The word *découpage* is fashioned from Middle French *decouper,* meaning "to cut out." "Decouper," in turn, pastes together the prefix *de-* ("from" or "away") and "couper" ("to cut").[24] This Venetian secretary is a phenomenal example of découpage. The genre for découpage treatment most often depicts rather realistically scenes or events from everyday life, pastoral landscapes, and/or cityscapes.

Furniture

The **desk (secretary)**, ca. 1730–1735, Venice, Italy, is from the Metropolitan Museum of Art. This is a splendid representation of Venetian furniture of its type and style. The two views are of the fall front closed and open (Figure 8.3). The medium is pine and linden wood. Its splendid quality begins with the carved finials adorning the top. The form on all sides is outlined with gilded trim. It is a tall piece with overall dimensions H 102″ × W 44″ × D 23″.[25] Keep in mind that Venetian palace and/or palazzo furniture was large scale.

Other features that add to the secretary's splendor are the arched doors with gold trim and mirror glass. The glass doors accentuate the height and assist proportionally to this visually balanced piece. Venetian mirrors were considered master pieces of art, painstakingly produced in a highly involved process.[26] Lastly, the defining feature—and most fascinating—is the colored découpage throughout the piece. Seen here is the use of Orientalism—imitating figures and motifs of the Eastern world. The genre is pastoral and the découpage looks convincingly like lacquered furniture. This is amazing considering the scenes are cutouts and pasted to the surface and varnished.

Figure 8.3
(Left) Desk (secretary) Italian, Venice, ca. 1730–1735. Fall front, mirrored glass. Pine, carved, painted, gilded and varnished linden wood decoration with colored decoupage prints. Overall: 102″ × 44″ × 23″. *(right)* Desk with doors open and fall front down.

Source: Metropolitan Museum of Art, New York, Department of European Sculpture and Decorative Arts. Public Domain OA [Open Access]. Fletcher Fund, 1925.

What makes these pieces 18th-century Italian?

Once the furniture moved beyond the Baroque form of expression and ornament, Italian furniture was influenced by the French Régence and Louis XV French Rococo style. The Italian interpretation resulted in dazzling furnishing and very extravagant designs. The furniture form was bold and exuberant, and had meticulously carved details that could be considered delicate at times—duplicitous in nature like the Venetian armchair. Although there were regional differences with 18th-century Italian furniture, collectively it can be described as extravagant in form and ornamentation. Particularly, Venetian furniture was most theatrical and colorful—capricious beyond description. The Venetian cabinetmaker's pieces were typically embellished with decorative lacquerwork and colorful paintwork, as seen with the secretary. Overall, what is important when identifying 18th-century Italian furniture is remembering that its visual quality is theatrical, extravagant in form and ornamental detail, colorful, and the materials are rich and luxurious.

18th century France—Rococo, ca. 1723–1774

History

As mentioned in the **Time period overview**, the French Rococo style flourished in the years following the transitional period of the Régence where Baroque forms were being gradually modified.[27] During this period in the 18th century, France continued to be the arbiter of style and a center for furniture design that influenced all of Europe.[28] Intrinsic to France's role at this point is the economic and societal positioning of the bourgeoisie, the French middle class. In 18th-century France, the middle class came to own much of society's wealth and means of production. Having attained a new financial position, the bourgeoisie began to emulate the newly established manner of life.[29] The encreasing affluence of the bourgeoisie led to increasing number of sumptuous dwellings, which in turn called for vast quantities of furntiure with myriad forms and purposes.[30] Private settings became desired with smaller rooms and furniture, and the atmosphere was intimte and informal.

Pivotal to the change in social attitudes, and the decorative arts, architecture, and interiors, was the role of women associated with King Louis XV. Historically speaking, women faced a life of limited opporunity, and few were capable of surpassing the traditional roles and gain power and influence.[31] However, Jeanne-Antionette Poisson rose beyond her bourgeoisie status to become the Marquise de Pompadour and gained the title of *maitresse-en-titre* to Louis XV, King of France.[32] Between 1745 and 1750, Madame de Pompadour became the king's mistress and remained powerful as the king's confidante until her death in 1764.[33] Madame de Pompadour has widely been known as a patron of the arts and literature, and influenced architecture and decorative arts during her time at court. While at court, Madame de Pompadour became the arbiter of fashion and the Rococo style. Under Madame de Pompadour's influence both at court and in private residences, the salon and social gatherings became the ritual.[34] And a new social attitude began to assert itself; the direction was toward relaxation and pleasure, and this led to subsequent changes in the arts.[35] Furniture reflected a desire for personal comfort and an interest in conversation, and convenience. There became a demand for private settings that were intimate and informal, with smaller rooms and smaller furniture. This change can be attributed to Madame de Pompadour's sense of femininity. Rococo is femininely characterized by elegance, lightness; it is fanciful and even at times fantastical. And, importantly, the execution of curvilinear minute decorative details such as *C*-scrolls and *S*-scrolls interlaced with shells, plant leaves, and floral motifs defined decoration and the ornamental approach.

To conclude, it is important to mention that an unparalleled level of perfection in craftsmanship prevailed during the period of Louis XV. During the 17th century, guilds were important in establishing stringent requirements in order to attain the master level of competence. However, in the 18th century, France statutes passed in 1730 and validated by Parliament in 1751 made it mandatory for the stamp of the master to appear on furniture as verification of its having come from the hand of a specific craftsman.

Console table, ca. 1735, Paris, France; armchair, 1754–1756, Paris, France; and commode, ca. 1765–1770, French

Aesthetics
The aesthetic explanation given here for France will apply to all three pieces on the pictorial timeline. Progressing from transitional Régence to the fully matured French

Rococo style aesthetically, the infallible characteristics of symmetry, straight lines, and Classical orders were replaced with asymmetry and curvilinear form. The decorative motifs and ornament are interlaced by use of the curvilinear—sinuous lines, undulating and serpentine. The interlacing quality of the curvilinear is the element of datum which delineates the Rococo style. This quality applies to everything, a furniture piece, decorative arts object, and interior envelope—all wall planes.

Rococo style furniture such as commodes and console tables will often have a serpentine silhouette. Seating pieces have a voluptuous form. Specific ornamental features and decorative details, as mentioned previously, are interlacing shells, plants, leaves, and floral motifs. The prevailing ornamental vocabulary is the use of the minutely carved *C*-scroll and *S*-scroll motifs connecting foliage with vine-like sinuous lines. Most often, Rococo is femininely characterized by elegance and lightness, and is fanciful and at times fantastical.

Furniture

The **console table**, ca. 1735, Paris, France, is attributed to French designer François Roumier (1701–1748). This first timeline example for French Rococo furniture is from the Art Institute of Chicago collection (Figure 8.4). The symmetric design of this table is reminiscent of the Baroque formality and identifies the piece as early French Rococo—transitioning from French Régence. Another feature of the console that indicates it is a transitional piece is that its appearance is visually broad. This absence of a slightness in form appears Baroque. The fanciful Rococo quality is not present here yet but will come a few years later, as will the asymmetry—both are indications of a mature Rococo style.

Figure 8.4
Console table, ca. 1700–1725, Italian, Rome. Gilded linden and gilt-bronze, with green porphyry stone. Size 38½″ × 69¼″ × 27¾″.

Source: Art Institute of Chicago, Department, European Decorative Arts, Gift of K. Wrigley through The Antiquarian Society.

However, the ornamentation and decorative motifs' impeccable articulation is noticeably Rococo. Observe the serpentine marble top and curvilinear carved ornament; next, the use of the carved *C*-scrolls and *S*-scrolls that shape the apron, legs, and stretcher. Also observe the central shell motif at the apron's center and center of the base stretcher. Lastly, notice the carved foliage interlacing all motifs seen at the apron, legs, and stretcher—all connecting sinuously. These qualities are unabashedly the French Rococo style.

The **Rococo armchair**, ca. 1753, France, is the next piece discussed and will seem familiar because it was introduced in Chapter 4 (Figure 4.10). The armchair is from the Boiserie from the Hôtel de Varengeville, Metropolitan Museum of Art, period room (Figure 8.5).

It is the quintessential *fauteuil* (armchair). A *fauteuil* will have upholstered arms that are slightly set back from the seat, with open sides and a cartouche-shaped back, as seen in this chair. The type of leg is cabriole shape and the wood that forms the legs continues as wood trim moving around the frame of the chair.

18th century

Figure 8.5
French armchair, 18th century, Louis XV, Rococo, ca. 1753. One of two made for Baron Johann Ernst Bernstorff, Dutch Ambassador to the court of Versailles. Beech wood, gilded gold frame, Beauvais tapestry upholstery.

Source: Metropolitan Museum of Art, New York, The Boiserie Hôtel de Varengeville, from the Period Room. French, Paris, ca. 1736–1752. Public Domain OA [Open Access]. Gift of John D. Rockefeller Jr., 1935.

This armchair illustrates this feature brilliantly. Its medium is beechwood, and frame is gilded gold.

It is normative for the wood of a *fauteuil* to be left natural, gilded gold, or painted. This frame is exquisitely carved with interlacing shells, foliage, and floral motifs, Notice the ubiquitous C-scrolls and S-scrolls seen on the chair's back frame and elsewhere, and lastly the delicately carved scroll foot. The scale is similar in size to a contemporary lounge chair. Its provenance fortunately is known; as mentioned previously, it is one of a two chairs made for the Dutch Ambassador to the court of Versailles.

This **commode**, ca. 1765–1770, French, will also appear familiar since it was introduced in Chapter 3 (Figure 3.9). It is attributed to Léonard Boudin (French, 1735–1807, master 1761) and Pierre-Antoine Foullet (French, 1746–1809).[36] It is an exquisite piece veneered in marquetry and ornamented with gilt-bronze mounts (ormolu), and its form displays the typical French Rococo 18th-century commode features—low, wider than it is tall, and placed on short cabriole legs (Figure 8.6).

Figure 8.6
Commode, ca. 1765–1770, French. Attributed to Léonard Boudin and Pierre-Antoine Foullet. Veneered marquetry with gilt-bronze mounts.

Source: Metropolitan Museum of Art, New York. Public Domain OA [Open Access]. Lehman Collection, 1975.

However, this commode's form, decorative motifs, and ornamental application places the piece toward the end of the French Rococo period. This is noticeable when examining its silhouette which is less curvaceous than earlier commode forms. There is a very slight serpentine front—a soft approach. The same can be said for the short cabriole legs. Their shape and gilt-bronze decoration (mounts) work together seamlessly, yet the curve of the leg is gentle, barely distinguished. Additionally, the adornment of interlacing gilt-bronze foliage abreast the marquetry is alluring and graceful, yet the C-scroll and S-scroll have become inexact here.

Toward the end of the 18th century, Neoclassicism resurfaces with vigor. The marquetry design is Classically referenced, which is a strong indicator of time. Visible on the right and left sides of the commode are Classical urns with different shapes, adjacent is an obelisk, and lastly there is an image of a building ruin with a round arch entrance—all placed concisely within the landscape scene.

The reason the Museum scholars state that this may be the work of French cabinetmaker Pierre-Antoine Foullet is that he was known for elaborate case pieces embellished with Classical urns or floral ornament, and landscape scenes with architectural ruins.[37] In the late 1760s, Foullet often worked in collaboration with Léonard Boudin, who suppled him with furniture to be veneered.[38] The medium is oak and pine veneered with stained maple, tulipwood, amaranth, and holly stringing, with marquetry of stained, shaded, and engraved maple, mahogany, amaranth, barberry and other marquetry woods. Mounts are gilt-bronze, the top is marble, and the rollers are brass.[39] The approximate size is 34½" × 48" × 24".[40]

What makes these pieces 18th-century French?

The Rococo style is the defining style for 18th-century France. It is a style that is easily identifiable and most original. Its features are designed to make an impression both pleasurable and stimulating. French Rococo furniture physiognomy is one of the easiest to implant in the mind because the specific features are somewhat formulaic—same decorative motifs and ornamental approach. Remembering these features will allow for a flawless identification. To begin, think curvilinear. Straight lines are replaced with curves—not only for furniture, but room shapes (corners), wall paneling (boiserie), moldings, and trim. There is a wholistic aesthetic approach from micro to macro, from object to room. French Rococo furniture has a shapely silhouette. Both silhouette and surface details are curvilinear, such as the serpentine curved fronts on consoles or commodes, the softly curved cabriole leg, and carved surface curvilinear motifs—natural forms. Forms like the *C*-scrolls and *S*-scrolls, shells, foliage, and bouquets acutely connected, interlaced by sinuous vine-like lines. The armchair from the timeline is a successful demonstration of this. Also, remember the hallmark for the style is asymmetrical. The ornamental application is asymmetrically arranged. Lastly and importantly, the overall appearance of a French Rococo piece will be light, elegant, fanciful, and, at times, fantastical.

18th-century England—Georgian Period, George I–George III

History

In 18th-century England, several factors converged to influence art, architecture, interiors, decorative arts, and furniture design. First, changes in England's political climate (Act of Settlement 1701) solidified the ruling Hanoverians, beginning with George I. Second, regarding the arts, the leading political party, the Whigs, promulgated the Classical cannon. Additionally, the power and prestige of the upper classes based on ownership of land and construction of country houses was a large influence. Country houses were stylistic models of the richer landowners who brought the latest fashions in furniture and new forms in architecture to their county seats.[41] All effected changes in furniture design, as did influence of French furniture design, the publication of furniture pattern books, and the leadership of native designers.[42]

As mention in the **Time period overview** in this chapter, the English version of the Rococo begins with the ruling monarch Queen Anne (1702–1714). Queen Anne style was the first to emphasize French Rococo curving forms, yet modifying the French style with British restraint. After Anne's death in 1714, thus ensues the Early Georgian period. The political party in power (Whig) became influential in matters of taste.[43] Salient was the Classical cannon during this time and the nascent architectural principles of Andrea Palladio. This Classical language was perpetuated by native designers—influential architects and cabinetmakers—and the publications of pattern books. The decades from George II to George III define the "Golden Age of English Furniture design" and a defining switch in medium from walnut to mahogany. Three important cabinetmakers are distinguished during this "Golden Age of English Furniture Design"—Chippendale, Hepplewhite, and Sheraton, already discussed in Chapter 3. Common pieces of furniture are side tables with marble tops, chairs with wide seats and splat backs, and breakfront case pieces, etc.

To summarize, from the Early Georgian to Late Georgian period numerous stylistic phases occur in architecture, interior design, decorative arts, and furniture design, such as Baroque, Palladian, Rococo, Chippendale, and Neoclassical. Intrinsic to these stylistic phases was the Classical cannon—Classical orders, use of symmetry, Classical proportions, Greco-Roman motifs used for ornament and decoration etc. However, it is perfectly acceptable to use the general classification of Georgian (Early–Late). Applying the general classification of Georgian, style, era, or period will serve one best on the journey to become erudite.

Gilt gold sofa, 1765, London, England; mahogany breakfront bookcase, 1764, London, England; and side chair, "ribband-back," ca. 1755–1760, British

Aesthetics

This aesthetic explanation will apply to all three English furniture pieces on the pictorial timeline. These furniture examples fit within the "Golden Age of English Furniture Design." What should come to mind visually regarding aesthetics is highly finished and sophisticated designs. The vocabulary is that of Classicism yet restrained. The restraint can be attributed to size. The English homes, although large in area, are smaller and more modest buildings than the Greco-Roman Classical architype—temples, halls, and baths.

Salient features of the Georgian style can be characterized succinctly. Mahogany is the wood of choice for the cabinetmaker; near the end of the 18th century fruitwood and satinwood were also used. Symmetry is a necessary component, mathematical ratios where applied for form making, which influence the piece's proportion and brought about visual balance. French furniture was still influential through publications, and therefore features of French furniture were adapted to English fashion. A good example is the design approach for the cabriole leg and variation on furniture feet, such as the English claw-and-ball foot.

Furniture

The **gilt gold sofa**, 1765, London, England, will also look familiar as it was introduced in Chapter 3 (Figure 3.49). It is part of a suite, "the Dundas sofas," 1765, and representative of work done by two of the most renowned designers of 18th-century England—architect Robert Adam and cabinetmaker Thomas Chippendale. The suite was for the London home of Sir Lawrence Dundas, 1st Baronet, at 19 Arlington Street. Robert Adam designed the sofas and Thomas Chippendale supplied the pieces (Figure 8.7).

The original furniture of 19 Arlington Street remained in the family for generations and in June of 2012 several pieces came to auction at Christie's UK, London. The sale was unique, dedicated to the 300th anniversary of Thomas Chippendale's (1718–1779) birth and furniture marking. Christie's printed marketing material made this statement about the event: "To celebrate the genius of Chippendale's designs and the perfection of his execution"—a clear indication of the sentiment for this English cabinetmaker's contribution to Britain's tangible heritage.

Christie's "Dundas sofas" were classified at auction as English Neoclassical furniture and advertised as "One of a pair of George III giltwood sofas," considered the first English Neoclassical pieces designed. This "the first" classification has resulted in the 19 Arlington Street suites of furniture as being highly recognized and valued. The George III Neoclassical classification is a reminder of the numerous stylistic phases occurring during the Georgian period.

Figure 8.7
Neoclassical giltwood sofa. One of a pair designed by Robert Adam. Workshop of Thomas Chippendale, 1765, for Sir Lawrence Dundas.
Source: Christie's Images/Bridgeman Images, 17–19 Garway Road, London W2 4PH, UK.

To reiterate from Chapter 3 the sofa is a voluptuous English Rococo form with the ubiquitous cabriole leg, yet overlaid with unmistakable Classical motifs; carved reading, anthemia, rosettes, and shells, griffins and sphinxes, etc. thus classified as the first English Neoclassical piece designed. The scale of the sofa is generous—H 45½" × W 86" × D 36". The result is a design and execution of extremely high value.

This **mahogany breakfront bookcase**, 1764, London, England, is designed by Thomas Chippendale. This piece will also be familiar, first introduced in Chapter 3 (Figure 3.51 and Figure 3.52). It is fortunate to have two images of the bookcase, especially a recent black-and-white photograph of the bookcase in the home of the owner at the time. The mahogany breakfront bookcase is also from the Dundas 19 Arlington Street collection. This piece sold on June 18, 2008 at Christie's, London

(Figure 8.8). The bookcase passed by family descent to the present owner and was sold by the Trustees of the 3rd Marquess of Zetland Will Trust.[44]

Sir Lawrence Dundas commissioned two mahogany bookcases from Thomas Chippendale, one for Arlington Street and the other for Aske, his estate in Yorkshire. The bookcases were delivered in 1764 and were identical in design with the exception that more expensive glass was used for the Arlington bookcase.[45] This mahogany breakfront bookcase is a brilliant example of cabinetmaker Thomas Chippendale's talent and keen design ability. He masterly produced what are considered the finest mid-century English Rococo and Neoclassical furniture of the time. Chapter 3 can be revisited for a look at Chippendale's background.

Figure 8.8
Mahogany breakfront bookcase design by Robert Adam. Workshop of Thomas Chippendale, 1764, for Sir Lawrence Dundas, 19 Arlington Place, London.
Source: Christie's Images/Bridgeman Images, 17–19 Garway Road, London W2 4PH, UK.

The mahogany breakfront bookcase, 1764, is a large piece— H 109½" × W 133¾" × D 23".[46] The term *breakfront* refers to the forward projection seen in the central section and is why case pieces are referred to as *breakfront*. The proportions on this bookcase are flawless—the top and bottom sections 2:1 and rhythmic symmetry about the central axis. Like the previous sofa design by Robert Adam, it is a mixture of the Classical vocabulary and Rococo style. The Classical is reflected in the pediment top with dentil molding and pilaster-like linear detail, and the paneled dado base with Classical beading and corner. The lively movement in the grain pattern of the mahogany veneer and corner scroll pattern begins the descent into the English Rococo. Also, a Chippendale Rococo signature is the use of a Chinese-style decorative patterning in the muntin design on the glass doors. The Chinese-style decorative motif was popularized with Louis XV French Rococo, known as *chinoiserie* and became popular in England in the mid-Georgian period (George II and George III). Chippendale's chinoiserie furniture over time became known as "Chinese Chippendale."

■ An Illustrated Guide to Furniture History

The last English pictorial timeline piece is a **side chair**, ca. 1755–1760, after the design of Thomas Chippendale. Because of the splat design, this chair type is referred to as a "ribband-back" or "ribbon-back" chair. This side chair is one of a pair and is in the collection of the Metropolitan Museum of Art (Figure 8.9). This ribbon-back chair was also introduced in Chapter 3 (Figure 3.32).

Whether or not his invention, the ribbon-back chair design is most frequently associated with Thomas Chippendale's name.[47] The design was included in all three editions of his notable publication *The Gentleman and Cabinet-Maker's Director*.[48]

The pair have no recorded history before the 1950s, but based on the chair construction, the type of mahogany, and the quality of the carving, they are dated to the years immediately following the publication of the *Director*.[49]

Figure 8.9
English Rococo ribbon-back chair, ca. 1755–1760. After the design of Thomas Chippendale.

Source: Metropolitan Museum of Art, New York, Department of European Sculpture and Decorative Arts. Public Domain OA [Open Access]. Gift of Irwin Untermyer, 1964.

The chair has a marvelously duplicitous appearance—delicate details, yet a visually powerful form. This intertwinement aesthetically begets a most beatific piece of furniture, seen in its gracefully carved bow at the crest of the back cascading into an annular stylized ribbon pierced splat. Also visible is the slightness of the cabriole leg and scroll foot, yet contradicted by the boldness of the carved knee with well-defined vine and scrollwork gracefully moving downward and terminated sensitively at the carved scrolled foot. It is easy to envision the assiduous craftmanship of Chippendale's workshop for this impeccable piece.

What makes these pieces 18th-century English?

The 18th century is a defining period for English furniture, as mentioned, with several factors converging in art, architecture, and interiors. There is a monumental change in furniture-design features due to a combination of factors, such as mahogany becoming the wood of choice by mid-century for fashion as well as for practical reasons, greater ease of working, relative freedom from warping and instability, and superior color, graining, and finish. And around this time the rise of the renowned cabinetmakers in whose studios new designs were being created for pattern books, providing stylistic choice in both furniture details and decoration—inspiring furniture fashion such as seen in the work of Thomas Chippendale (Figure 8.8), an excellent example of this period. As part of this convergence, French design and Asian motifs became inspiration influencing the English cabinetmakers' treatment of furniture form and decorative detail, of which the exuberant carving and voluptuous English Rococo Gilt Gold Sofa (Figure 8.7) is a fine example, although for the sofa lime wood was used instead of mahogany. Lastly, the mid-18th century "Age of Mahogany" resonates in the gracefully carved mahogany "ribband-back" side chair (Figure 8.9), with its exquisite decorative detail, carved bow, and cascading ribbon. These timeline pieces are outstanding examples and representative of 18th-century England's tour de force in furniture design.

18th America—Late Colonial, ca. 1720–1780

History and period overview

This last section moves across the Atlantic Ocean to America, Late Colonial period. Aspects of this section will seem familiar since they were introduced in Chapter 3.

This period of American history coexists with the reigns of the House of Bourbon, Louis XIV–Louis XVI, and the Hanoverians, George I–George III. European examples of design are followed in Colonial America, yet the style arrives more than a decade later. Late Colonial American style is defined by Queen Anne, ca. 1720–1780, Chippendale style, 1750–1790, and Rococo style, ca. 1750–1777, referred to as Chippendale Rococo style. By the century's end, as in France and England, Classicism prevailed and in America the furniture style that referenced the Classical vocabulary ushered in the 19th century—the Federal style, ca. 1780–1820.

By the Late Colonial period in America, the rich merchants had become social leaders and patterned their social lives after the aristocrats of the old country, even though they were not of that class in the old country. Their houses, interiors, and furnishings copied the styles of England and the Continent. The middle-class colonists were freemen, and as they became owners of property, they sought after higher-grade furnishings and materials. For this group, furniture, like architecture, became the barometer of mainstream taste.

The physical form of 18th-century American furniture is intrinsically linked to national identity and region. As a result, European prototypes such as Queen Anne and Chippendale Rococo were favored but were given regional features. The American cabinetmaker relied on the pattern books published by the French and English cabinetmakers, architects, and designers, yet were fearless in their interpretation of these designs. The result was an unbridled virtuosity in the design and craftsmanship from northern to southern regions. As mentioned in Chapter 3, the regions of Newport, Boston, Philadelphia, and Charleston designed and produced furniture that expressed regional differences. Fortunately, many pieces are still in existence at cultural institutions and are available for the public to view.

Early Queen Anne bonnet-top secretary, ca. 1750, Boston, Massachusetts

Aesthetics

This first piece from the pictorial timeline is an Early Queen Anne bonnet-top secretary. The furniture features prevalent in England's Queen Anne style are applied to

American furniture. American Queen Anne, like England's Queen Anne style, is a restrained interpretation of French Rococo curvilinearity.[50] There was a softening of the curve, which typically was revealed in the silhouette for certain pieces. American Queen Anne style, like that of England's Queen Anne, had little carving or applied ornament. The wood grain patterning was valued over applied ornament. The cabinetmaker in America also relied on the beauty of the wood grain as the most decorative feature.[51] The idea of an exquisite veneer pattern being a major element of the design and aesthetic is visible on the doors of the timeline piece. American Late Colonial Queen Anne, like the English, incorporated the soft curves of the French Rococo, usually in tall case furniture such as tall chests, secretaries, breakfronts, bookcases, and tall case clocks. The tops of these pieces allowed the soft curve to translate easily through the use of a bonnet or hood—a single, double, or hooded-pediment which is reflected in the case furniture's silhouette. Please refer to Chapter 3's America—Late Colonial section for case piece top configurations (Figure 3.70).

Furniture

This **Early Queen Anne bonnet-top secretary**, ca. 1750, Boston, Massachusetts, is attributed to Benjamin Frothingham. It was introduced in Chapter 3 (Figure 3.85). This Early Queen Anne Bonnet-Top Secretary currently can be viewed at Bernard & S. Dean Levy Inc., New York, a long-established (1901) renowned antique resource (Figure 8.10). This piece excellently demonstrates the restraint and serene essence of Benjamin Frothingham's Early Queen Anne interpretation.

Benjamin Frothingham (1734–1809) presumably was trained in the Boston shop of his father who was a joiner.[52] Frothingham established his own shop in the neighborhood of Charlestown, Boston, Massachusetts, in 1754, and was in business until his death.

This elegant American secretary imbues balanced proportions. Its height is tall at 8 feet—its size overall is W 38½″ × H 98¾″ × D 22″.[53] Typical of secretaries, it has two sections. Above is shelf storage and below a chest of drawers, with a fall front which lowers and becomes a writing surface (Figure 3.85). Behind the fall front are Classically orchestrated pigeonholes and drawers (Figure 3.85).

Between all three sections, including the fall front, there is a calm appearance and sense of balance. The secretary's top portion and bottom

Figure 8.10
Queen Anne bonnet-top secretary, ca. 1750, Boston, Massachusetts, Attributed to Benjamin Frothingham. Primary wood sabicu and mahogany.

Source: Courtesy of Bernard & S. Dean Levy, Inc. Antique Store, New York, N.Y.

portion appear proportionally equal. This can be attributed to several factors, beginning with the graduated drawer size and the richly patterned veneer on the double arched doors which vertically direct the eyes upward. As the eyes move up the double arches, the doors terminate at the bonnet-top pediment.

It is an excellent example of what was discussed under **Aesthetics** about tall case furniture—English and American makers translating at the top of the tall case piece the soft curves of the French Rococo. Lastly, a mention of an impeccable feature: the slender corkscrew finials with spiraling movement which terminate this Early Queen Anne bonnet top secretary majestically.

Chest of drawers (block-front chest), Newport, Rhode Island, ca. 1765

Aesthetics

The second piece on the pictorial timeline is a Newport, Rhode Island, block-and-shell piece. The block-front chest was introduced in Chapter 3 (Figure 3.59). The physiognomy is formulaic. Block-front chests from region to region are remarkably alike in overall design, decorative detail, and construction.

The well-proportioned block appears nearly square from the front view. The front is divided across in three vertical sections that typically have slightly convex left and right ends and a concave center. The form will always rest on feet, either block shape or ogee shape. There will be four drawers, three will graduate in size except the top drawer which ends the vertical sections with shell motifs at the top of each section. The three graduating drawers are void of ornament. Regarding the ubiquitous use of graduated drawers for historic furniture, Graham Blackburn, furnituremaker and publisher (Blackburn Books) states: "Graduated drawer sizes, I should point out, is only one way in which esthetic proportionalism may be achieved and is far from dead." He mentions further: "In the eighteenth century when professional, high-end furniture was made by furniture makers and cabinetmakers who had served long apprenticeships, as much emphasis was placed on proportion as on function and structure." Well-designed furniture emphasizes "Three pillars of Design: Function, Structure, and Proportion."[54]

Aside from the wood grain, the only ornament of the chest of drawers is the brass shape pulls and decorative back plates, scalloped and curvilinear in shape. Most of the brass was manufactured across the Atlantic, in Birmingham, England.[55]

Furniture

This **chest of drawers**, ca. 1765, Newport, Rhode Island, is attributed to John Townsend (1732–1809) and will look familiar as it was also featured in Chapter 3 (Figure 3.59). It is a fine example of American regionalism in furniture making and virtuosity in design and craftsmanship seen from the northern to southern regions of the nation. The piece is from the collection of the Metropolitan Museum of Art (Figure 8.11).

John Townsend was perhaps the greatest master of block-and-shell furniture, the signature style of Rhode Island cabinetmakers.[56] This chest is one of eight known case pieces that he signed or labeled.[57] Two of the pieces, including this one, are dated 1765; the others are from around 1790, suggesting how long-lived this style was.[58]

The harmoniously proportioned chest is the result of several factors, beginning with its squarish front raised on concisely carved scroll feet; next, balanced repetition of the convex and concave three vertical sections ending at the top with its own shell motif. The graduating drawer size also contributes to the proportional harmony. The top and fourth drawer are exempt, yet the shell motifs provide a visual hierarchy and way to end the form. Lastly, the mahogany woodgrain pattern is also important to the proportional harmony. The horizontal wood complements the drawer width, and on the side the vertical grain accentuates its height and depth. For the medium, in addition to mahogany, the secondary woods are tulip poplar, pine, and chestnut. The overall dimension is 34½" × 37½" × 20¾".[59]

Figure 8.11
Chest of drawers, ca. 1765 (block-front-chest). Attributed to John Townsend, Newport, Rhode Island. Mahogany, tulip poplar, pine, and chestnut.

Source: Metropolitan Museum of Art, New York, The American Wing. Public Domain OA [Open Access]. Rogers Fund, 1927.

Side chair, ca. 1769, Philadelphia, Pennsylvania

Aesthetics

From observation of this last piece, a Philadelphia mahogany side chair, with its ample proportions, saddle seat, and scalloped skirts, the chair at first glance appears English.[60] On closer examination, the construction and naturalistic carving communicate quintessentially Philadelphian. The chair's form—the boldness of the curvilinear back and crest, and plasticity of the carved splat—is a testament of its Philadelphia pedigree. Obvious features are the decorative ornament and design motifs of the intricately pierced carved splat with compound curves and surface scrollwork; the virtuosity exercised in all the three-dimensional carved design motifs; the unbridled stylized foliage connecting the skirt of the chair then on to the knee of the cabriole leg terminating in a realistic animal paw foot. This fearless and unbridled approach represents splendidly the American cabinetmaker's virtuosity in interpreting pattern book designs. What must be remembered is the regional differences: the exuberance in carving is characteristic of Philadelphia Chippendale style or Philadelphia Rococo.

Furniture

This next piece, a **side chair**, ca. 1769, Philadelphia, Pennsylvania, is attributed to Benjamin Randolph (1737–1792), possibly carved by Hercules Courtenay

18th century ■

Figure 8.12
Side chair, ca. 1769, Pennsylvania. Attributed to Benjamin Randolph, possibly carved by Hercules Courtenay. Mahogany, northern white cedar, with intricately carved pierced splat and surface scrollwork.

Source: Metropolitan Museum of Art, New York, The American Wing. Public Domain OA [Open Access]. Purchase, Sansbury-Mills and Rogers Funds, Emily Crane Chadbourne Gift, Virginia Groomes Gift, in memory of Mary W. Groomes, Mr. and Mrs. Marshall P. Blankarn, John Bierwith and Robert G. Goelet Gifts, The Sylmaris Collection, Gift of George Coe Graves, by exchange, Gift of Mrs. Russell Sage, by exchange, and funds from various donors, 1974.

(1774–1784). It is another familiar furniture piece from Chapter 3 (Figure 3.85). The chair is from the collection of the Metropolitan Museum of Art (Figure 8.12).

Randolph made furniture in the Queen Anne and Philadelphia Chippendale styles. In 1767, he bought a shop and advertised himself as "cabinetmaker."[61] Benjamin Randolph's clientele were prominent citizens. Randolph was commissioned to make the lap desk on which Jefferson drafted the Declaration of Independence (Figure 3.73).

This chair was made during Philadelphia's "Golden Age" of furniture production. It is quintessential Philadelphian and is part of a well-known suite of furniture made for General John Cadwalader's (1742–1786), house on Second Street.[62] Benjamin Randolph and American cabinetmaker Thomas Affleck were both commissioned to work on the house.[63]

The medium is mahogany with a secondary wood of northern white cedar. Its size is H 37" × W 22½" × D 23".[64] Several key features mentioned under **Aesthetics** categorize the side chair as Philadelphian. But the obvious are the pierced carved splat with compound curves and surface scrollwork, and the virtuosity exercised in the carved design motifs that move from surface to surface, from chair back, arms, seat apron, knee, down the leg, and lastly shape the feet.

It is written that the Cadwalader residence was reputed to have the richest parlor furnishings in pre-Revolutionary Philadelphia[65] and was a splendid and exceptionally pure instance of Rococo-style taste in America.[66] The design achievement of this side chair exemplifies this notion excellently.

What makes these pieces American—Late Colonial?

American furniture can be challenging to identify because the American cabinetmakers emulated the furniture design of Europe, especially England. Therefore, the same characteristics are visible—naturalistic carving, foliage and interlaced patterns, cabriole leg, pierced splat, chinoiserie, etc. Upon first observation, a furniture piece could easily appear English. Additionally, American designs were taken from pattern books purchased from abroad, such as Thomas Chippendale's *The Gentleman and Cabinet-Maker's Director*. Being aware of several aspects will assist this identification. In most regions, with the exception of Philadelphia, American furniture is subdued in respect to form and surface ornamentation— stylistically different from English and Continental chairs. This is noticeable with the bonnet-top secretary. Within one piece, there will be a blend of influences— English, French, Flemish etc. This is an aspect that Philadelphia cabinetmakers celebrate brilliantly, visible with Randolph's Philadelphia side chair. Lastly, as one

■ An Illustrated Guide to Furniture History

Plate 8.1
Dining Room from Kirtlington Park, 1748, Oxfordshire, England, Design by John Sanderson for Sir James Dashwood, 1st Baronet. Rococo decoration (plaster work) and Neoclassical interior architecture.

Source: Metropolitan Museum of Art, New York, Annie Laurie Aitken Galleries, British Galleries, Period Room. Dining Room from Kirtlington Park, 1748. Public Domain OA (Open Access). Fletcher Fund, 1931.

gets more familiar with this time period, regional specialized furniture will become noticeable and identifiable—like the timeline's Townsend block-front chest made popular in Rhode Island; from Boston the chair form with a vase-shaped splat and *S*-curved cabriole legs (Figure 3.53); and, in the southern part of the colonies, the double chest of Charleston (Figure 3.107, Figure 3.108, and Figure 3.109).

To conclude this chapter on 18th-century Italy, France, England, and America, the room chosen to provide the reader context and an idea of a total environment is a dining room from a country house located in Oxfordshire, England. Kirtlington Park (1742–1745) was built for Sir James Dashwood, 1st Baronet, and the interiors were designed by architect John Sanderson. Before its removal in 1931, the dining room at Kirtlington Park was widely regarded as one of the most beautiful Rococo rooms in England.[67] Today, the dining room (ca. 1748) is installed as an English period room in the British Galleries at the Metropolitan Museum of Art (Plate 8.1).

The Kirtlington Park dining-room furniture is not original, but furniture of the period has been selected for the dining room's display. The room's aesthetic quality is English Rococo and Neoclassical. The Neoclassical detailing is prevalent in the interior architecture details. Notice details such as the Classical molding surrounding the window and door casing and pediment door head; also the dentil work at the ceiling with frieze below. The characterization of the most beautiful Rococo room in England is visible in the Rocco plaster decoration. It has a sculptural quality and naturalistic modeling.[68] The plasticity of the plasterwork is bold—three-dimensional and appearing to engulf the wall surfaces and room volume. The Rococo plaster decoration exhibits typical Rococo ornamentation—shells, scrolls, fruit, bouquets, and foliage in curvilinear patterns interlaced and sinuous, encapsulating whatever surface touched. The room's abundant plasterwork and sculpture-like quality attributes to the Kirtlington Park dining room's reputation as one of the most beautiful Rococo rooms in England. Further evidence of this quality is seen with the decorative built-in pier mirror frames, and decorative trim around the two large painting frames on opposite walls, also within the pedimented doors. At the ceiling plane, it is visible on the ceiling panels and the frieze below. The same treatment happens at the chimneypiece surround, not visible in this view. The concept that the Rococo style was meant to create an impression both pleasurable and stimulating is exemplified perfectly with the Kirtlington Park dining room.

This concludes Chapter 8 and the investigation of 18th-century Italy, France, England, and America. In Chapter 9—Precursors to Modernism, the timeline moves to the dawn of Modernism, the late 19th century. In respect to this book, the pictorial timeline pieces are given the classification of precursor—forerunner to what is commonly known as early the Early Modernist period.

NOTES

1. www.britannica.com/art/Baroque-architecture.
2. Judith Miller, *Furniture World Styles from Classical to Contemporary* (New York: Dorling Kindersley, 2005), 80.

■ An Illustrated Guide to Furniture History

3   Douglas Ash ... [et al.], *World Furniture: An Illustrated History* (New York, London, Sydney, Toronto: Hamlyn Publishing Group, 1976), p.154.
4   Ibid.
5   Ibid.
6   https://en.wikipedia.org/wiki/Italian_Rococo_interior_design.
7   Judith Miller, *Furniture World Styles from Classical to Contemporary* (New York: Dorling Kindersley, 2005), p.82.
8   Judith Gura, *The Guide to Period Styles for Interiors from the 17th Century to the Present* (New York: Fairchild Books, Bloomsbury Publishing, 2016), p.34.
9   Ibid., p.44.
10 Sherrill Whiton and Stanley Abercrombie, *Interior Design and Decoration* (New Jersey: Prentice Hall, Pearson Education, 2002), p.362.
11 Ibid.
12 Judith Gura, *The Guide to Period Styles for Interiors from the 17th Century to the Present* (New York: Fairchild Books, Bloomsbury Publishing, 2016), p.54.
13 Ibid.
14 Judith Miller, *Furniture World Styles From classical to Contemporary* (New York: Dorling Kindersley, 2005), p.82.
15 Ibid.
16 On-line Open Image Collection, Object Label, Metropolitan Museum of Art, New York, 2020.
17 Ibid.
18 Ibid.
19 Ibid.
20 On-line Collection, Object Label, J. Paul Getty Museum, Los Angeles, CA, Object Number 87.DA.2.
21 Ibid.
22 On-line Collection, Object Label, Metropolitan Museum of Art, New York, New York, 2020.
23 Ibid.
24 https://en.wikipedia.org/wiki/Decoupage.
25 On-line Collection, Object Label, Metropolitan Museum of Art, New York, New York, 2020.
26 www.invitinghome.com/the-rise-of-venetian-mirrors/?v=1d20b5ff1ee9.
27 Robert Bishop and Patricia Coblentz, *The Smithsonian Illustrated Library of Antiques. Furniture I: Prehistoric Through Rococo* (New York: Cooper-Hewitt Museum, The Smithsonian Institution's National Design Museum, 1979), p.84.
28 Ibid.
29 Robbie G. Blakemore, *History of Interior Design & Furniture: From Ancient Egypt to Nineteenth-Century Europe* (New Jersey, John Wiley & Sons), p.222.
30 Robert Bishop and Patricia Coblentz, *The Smithsonian Illustrated Library of Antiques Furniture I Prehistoric Through Rococo* (New York: Cooper-Hewitt Museum, The Smithsonian Institution's National Design Museum, 1979), p.84.
31 Tricia Tait, "Madame de Pompadour." Kings College, History Department, 2005.
32 Ibid.
33 Ibid.
34 Robert Bishop and Patricia Coblentz, *The Smithsonian Illustrated Library of Antiques. Furniture I: Prehistoric Through Rococo* (New York: Cooper-Hewitt Museum, The Smithsonian Institution's National Design Museum, 1979), p.88.
35 Robbie G. Blakemore, *History of Interior Design & Furniture: From Ancient Egypt to Nineteenth-Century Europe* (New Jersey, John Wiley & Sons), p.222.
36 On-line Collection, Object Label, Metropolitan Museum of Art, New York, 2020.

37 Ibid.
38 Ibid.
39 Ibid.
40 Ibid.
41 Robbie G. Blakemore, *History of Interior Design & Furniture: From Ancient Egypt to Nineteenth-Century Europe* (New Jersey, John Wiley & Sons), p.249.
42 Sherrill Whiton, Stanley Abercrombie, *Interior Design and Decoration* (New Jersey: Prentice Hall, Pearson Education, 2002), p.413.
43 Robbie G. Blakemore, *History of Interior Design & Furniture: From Ancient Egypt to Nineteenth-Century Europe* (New Jersey, John Wiley & Sons), p.247.
44 Christie's UK, The Auction of 12: Exceptional Furniture, Chippendale Furniture sale, 2008.
45 Ibid.
46 Ibid.
47 On-line Collection, Object Label, Metropolitan Museum of Art, New York, 2020.
48 Ibid.
49 Ibid.
50 Treena Crochet, *Designer's Guide to Furniture Styles* (New Jersey: Prentice-Hall, 1999), p.146.
51 Ibid.
52 Morrison H. Heckscher and Leslie Greene Bowman, *American Rococo, 1750–1775: Elegance in Ornament* (New York: The Metropolitan Museum of Art and Los Angeles County Museum of Art, distributed by Harry N. Abrams, New York, 1991), p.137.
53 Bernard and S. Dean Levy, Inc. Furniture listing description, New York, 2020.
54 Graham Blackburn, quotation from email, Tuesday, June 9, 2020.
55 Margaret Culbertson, "A Brass Catalogue," Episode No. 2824, Collection of Kitty King Powell Library, Bayou Bend Collection, Museum of Fine Arts, Houston, 2012.
56 On-line Collection, Object Label, Metropolitan Museum of Art, New York, 2020.
57 Ibid.
58 Ibid.
59 Ibid.
60 Ibid.
61 https://en.wikipedia.org/wiki/Benjamin_Randolph_(cabinetmaker).
62 Morrison H. Heckscher and Leslie Greene Bowman, *American Rococo, 1750–1775: Elegance in Ornament* (New York: The Metropolitan Museum of Art and Los Angeles County Museum of Art, distributed by Harry N. Abrams, New York, 1991), p.214.
63 Ibid.
64 On-line Collection, Object Label, Metropolitan Museum of Art, New York, 2020.
65 Ibid.
66 Morrison H. Heckscher and Leslie Greene Bowman, *American Rococo, 1750–1775: Elegance in Ornament* (New York: The Metropolitan Museum of Art and Los Angeles County Museum of Art, distributed by Harry N. Abrams, 1991), p.217.
67 William Rieder … [et al.], *Period Rooms, in the Metropolitan Museum of Art Harry* (New York: Metropolitan Museum of Art, Harry N. Abrams, 1996), p.137.
68 Ibid., p.141.

9 Precursors to Modernism

Europe Arts and Crafts Movement, Art Nouveau, and Vienna Secession (or Wiener Werstätte), and American Arts and Crafts

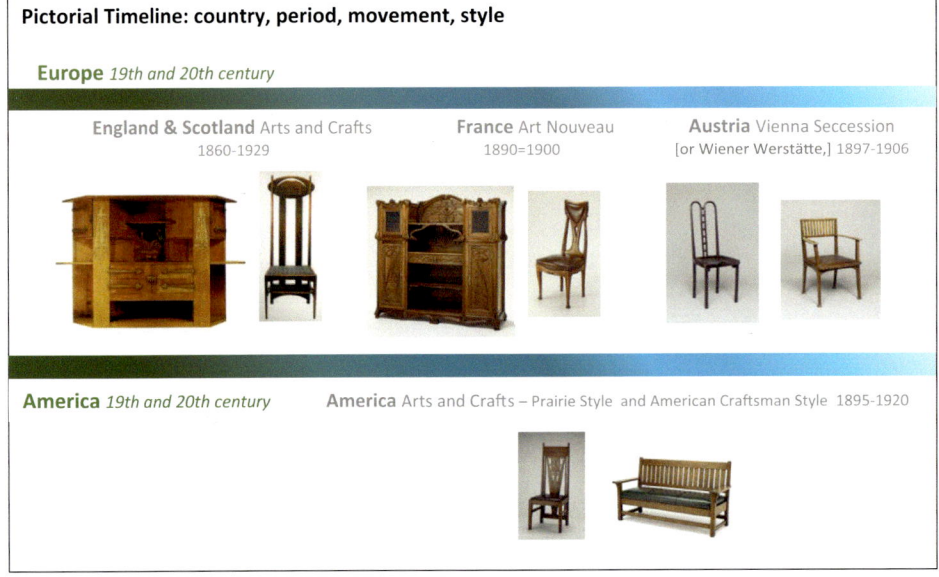

9.1
Pictorial timeline—Precursors to Modernism: Europe Arts and Crafts Movement, Art Nouveau, and Vienna Secession (or Wiener Werstätte), and American Arts and Crafts

TIME PERIOD OVERVIEW

As the pendulum moves through the 19th century, at its end there seemed to be a concerted effort by architects, designers, and artists to reject historicism and the past tradition of referencing Greco-Roman precedent. There was an intentional move toward an expression with no relation to the past. Thus began the rise of Modernism. Therefore, it can be acknowledged that Modernism is an invention of late 19th and early 20th century as a reaction to the supposed chaos and eclecticism of various earlier 19th-century revivals of historical forms. Movements and stylistic approaches from the late 19th century can be considered precursors to Modernism both in Europe and America—the avant-garde in European architecture, interiors, and decorative arts. Movements to be discussed in this chapter are Arts and Craft, Art Nouveau, and Viennese Secession. Chapter 9's pictorial timeline focuses on the European countries of England, Scotland, France, and Belgium. These countries are considered design leaders at this time. As the Arts and Crafts movement makes it way to the United States, its influence affects the aspirations of architects, designers, and artists who strove toward Modernism. Therefore, parallel on the timeline is the America Arts and Crafts movement examined in relation to the nation's regions and classification of the Prairie Style and Craftsman Style.

For this chapter, the precursors to Modernism selected for the pictorial timeline are those canons reflecting Western intellectual traditions: Arts and Craft, Art Nouveau, and Vienna Succession. The makers—architects and designers—are widely known and esteemed, and their influential works are essential to understanding the time period in Europe and America. This section will briefly include their histories in tandem with investigating the furniture piece that the architect and designer designed. The chosen eight examples epitomize the design of that region and movement.

Lastly, a reminder, as the section is reviewed, do not get ahead of yourself and decide which furniture piece to analyze prior to finishing the entire chapter.

ENGLAND AND SCOTLAND: ARTS AND CRAFTS, 1860–1929

History

As a British phenomenon, the term "Arts and Crafts movement" came into being during the second half of the 19th century and continued into the early part of the 20th century. The movement began in Victorian England, the cradle of the Industrial Revolution, and provided a moral critique of the values of Victorian society. The movement was a reaction to the period of industrialization in Britain—a reaction against mass-produced items, such as furniture and textiles. There was a desire by many pepetuating the Arts and Crafts ethos to celebrate a return to simplicity and individual creativity. Some felt it necessary to step back a century or more to a time when everything was decorated and crafted by hand. Work that often referenced Medieval times, the romantic, or folk styles of decoration was preferred. Other makers embraced the new period of industrialization and worked with it. At its inception, Arts and Crafts centered on the redefinition of work, the authority of the artist-craftsman, the preference for handmade rather than machine-produced objects, and the theory that beauty unifies by producing moral uplift for people of all classes.[1]

The beginning of the Arts and Crafts movement is often associated with William Morris as the pioneer of its design reform. His association as reformer begins with his friendship with the Pre-Raphaelites and later the design of his new home, the Red House, in 1860, located at Bexleyheath in Southeast London. The architect was Phillip Webb. Webb's Red House is considered the first Arts and

Crafts house built in England. Without detracting from Morris's importance as a pioneer of design reform, it is necessary to mention other great protagonists, in a real sense revolutionaries—thinkers and writers, architects and designers, artist and crasfsman.[2] If one chooses to further investigate this movement in relation to the built environment and look at works beyond those associated with the pictorial timeline, a suggestion would be to consider, in addition to William Morris, the work of Charles Ashbee, Phillip Webb, William Lethaby, C.F.A. Voysey, and A.H. Mackmurdo.

The Arts and Crafts movement not only had an impact in respect to the built environment but it spread across disciplines. Individuals making a living in decorative arts and fine arts became followers of the movement, such as ceramicists, textile designers, and jewelry designers. For these creatives, the notion of stepping back in time influenced their work, and there was an emphasis on simple forms, natural materials, and utility of design.

In closing this segment, it is necessary to mention that there resides a dicotomy in regard to the Arts and Crafts movement. The philosophical intent in its inception is admirable—that beauty unifies by providing a moral uplift for people of all classes. However, the reality is that not all classes were the beneficiaries. Britain was the richest and most powerful nation at this time and its people probably the most free people in the world. Even so, the upper and middle classes were the only people who could enjoy individual freedom in Victorian England; they were free of the grinding proverty of the lower orders, the inverted snobbery of the lower middle class, and the increasingly rigid formality of the aristocracy.[3] It was the upper and middle classes that the Arts and Crafts architects were commissioned to design for, evolving into a easy new style that was most often seen in the small country houses of a free, proud individualist. This was a breed who, in three decades between 1880 and 1910, were the patrons of some of the finest and most original architecure and artifacts ever produced in Britain.

Buffet, ca. 1897, England, Arts and Crafts, and high-back chair with oval back-rail, ca. 1898, Arts and Crafts, Scotland

Aesthetics
This information will apply to both timeline pieces from England and Scotland. Arts and Crafts vocabulary, whether referencing the built environment or decorative and fine arts, is most often described using general terms or phrases such as Medieval, Gothic, vernacular, simple forms, natural materials, and utility of design. Thinking more specifically will assist in an expedient way with identification. British Arts and Crafts furniture include such specific features. The form appears solid and strong, displaying truth of material and function. The design is simple, and the preferred geometry is rectalinear. Typically, there is limited applied decoratve ornament. Metal will often be used as a feature on the piece for hardware or decorative motifs. The type of metal can be either wrought iron, copper, or brass. The fastening devices are purposely exposed, such as nail heads, pegs, screws,

and bolts. Solid wood is used instead of veneer, and the species are native to the region. The wood is most often quarter-sawn or plain-sawn, stained medium to very dark, sometimes painted. The painted hues that dominate are off-white and shades of yellow, green, and blue.

Furniture

The **buffet**, ca. 1897, England, Arts and Crafts movement, is the work of Mackay Hugh Baillie Scott (1865–1945), a highly praised English Arts and Crafts architect (Figure 9.1). The buffet was designed for a dining room of Glencrutchery House, Douglas, Isle of Man. Baillie Scott's professional practice was broad and successful, and flourished in the area of residential architecture. Baillie Scott, when designing a piece like the buffet for a client, would likely have also designed the dining table and chairs, which would have possessed similar characteristics. This idea is no different from earlier centuries, where rooms consisted of a suite of furniture designed with a similar appearance.

Figure 9.1

Large buffet cabinet, 1897, Arts and Crafts, Isle of Man. Designed by Mackay Hugh Baillie Scott for the dining room at Glencrutchery House. Oak with repoussé copper panel and gilt inlay.

Source: Christie's Images Limited. © 2020 Christie's Images, London. © Photo SCALA, Florence.

The buffet's appearance harkens to the Medieval period, a characteristic of the Arts and Craft canon. This can be recognized in both its form and material. The use of oak, the vertical post, and the angled edge box-like shape make it appear strong and durable, a feature associated with Medieval furniture. The lower section with the hinged doors resembles a Medieval chest or coffer. Notice, however, that there is little ornamentation except for the repoussé copper panel at the center of the piece which appears to be stylized flora. Also note the elongated gilt-inlayed designs on both vertical posts, resembling an inverted fleur-de-lis or perhaps a sword-like armament. The gilt wrought-iron hinges and lock plates are functional, but can be considered decorative due to their design and finish material.

Baillie Scott, like many other architects, insisted on designing the utilitarian parts of a home including its furnishings. Through his long career, his vocabulary progressed into simple forms relying on truth of material and function as seen in the piece above. He favored the vernacular furniture reminiscent of a former age, and believed that craftsmanship should be exposed, exhibiting a strong structural sense of utility and fitness for purpose. There was a strong sense of "folk art" in his designs and an ambience or reflection of something home-like, which is visible in the buffet.

What makes this an Arts and Crafts piece from England?

This piece successfully demonstrates features deemed essential for Arts and Crafts classification—in general, the simple form and use of the vernacular. Specifically, the quality resides in the use of solid oak, lightly stained, the incorporation of metal seen in the lock plates and wrought-iron hinges, and the copper panel repoussé, centrally placed on the back of the buffet depicting boldly what appears to be stylized regional flora. Lastly, the desire of Arts and Crafts designers to create original design(s)—a good example here is the gilt inlay design on the vertical supports. This gilt design appears to be a cross between an inverted fleur-de-lis and a sword that a Medieval knight might carry. Baillie Scott's design approach and chosen features create a visually appealing piece and no doubt express the simple form and utility of this design.

To conclude, Mackay Hugh Baillie Scott produced nearly 300 buildings over the course of his career. One of his most notable projects is Blackwell House, 1898–1908, situated in the Lake District of northwestern England. He always designed his interiors with the family in mind. His houses were designed with large hallways, which he referred to as "Living-Halls," an area for the family to meet, greet, and converse. This feature occurs in Blackwell House. If one is interested in learning more about Mackay Hugh Baillie Scott's work, Brian D. Coleman's book *Historic Arts and Crafts Homes of Great Britain* or Diane Haigh's, *Baillie Scott: The Artistic House* would be a good place to begin.

Furniture

The next timeline piece is the **high-back chair with oval back-rail**, ca. 1898 (Argyle chair), Glasgow, Scotland, Arts and Crafts, was designed by Charles Rennie Mackintosh (1868–1928) architect, designer, and artist (Figure 8.2). The chair was part of the collection at the Glasgow School of Art, Glasgow, Scotland, but tragically this item was lost in the fire in the Mackintosh Building at the Glasgow School of Art on May 23rd, 2014.[4] Other known examples are in the Museum of Modern Art in New York and the Victoria and Albert Museum in London.

Stylistically, the chair is the most advanced piece of furniture designed for Argyle Street and was used by Mackintosh again in his own flat.[5] It is also one of the most recognized furniture pieces from this period in design history. There are two versions of the chair with different seat types, horsehair and rush. The one seen here is horsehair. The medium is oak, dark stain, and the chair dimensions are approximately H 54" × W 20" × D 18". It is an unusually tall side chair at nearly six feet. Its stylistic expression celebrates its constituent parts. This is seen first in its vertical quality—the flat and rounded stiles of the back which at the base frame into a rectangular plane with semicircular cutout and at the top engage into an oval back-rail with a crescent-shape cutout. Its essence appears to be about connection, construction, and individual details—how these parts work in relation to one another. The aesthetic quality is the expression of this relationship.

Mackintosh was commissioned by Catherine (Kate) Cranston to design her Argyle Street Tea Rooms, the Ingram Street Tea Rooms, and the Willow Tea Rooms

Precursors to Modernism ■

on Sauchiehall Street from the late 1990s to 1912.[6] The Willlow Tea Rooms exist today, although not in their original state.[7] = Mackintosh transformed not only the interior space but also the exterior of a Victorian row house. The façade was stripped of its Victorian pretensions and given deep window reveals with no molding and shallow sensual curves.[8] It was an architectural revelation for Glasgow and the tea rooms became an overnight success for Miss Cranston. Charles Rennie Mackintosh designed this chair for Argyle Street Tea Rooms, and most often design professionals will refer to this chair simply as the Argyle chair.

Cranston was savvy, innovative, and aware of social need—providing amenities and a space designed in the latest style would attract patrons. The upper classes deemed this important. This awareness of the needs of the upper classes was Kate Cranston's reason for commissioning Mackintosh—architect, designer, and artist. As an architect, Mackintosh was concerned about the inside as well as the outside of his buildings, and much of his furniture was conceived as integral elements of carefully composed interiors. An interesting aspect professionally is that he collaborated with his artist wife Margaret Macdonald throughout his career. Margaret was a student of the Glasgow School of Art. The amount of Margaret Macdonald's influence has never been documented. In the publication *Charles Rennie Mackintosh*, Pat Kirkham states: "This essay does not attribute separate elements of a piece of furniture or room design to one or the other, nor does it establish a fifty-fifty input in order to prove and 'equality'; rather, it insists that the mutual influences were both, complex and compound."[9]

Figure 9.2
High-back chair with oval back-rail (Argyle Chair), 1898, Glasgow, Scotland (Arts and Crafts, Scotland). Designed by Charles Rennie Mackintosh for the Argyle Tea Rooms, Argyle Street, Glasgow, Scotland.

Source: Glasgow School of Art, Glasgow, Scotland. Creative commons Zero (CC0).

Makintosh was born in Glasgow, Scotland, where he had his life-long professional practice. All the furniture designed by Mackintosh between 1893 and 1896 falls within the parameters of the Arts and Crafts movement, then at its height.[10] Although the reference made to his early furniture design is Arts and Crafts, his body of work overall formulated a new vocabulary of architecture and design by distilling and combining essential elements from Scottish baronial and vernacular architecture, the English Arts and Craft movement, Japanese designs, and organic growth. The Argyle chair bears resemblance to that distillation.

What makes this an Arts and Crafts piece from Scotland?

Like the previous example, the essential features begin with the form and use of the vernacular. In this case, the material is a dark-stained oak. The seat has been reupholstered

243 □

with horsehair, which would have been used at the time. Incorporated here to express connection are not metal fasteners like those of Baillie Scott's buffet; instead, Mackintosh expresses the connection and construction by designing the chair's parts so that the relationship—how the parts attach to one another—is visually obvious. The aesthetic quality is the expression of this relationship: the way the stiles are engaged and flush with the pierced oval, yet the outer turned pieces on the left and right are attached on top of the oval, and the structure of the back touching the floor to support the back and seat in which the turned stretchers are anchored. This chair successfully represents the premise that a design vocabulary can derive from function and utility. There is no doubt that the attractiveness of this chair has to do with the juxtaposition within the form: flat versus turned, low versus tall, and the lack of applied ornament. This successful chair is likely a result of Mackintosh's distillation and an essential part of his new vocabulary.

FRANCE: ART NOUVEAU, 1890–1900

History

The next precursor to Modernism on the timeline to be examined is Art Nouveau. Art Nouveau in French means "new art." It began in France during the late 19th century, and as a decorative style it flourished throughout early 20th century. Like the Arts and Crafts movement, it crosses over into many disciplines—architecture, interior design, fashion, decorative arts, including furniture design, jewelry, pottery, metalwork, and glasswork. Also like the Arts and Crafts movement, Art Nouveau creatives purposely rejected historicism, inventing an original and authentic style at the dawn of the 20th century.

In his publication *Modern Architecture Since 1900*, architecture historian William J.R. Curtis states: "Art Nouveau was actually the first stage of modern architecture in Europe. If modern architecture be understood as implying primarily the total rejection of historicism."[11] He further mentions that although Art Nouveau artists rejected historicism, they could not altogether reject tradition. What becomes evident is that Art Nouveau architects, designers, and artists switched their allegiances from familiar traditions to an ideology and practices considered unfamiliar and not recent. Therefore, similar to the Arts and Crafts movement, Art Nouveau was a reaction against Greco-Roman Classicism—the French Beaux-Arts tradition widely practiced in the 1870s and 1880s.[12] This response to Classicism is the common denominator among the precursors of Modernism.

Art Nouveau is one of the few periods whose greatest achievements are found in both interior design and designed objects. The interiors where typically designed by the architect. A commission at this time would include the architecture, interior architecture, interior design, furniture design, and decorative art objects. Architecture curricula for European universities resulted in architects being adept at interior design and often accomplished furniture designers. Art Nouveau pieces were highly ornamental. The single most important principle motivating the Art Nouveau artist was the belief that artistic forms should take their inspiration from the natural world, often incorporating these motifs; flowers, vines, birds, and insects all served as source materials.[13] The two-dimensional and three-dimensional design vocabulary that developed is characterized by curvaceous and sinuous lines—lines that are spiral or whiplash and tendril-like. The lines can be smooth and graceful or energetic. The stylized linework in three-dimensional design simultaneously express axial and radial directions. Asymmetry is typical. The Art Nouveau elaborate forms quietly nurtured the seeds of Modernism. Additionally, new technologies in printing and publishing helped Art Nouveau to quickly reach a global audience. Art magazines, illustrated with photographs and color lithographs, played an essential role in popularizing the new style.[14]

Display cabinet, ca. 1895–1905, Art Nouveau, France, and side chair, ca. 1900–1913, Art Nouveau

Aesthetics

Whether referencing the built environment or decorative and fine arts, the Art Nouveau vocabulary is most often generally described as curvaceous, sinuous lines, spiral, whiplash, smooth, energetic, asymmetrical, and use of natural motifs from nature: flowers, vines, birds, and insects. It is descriptively reminiscent of the Rococo style, but formally different in regard to application. The benefit at looking specifically at descriptive elements, instead of in generalities, will asssit with an effective identification. Specifically, Art Nouveau is an aesthetic of abstraction; a particlar type of flower, vine, bird, or insect will not necessarily be recognized literally. The abstraction comes via the varried linework—sinuous, spiral, whiplash, etc. This is the key difference in regard to the Rococo comparison. What is evident is that the entire Art Nouveau design, rather than happening three-dimensionally or two-dimentsionally, encompasses the full surface it touches, which is noticeable in the timeline display cabinet and side chair. The touched surface is begotten from curvaceous linework, which can be sinuous, spiral, tendril-like, smooth, energetic, and asymmetrical. The linework can change scale, slender at times and thicker at other times, and go in differ axial directions simultaneaously. The most crucial aspect is that the curvaceous quality encompasses the full surfaced touch. Second, for three-dimensional forms such as furniture, the curvaceous multidirectional line creates relief and a sculpture-like quality, as seen in both timeline pieces.

Furniture

The first Art Nouveau timeline piece, a **display cabinet**, ca. 1895–1905, France, is the work of Louis-Désiré-Eugène Gaillard (1862–1933), French, and resides in the European Decorative Art collection of the Art Institute of Chicago (Figure 9.3).

The display cabinet's massing is simple; the front view appears almost square with a right and left volume and void in the center. Its simplicity ends here, however. The ornament on the display cabinet is a testament to Art Nouveau originality and authenticity. The material is a rich medium-tone walnut with pulls of gilt bronze, and glass in the top doors. It is a tall and wide piece—H 74¼″ × W 76″ ×

D 24¼"—yet visually the display cabinet seems perfectly proportioned due to its mass-to-void ratio and visual movement of the linework relief.

The Art Nouveau quality is visible in the use of the sinuous and energetic lines in relief. The curvacious lines move boldly on the front face of the cabinet doors and drawers and around the body of the cabinet, both axially and radially, defining the shape of its outline. The outlining is essential for the style, reinforcing the notion that the curvaceous quality encompasses the full surface of the planes touched and perimimeter. Notice that the linework around the edge on this display cabinet resembles a thick ribbon, more so than a vine, but regardless the movement is form defining. Lastly, the inspiration from nature is seen in the central arched portion where the vine-like patterning and floral motif are expressed brilliantly in the center; also, a floral motif crowns the top of the glass doors, a final reminder that the curvaceous quality encompasses the full surface touch.

Louis–Désire-Eugène Gaillard was an advocate of modern design, and on record mentioned is the fact that Gaillard abandoned his career in law for a career in design.[15] One could assume due to an interest and or passion for Art Nouveau style. Gaillard would have designed a display cabinet such as this one for a salon, parlor, or perhaps a hallway. The open shelving resembles an étagèr, yet the left and right doors with glass front upper display is not typical for an étagèr design. It's possible that the untypical is what makes the display cabinet visually appealing. Its design is a superb display of Louis–Désire-Eugène Gaillard's creative acumen and technical virtuosity.

Figure 9.3
Display cabinet, ca. 1900, Art Nouveau, France. Louis-Désire Eugène Gaillard. Walnut, gilt bronze, and glass.
Source: Art Institute of Chicago, European Decorative Art Gallery. Creative Commons Zero (CC0). Through prior acquisitions of the George F. Harding Collection, Mr. and Mrs. Lester Abelson and the Blackstone Memorial Fund.

What makes this an Art Nouveau piece?

The display cabinet excellently exhibits all the qualities that were included in the **Aesthetics** category explanation. The abstraction of form for the motifs adorning the façade is evident. A vine or possibly a leaf or ribbon? The curvaceous energetic line changes scale, at times slender and then thicker. This scale change is obvious when one looks at the motif on the door panels versus the cabinet's edges. On the door panels there are radiating motifs, tendril-like at the ends and at other times serpentine in quality. A similar motif is visible on the horizontal center front panel and back semicircular panel—the latter, however, definitely depicting nature and a type of flower. The material is solid walnut, with gilt bronze, also called ormolu, and brass pulls. What should be obvious to the observer is that Art Nouveau ornament is original and authentic. There is no reference to precedent. Important to remember is that the ornament not only adorns the surface but moves on to the outline and defines the silhouette. Most crucial is that the curvaceous quality encompasses the entire surface it touches, very similar to the Rococo style. This quality applies to everything from a furniture piece, decorative art objects, or interior envelope.

Furniture

The next timeline piece, a **side chair**, ca. 1900–1913, France, Art Nouveau, is the work of French architect and designer Hector Guimard (1867–1942). His Art Nouveau architectural and decorative work is instantly recognizable and distinguishable, and held in high regard by experts in the design world. For many, Guimard is considered one of the most notable Art Nouveau architects, interior designers, and furniture designers of the time. The best of his architectural decorative work was done during a relatively brief 15-year period.[16] Nevertheless, it is the work from these years of prolific creative activity that is seen throughout Paris—in buildings, interiors, and the famous designs for the Paris Metro stations. The chair resides in the European Decorative Arts collection of the Art Institute of Chicago (Figure 9.4).

Figure 9.4
Side chair, 1900–1913, Art Nouveau. Designed by Hector Guimard. Pearwood and tooled leather.

Source: Art Institute of Chicago, European Decorative Art Gallery. Creative commons Zero (CC0). Through prior gifts of Mr. Walter Brewster, Mrs. James cook, Mr. Joseph Nash Field, Mrs. T. Clifford Rodman, Mrs. Clive Runnels, Mr. and Mrs Martin Ryerson, Mrs. Norman Schloss, Mrs. Sidney Schwartz, Mrs. Diego Suarez.

This side chair would have likely been part of a dining-room suite where all the furniture would have a similar appearance. The medium is pearwood and tooled leather. The size of the chair is H 42½″ × W 18″; seat diameter 18½″.

The pearwood, slightly polished to a deep gold tone, appears soft to the touch. This intriguing softness seems to epitomize the chair. The body and silhouette are defined by light-relief curved lines. These lines are less curvaceous than what is typical for Art Nouveau. The relief lines on this side chair resemble a draped or folded textile. The draping and folds begin at the heart-shaped crest rail—the curves softly enfolding its leather. The same lines descend, shaping the right and left stile and splat. Both stiles are formed in an outward direction and the splat slightly inward, conforming to the human back. The draping continues at the splat, then stops, leaving a pierced open area in the center and continuing on to the seat.

The leather seat shape is also defined by a curvilinear line happening at the base of the seat and on the leather as an embossed curvilinear design. The leather seat curves gently down at the seat rail, reinforcing the relief lines on the rail which appear like tautly gathered fabric. The line movement continues down the leg to the feet, where the draping terminates on a diminutive block.

It is believed that Guimard's idiosyncratic form of Art Nouveau derived from his association with French architect and author Eugène Viollet-le-Duc.[17] Guimard attended the École Nationale Supérieure des Arts Décoratifs in Paris, where he became acquainted with the theories of Eugène Viollet-le-Duc. It is believed these rationalist ideas had an impact on Guimard. Regardless of the impetus, Guimard's vocabulary seems to encapsulate the spirit of Art Nouveau "new art."

What makes this an Art Nouveau piece?

This side chair, like the display case previously seen, strongly exhibits all the qualities brought forth in the **Aesthetics** category explanation above. The abstraction of motif is evident, but gentler than was seen in the display cabinet. The sinuous line is less energetic and curvaceous, and appears as controlled energy. The ornament—applied linework—is not a fantastical aspect; its quality is controlled, revealing itself on the surface and in the three-dimensional form of the side chair. The chair's frame moves in and out, swelling and receding on all surfaces, beginning with the feet and legs, enveloping the seat, moving up toward the back, and reaching its apex in the heart-shaped crest rail. The lines of the applied ornament appear like a draped textile more so than vine. The tooled leather pattern feels most organic. The design success of this side chair resides in its balanced, graceful, and elegant silhouette. It is a good example of Guimard's idiosyncratic form of Art Nouveau.

AUSTRIA: VIENNA SECESSION, 1897–1906 (WIENER WERSTÄTTE), 1903 ESTABLISHED

History

The Vienna Secession was an art movement formed in 1897 by a group of Austrian Artists. The movement included architects, painters, and sculptors, and was founded by Gustav Klimt, Koloman Moser, Josef Hoffmann, Joseph Maria Olbrich, Max Kurzweil, and Wilhelm Bernatzik.[18] The architect Otto Wagner is recognized as an important member but was not a founding member. Around 1903, Koloman Moser, graphic designer and painter, and Josef Hoffmann, architect, established an enterprise connected to the Secession movement, a productive cooperative of artisans in Vienna known as the Wiener Werkstätte (Vienna Workshop).

The Secessionists objected to the prevailing conservatism and traditional orientation toward historicism in the arts. The group sought to separate themselves from the art and design establishment, to discover a new modern aesthetic, to erase the distinction between the fine and applied arts, and to improve public taste.[19] In this objective, they had much in common with the English reform movement—Arts and Crafts. Yet unlike many of the English reformers, the key concepts for the Vienna Secession designers were the understanding that industrialization had radically changed the process of design and the acceptance of the machine as a valid alternative to hand craft, though not necessarily a replacement for it. The Secessionists, although taking steps away from tradition, did not break entirely with the past.

One of the tenets of the new Modernist aesthetic was expressed in a widely published 1908 essay by theorist Adolf Loos (1870–1933). Entitled "Ornament and Crime," Loos posited that ornament was not a natural product of modern society and was therefore no longer appropriate. The essay was used to justify the rejection of ornament by Modernists.

The Secessionists erected an exhibition hall in Vienna as an architectural manifesto for their cause. It was the work of architect Joseph Maria Olbrich. The building is simply known as the Secession Building and still stands today. Its current life is not vastly different from its original intent—it is an exhibition gallery for the city and is one of the city's architectural treasures.

In conclusion of this **History** section, it is important to mention that it is often said, unlike other movements, there is no one style that unites the work of artist who were part of the Vienna Secession.[20] However, there are specific qualities in the work of the members that recur and bear resemblance. These qualities will be discussed below.

Side chair, Model No. 371, ca. 1901–1911, Austria, Vienna Secession, and Armchair No. 8, 1898–1899, Austria, Vienna Secession

Aesthetics
This aesthetic explanation will apply to both Vienna Secession chairs on the pictorial timeline. When examining the work of Vienna Secession, it is apparent that all elements of a project are part of a coheret plan and designed to coalesce.[21] Secessionist interiors and furniture design are notable for their striking rectilinear quality and their elegant simplicity. The Secession interior as well as furniture is defined by the interplay of horizontal and vertical lines. As mentioned earlier, although they took steps away from tradition, the Vienna Secessionists did not break entirely with the past. Ornament is visible in their work and stylized floral or geometric motifs is not uncommon. They did not eschew pattern, but they stripped it down to the barest essentials: the pure geometry of checkerboards, squares, and sometimes circles.

Lastly, although interior design and furniture design thrived for Werstätte designers, they were extremely prolific in metalwork and other accessories: silver and silver plate used for elegant lighting fixtures, clocks, bowls, boxes, and vases decorated with hammering or perforated grid patterns.[22] The workshop also produce striking works of color-accented glass, as well as ceramics and jewelry.

■ An Illustrated Guide to Furniture History

Furniture

Side chair, Model No. 371, ca. 1901–1911, Vienna Secession, Vienna, Austria. This chair is the design of Josef Hoffmann (1849–1914) and resides in the European Decorative Arts collection of the Art Institute of Chicago (Figure 9.5). It was designed for the first-floor dining room at the Purkersdorf Sanatorium, Wien-Umgebung, Lower Austria. Josef Hoffmann designed the building for the industrialist Victor Zuckerkandl (1904–1905).

Model No. 371 was made by Jacob Kohn together with his son Josef Kohn, J & J Kohn, founded in 1849. They became one of the leading furniture makers in Austria-Hungary. Kohn worked together with artists of the Wiener Werkstätte and Josef Hoffmann in the design of many pieces.[23] Kohns' business received many awards and prizes for their work.

The side chair's medium is beech and wood laminate. Its size is approximately H 43" × W 17½" × D 19½". Visible in the chair are those qualities mentioned under the **Aesthetics** section. The design of the chair is minimalist in approach, with no applied ornament or reference to past tradition. Chair No. 371 is stripped down to its barest essentials, becoming a repetition of simple shapes and lines. It is not uncommon for Secession designers to use geometry, and here the splat becomes a single row of seven spheres embraced by the tall, narrow arches of bent wood that form the back.

The diameter of the rods that form the back legs and arches taper gradually from their widest point at the foot (for greater stability) to the smallest diameter at the crest to make the tight curve.[24] The spheres are the juncture of the front legs and underside of the seat. They are recurring motifs in Hoffmann's furniture and elements of his new 20th-century vocabulary.[25]

The sphere as a recurring motif on Hoffmann's furniture design can have a structural role as well as an aesthetic one.

As mentioned in the **History** segment, Josef Hoffmann was a founding member of the Vienna Secession, seen as a radical anti-historicist movement, and, together with Koloman Moser, created the Wiener Werstätte Cooperative workshop.[26] Therefore, it is not uncommon to interchange Werstätte and Secession.

Although Hoffmann's designs were influenced by the British Arts and Crafts movement, and while he did not necessarily reject traditional decoration, he succeeded in making it serve structural principles.[27] This worked implicitly with his ability and desire to embrace the industrial

Figure 9.5
Side Chair, Model No. 371, ca. 1906, Vienna Secession, Vienna, Austria. Designed by Josef Hoffmann. Beech and wood laminate.

Source: Art Institute of Chicago, European Decorative Art Gallery. Creative commons Zero (CC0). Gift of Fern Gand Manfred Steinfeld.

age. His design vocabulary concentrated on abstract and geometric shapes.[28] This side chair is an excellent example of that quality.

Hoffmann's professional direction is linked to his association with Otto Wagner, when he studied architecture at the Vienna Academy, between 1901 and 1905. At the Academy he was taught by Otto Wagner. Wagner was proponent of Architectural Realism, which was a theoretical position that enabled him to mitigate the reliance on historical forms. At the time of their encounter Wagner was well advanced on his path toward a more radical opposition to the prevailing currents of historicist architecture which will be seen in the next timeline example.

Armchair No. 8, 1898–1899, Vienna Secession, Vienna, Austria, is a design of Otto Wagner (1841–1918), architect, urban planner, and teacher (Figure 9.6). Otto Wagner was born in the Penzing district of Vienna. He studied in Vienna and Berlin. His first buildings were in the historical style, but by the 1880s he became a proponent of architecture "Realism."[29] His architecture commissions included his design of furniture to complement the design of the building.

In 1894, he became professor of architecture at the Academy of Fine Arts, Vienna, and, as mentioned earlier, Josef Hoffmann was one of his students. It was through his academic position that Wagner disseminated his ideology—an architecture based on modern materials and modern construction methods. He published a textbook in 1896 entitled *Modern Architecture*, based on his lectures at the Academy in which addressed the role of the architect. This thinking aligned him with his Succession brethren. By 1897, he joined Moser and Hoffmann, Klimt, and Olbrich after they founded the Vienna Secession.

Armchair No. 8 clearly expresses Otto Wagner's theories and principles of simplicity and functionality. Not uncommon in the design approach of Vienna Secession designers, the armchair's form has minimal ornament. It is on a slight scale 35½" × 26", diameter 23¼") yet appears sturdy.[30]

Figure 9.6 Armchair No. 8, Vienna Secession, Vienna, Austria. Designed by Otto Wagner. Polished walnut, mother-of-pearl, and brass with leather seat.

Source: Art Institute of Chicago, European Decorative Art Gallery. Creative commons Zero (CC0). Restricted gift of Mr. and Mrs Manfred Steinfeld.

Structurally, the chair's frame consists of vertical stiles horizontally aligned to form the crest rail. The back frame and legs have a delicate angle, but this angle appears to plant the chair solidly on the floor, contributing to its visual sturdiness. The seat rails are formed from flattened arches that visually communicate the structural principle of the arch as a strong compression member. It is therefore capable of supporting the seated human body.

Regarding the aesthetics of Armchair No. 8, it was Otto Wagner's preference to combine traditional materials with new materials, such as aluminum.[31] Here he uses only a combination of traditional materials which works splendidly for Armchair No. 8. The medium is a polished walnut and its honey tone emits a sense of warmth. The chair's arms display small round insets of mother-of-pearl. This is the extent of ornament yet it seems to add just enough luxuriousness. In the front of the leather seat is an embossed straight-line pattern within a curved shape which spans from side to side of the seat. The lines and curve appear to emphasize where to sit. The visual completeness is rounded off by the exposed brass nail heads that wrap around the seat and the brass plate seen at the foot. One could ask if this touch is functional or ornamental. The answer could be both; regardless, the decision results in a visually inviting seating piece.

What makes these Vienna Secession (or Wiener Werstätte)?

As mentioned above, there is no one style that unites the work of these designers, yet there are specific qualities in the members' work that recur and bear resemblance which is evident in the side chair for the Purkersdorf Sanatorium and Armchair No. 8—qualities such as the reductivism or minimal aesthetic, where the treatment of the form and detailing become the aesthetic. With the Hoffmann chair, this is reflected in the use of the laminated bent wood and spherical forms centrally located at the back and the underside of the seat at the chair legs. With Wagner's armchair, it is the vertical slat crest rail and simple splayed-leg form of his chair and use of the deep honey-tone walnut. The Secessionists did not reject curvilinear forms but used the curve with discretion. Implemented in their work mostly was an interplay of horizontal and vertical lines; this vertical emphasis is visible in both timeline chairs. The linear emphasis in architecture and decorative arts for the Secessionists appears repeatedly in their use of geometry, checkerboards, squares, and spheres. This emphasis is seen with the tall vertical arched back members for the Purkersdorf chair and the linear emphasis in the back and legs of the Armchair No. 8.

Lastly, often with Vienna Secession furniture the materials used were quite elaborate, such as rare woods, mother-of-pearl, or semi-precious stones and inlays of contrasting materials. This would apply to furniture, lighting fixtures, bowls, boxes, vases, etc. Mother-of-pearl was used as a decorative motif on the arms of Armchair No. 8; however, the material of the Purkersdorf Sanatorium side chair is a simple stained beech. A final mention, decorating with hammering or perforation was employed. Although neither timeline example contains this feature, keeping this in mind will be beneficial.

AMERICA: ARTS AND CRAFTS, 1895–1920

History

There is no sharp line that divides the 19th century and 20th century; the only absolute division is the numerical date. At the end of the 19th century, contexturally the social, cultual, and artistic attitudes and expressions continue into the early 20th century. When thinking about the late 19th century as the beginning of Modernism, what becomes evident is that by the century's end the battling discourse—concerning an intellectual and physical presence of Modernism and the modern world—has been largely reconciled. For design and the world of the built environment, the 19th century set the foundation for the Modernist vocabulary—a movement away from Classical precedent and Greco-Roman forms and ornament for inspiration. By its end, there was space for the original and authentic, thus framing 20th-century modern idealogy which continues to impact contermporary society.

The Arts and Crafts movement, based on the Brisish model, flourished in the United States in the first quarter of the 20th century.[32] The formal introduction of the Arts and Crafts movement was an exhibition at Copley Hall in Boston 1897. The exhibition was organized by the Society of Arts and Crafts, Boston. This exhibiton introduced to America England's Arts and Craft model and the work of its prominent British designers. A key factor that shaped 19th-century design also would shape 20th-century design, which was expositions, exhibitions, competitions, world fairs, and publications. The opportunity for artists, designers, and makers to see the work of others and exhibit their own work, such as in the exhibition in Boston, helped propel 20th-century "modernity" forward.

American creatives—artists, ceramicists, jewelry desingers, architects, furniture designers, and furniture makers—were sympathetic to the unifying principles of the Arts and Crafts movement of the British Isles. Principles such as the return to traditional skills, simplicity of form, and the idea that materials and technique dictate shape and decoration were appreciated by American creatives. The American milieu, however, resulted in a different interpretation of the syle. The vastness of the United States and regional differences played an important role in the interpretation of the English Arts and Crafts style. Depending on the region, the Arts and Crafts movement came to be known by various titles: in the eastern portion of the country, the renaming became *Craftsman style*; in the Midwestern portion of the country, it was *Prairie Style*; and on the West coast, it became *Mission Style*.

Additionally, unlike their British counterparts, American furniture makers valued the role of the machine in manufacturing their designs, and they used mechanized processes to produce chairs, cabinets, and cupboards in the Arts and Crafts style.[33] This is particularly visible with the Prairie Style, originating in the Midwestern part of the United States. In architecture referenced as "Prairie School," there was a commitment to developing an indigenous North American style of architecture which was in alignment and shared the ideology of the Arts and Crafts movement.[34] Prairie School architecture was exemplified by long and low lines believed to evoke the expanses of the prairie landscape—flat, wide, and long, typical of the Midwestern region prior to pioneer settlements. Specific architecture features are horizontality both in three-dimensional form and two-dimensional shape—roofs are long and wide, pitched, hipped, and at times gabled with overhanging eaves. Windows are grouped in horizontal bands.[35] There is attention given to solid construction, disciplined use of ornament, and integration with the landscape. This translated impeccably to Prairie Style furniture and interiors.

The Prairie School architects, designers, and craftsmen embraced a return to traditional skills, hand craftmanship, simplicity of form, and the idea that form and shape derive from materials and technique. The decorative or aesthetic quality is a result of the type of material and construction. In regard to furniture design and construction, the idea was to look handcrafted, and the pieces might often be finished by hand, but in America these pieces were machine-made. American Arts and Crafts design did have variation regionally, but collectively it shares features such as a sturdy form, and the emphasis on linear lines—it was therefore predominantly rectilinear. Also important is the link between form and function. The way a piece was constructed held importance and its assembly was exposed. It is not unusual to be able to see the connectors—wood pegs, metal nails, wood bracing, metal nail heads. Indigenous species are the medium used. Wood is used in its natural state, often rift-sawn, quarter-sawn, or plain-sawn, and was sometimes stained. Applied ornament was used minimally.

Side chair, 1910, Prairie (style) School, Chicago, Illinois, and settle, 1909, Craftsman Furniture style, Eastwood, New York

Aesthetics
This section will apply to both American Arts and Crafts timeline pieces—the Midwest Prairie (style) School side chair and the settle, representing the East Coast Craftsman Furniture style. A *settle* refers to a wooden bench, usually with arms and a high back, and long enough to accommodate three or four sitters. In some respects, it can be equated to a sofa or settee.

Both pieces share those features that collectively identify them as American Arts and Craft furniture, regardless of being designed and made in different regions of the country. In looking at the form of the side chair and settle, what becomes obvious is that the form is sturdy and predominantly rectilinear, and there is an emphasis on clean geometric lines. Omnipresent is the linear line as seen in the chair back and stiles of the settle's back. These furniture pieces have no applied ornamentation. Features were amalgamated into the design of the furniture, such as construction, assembly and the aesthetic quality, becoming indistinguishable. This is noticeable when looking at the settle's under-arm bracing and square peg on its top joining it to the leg. The medium is oak, a native species to both regions, and there is no desire to hide the wood grain pattern resulting from being rift-sawn, plain-sawn, and/or quarter-sawn. The imaginative and authentic pierce splat design for the side chair is a perfect example of function and aesthetic being intrinsically linked.

Furniture
The **side chair**, 1910, Chicago, Illinois, Prairie Style, is designed by Prairie School architect George Grant Elmslie (1869–1952). The chair is in the American Art Gallery at the Art Institute of Chicago (Figure 9.7). George Grant Elmslie was born

in Scotland but spent his entire career practicing architecture in Chicago and the Midwest. His career path is outstanding, and Elmslie worked for a number of esteemed Chicago Prairie School architects. Designing the building and the space within was part of the Prairie School holistic approach to architecture. The side chair design is masterfully exemplifying this approach.

Figure 9.7
Side chair, 1910, Prairie Style, Chicago, Illinois (American Arts and Crafts). Designed by George Grant Elmslie. Oak, laminated oak, horsehair.
Source: Art Institute of Chicago, American Art Gallery. Creative commons Zero (CC0). Mrs. William P. Boggess II Fund.

Elmslie's esteemed work lineage begins as an apprentice in the office of William LeBaron Jenney, "father of the skyscraper"; next, the office of Dankmar Adler & Louis Sullivan; then for Sullivan's practice where he was responsible for detailing the ornamentation for Sullivan's most highly regarded commissions, such as the Wainwright Building in St. Louis and National Famers Bank in Owatonna, Minnesota.

The side chair masterfully translates the use of Sullivan's "Ornamentalism" vocabulary. This is evident in the design of the triangulated splat. Its pierced openings around the edge and center remind us of the natural world, yet the rectangular plane and linear strips recall the man-made—orchestrated geometry. The triangular plane of the splat serves both a functional role and ornamental role.

The chair has a sturdy appearance typical of American Arts and Crafts furniture. Also typical is the medium—quarter-sawn cut and laminated oak. The seat upholstery is leather with jute webbing. The original seat was horsehair upholstery. The chair height and overall size is H 50⅛"× 19¼" × 16¼".

Clearly George Grant Elmslie's imagination had no limits. The chair is imaginative and authentic. Its originality embraces the Prairie School architect's vision of developing an indigenous North American style.

This **settle**, ca. 1909, Eastwood, New York, Craftsman Furniture, designed by Gustav Stickley (1858–1942) (Figure 9.8). Made by the Craftsman Workshops (Gustav Stickley Company), Eastwood, New York, 1898–1915. Stickley's parents,

German émigrés, came to Osceola, Wisconsin, in the mid-19th century. The extent of Gustav's training in furniture design and making was working in his uncle's chair factory in Brandt, Pennsylvania. His first business enterprise was with his four brothers until 1895; by 1898, he had opened the Gustav Stickley Company. In 1898, he also traveled to Europe to the British Isles where he was exposed to the well-established styles of the Arts and Crafts movement.[36] After his European travels, his ideology for his furniture design became nostalgic in its evocation of handicraft and the pre-industrial era, and proto-modern in its functional simplicity.[37]

In the summer of 1900, Gustav Stickley created his first Arts and Crafts works for an experimental line called New Furniture.[38] The furniture reflected the American Arts and Crafts ideology—simplicity, sturdy form, honesty in construction, and truth of materials. Also characteristic of his experimental line was unadorned furniture free of applied ornamentation, the aesthetic linked to function. The wood grain was exposed, typically rift-, quarter-, and plain-sawn oak and exposed joinery—mortise-and-tenon which emphasize the structural quality of the piece.

In October 1900, Stickley published the first issue of *The Craftsman* magazine, a vehicle for publicizing both his designs for decorative arts and his philosophy for good design.[39] Good design was synonymous with England Arts and Crafts style. The publication also gave him ample opportunity to promote his belief in coordinating the interior and exterior.[40] In 1903, he changed the name of his company to the Craftsman Workshops, and began a concerted effort to market his works, which included not only furniture but textiles, lighting, and metalwork.

Figure 9.8
Settle, 1909, Craftsman Furniture, Eastwood, New York (American Arts and Crafts). Designed by Gustave Stickley. Oak and leather upholstery (replacement).
Source: Art Institute of Chicago, American Gallery. Creative commons Zero (CC0). Gift of Mrs. and Mrs. John J. Evans Jr.

The settle's craftsman style characteristics are clearly visible. What must be remembered is that the American Arts and Crafts makers did not shy away from modern woodworking machinery. Stickley's furniture, like George Grant Elmslie's chair, was fabricated using both hand-working techniques and modern woodworking machinery.

The American Arts and Crafts preference for linear lines is evident in the settle's horizontal seat rail and stretchers and vertical stiles which form its back. The medium is the ubiquitous oak, and its size is H 38" × W 71 1/16" × D 22". The leather upholstery is not original. The bracing under the arm and square peg exposure on top of the arm and bracket underneath reveal its assembly. The directional wood grain reinforces its form horizontally and vertically, plain-sawn on the back stiles and quarter-sawn or rift-sawn front rail. The settle appears sturdy, simply designed, and unmistakably American Arts and Crafts, Craftsman style. Gustav Stickley's work, like that of the Prairie Style, recalls the ideals of developing an indigenous North American style. It is fortunate and invaluable to the nation's cultural heritage that the Stickley company (www.stickley.com) is still in operation today honoring the Arts and Crafts movement of the early 20th century.

What makes these American Arts and Crafts—Prairie style and Craftsman style?

There is no mistake in saying that American Arts and Crafts closely follow the Arts and Crafts movement of the British Isles in respect to doctrine and both formal and aesthetic vocabulary. Upon first glance, it can be a challenge to distinguish the difference. However, the difference is linked to the indigenous yearning by the architect and designer, the desire to make Arts and Crafts American and native to a region—Midwestern, Eastern, Western etc. The common and obvious characteristics collectively that define American Arts and Crafts, and form and aesthetic for Prairie Style and Craftsman style succinctly can be listed as such; the piece visually has an appearance of being handcrafted and nostalgic—from some past. There is honesty in construction and materials. The form is sturdy and rectilinear, and the emphasis is on clean geometric lines, most often rectilinear. The medium is oak rift-sawn, quarter-sawn or plain, and exposing the grain is welcome. The pieces are usually unadorned; applied ornament is minimal. Linked are the aesthetics, function, and construction features, which are amalgamated into the design as a whole.

To conclude Chapter 9 and to provide the reader context and an idea of a total environment, an Art Nouveau dining room has been selected. The Salle à Manger Masson was designed by Eugène Vallin (1856–1922), architect, furniture designer, and manufacturer, and is installed at the Musée de l'École de Nancy (Plate 9.1). Eugène Vallin's Art Nouveau oeuvre is highly regarded and directly linked to his affiliation with École de Nancy (Nancy School), a group of Art Nouveau artisans, architects, and designers working in Nancy, ca. 1890–1914. The dining room was offered to the city of Nancy in 1938.[41] Its dimensions are slightly different from the original room, due to modifications made for its installation in the museum in 1961.[42]

The dining room was designed for Charles Masson, ca. 1903–1906.[43] The room's impeccable design epitomizes the Art Nouveau "new art" completely, and importantly the room brilliantly demonstrates the crucial Art Nouveau design feature of encompassing the full surface of the planes touched. Evident in the dining

Plate 9.1
The Salle à Manger Masson, 1903–1904, Nancy, France. Designed by Eugène Vallin. Artwork, the work of Victor Prouvé. Installed at the Musée de l"Ecole de Nancy.

Source: Mark Hinchman, *History of Furniture A Global View* (New York: Fairchild Books, A Division of Condé Nast Publications, Inc., 2009), p.430.

room is the Art Nouveau design vocabulary—highly ornamental and stylized relief linework that is curvaceous and sinuous. Some lines are smooth and graceful, and others more energetic. At certain junctures, the lines simultaneously move axially and radially. Asymmetry is preferred over symmetry. Natural motifs are used—harmonic foliate lines and shapes appear inspired by nature yet abstracted and stylized.

Vallin chose to reinterpret the traditional bourgeois dining room in accordance with the École de Nancy canons.[44] Important to the room is the central Art Nouveau design copper candelabra hanging from the room's center that simultaneously projects axial and radial and diffuses its light on three levels, creating a warm ambience for the space. The room's corners softly curve, and Vallin added six bouquets of tree tulip light fixtures in the area which accentuate the shape when illuminated. The ceiling is made of four pasted canvas panels divided by curved wood molding and illuminated by the candelabra's upper lights. Three allegoric panels were painted by Victor Prouvé, evoking the five senses through feminine figures. The carved wood on the buffet reflects food and drink, and on the chimney a lumber jack is a reminder not only of the wood in the chimney, but also of the material making up this room. Leather panels with rose motifs cover the walls. Several of Vallin's furniture pieces shown here are from other commissions, such as the buffet on the left and two small tables. It is fortunate to have the reinstallation of the Salle à Manger Masson for it convincingly demonstrates the merits of the Art Nouveau style.

This concludes Chapter 9. Chapter 10 moves further into the 20th century. Touched upon will be pivotal canons that contributed to the Modernist design direction in Europe; additionally, America will be touched upon.

NOTES

1. Art Institute of Chicago, Exhibition Brochure, *Apostles of Beauty, Arts and Crafts from Britain to Chicago*, November 7, 2009–January 31, 2010.
2. Brian D. Coleman *The Arts and Crafts Homes in Great Britain* (Layton, Utah: Gibbs Smith, 2005), p.vii.
3. Peter Davey, *Arts and Crafts Architecture* (London: Phaidon Press, 1997), p.11.
4. On-line Collection, Object label, Glasgow School of Art, Glasgow, Scotland, 2020.
5. Ibid.
6. Dennis French, Design 1900online.com, Europen Design & Architecture 1900, Tea Rooms, 2008.
7. Ibid.
8. Ibid.
9. Pat Kirkham, *Charles Rennie Mackintosh* (New York, London, Paris: Glasgow Museums and Abbeville Press, 1996), p.230.
10. Ibid.
11. William J.R. Curtis, *Modern Architecture since 1900* (Prentice Hall, 1996), p.54.
12. Ibid.
13. March Hinchman, *History of Furniture: A Global View* (Fairchild Books, 2009), p.431.
14. https://en.wikipedia.org/wiki/Art_Nouveau#Origins.
15. https://en.wikipedia.org/wiki/Eugène_Gaillard.

16 https://en.wikipedia.org/wiki/Hector_Guimard.
17 Ibid.
18 https://en.wikipedia.org/wiki/Vienna_Secession.
19 Ibid.
20 Ibid.
21 Judith Gura, *The Guide to Period Styles for Interiors: From 1st Century to Present* (New York: Fairchild Books, 2016), p.261.
22 Ibid., p.262.
23 https://en.wikipedia.org/wiki/Wiener_Werkstätte
24 Ghenete Zelleke, Eva B. Ottillinger, and Nina Stritzler, *Against the Grain: Bentwood Furniture from the Collection of Fern and Manfred Steinfeld* (Art Institute of Chicago, 1993), p.86.
25 Ibid.
26 www.dwr.com/designer-josef-hoffmann?lang=en_US.
27 Ibid.
28 Ibid.
29 https://en.wikipedia.org/wiki/Otto_Wagner.
30 On-line Collection, Object label, Art Institute of Chicago, European Decorative Art Gallery, 2020.
31 https://en.wikipedia.org/wiki/Otto_Wagner.
32 Judith Miller, *Furniture World Styles from Classical to Contemporary* (New York: Dorling Kindersley, 2005), p.336.
33 Ibid., p.322.
34 https://en.wikipedia.org/wiki/Prairie_School.
35 Ibid.
36 Treena Crochet, *Designer's Guide to Furniture Styles* (New Jersey: Prentice Hall, 1999), p.206.
37 https://en.Wikipedia.org/wiki/Gustav_Stickley.
38 Ibid.
39 Judith Miller, *Furniture World Styles from Classical to Contemporary* (New York: Dorling Kindersley, 2005), p.399.
40 Treena Crochet, *Designer's Guide to Furniture Styles* (New Jersey: Prentice Hall, 1999), p.206.
41 https://izi.travel.en/1588-eugene-vallin-and-victor-prouve-dining-room-masson-1903-1906/en, 2020.
42 Ibid.
43 Ibid.
44 Ibid.

10 Modernist movements

Deutscher Werkbund, Bauhaus, De Stijl, International Style

10.1
Pictorial timeline—Modernist movements: Deutscher Werkbund, Bauhaus, De Stijl, International Style

TIME PERIOD OVERVIEW

By the beginning of the 20th century, large commercial furniture manufacturers used machines to produce standardized pieces, usually period pieces.[1] What prevailed by the dawn of the 20th century was an acceptance of the machine's necessity for furniture design and production. As the Modern style took hold, what dictated was a style of functional design for machine production and contemporary living.[2]

To form an understanding of Modern furniture contextually, it will be necessary to have background on Modern architecture and some of its early movements

261

which impacted other aspects of the built environment including furniture design. It is not unusual to relegate Modernism to a simplified iconic entity.[3] However, over the years historians and scholars have acknowledged that Modernism is a pluralistic phenomenon.[4] Between about 1890 and the 1920s, a number of positions emerged which claimed "modernity" as a chief attribute, and by the 1930s it seemed as if a broad consensus had at last been achieved.[5] The notion and significance of "modernity" differed from place to place, even from mind to mind, but the essential preconditions including the mechanization of the city, the introduction of new materials such as iron, glass, and steel, experimental clients, and creative architects intent on expressing the new state of things in spaces and forms are consistent.[6]

Imperative to keep in mind is that the architects and designers were not merely designing but purposely forging a movement.[7] The architecture, which was to have expunged tradition, founded a tradition of its own.[8] Modern architecture itself eventually created the basis for a new tradition with its own themes, forms, and motifs. Intrinsic to the tradition of the Modern style are architecture movements impacted by people, location, and shared aims. The Modern style was elastic enough for divergences and to permit individual interpretation.[9]

Now for a review of a few of these movements which signaled a new 20th-century design direction for architects, interior designers, artisans, and manufacturers, and an introduction to the leading protagonists. Much of the early creative work took place in Germany, Austria, Holland, and France, and later spread throughout the Continent and leaped "across the pond" to the United States. A listing of a few key movements and architects associated with the rise of the Modern movement will provide some background. It is fitting to start with Germany in 1907 and the establishment of the Deutscher Werkbund associated with founders Hermann Muthesius, Peter Behrens, Walter Gropius, and others, and also the German Jugendstil, 1910, which was the German counterpart of Art Nouveau, associated with Richard Riemerschmid. In Germany emerged the Bauhaus School, 1919–1933; those associated with it include Walter Gropius, Ludwig Mies van der Rohe, and Marcel Breuer. In the Netherlands, Modern architecture was impacted by the art movement known as De Stijl, or "The Style," also referred to as Neo-plasticism. Well-known artists associated with De Stijl are the founder, artist and author Theo van Doesburg, painter Piet Mondrian, and architect Gerrit Rietveld. By the mid-1920s, France takes the stage for Modernist design activity. In 1925, a World Fair was held in Paris designed by the French government—the *Exposition Internationale des Arts Décoratifs et Industriels Modernes*, which was to highlight the new Modern style of architecture, interior design, furniture design, and decorative arts. The Exposition introduced and promoted what was to be the new French Modern style, Art Deco—an abbreviation of *Arts Décoratifs*. This term has been in use only since the 1960s. This style, for Modernism in which functionalism was valued, was not modern enough. An aversion to the style, and to the Societé des Artistes Décorateurs (SAD—Society of Decorative Artists) which sponsored the annual Salon des Artistes Décorateurs promoting Art Deco as the new Modern, resulted in an alternative, the Union des Artistes Modernes (UAM). This membership included architects with a vastly different interpretation of "modernity," such as Charles-Edouard Jeanneret (known as Le Corbusier), Pierre Jeanneret, Charlotte Perriand, Pierre Chareau, Eileen Gray, and Jean Prouvé.

Lastly, one of the most viable ways to promote "modernity" was through exhibitions, publications, and affiliations with professional organizations. From 1928 to 1959, the Congrès Internationaux d'Architecture Moderne (CIAM—International Congresses of Modern Architecture) was responsible for a series of exhibitions, expositions, and competitions organized by the most prominent architects of the time from countries across Europe. The objective was to spread the principles of Modern architecture and design that later became known as Internationalism. From this period on, there was considerable effort in distinguishing the characteristics of 1930s Internationalism. Associated with CIAM were many of the same individuals involved in the UAM—members included Le Corbusier, Pierre Jeanneret, Charlotte Perriand, Eileen Gray, Walter Gropius, and Ludwig Mies van der Rohe.

Modern architecture, the style emerging in Europe in the 1920s and 1930s, was first recognized in the United States in 1932, when historian Henry-Russell Hitchcock and architect Philip Johnson coined the term "International Style" as a result of their collaborative exhibition for the Museum of Modern Art, in New York, titled "Modern Architecture: International Exhibition," New York, February 10–March 23, 1932.[10] They appropriated the term "International Style" to describe the plain, unadorned European architecture of rectilinear forms built of steel, reinforced concrete, and glass[11]—the style that would throughout the next several decade transform the skylines of many major cities around the world. The architecture vocabulary of the International Style became that expressive language of simple, floating volumes, clear-cut geometries, and white facades of concrete. This ideology was shared by a diverse group of architects—J.J.P. Oud, Gerrit Rietveld, Walter Gropius, and Ludwig Mies van der Rohe. Other movements within the Modernist canon to be noted are Expressionism, Regionalism, and Functionalism.

This chapter's furniture selection for the pictorial timeline is what the author deems most influential in terms of early 20th-century design and the production for furniture of "modernity."

DEUTSCHER WERKBUND 1907–1914, GERMANY

History

The Deutscher Werkbund movement was founded by Hermann Muthesius in 1907, with the aim to forge a closer relationship between German industrialists and artists to develop a German identity through design and architecture and to upgrade the quality of design—German National design. The structure of the Werkbund was an emulation of what Muthesius had seen in the English Arts and Crafts movement.[12] However, a critical difference was that eventually formal attitudes would emerge in which an adulatory view of mechanization was to be found.[13] Mechanization came to be regarded as a sort of essential motor to the forward march of history, requiring an appropriate expression in architecture and design.[14] Linked to German National identity ideologically was the elevation of general taste to a position of supremacy in world markets and affairs, and the moral tenor of life was to be raised through the impact of well-designed objects in the marketplace, in the home, and in the workplace.[15]

The Werkbund expanded on adopting concerns that craft and design influenced people's lives and propagated a rejection of historicism in favor of vernacular architecture suited to the modern age. However, the Deutscher Werkbund sought to combine promotion of craft with industry, integrating machine production. The Werkbund embraced technology to design objects and buildings that fulfilled the changing needs of society—a relevant ideology since, between 1894 and 1904, the value of Germany's foreign trade doubled, and by 1913 Germany overtook Great Britain in percentage of world production. By 1914 there were over one thousand members.[16]

Peter Behrens, architect, artist, and industrial designer, was a founding member of the Deutscher Werkbund and a leading German architect early during the Modern movement. Behrens epitomizes the Werkbund's preoccupations with representing industry as both noble and part of German identity.[17] He believed that the industrial tasks must be seen as the essential cultural ones of the time.[18] Peter Behrens' commission to design for the electrical company Allgemeine Elektricitäts-Gesellschaft (AEG) was the first large-scale architecture commission that demonstrated the viability and vitality of the Werkbund's "modernity" initiatives and objectives. From 1908 to 1914, the establishment and evolution of Behren's architecture work for AEG is an essential link to the rise of the Modernist style. Behrens successfully formed a corporate identity for AEG, through graphic design, advertising, products, and also architecture. Not only did the AEG company change the nature of mass production with its decision to hire a talented architect, designer, and artist such as Behrens, but the erection of the AEG Turbine Hall (1908–1909) was a transforming moment for architecture, solidifying a change in a Modern direction firmly rooted in the "Avant-Garde."[19] Additionally, because of AEG's immense size, the introduction of design to industrial production heralded AEG's ever-increasing economic power.

By 1914, the Werkbund Exhibition in Cologne showed the split between the group—Expressionistic forms and ideas versus Rationalism. Debates among the founding members led to the weakening of the Deutscher Werkbund and after World War I the group lost influence. The Deutscher Werkbund was an incredibly important and influential movement appropriate for the Zeitgeist (spirit of the time) and creative rhythm of the moment. The idea that architects and designers could be part of mass production and industrial design continued to develop in Germany with the Bauhaus School headed by Werkbund affiliate architect Walter Gropius.

Side chair, 1902, Germany, Modernism

Aesthetic
This first timeline piece of Peter Behrens recalls the desire of Deutscher Werkbund to link industry, art, formal invention, and standardization. In looking at this side

chair, there is an acknowledgment of the machine age, Classical principles, and handcraft. The chair's erect form seems machine-driven and the orchestration of the vertical and horizontal framing members is reminiscent of the formularization of "Classical Orders." However, an overriding quality of the chair appears craftlike and handmade. Evident is an appreciation of straightforward use of natural materials; the ebonized wood and rattan seem to hint at this. As well as the functional construction and unadorned form, the attractiveness resides in the chair's straightforward presence and how its geometry comes together to complete the form. This side chair appears stable and solid, and the design emits truth in material and construction, reminiscent of Arts and Crafts furniture of the British Isles.

Figure 10.1
Side chair, 1902, Germany, Deutscher Werkbund. Designed by Peter Behrens. Ebonized oak and woven rattan.

Source: Art Institute of Chicago, European Decorative Art Gallery. Creative commons Zero (CC0). Restricted gift of Mr. and Mrs. Manfred Steinfeld.

Furniture

This **side chair**, 1902, Germany, Deutscher Werkbund, is designed by Peter Behrens (1868–1940) for the Wertheim department store in Berlin (Figure 10.1). The chair resides at the European Decorative Art, gallery at the Art Institute of Chicago. The medium is ebonized oak and woven rattan is used for the seat. Its size is H 39″ × W 17¾″ × D 21½″.[20]

The chair was created for a model dining-room display at the Wertheim department store in Berlin. It was one of 12 architect-designed rooms installed at the store.[21] The concept of having the architect-designed spaces was to disseminate the philosophy of Modern design to consumers. The geometric forms of the chair translated to the lighting, wallpaper, and carpet of the room.[22]

The chair is geometrically articulate—for example, the vertical and horizontal framing members, the splat which is a wide solid straight line capped off at the top and bottom with a rectangular member. Softness is added with the splayed right and left stile gently arching outward and terminating in lightly sculpted legs. There is no need for applied ornamentation; the geometric form and various components—straight and curved, textured and smooth, light and dark—create a visually pleasing whole.

Peter Behrens designed buildings, furniture, metalwork, ceramics, glass, textiles, and other objects. His formal education was in fine art not architecture, and his career path began as artist and educator. He became interested in subjects related to reform of lifestyles, which led to his architecture associates and ultimately his affiliation with the Deutscher Werkbund. His thriving architecture office was seminal for the Modern movement and germane to his architectural assistants' careers that his affiliation would set in motion. These men—Walter Gropius, Adolf Meyer, Ludwig Mies van der Rohe, and Le Corbusier—would become legendary Modernists of the 20th century, exercising the Modern language in the most remarkable buildings around the globe.

THE BAUHAUS SCHOOL, 1919–1933

History

The Bauhaus School began in Weimar, Germany, in 1919. Its founder, Walter Gropius, was the director through 1925 and remained actively involved until its closing. His initial idea for the school centered on the notion of combining crafts and the fine arts. The approach was to level out the past tradition of hierarchy of arts where fine arts, sculpture, and painting were at the top; therefore, the practical crafts such as architecture and interior design, textiles and woodwork, would be placed on a par. However, Weimar officials and residents regarded the new school's ideology and presence as foreign; this foreign-ness was irreconcilable, causing the school to change locations. The school relocated to Dessau. The Mayor of Dessau, by contrast, showed considerable sympathy for the ideals of the school.[23] The school moved to Dessau by 1926 and this was the Golden Age of the Bauhaus.[24] Within a year, a site had been chosen and Walter Gropius designed the new buildings for the school. This was an opportunity for him to create an exemplary Modern work in which all the arts would be synthesized.[25] Gropius brought to the Bauhaus teachers and masters from multiple disciplines whose reputations remain commendable a century later: the painters Wassily Kandisky and Paul Klee, designers Lázló Mohaly-Nagy, Josef Albers, and Anni Albers, metalworker Marianne Brandt, weaver and photographer Gertrud Arnd, and architects Marcel Breuer, Mart Stam, and Ludwig Mies van de Rohe, the latter serving as Bauhaus director the year it closed.

The school was arguably the single most influential Modernist art school of the 20th century.[26] It was deeply concerned with intellectual and theoretical aspects of its subject. It became famous for its pedagogical approach, a model that involved the entwinement of art, society, and technology. Pertaining to teaching, it emphasized experimentation and problem-solving and the reconceptualization of the artistic process. The school's approach to design attempted to unify the principles of mass production with individual artistic vision and strove to combine aesthetics with everyday function. In 1933, under the directorship of Mies van de Rohe, the school closed due to pressure from the Nazi regime which labeled the education institution as a center of communist intellectualism.[27] Although the school closed, the staff were exalted and left Germany, emigrating all over the world and continuing to spread the Bauhaus idealistic precepts.

Throughout the 20th century, the Bauhaus ideology proved to be enormously influential, especially for higher education. It led to rethinking and reshaping curricula for the art and design departments of many colleges and universities.

Throughout the century, the school's precepts became some of the most powerful currents of thinking for design education, impacting art, architecture, graphic design, interior design, industrial design, typography, and textile design. The idealistic goals of the Bauhaus, some would argue, still resonate and continue to have some impact on contemporary art and design education.

Wassily Chair (Model No. B3), 1925, Bauhaus, Dessau, Germany, Cesca Armchair (Model No. B32), 1928, Germany

Aesthetics

Keeping in line with the school's philosophy, Bauhaus furniture design was revolutionary and experimental. The Bauhaus designers embraced the increasing prevalence of machines in factories and mass production and standardization, yet envisioned that the designer would function as a mediator between invention and standardized form. For the designer, the ideas evolved around developing a system of forms that symbolized the modern world. The major part of this equation was embracing the technological advances of the late 19th and early 20th century and experimenting with new materials and existing materials in new ways. The result would produce designs with forms that are simple, harmonious, geometric, airy, and lightweight in appearance and have an industrial-like practicality. The designs would be inexpensive enough for an average citizen to purchase readily. A key material used would be steel tubing—standard gas pipe and pipe joint fittings. The use of steel tubing took on a new dimension for furniture design, particularly chair design. Experimental prototypes using tubular steel were explored, implementing the use of chrome-plated steel and cantilever seats, and with the overriding idea that the design could be standardized and mass-produced for the average citizen. Unfortunately, over time the traditional chrome plating proved bad for the environment. Fortunately, environmentally responsible processes are used today. New "green" trivalent chromium eliminates the health and environmental concerns and uses spray chrome, a safer alternative to chrome plating.

Furniture

The next timeline piece, the **Wassily Chair (Model No. B3)**, 1925, Germany, designed by Marcel Breuer, American, born in Hungary (1902–1981). The chair is part of the Cooper Hewitt Smithsonian Design Museum Collection (Figure 10.2).

Marcel Breuer was a protégé of the Bauhaus founder and director, Walter Gropius. At 19 years old, Breuer was one of the youngest students to enter the Bauhaus, joining in 1920, a year after the school's opening.[28] He was one of the most influential and prolific graduates of the school. Model No. B3, a tubular steel armchair, was one of Breuer's first projects upon returning to the Bauhaus as a teacher. He designed the chair for Wassily Kandinsky's living quarters at the Dessau, Bauhaus, and later renamed it the Wassily Chair.

The Wassily Chair utterly transformed the language of chair design.[29] It was revolutionary in the use of tubular steel and its method of manufacturing. Its chrome-plated tubular steel frame has a square geometry and possess those qualities mentioned under **Aesthetics**, such as simple form, airy and lightweight in appearance. Its constituent parts—the slanted tubular back and seat, looped arms and seat frame—work harmoniously together with the canvas upholstery as the natural element that brings all parts together. Today, however, leather upholstery has replaced the canvas. The size is H 28 11/16" × W 30 5/16" × D 26¾".[30] The manufacturing of the chair came several years after the design, ca. 1927–1928.

Figure 10.2 Wassily Chair, 1925, manufactured ca. 1927–1928. Design by Marcel Breuer (American, b. Hungary, 1902–1981). Probably manufactured by Standard-Möbel (Dessau, Germany). Chrome-plated steel, canvas H 72.8 x W 77 x D 68 cm.

Source: Cooper Hewitt, Smithsonian Design.

The next timeline piece is the **Cesca Armchair, (Model No. B32)**, 1928, Germany, reissued ca. 1971, Knoll International, New York.[31] This chair is also designed by Marcel Breuer. It resides at Yale University Art Gallery, New Haven, Connecticut, in the American Decorative Arts Collection (Figure 10.3).

Similar to the Wassily Chair, the Cesca Armchair represents how Marcel Breuer marries traditional craftsmanship with industrial methods and materials. Its cantilevered form exploits the possibilities unique to the material and gives the chair added flexibility and comfort.[32] Its frame is polished tubular steel and black painted beechwood, and the seat features woven cane inserts and a beech frame. The Cesca Armchair's size is H 31" × W 23" × D 21¾".[33] The chair comes with arms or without, and with other types of seating materials.

Figure 10.3 Cesca Armchair, 1928, Germany. Designed by Marcel Breuer. Polished tubular steel frame, and black painted beechwood, with woven cane seat.

Source: Yale University, The American Decorative Art Gallery, New Haven, Connecticut. Creative commons Zero (CC0). Knoll International, New York, N.Y. Millicent Todd Bingham Fund.

Marcel Breuer named the chair after his daughter Francesca. The family's nickname for her was Cesca.[34] Knoll introduced the Cesca Armchair in 1968 following its acquisition of Gavina Group, an Italian furniture manufacturer that represented Breuer's designs. Breuer's work was in many ways a perfect demonstration of the Bauhaus ideals of art meeting industry and his more rational approach. Bauhaus furniture had a tremendous impact on 20th-century furniture design and beyond. Twenty-first-century architects and designers specify Bauhaus furniture such as the Wassily Chair and Cesca Armchair for projects today, as well as for personal possession. It is reassuring to the design community that Bauhaus furniture continues to be manufactured in many parts of the world.

DE STIJL, CA. 1917–1931, NETHERLANDS

History

The De Stijl—The Style—movement existed in the Netherlands from around 1917 to 1931. Its central figures and founders were visual artists. Key individuals were the painters Theo van Doesburg and Piet Mondrian and architects Gerrit Rietveld and J.J.P. Oud among others. Theo van Doesburg published a journal of the same name helping to promote their philosophy and innovative ideas. The movement's contribution to the "modernity" Zeitgeist envisioned establishing a universal visual language. The language embraced a pared-down aesthetic centered on basic visual elements such as geometric shapes, simple forms, primary colors, and asymmetrical arrangements. The language outcome was balanced composition conveying harmony and visual abstraction. This approach is also referred to as Neoplasticism. Succinctly, Neoplastic art and architecture compositionally focused on the elemental forms of point, line, and plane, which, when constructed three-dimensionally, translates visually as volume.

De Stijl members' attention did not center only on the fine arts, but crossed art platforms that included architecture, interiors, industrial design, typography, literature, and music. De Stijl protagonists' ambition was to define an appropriate symbolic visual expression for Modernism, and the distillation was a formal language of tensely related, simple forms and shapes. This idea, noticed by architects, resolved into a compelling unit in the realm of architecture. Architects and designers striving for similar purpose were affected by De Stijl ideology and the group's works. Bauhaus architects Walter Gropius and Marcel Breuer, as well as Gerrit Rietveld and others, began to incorporate these spatial concepts in architecture. This interrelationship with De Stijl helped propel the International Style of the 1920s and 1930s.

Red/Blue Chair, 1917, Netherlands, De Stijl

Aesthetics

In general, the formal language of De Stijl seen in art consists of simple forms and shapes, balanced compositions that resolve into a compelling unit. This is visible in the Red/Blue Chair design. Keep in mind De Stijl's characteristics of asymmetry, simple geometry—lines, circles, squares—and use of primary colors. The Red/Blue Chair is controlled symmetry instead of the esteemed asymmetry valued by De Stijl creatives, yet one could surmise that the Red/Blue Chair is a three-dimensional equivalent of De Stijl characteristics. The chair's form is an impressive reinterpretation of De Stijl features—points, lines and planes. Notice its simple construction with very few components. The De Stijl line here translates to joinery—struts and rails with each line terminated and accentuated with yellow paint. De Stijl use of squares and rectangles translates to the back and seat of the chair painted in primary red and blue. The chair, like De Stijl art, is a balanced composition conveying a well-orchestrated and harmonized unit.

Furniture

The **Red/Blue Chair**, ca. 1918, Netherlands, was designed by architect Gerrit Rietveld (1888–1964). The chair is in the collection of the Museum of Modern Art, New York (Figure 10.3). It is considered a pivotal work of early De Stijl. Gerrit Rietveld's design attempts to find a functioning equivalent in three dimension of a rectilinear abstract painting.[35] The chair was originally designed with a natural wood finish.[36] Rietveld painted the chair around 1923 as a result of his association with De Stijl.[37] Rietveld aimed for simplicity in construction. The pieces of wood that compose the Red/Blue Chair are in the standard lumber sizes readily available at the time.

The chair's medium is painted plywood, and the size is H 34⅛" × W 26" × D 33", seat H 13".[38] The form is a manipulation of rectilinear volumes and an exploration of the interaction between vertical and horizontal planes. The vertical and horizontal struts and rails are painted black and each appears to run beyond the other, terminated by a yellow-accented end. The bypassing linear planes with painted ends suggest that one element is floating independently of another. The visual implication is that all parts appear to be hovering in a tangible continuous space.[39]

Rietveld's chair bears symbolic significance as a prototype for machine art and the character of a standardized object.[40] Yet the chair is a one-off handmade object or "custom" piece. Such a piece designed for a client would typically cost considerably more to produce. Rietveld's intention for much of his furniture was that it would eventually be mass-produced rather than handcrafted.[41]

Figure 10.4
Red/Blue Chair, ca. 1918, Netherlands. Designer Gerrit Thomas Rietveld. Plywood construction, painted red, blue, black, and yellow.

Source: Museum of Modern Art, New York, N.Y. Department: Architecture and Design. Gift of Phillip Johnson Rietveld, Gerrit (1888–1964) © ARS, NY. Red and Blue Chair, c. 1918, Gift of Philip Johnson. Digital Image ©The Museum of Modern Art/Licensed by SCALA / Art Resource, NY.

The Red/Blue Chair was used in a residence that is considered the first actual building to embody the full range of De Stijl formal, spatial, and iconographic intentions—the Schröder house in Utrecht, Holland.[42] This iconic landmark of Utrecht is currently an UNESCO World Heritage site.

INTERNATIONAL STYLE, 1920–1930S

The term International Style is typically used interchangeably with the Modern movement in architecture. As mentioned in the **Time period overview**, the moniker was the invention of Museum of Modern Art curators Henry-Russell Hitchcock and Philip Johnson, for the 1932 "Modern Architecture: International Exhibition."

Shortly afterward, Hitchcock and Johnson published the exhibition catalog from the show as a book, *The International Style*. Their book is significant for historians and scholars today. The show and publication become the genesis of a Modern Architecture Movement in the United States. Another impactful moment was the outbreak of World War II causing European Modernists to cross the pond. In the 1930s Europeans began to take up residence and start architecture practices in the United States. Two critical players became heads of two eminent architecture schools, Gropius at Harvard Graduate School of Design (GSD) and Mies at the Armour Institute, later the Illinois Institute of Technology (IIT). Fellow Bauhaus colleagues and emigrés joined them, Marcel Breuer at the GSD and László Moholy-Nagy at IIT.

A preeminent research center for arts and culture, the Getty Research Institute (GRI) offers a most succinct description for the International Style:

> The style of architecture that emerged in Holland, France, and Germany after World War I and spread throughout the world, becoming the dominant architectural style until the 1970s. The style is characterized by an emphasis on volume over mass, the use of lightweight, mass-produced, industrial materials, rejection of all ornament and color, repetitive modular forms, and the use of flat surfaces, typically alternating with areas of glass.[43]

The International Style in the United State became admired by architecture practitioners, faculty, and students. This constituency was in awe and willing to pay homage in commissions, competitions, and student projects. The European International architects were given the moniker "White Gods" because the building material used was usually whitewashed concrete or stucco. Architects and the greater design community kept their fervor for the International Style well into the 20th century; around the 1970s, it began to wane and allowed other movements to take the stage such as Brutalism, Postmodernism, Deconstructivism, and High-tech.

Upon closing this **History** segment, there is one last component to the "modernity" framework. Outside of Germany and Holland, the other major center of early Modernist design activity was France.[44] One of the most notable protagonists essential to the Modern movement was Charles-Édouard Jeanneret (1887–1965), known by the moniker Le Corbusier, architect, writer and artist. Before settling in Paris Le Corbusier spent time in Germany working in the architecture office of Peter Behrens. After leaving Germany in the early 1920s, Le Corbusier and his cousin Pierre Jeanneret (1896–1967) opened an architecture office in Paris. In 1927, the men did something unprecedented, Le Corbusier and Jeanneret hired a female architect, Charlotte Perriand (1903–1999), to work in their office. This was a result of Le Corbusier seeing her project "Le bar sous le toit" at the Salon d'Automne in Paris. From this point on, the eminent trio helped define and epitomize Modernism and the International Style architecturally as well as in interior design and furniture design. The collaboration of Le Corbusier, Jeanneret, and Perriand was seminal to Modern architecture and without a doubt Modern furniture history. Their prototypical models became symbolic for "modernity" and are still revered today.

Barcelona chair, Spain, 1928–1929, MR 534 Chair, Germany, 1927, LC1, Sling Chair, France, 1928, LC2, Grand Comfort, France, 1928, LC4, Chaise Lounge, France, 1928

Aesthetics

This aesthetic explanation will apply to all furniture pieces on the pictorial timeline under the International Style. The fundamental principle and aesthetic order of the International Style's origins begin in the 1920s and by the 1930s had blossomed into its own style communicating a message about "modernity" and aesthetic vocabulary. The Bauhaus School was the leading proponent. So the genesis is partially linked to a German design philosophy—the Bauhaus acknowledgement of the inherent relationship of form and function influenced the furniture being designed, as well supporting mass production and standardization. The goal was to create mass-produced and easily affordable furniture. Aesthetically, all International Style furniture could be characterized as simple forms with an industrial quality. There is no superfluous decoration. The material and form define the aesthetic—the use of sleek materials, tubular steel, chrome plating, plastic, glass, and leather. A softer version was the introduction of rattan and wood. These iconic pieces from this period in design history are used by contemporary architects and designers.

Furniture

The first piece, the **Barcelona chair**, 1929, Germany, was designed by Ludwig Mies van der Rohe (1886–1969) for the German Pavilion at the International Exhibition in Barcelona, Spain, 1928 (Figure 10.5). The chair resides at Kunstmuseum, The Hague, Netherlands. It was designed a few years before Mies was forced to leave his position in Dessau as the last Bauhaus director due to the events in Germany leading to World War II.

Figure 10.5
Barcelona Chair, 1929, Germany. Designed by Ludwig Mies van de Rohe. Bent chrome-plated flat steel frame with leather strap supports for leather back and seat cushion. Back and seat cushions are tufted.

Source: Kunstmuseum, Den Haag, Netherlands, Furniture Collection.

This icon of the Modern movement is one of the most recognized pieces of furniture of the last century. The Barcelona chair exudes a simple elegance that epitomizes Mies van der Rohe's most famous maxim—"less is more."[45] Scholars make the argument that its form is akin to the Greek Klismos. This is attributed to Mies's Classical training and understanding of

Classical design. Whether this is the case or not, there is no doubt that it is a sensational translation as a Modern icon and features associated with "modernity" are obviously visible. Notice the raked back of the chair's frame and X-shaped side profile formed of bent chrome plated flat steel. Seventeen leather straps are used to support the leather cushions. The tufting on the cushions consist of 40 squares, the grid paying homage to geometry and held in place with leather covered buttons. The overall size H 29½" × W 29½" × D 29½".[46]

Figure 10.6
MR Chair, 1927, Germany. Designed by Ludwig Mies van de Rohe and Lilly Reich. Nickel-plated bent tubular steel frame. *(left)* Without arms, leather seat and back, *(right)* with arms, rattan continuous seat and back.
Source: Courtesy of Knoll International SpA.

Next on the timeline is the **MR Chair**, 1927, Germany (Figure 10.6), also designed by Ludwig Mies van de Rohe with collaborator Lilly Reich. During the late 1920s and 1930s, Lilly Reich and Mies collaborated on multiple projects. Reich was a German Modernist designer who in 1920 was appointed to the Deutscher Werkbund board of directors, becoming the first woman to help lead the German association. Although Reich and Mies kept separate design studios, they collaborated on furniture, exhibitions, and interior design and "exchanged artistic ideas constantly," according to art historian and scholar Christiane Lange.[47]

The material choice for the chair—a nickel-plated bent tubular steel frame—was inspired by Bauhaus colleague Marcel Breuer. The steel tubing is not used in a minimalist way but to form elegant curves that fall just short of being extravagant.[48] The forms are thought to be Modern derivatives of 19th-century iron rocking chairs.[49] The MR Chair exists with and without arms and a variety of back/seat materials. The approximate size without arms is W 19" × D 27" × H 31", seat H 18".[50]

Figure 10.7
LC 1 Sling Chair (Fauteuil Basculant No. B 301), 1928, Paris. Designed by Charles-Édouard Jeanneret-Gris, Charlotte Perriand, and Pierre Jeanneret. Chrome-plated bent tubular steel and leather upholstery.
Source: Cassina S.p.A. Italy. Courtesy of Cassina.

The next timeline piece, **LC 1 Sling Chair, (Fauteuil Basculant No. B301)**, 1928, France, was designed by the trio, Charles-Édouard Jeanneret (1887–1965), Charlotte Perriand (1903–1999), and Pierre Jeanneret (1896–1967). The chair is currently produced by an Italian manufacturing Cassina company specializing in creating high-end designer furniture (Figure 10.7). Cassina produces other pieces of the eminent trio. In 1928, the chair was originally produced by the renown Thonet company. The company's reputation as the foremost bentwood manufacturer aided in Thonet's ability to produce many early Modernist furniture designs. The LC 1 is industrial looking and its size is slight. Overall size, H 25 3/5" × W 23 3/5" × D 25½", seat H 15 1/5" and arms H 22 9/10".[51] The original prototype was chrome-plated bent tubular steel and canvas. Other versions included calf skin which gives the LC 1 a more luxurious presence. Its slight bent tubular frame has minimal parts, appearing efficient and comfortable. Notice the seat and back have about a 60-degree slant. The arms are simply leather strips slung between the tubular steel frame. It is reminiscent of an industrial conveyer belt.

Next is **LC 2, (Fauteuil Grand/Gran Comfort)**, 1928, another design by Le Corbusier, Pierre Jeanneret, and Charlotte Perriand. It is currently produced by Cassina, Italy (Figure 10.8). The chair was first exhibited at the Salon d'Automne in Paris in 1929.[52] This annual art exhibition has been held in Paris since 1903. Its genesis was a reaction to the conservative policies of the official Paris Salon. This massive exhibition almost immediately became the showpiece of developments and innovations in 20th-century painting, drawing, sculpture, architecture, and decorative arts.

Figure 10.8 LC 2 (Fauteuil Grand Comfort), 1928, Paris. Designed by Charles-Édouard Jeanneret-Gris, Charlotte Perriand, and Pierre Jeanneret. Chrome-plated bent tubular steel with seat, back, and arm cushions upholstered in leather.

Source: Cassina S.p.A. Italy. Courtesy of Cassina.

The Grand Comfort was an archetypal armchair in the new and modern conception of furnishings understood as "domestic equipment."[53] The separation of the metal frame and the cushions express a rationalist approach to industrial production.[54] The form of the chair is visually clear. Its shape is cube-like. Its large, sumptuous cushions give a sense of modern luxury. The tubular steel structural frame is like a rectilinear basket holding the rather large loose cushions in their respective position. The cushions fit into the frame like pieces in a puzzle, each having its specific place and role, in this case—arm, back, and seat. The size is H 26 4/5" × W 27 3/5" × D 21 1/5".[55] The chair was re-issued by Cassina and produced exclusively since 1965.

The next piece **LC 4 Chaise Lounge (B306 Chaise Lounge)**, 1928, is the last piece designed by Le Corbusier, Charlotte Perriand, and Pierre Jeanneret. This piece is also currently produced by Cassina, Italy (Figure 10.9). The iconic LC 4, given its design and purpose, is another memorable 20th-century Modern furniture piece. Equally recognizable is the black-and-white photograph of Modernist pioneer and avant-garde designer Charlotte Perriand shown reclined in the LC4. Both lounge and photo no doubt throughout the decades have become fixed in the memory of design and architecture students and professionals (Figure 10.10).

The debut for the lounge was at the Salon d'Automne, Paris, 1928. Originally named B306 Chaise Lounge, this resplendent daybed looks more like a piece of equipment than a furniture piece.[56] The form is simple, consisting of three

Figure 10.9
LC 4 Chaise Lounge (B 306 Chaise Lounge), 1928, Paris. Designed by Charles-Édouard Jeanneret-Gris, Charlotte Perriand, and Pierre Jeanneret.

Source: Cassina S.p.A. Italy. Courtesy of Cassina.

Figure 10.10
Charlotte Perriand resting on the chaise lounge, LC 4 Chaise Lounge (B 306 Chaise Lounge), 1928. Designed by Le Corbusier, Charlotte Perriand, and Pierre Jeanneret.

Source: Photograph DR-Archives Charlotte Perriand (1903–1999). © 2020 Artists Rights Society (ARS), New York/ADAGP, Paris/Art Resource, Inc., New York. Photo Credit: Banque d'Images.

parts—the black enamel steel H base, and the trivalent arcuated chrome-plated steel frame attached at three points to the bent plane, top, center, and end. The anthropomorphically inspired reclining plane bends in two places. The frame can be positioned for any angle of inclination. The position of the tilt is decided upon by the sitter. Once sat upon, it remains in a fixed position—guaranteed by the friction through rubber tubes that cover the cross bar of the base.[57] The medium is trivalent chrome-plated tubular steel with rubber stretchers. The upholstery leather or pony skin speaks to the Modernist interest in the primitive.[58]

To conclude Chapter 10 and provide the reader context and a total environment, the interiors of two notable examples of 20th-century design have been selected (Plate 10.1 and Plate 10.2).

■ An Illustrated Guide to Furniture History

Plate 10.1
(above) Interior space designed for "Inner Equipment of a Home," at the 1929 Fall Salon. Design by Le Corbusier, Charlotte Perriand, and Pierre Jeanneret. *(below)* View 2, Interior space designed for "Inner Equipment of a Home," 1929 Fall Salon. Designed by Le Corbusier, Charlotte Perriand, and Pierre Jeanneret.

Source: Le Corbusier Foundation, Paris. *(above)* Ref # L3(7)89, Photographer: G. Thiriet. *(below)* Ref # L3(7)97, Photographer: G. Thiriet. © 2020 Artist Rights Society (ARS), New York/ADAGP, Paris.

© F.L.C./ADAGP, Paris/Artists Rights Society (ARS), New York 2020.

Plate 10.2
Villa Tugendhat, 1929, Brno, Czech Republic. Designed by Ludwig Mies van der Rohe and Lilly Reich. *(above)* Living area looking towards curved wall of dining area, with Barcelona and Tugendhat chairs. *(below)* Dining area with Brno tubular chairs at round dining table.

Source: Courtesy of Photographer, Mr. Zidlicky and the Villa Tugendhat, Brno, CZ.

■ An Illustrated Guide to Furniture History

This concludes Chapter 10. Chapter 11 will focus on four individual Modernists of the French Avant-Garde due to their idiosyncratic nature and approach which transcends the Modernist direction of their contemporaries. The four are Eileen Gray (1878–1976), Pierre Chareau (1883–1950), Jean Prouvé (1901–1984), and Charlotte Perriand (1903–1999).

NOTES

1. William C. Ketchum, Jr., *The Smithsonian Illustrated Library of Antiques Furniture II Neoclassical to the Present* (New York: Cooper-Hewitt Museum, The Smithsonian Institution's National Design Museum, 1979), p.87.
2. Ibid.
3. Mark Hinchman, *History of Furniture: A Global View* (New York: Fairchild Books, A Division of Condé Nast Publications, 2009), p.479.
4. Ibid.
5. William J.R. Curtis, *Modern Architecture Since 1900* (New Jersey: Prentice-Hall, Simon & Schuster, 1996), p.12.
6. Ibid., p.33.
7. Mark Hinchman, *History of Furniture: A Global View* (New York: Fairchild Books, A Division of Condé Nast Publications, 2009), p.179.
8. William J.R. Curtis, *Modern Architecture Since 1900* (New Jersey: Prentice-Hall, Simon & Schuster, 1996), p.12.
9. Henry-Russell Hitchcock and Philip Johnson, *The International Style* (New York: W.W. Norton & Company, 1932), p.239.
10. On-line Collection Description, Museum of Modern Art, New York, New York, 2020.
11. Ibid.
12. William J.R. Curtis, *Modern Architecture Since 1900* (New Jersey: Prentice-Hall, Simon & Schuster, 1996), p.100.
13. Ibid., p.99.
14. Ibid.
15. William J.R. Curtis, *Modern Architecture Since 1900* (New Jersey: Prentice-Hall, Simon & Schuster, 1996), p.100.
16. University of Chicago, "The Deutscher Werkbund", A Dictionary of Modern Architecture, November 17, 2015, https://voices.uchicago.edu/201504arth15709-01a2/2015/11/16/deutscher-werkbund,.
17. Ibid.
18. Ibid.
19. Leonardo Benovolo, *Modern Movement*, Vol. II (Cambridge, MA: MIT Press, 1977), p.384.
20. On-line, Collection Object Label, Art Institute of Chicago, European Decorative Art, Gallery 246, 2020.
21. Ibid.
22. Ibid.
23. William J.R. Curtis, *Modern Architecture Since 1900* (New Jersey: Prentice-Hall, Simon & Schuster, 1996), p.195.
24. Ibid, p.196.
25. Ibid., p.195.
26. The Art Story Foundation, "Bauhaus," www. theartstory.org/movement/Bauhaus.
27. Ibid.
28. Jon Astbury, "Marcel Breuer: the Bauhaus Furniture Master with Passion for Architecture." *Dezeen*, November 17, 2018.

29 Charlotte and Peter Fiell, *1000 Chairs in the 20th Century* (Germany: Taschen Bibliotheca Universalis, 1997), p.105.
30 On-line Collection, Object Label, Cooper-Hewitt, Smithsonian Design Museum, New York, 2020.
31 Knoll On-line Object Description, Knoll International, New York, 2020.
32 Ibid.
33 On-line Object Label, Yale University Art Gallery, American Decorative Arts Collection, New Haven, Connecticut, 2020.
34 https://en.wikipedia.org/wiki/Cesca_Chair.
35 William J.R. Curtis, *Modern Architecture Since 1900* (New Jersey: Prentice-Hall, Simon & Schuster, 1996), p.156.
36 Charlotte and Peter Fiell, *1000 Chairs in the 20th Century* (Germany: Taschen Bibliotheca Universalis, 1997), p.94.
37 On-line Collection, Object Label, Museum of Modern Art, New York, 2020.
38 Ibid.
39 William J.R. Curtis, *Modern Architecture Since 1900* (New Jersey: Prentice-Hall, Simon & Schuster, 1996), p.157.
40 Ibid.
41 On-line Collection, Object Label, Museum of Modern Art, New York, 2020.
42 Ibid.
43 https://en.wikipedia.org/wiki/International_Style_(architecture).
44 Mark Hinchman, *History of Furniture: A Global View* (New York: Fairchild Books, A Division of Condé Nast Publications, 2009), p.492.
45 Mandi Johnson, "Interior Styling, Design Style 101: International Style." *Home Décor 101*, October 9, 2015.
46 On-line Object Label, Kunstmuseum, Den Haag, Netherlands, 2020.
47 Rebecca Veit, "Lilly Reich was More than Mies' Collaborator." *Core 77*, August 2, 2016.
48 Mark Hinchman, *History of Furniture: A Global View* (New York: Fairchild Books, A Division of Condé Nast Publications, 2009), p.486.
49 Knoll On-line Object Description, Knoll International, New York, 2020.
50 Ibid.
51 Ibid.
52 Cassina On-line Description, Cassina S.p.A, Meda, Italy, 2020.
53 Ibid.
54 Ibid.
55 Ibid.
56 Judith Miller, *Furniture: World Styles from Classical to Contemporary* (New York: Dorling Kindersley), p.433.
57 Cassina On-line Description, Cassina S.p.A. Meda, Italy, 2020.
58 Mark Hinchman, *History of Furniture: A Global View* (New York: Fairchild Books, A Division of Condé Nast Publications, 2009), p.495.

11 Early Modernist designers and architects

Pierre Chareau (1883–1950), Eileen Gray (1878–1976), Jean Prouvé (1901–1984), Charlotte Perriand (1903–1999)

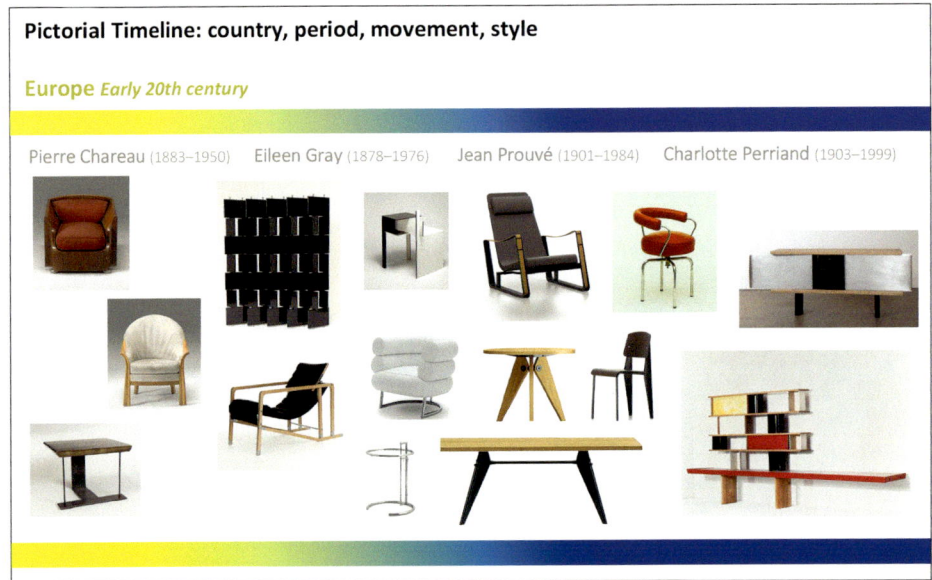

11.1
Pictorial timeline—Early Modernist designers and architects: Pierre Chareau (1883–1950), Eileen Gray (1878–1976), Jean Prouvé (1901–1984), Charlotte Perriand (1903–1999)

TIME PERIOD OVERVIEW

The affinities for the Modern movement of the four architects/designers discussed in this chapter are surely discernible in their design work. However, their creations possess an originality that can be misleading categorically within the context of the movement. The oeuvre of Pierre Chareau (1883–1950), Eileen Gray (1878–1976), Jean Prouvé (1901–1984), and Charlotte Perriand (1903–1999)—referencing her design work post Le Corbusier and Jeanneret—are distinct, individualistic, and, some would argue, idiosyncratic. Each of these four individuals is very much their own person, and their designs, whether architecture, interior, or furniture, reflect this. Referentially, their work can be considered to follow the premise of the Modern movement, functional and influenced by the industrial nature. However, there is an authenticity to their work and original quality that doesn't hesitate to embrace both functionalism and the decorative. This is not apparent in the work of their contemporaries. The author does not frame this idea as being better, yet simply values the uniqueness. The result is designs that are genuine, not a copy or imitation, but an authentic expression—architecture, interior, or furniture—of their three-dimensional definition of "modernity." This authenticity is overt in their architecture, interiors, and furniture designs. Speaking architecturally, examples would be Pierre Chareau's 1929 Maison de Verre (House of Glass), Paris; Eileen Gray's villa E-1027 in Roquebrune-Cap-Martin, France, a Modernist white rectangle perched on a cliff; Jean Prouvé's Maison Tropical, designed to address the shortage of housing in French colonies in West Africa during the 1950s; and, lastly, Charlotte Perriand's work and contribution to Les Arcs, a 1960s ski resort in France. Perriand successfully pushed the boundaries of prefabrication to make producing high-quality mass housing possible in the short summer building season.

PIERRE CHAREAU (1883–1950), PARIS, FRANCE, NEW YORK CITY, USA

History
Pierre Chareau was best known during his lifetime as an interior and furniture designer.[1] The enigma of Chareau's work is at least in part a reflection of a lack of information about the man's history, philosophy and manner of working, personality, and professional objectives,[2] and his uniqueness—Jewish background, the breadth and depth of his work designed between the two Wars, before fleeing Nazi-occupied France. Pierre Chareau was a pivotal figure in Modernism. Unapologetically, the Parisian Avant-Garde appears intrinsically connected to his designs. The nature of his work is interdisciplinary, linking architecture, fine arts, and style. Chareau was a radical innovator in the use of materials, and as well as chic homes, he also designed furniture for Avant-Garde films.

Although Chareau had notoriety in his own day, the beginning of formulating a clearer, deeper understanding of Chareau's greatness can be traced to 1984.[3] This year was the first attempt to assemble a descriptive catalog covering his designs and exhibitions.[4] Regardless of his competence and ultimate mastery of his crafts as designer and furniture maker, until this point the dissemination of Chareau's oeuvre was non-existent. Information about his life came from his family and friends. Fortunately, his wife of 46 years, Dollie, left letters and accounts of their life together, although the information is sparse and often anecdotal.[5]

He began his career working as a draughtsman in the Paris offices of Waring & Gillow, a large British company specializing in furniture and interior design, around 1899 or 1900. During this period, he created furniture for ocean liners and hotels. He left in April 1914, and in 1919 he established his own studio.

He soon joined the Société des Artistes Décorateurs (SAD) which sponsored the annual Salon des Artistes Décorateurs for designers and artist to exhibit their work. His recognition at exhibitions allowed him to begin producing custom furniture and light fixtures for wealthy clients, using luxurious materials like exotic woods, silver, bronze, and alabaster. In 1929, Chareau became a member of Union des Artistes Modernes (UAM), aligning himself with an influential group of committed Modernist designers who had become disillusioned with the conservatism of the SAD.[6] Also, in 1928 Chareau became associated with Congrès Internationaux d'Architecture Moderne (CIAM, International Congresses of Modern Architecture). As mention previously, members included Le Corbusier, Pierre Jeanneret, Charlotte Perriand, Eileen Gray, Walter Gropius, and Mies van de Rohe.

In the late 1920s, Pierre Chareau designed the Maison de Verre (House of Glass) in Paris, a Modernist masterwork that to this day has influenced a wide range of architects and designers.[7] The Maison de Verre was commissioned by Dr. Jean Dalsace and his wife, Annie. Pierre Chareau collaborated on this project with the Dutch architect Bernard Bijvoet and the French metal craftsman Louis Dalbet. It was built between 1928 and 1932 and is a stunning example of Modern architecture of the 20th century with custom furniture designed for the home. It is located in Paris, at 31 Rue Saint-Guillaume in the 6th Arrondissement.

The fascinating structure has translucent glass-block facades, supported by an exposed steel frame structure. Its interior spaces are separated by movable, sliding, folding, or rotating screens in glass and sheet or perforated metal. Custom furniture was made specifically for the interior spaces—sofas, chairs, tables, and bookcases. Other mechanical components include an overhead trolley from the kitchen to dining room and a retracting stair. The steel structure is exposed, so the beams and mechanical systems are visible from within and from the outside; in essence, both the utilities and structural system define the aesthetics.

It is fortunate that in 2005 art historian and collector Robert M. Rubin and his wife Stéphane Samuel purchased the house to restore and live in. Thanks to Mr. Rubin's stewardship, the Maison de Verre is vital and intact nearly 100 years after it was built.

In about 1940, after fleeing Paris during its German occupation, Chareau emigrated to the U.S., spending the last decade of his life in New York City (1940–1950). When he moved to New York, his career largely came to a standstill, even though he continued to produce drawings for furniture. Chareau did, however, design two houses, one in East Hampton, Long Island, 1947, for the artist Robert Motherwell, which was sadly demolished in 1985, and the other in upstate New York, which has been changed beyond recognition.

While living in Paris, Chareau and his wife, Dollie, were passionate about the arts and they became collectors, amassing an impressive art collection. Their collection included works of artists such as Piet Mondrian, Amedeo Modigliani, Fernand Léger, Max Ernst, Robert Motherwell, and Pablo Picasso.[8] While living in New York, they began selling some of the art collection. Two renowned institutions were beneficiaries—the Museum of Modern Art in New York and the Baltimore Museum of Art.

In conclusion of this **History** section about Pierre Chareau, it is a delight to share that the first U.S. exhibition and tribute to the French furniture designer and architect's oeuvre happened relatively recent at New York City's Jewish Museum (November 4, 2016–March 26, 2017). The show pulled together more than 180 works from private and public collections in Europe and the United States. The exhibition received outstanding reviews and press coverage—acknowledgment of the superb oeuvre of Pierre Chareau.

Armchair, 1924–1926, France, Armchair, 1925, Paris, France, Table Model SN3, ca. 1927, France

Aesthetics

Pierre Chareau developed a style that incorporated elements of Cubism and bridged the gap between Art Deco's dynamic geometry and the crisp rectilinearity of functionalist Modernism.[9] Chareau's designs consisted of strong geometry, angular and curved, which is evident in the pictorial timeline pieces. Like his contemporaries, Pierre Chareau was an important proponent of Modernism and advocate for the use of industrial materials in domestic design; however, his choice of materials was not those of his contemporaries, many whom favored chrome-plated tubular steel, glass, leather, etc. Instead, he married beautiful hardwoods and veneers with richly worked iron, playing with planar forms and endowing works with an almost Japanese purity.[10]

It is important to keep in mind that Pierre Chareau's furniture was not for mass production, a common furniture design objective for Modernists. Chareau's pieces, although reproducible, were specific to the commission, its design program, and client. These pieces would include exotic woods and stone such as alabaster, wrought iron, silver, and bronze incorporated in the design. He had a fascination with the qualities of metal as a material for furniture and preferred to juxtapose the iron with wood or with leather or wicker.[11] His collaboration with ironworker Louis Dalbet, who employed a hammer wrought-iron technique imported from the East, appealed to Chareau's design sense. Chareau also used veneers and combined silver-plated or nickel-plated components with subtle rich colors and wood grain (Figure 11.1 and Figure 11.2).[12] In his designs, he purposely emphasized the hand-worked and the traditional techniques of cabinetmaking and metal working. His rationale in pursuing traditional techniques could have resulted from his absorption of the influences of his era and his milieu, and his ability to bridge the gap between the Art Deco style and Modernist functionalism.

Lastly, an essential part of Chareau's hallmark of inventiveness was mobility. This mobility could lend itself to the furniture piece as a whole or individual parts and to the architecture and architectural details. This concept allowed the object to be transformed. He appeared to be the first to elevate the concept of mobility, especially making it fundamental to his furniture designs. Such pieces are not represented in this section, but the reader is encouraged to investigate some of his projects, such as the Maison de Verre to gain insight on this aspect of his work.

Furniture

The first timeline piece of Chareau's to discuss is an **armchair**, 1924–1926, France, located at the Virginia Museum of Fine Arts, in the Decorative Arts after 1980 galleries (Figure 11.1). This original form is an unusual approach to an armchair. The chair demonstrates Chareau's preference for strong geometry, angles, and curves. It is cube-like and boxy with subtracted areas that leave the seat portion most forward. But as the eye continues to observe, one detects a softened profile—the back slightly curves, its sides flared out, and there are curved angles in the front.

Figure 11.1 Armchair, 1924–1926, France. Designed by Pierre Chareau. Rosewood veneer with metal bun feet, and upholstered seat cushion and back cushion.

Source: Courtesy of Virginia Museum of Fine Arts, Decorative Arts after 1890 Collection. Gift of Sydney and Frances Lewis.

The shape of the back cushion accentuates the flaring back and arms with curved angles. The whole form rests perfectly on the formed metal bun feet. There exists a sofa-canapé of the same design, but with a walnut veneer. The chair's medium is rosewood veneer, and the elegance in its finishing is typical of his furniture pieces—straight grain pattern and highly polished finish. The cushions are upholstered, and the fabric color is a perfect complement to the rosewood. The scale of the chair is not large, even though visually the cube-like geometry gives the impression of a rather large armchair. The overall size is H 23⅜" × W 27 9/16" × D 31½".[13]

The next timeline piece, an **armchair**, 1925, Paris, is also an upholstered chair from the Virginia Museum of Fine Arts, Decorative Arts after 1980 galleries (Figure 11.2). This is yet another unconventional form which deviates from his Modernist colleagues whose "modernity" reflected the need to produce furniture that was standardized, mass-produced, and factory-made. This chair design is reminiscent of a conventional rounded-back upholstered armchair. Yet its constituent parts and overall form are unconventional.

Figure 11.2 Armchair, 1925, France. Designed by Pierre Chareau. Bleached mahogany, fully upholstered.

Source: Courtesy of Virginia Museum of Fine Arts, Decorative Arts after 1890 Collection. Gift of Sydney and Frances Lewis.

The relationship of the back, arms, seat, and legs is unique. The back gently curves and the arms of the chair become slightly flared. The wedge-shaped wood on top of the arm is unusual in the way it meets the suede upholstery. Neither wood, upholstery, nor form dominate; all seem to simply coexist. The medium is a bleached mahogany, which takes on a luminous gold quality.[14] The wood portion continues downward from the top of the flared arms becoming molded chair legs in cruciform or lyre-shape. The splayed legs give the appearance of being solidly planted on the ground plane. The wood seat rail visually reinforces this. The overall size is somewhat diminutive at H 33¼" × W 26½" × D 24½".[15]

Figure 11.3
Table Model SN 3, ca. 1927, France. Designed by Pierre Chareau. Metal work by Louis Dalvet (French, 1885–1950). Cut mahogany and wrought iron.

Source: Copper-Hewitt, Smithsonian Design Museum. Gift of David Teiger Trust, 2016-36-1, Photo: Matt Flynn (Smithsonian Institution).

The last piece, **Table Model SN3**, ca. 1927, France, demonstrates the collaborative effort between Pierre Chareau and Louis Dalbet. The chair was designed by Pierre Chareau and made by ironworker Louis Dalbet (Figure 11.3). It resides in the Product Design and Decorative Arts department at the Cooper-Hewitt, Smithsonian Design Museum collection. The table was made for the smoking room at the Grand Hôtel de Tours, built in 1927 by local architect Maurice Boille.[16] The Grand Hôtel de Tours is located east of Paris in France's Loire Valley.

Pierre Chareau was in charge of the hotel's interior decoration and furnishings which exemplified the sophistication and quality of the best French Modern design.[17] SN3 side tables and stools could be found throughout the bar and smoking lounge. The SN3 is an ideal example to demonstrate Chareau's preference for juxtaposing iron with wood in his designs. The result bridges the Japanese aesthetic with the rectilinearity of functionalist Modernism. Its medium is cut mahogany and wrought iron. The size is H14¼" × W19½" × D15¼".

Throughout his career, Pierre Chareau recognized and appreciated the role of craftsmen in executing his pieces, and he preferred designing for serial or unique production by skilled craftsmen even when working with industrial materials.[18] Metal, especially iron, had become an important medium for Chareau in the 1920s and 1930s.[19] He met the ironworker Louis Dalbet in 1923, and the pair began collaborating immediately. The fruits of their partnership were acknowledged at the 1924 Salon d'Automne. From that point on, Dalbet was the only ironworker with whom Chareau worked. Lastly, this particular piece is especially significant is it descended through the Dalsace family, owners of the Maison de Verre.[20]

EILEEN GRAY (1878–1976), PARIS, FRANCE

History

The innovator Eileen Gray was one of the earliest women designers to gain recognition.[21] She was a pioneer in Modern design and architecture and one of the few women to practice professionally in those fields before World War II.[22] Born Kathleen Eileen Moray Smith on August 9, 1878, at Brownswood House, Enniscorthy, County Wexford, Ireland, Gray's heritage is Scots-Irish—her family was a distinguished upper-class household.[23] Her mother was grand-daughter of the tenth Earl of Moray and in 1895 inherited the title Baroness Gray.[24] Her daughter—the woman who came to be known as Eileen Gray—architect, interior designer, furniture designer, painter, and photographer, is one of the foremost woman creatives of the 20th century. Currently, one can see the latest stage in the revival of interest in Gray's career. Most recently, an exhibition titled "Eileen Gray," was installed at Bard Graduate Center Gallery, New York City, February 29–July 12, 2020, receiving an abundance of accolades. Deservingly, Eileen Gray is being recognized as a pioneering woman in what was a predominantly male field of Modern architecture, and appreciation for the legendary designer and architect's work continues to flourish.

Eileen Gray, like Peter Behrens, started as a painter. In the early 1900s, she had been one of the very first women students at the Slade School in London.[25] Also around this time she was introduced to the Asian traditional lacquer technique—somewhat serendipitously, when she happened to encounter the process at shop D. Charles at 92 Dean Street, London. She spent a short period of time at D. Charles becoming familiar with the art of lacquer, and this exposure was the genesis for developing her talent in the area of Asian traditional lacquer. Gray moved to Paris in 1907 and continued her art training at the Académie Colarossi and Académie Julian. The apartment she found during this time, 21 rue Bonaparte in the 6th Arrondissement, is where she lived until her death. In 1910, Gray and her fellow Slade School friend, Evelyn Wyld, established a workshop to produce carpets and wall hangings.[26] Gray also continued her pursuit of the traditional lacquer technique with Japanese artist Seizo Sugawara, with whom she formed a successful partnership. In 1922, she opened her Paris shop, Galerie Jean Désert, at 217 rue du Faubourg-Saint-Honoré, where she sold furniture and rugs. Gray's rugs demonstrated her creativity with geometric forms, and by the early 1920s, she was designing furnishings in tubular metal and other modern materials. Gray also offered interior design services. Her elite client list included Madame Mathieu Lévy (Suzanne Talbot), Jacques Doucet, and the Maharajah of Indore. The Galerie also served as an exhibition space for Modern art, making Gray, albeit working under a male pseudonym, one of the first women gallerists.[27] In 1923, Gray exhibited her design Boudoir de Monte Carlo at the 14th Salon des Artistes Décorateurs. This exhibition made a great impression on the Modernist–De Stijl architects Jan Wils and J.J.P Oud, as well as Le Corbusier, and Peter Behrens from Germany. This interaction led to Gray being featured in the Dutch Avant-Garde journal *Wendigen* in 1924.[28] This total transformation of the environment by a designer seen at Salon des Artistes Décorateurs is not unusual in contemporary times, but in the1920s this was not the norm and represented something of a departure. The villa she designed in Roquebrune-Cap-Martin, France, further demonstrates impeccably Gray's ability to totally transform an environment.

Eileen Gray entered the architectural mainframe late in life. She was 48 when she began working on E-1027, her first building at Roquebrune-Cap-Martin. As recently as 2006, the E-1027 was in a dilapidated state, but fortunately Cap Moderne was set up in 2014 to manage E-1027 and has begun to reconstruct what has been destroyed over the decades.[29]

The villa E-1027 is essentially a white rectangle perched upon the cliff's face at Cap-Martin—clearly a Modernist building.[30] The villa was intended as a peaceful retreat for Gray and her then romantic partner, Romanian architect, writer and editor Jean Badovici. In the design of E-1027, Gray adopts some aspects of the French-Swiss architect Le Corbusier's five points of new architecture published in his seminal 1923 book *Vers Une Architecture*, such as concrete piles, open-plan rooms, a roof garden, horizontal windows, and a "free" façade.[31] Gray's response to the spatial principles and forms of Le Corbusier was to introduce new elements into the design, reacting against what she saw as the over-intellectualized approach of the architectural Avant-Garde, which she found too doctrinaire and lacking in humanism.[32]

E-1027 exemplifies Gray's approach to architecture, focusing on the relationship of the building and its occupant, with an emphasis on bodily experience, convenience, and comfort.[33] Gray's architecture is noteworthy for using light and space in original and inventive ways. She believed strongly that a house must be in tune with and respond to its setting and environment.[34] Privacy is a main objective of E-1027. On the exterior, floor-to-ceiling concertina windows open to the Mediterranean Sea, providing light and views, yet rolling shutters and two strips of canvas shield the villa's interiors from being seen, thereby also blocking harsh afternoon sunlight and framing the seaside vista.[35]

Eileen Gray's furniture demonstrates her versatility as a designer. In her earlier pieces, she explored exotic materials and forms for affluent clients that one might say were bizarre, luxurious, and eccentric.[36] As the 1920s move on, in tandem with her exposure and interaction with Modernist architects, she began experimenting with new furniture forms, and used furniture to manipulate space.[37] In the late 1920s, as Gray had done for clients, she designed furniture specifically for E-1027. These furnishings have become iconic Modernist pieces such as the Fauteuil Transat (Transat chair) and adjustable glass and metal circular table.

Although Eileen Gray was a prolific designer from early on in the 20th century, it took an essay by Joseph Rykwert in 1967 to bring her deserved recognition. By that time, the house had been credited as entirely the work of Badovici and even Le Corbusier.[38] From the 1920s onward, and throughout the rest of her life, Gray produced architectural projects for private and public commissions, including homes for her own use in France: E-1027 (1926–1929) in Roquebrune Cap-Martin, Tempe a

Pailla (1931–1934) in Menton, and Villa Lou Pérou (1954–1958) in St. Tropez. In 1976, Eileen Gray died in Paris at the age of 98.[39] Since the 1970s, Aram Designs Ltd, UK, has held the worldwide license for Eileen Gray Designs. One of her last tasks was to work with Zeev Aram on the introduction of her designs into the world market.[40]

Black Lacquered Screen, ca. 1922–1923, France, Table (Black and White), 1922–1924, France, Transat Chair, ca. 1925–1927, France, Bibendum Chair, 1926, France, E-1027 Adjustable Table, 1927, France

Aesthetics

During her early years, Gray designed many lacquered items such as decorative screens but also furniture pieces with a lacquered component and area rugs. At this time, her design vocabulary albeit original, took its cue from the Art Deco style which was prevalent in Paris, so the use of angular shapes and geometric designs defined the aesthetic. These pieces could be considered highly personal, eccentric, and decorative, incorporating the use of luxurious materials. In her later interior design projects, furniture was often made specifically for that particular project. Around 1924, due to her familiarity with the De Stijl, Gray's work embraced an abstract pared-down aesthetic and reflected the Neoplastic ideology. This is visible in the black-and-white table design included in the **Furniture** section (Figure 11.4). As she continued to interact with her Modernist contemporaries—some of the leading architects of the day—she adopted the vocabulary of Modernism for her furniture, architecture, and interior designs. These Modernist pieces were no less personal but much more restrained.[41] The furniture as well as the architecture she created consisted of clean lines and simple geometry, and incorporated the use of chrome-plated tubular steel, glass, leather, and neutral colors. The pieces in the next section, the Transat Chair, Bibendum Chair, and E-1027 Adjustable Table—are good examples of Gray's nonconformism, exercising her interpretation of "modernity."

Furniture

Gray's first timeline piece, a **Black Lacquered Screen, ca. 1922–1923,** France, is from the Decorative Arts After 1890 collection, at the Virginia Museum of Fine Arts (VMFA) (Figure 11.4). This piece is considered an iconic Art Deco screen and it is one of several variations.[42] Eileen Gray designed the screen and mixed/made the lacquer. However, the craftsman and lacquerer is Pierre Bobot.[43] It was inspired by a screen and wall treatment Eileen Gray created for Madame Mathieu Lévy (Suzanne Talbot), the renowned Parisian fashion designer.[44]

Figure 11.4 Black Lacquered Block Screen, ca. 1922–1923, France. Pierre Bobot. Wood blocks, with black lacquer and aluminum connectors.

Source: Courtesy of Virginia Museum of Fine Arts, Collection: Decorative Arts after 1980, Lewis Decorative Arts Galleries. Gift of Sydney and Frances Lewis.

After opening her gallery Jean Désert in Paris, several other versions of the screen were made in black or white.

The screen's medium is lacquer, wood, and aluminum. Its construction consists of interlocking blocks handmade by Gray and lacquered. Each block is anchored at the top and bottom with the metal rods. The panels have a glossy lacquer finish that emits a reflective and slick appearance. Its size overall is H 71⅝" × 70¼" × ¾".[45]

Figure 11.5
Table (Black & White), ca. 1922–1924, France. Designed by Eileen Gray. Oak and sycamore, painted black and white.

Source: Courtesy of Virginia Museum of Fine Arts, Decorative Arts after 1980 Collection. Gift of Sydney and Frances Lewis.

The next timeline piece is a **Table (Black and White), 1922–1924**, France. This table also resides in the Virginia Museum of Fine Arts, Decorative Arts After 1890 collection (Figure 11.5). The table, aside from being black and white, is reminiscent of designs from the De Stijl movement. Its design emphasizes the Neoplastic language of geometry—straight lines, squares, and rectangles. The planar surfaces with a formal polarity of horizontal and vertical axes become a series of opposing forces. The table's medium is painted oak and sycamore. The overall dimension is H 24¾" × W 25 3/16" × D 33 1/16".[46]

Figure 11.6
Transat Chair, "Fauteuil Transatlantique," 1925–1927, France. Designed by Eileen Gray. Wood, lacquer, and chromed brackets.

Source: Image supplied by Aram Designs Limited, holder of the worldwide licence for Eileen Gray designs.

The next piece, the **Transat Chair, ca. 1925–1927**, France, is an iconic piece, originally referred to as the Fauteuil Transatlantique (Figure 11.6). This chair is from the collection of Aram Designs, London, the holder of the worldwide license for Eileen Gray Designs.

Its genesis—the deckchairs used on transatlantic steamships. In the 1920s and 1930s, high style and high society made ocean liners famous. The ocean liner became a luxurious way for the affluent to travel. Lounging on the liner's deck to be seen and to see others became a necessary social practice of ocean liner travel.

Gray's Fauteuil Transatlantique was inspired by the practical reclining chairs used on the decks of ocean liners.[47] The practical deckchair could be folded and stored, and was designed to meet the demand for outdoor lounging. The chair's name reflects the great vessels that crossed the Atlantic Ocean—sometimes called "transatlantiques" in French.[48] Ocean liners at this time were symbolic of speed and style. Both these concepts are revealed in the chair's design—the low-slung seat with separate head section and lacquered arms. The wooden side frames are designed with rigorous geometry, tenon joints, and chrome brackets. The frame design varied, with either wood or a lacquered finish. The seat is reminiscent of a deckchair's sling with a pivoting head section.[49] The size is H 21⅝" × W 41 11/16" × D 31⅛".[50] This iconic chair's Modern design evokes the romance of long journeys at sea.

The chair was designed to be used on the outdoor terrace of villa E-1027 at Roquebrune-Cap-Martin. It is a testament to its Modern appeal that it was also chosen by architect Ekhart Muthesius to furnish the palace of Maharaja of Indore during the same time period.

The next piece, **Bibendum Chair, 1926**, France, is another item from Aram Designs, London (Figure 11.7). Eileen Gray used this chair for several clients' interior projects. The design was influenced by the famous "Bibendum" Michelin Man of inflated tires.[51] Gray jokingly referred to this chair as her response as a feminist to Le Corbusier, Perriand, and Jeanneret's (LC2) Grand/Gran Comfort.[52] In this response, Gray's piece displays an original and feminine take on the geometries and proportions prevalent at the time.

Figure 11.7 Bibendum Chair, 1926, France. Designed by Eileen Gray. A semi-circular form, comprised of three stacked fully leather upholstered tire-like rolls which define the chair back and arms, with a chrome-finished steel base.

Source: Image supplied by Aram Designs Limited, holder of the worldwide licence for Eileen Gray designs.

The chair is a minimalist piece composed of three fully upholstered tire-like rolls which comprise the seat, back and arms, supported by a chrome-finish steel base. The three tire-like rolls that make this chair visually bold and enticing were comparable to the proportions and silhouette of the Michelin Man.[53]

The final timeline piece of Eileen Gray, the **E-1027 Adjustable Table, 1927**, France, is also from the Aram Designs collection (Figure 11.8). It was designed for her villa E-1027, Roquebrune-Cap-Martin. Eileen Gray had an interest in multi-functional furniture.[54] She wanted the table to have multiple functions. It could be used over the knees while sitting,

Figure 11.8 Adjustable Table, 1927, France. Designed by Eileen Gray. The frame is polished chromium-plated tubular steel with glass in-set top.

Source: Image supplied by Aram Designs Limited, holder of the worldwide licence for Eileen Gray designs.

but also as an occasional side table or bedside table when needed. So its height is adjustable.[55] The use of the Modernist vocabulary is clearly visible in its minimalist character and the articulate use of geometry and tubular steel circular top and base. Notice the base's circular form is unclosed, appearing to distinguish a different function from its top. The frame is polished chromium-plated tubular steel with glass inset for the table top. The top and base are linked together by a vertical frame which allows for movement. The table is a simple yet elegant Modernist design. In its original conception, the glass top could be clear or tinted and the steel frame had several finish options. These options are still available today. Within the architecture and design community, this iconic piece is readily utilized today.

JEAN PROUVÉ (1901–1984), NANCY, FRANCE

History

Jean Prouvé, metalworker and self-taught architect, left behind a complex and diverse oeuvre. He spent the majority of his life where he grew up as a child, in north-eastern France, in the city of Nancy in the Lorraine region. Nancy continued to be his home and headquarters. His design skills were not limited to one discipline in the sense that his work included architecture, industrial design, engineering, and furniture design. Nils Peters, author of *Prouvé, 1901–1984: The Dynamics of Creation*, states: "For a long period of time the lifework of artistic blacksmith, designer, and manufacturer Jean Prouvé seemed either misunderstood or forgotten."[56] However, in recent years his work has attracted again the interest of both the architectural and design world and broader public.[57] This has been facilitated by two factors. First, in 2002, Vitra International, in close cooperation with the Prouvé family, began to issue re-editions of designs by this great French constructeur. This was designation Swiss architect Le Corbusier gave Jean Prouvé—constructeur blending architecture and engineering.[58] Vitra is a seminal Swiss family-owned furniture company and manufacturer of the works of many internationally renowned designers. In the 1980s, the Vitra Campus was established. Over a period of time, different facility buildings of contemporary architecture has been built within the campus as a collaboration between Vitra and prominent architects. Second, Parisian dealer Patrick Sequin, of the Gallerie Patrick Seguin in the Bastille district of Paris, has made it his business to ensure the legacy of the mid-century designer and architect. His collecting and selling Prouvé's work—prefabricated architecture and furniture designs—has made Prouvé's work accessible to anyone.[59]

Prouvé's creativity can likely be attributed to being the son of an artist father, Victor Prouvé, and pianist mother, Marie Duham. He grew up surrounded by the ideals and energy of L'École de Nancy, the art collective that his father co-founded with Émile Gallé. L'École de Nancy's goals were to make art readily accessible and to forge links between art and industry, as well as between art and social consciousness.

Prouvé's professional direction was partly due to the outbreak of World War I. His intention was to study engineering but due to wartime conditions and financial strain his father arranged for him to apprentice and learn the art of blacksmithing.[60] In the early 1900s, Nancy was a center for the blacksmith's trade and steel industry, and also well known as a center for the crafts trade, especially for manufacturing furniture and glass, so the directional choice is understandable. His first apprenticeship was with blacksmith Émile Robert in Enghien (near Paris), but he soon moved to the Parisian metal workshop of Aldabert Szabo.[61] After completing his training, he opened his Atelier Jean Prouvé.

His professional breakthrough came in 1927, when he received a commission from the Modernist architect Robert Mallet-Stevens, to design an interior entrance for Reifenberg's city villa in Paris. This opportunity opened the way into the circle of Le Corbusier and other Modernists.[62] In 1930, together with Mallet-Stevens, Charlotte Perriand, Le Corbusier, Pierre Jeanneret, Eileen Gray, and others, he cofounded the Union des Artistes Modernes (UAM).[63]

By the 1930s, his atelier was manufacturing furniture and architectural components for schools, factories, and other buildings, and after World War II, when school and dormitory furniture and other necessities where in short supply, his products were in greater demand. In 1947, Prouvé established an atelier and factory in Maxéville, a suburb of Nancy. Prouvé's studios produced literally everything.[64] His products ranged from the micro to macro, essentially anything that suited industrial production methods—numerous furniture designs and lighting, door and window fittings, façade elements, prefabricated houses, modular building systems, and large exhibition structures.

Prouvé began collaborating with some of the best-known French designers of the day, including Le Corbusier and Charlotte Perriand. A classic Modern example of his metal furniture is his furniture design for the student dormitory at Cité Universitaire in Nancy, a result of a competition. Prouvé emerged as one of the four winners.[65] His task included the design of beds, desks, bookshelves, armchairs, and standard chairs. All furniture was conceived to require the least possible expenditure on materials during the production phase. This made it possible to produce furniture both light and inexpensive without forfeiting robustness.[66] The Cité armchair (Figure 11.9) and Standard Chair (Figure 11.10) are currently in Vitra's collection. These pieces will be discussed in depth under the **Furniture** section.

Regarding Prouvé's architecture, in 2008 an interesting happening occurred between hotelier André Balazs and the Design Museum and Tate Modern, London, in which Prouvé's La Maison Tropicale was brought to London and erected outside the Tate Modern. Jean Prouvé designed and manufactured three prototype Les Maisons Tropicales for West Africa between 1949 and 1951, designed to address the shortage of housing and civic buildings in France's African colonies. Prouvé aimed to design for the demands of the climate and included a veranda with an adjustable aluminum sun screen. The Brazzaville house is made from folded sheet steel and aluminum. For ease of transport, all the parts were flat and lightweight, and could be neatly packed into a cargo plane. The inner walls are made of fixed and sliding metal panels with blue glass portholes to protect against UV rays, and a double roof structure was designed to produce natural ventilation. Les Maisons

Tropicales prototypes were also shown in the Centre Pompidou, Paris, 2006, and in New York in 2007. These acquisitions a result of Patrick Seguin's commitment to the memory of Jean Prouvé as a central figure of 20th-century architecture and design; Seguin is the proprietor of Parisian Gallery Patrick Seguin.

By the later part of the 20th century, Prouvé served as a consulting engineer on a number of important architectural projects in Paris. He left his mark on architectural history again in 1971, when he played a major role in selecting the design of Renzo Piano and Richard Rogers for the Centre Pompidou as chairman of the competition jury.

Jean Prouvé has long been an influential force among Modern designers, especially constructionally minded architects such as Norman Foster and Renzo Piano, and his vintage Modern design has been sought after for years by connoisseurs and museums specializing in Modern design.[67] Prouvé's work has remained relatively unknown to the general public, but thanks to Vitra and the Jean Prouvé estate, that has changed recently, and there has been a resurgence of his original Modern design creations.

Cité Armchair, 1930, France, Standard Chair, 1934/1950, France, Guéridon Table, 1949, France, EM Table, "Entretoise Métallique," 1950, France

Aesthetics

Jean Prouvé introduced the machine age and industrial engineered Modern design aesthetic using primarily folded, bent, and corrugated metal for interiors, furniture design, and architecture.[68] Prouvé's work was the result of constant searching and improving.[69] He regarded himself as more of an engineer and constructor than a designer.[70] He believed it was important to work with materials and create designs in a way that revealed the construction process. Ideologically, he embraced the mass-producing of furniture on industrial machinery. He never designed for the sake of form alone, concentrating instead on the essence of materials, connections, and production. His commitment to developing machinery and new methods for production and to continuing to experiment with different materials such as sheet steel, folding the sheet metal to allow for hollow sections, resulted in the most classic Modern designs. His innovative method of folding sheet metal was utilized in a series of tables that have the perceived lightness of bridges and the presence of architecture. These pieces will be looked at more closely under the **Furniture** section. Jean Prouvé strove for the most constructionally and materially efficient designs. Swiss architectural historian Bruno Reichlin described Prouvé's work as a vivid example of "poetic functionalism."[71] This phrase can be clearly understood upon viewing Prouvé's furniture designs in the next section.

Furniture

This first timeline piece, **Cité Armchair, 1930**, France, produced by Vitra International, as mentioned was designed for a competition (Figure 11.9). Prouvé was awarded the prize, enabling him to design furniture for the student residence halls at the Cité Universitaire in Nancy. These designs demonstrated his preference for flat steel sections over tubular steel used by his Modernist contemporaries. For the Cité Universitaire residence halls, his industrial engineered Modern design aesthetic was employed for chairs, beds, desk, tables, and bookshelves. The commitment to express and not deny the essence of materials and connections is evident in the Cité Armchair design. The design is articulate, its form appearing efficient and comfortable. Its rectangular geometry is comprised of powder-coated steel runners and leather belt armrest. The dimensions are H 33″ × W 26¾″ × D 37½″ and the seat height is 8¼″.[72]

Figure 11.9 Cité Armchair, 1930, France. Designed by Jean Prouvé. The frame consists of powder-coated steel runners and leather belt armrest with fully wood seat and backrest. The Vitra collection offers a variety of woods and colors for the steel frame.

Source: Courtesy of Vitra.

The armchair's ergonomic quality is visible in that the chair is angled and slightly tilted backward for ease of motion in and out. Additionally, notice the fully upholstered seat and back. The design outcome for the Cité Armchair's was so satisfying that Prouvé, used it in the living room at his home in Nancy, France.[73]

The **Standard Chair, 1934/1950**, France, will be the next piece discussed (Figure 11.10). It is also part of the Vitra collection of Prouvé's furniture. The Standard Chair has become a recognized and highly utilized Prouvé design within the architecture and design community. Prouvé's ideas about efficient design and his focus on materials, connection, and production are evident in his combining of steel and wood for Standard Chair's design. The outcome is duplicitous, appearing utilitarian yet moving beyond its utilitarian role with the orchestration of combined materials which render a harmonious and visual appealing piece. This result is due to a combination of manipulations such as the chair's back leg geometry, straight flat steel profile on one side, yet triangulated on the other and tangent with the right-angle slender steel tube doubling as seat support and front chair legs. Lastly, regarding materiality, the emphasis is on the bending property of wood—the backrest, which conforms perfectly to the human shoulders, and seat shape with dropped edge for ease of seating. Currently, Vitra has made available a sizable selection of colors that can be chosen for the steel portion of the chair, as well as a variety of woods for the back rest and chair seat. The overall dimensions are H 32¼″ × W 16½″ × D 19¼″, seat height 18¼″.[74]

Prouvé's **Guéridon Table, 1949**, France, or **"Guéridon cafeteria,"** is another piece in the Vitra collection (Figure 11.11). This table was designed for a student housing commission and was produced in numerous series in a variety of materials for the University of Paris.

Figure 11.10
Standard Chair, 1934/1950 France. Designed by Jean Prouvé. Steel frame, flat and tubular with a wood seat and backrest. The Vitra collection offers a variety of woods and colors for the steel frame.
Source: Courtesy of Vitra.

Figure 11.11
Guéridon Table, 1949, France. Designed by Jean Prouvé. The table is constructed entirely of wood. Triangulated legs are organized in a triangle formation, inherently rigid. The connectors are powder-coated steel struts.
Source: Courtesy of Vitra.

Possibly, the choice to design a Guéridon table is linked to the table's history. The Guéridon table originated in France toward the mid-17th century. It typically was a small table with one or more column-like supports. Its style and use were humble—it was a utility piece used for candlesticks, vases, or other decorative objects. The contemporary equivalent would be a pedestal table or occasional table.

The design of this table's distinctive structural clarity communicates Prouvé's belief in creating designs in a way that reveals the construction process, as well as his commitment to concentrate on the essence of materials and connections. This is visible in the triangulated shape legs, organized in a triangle formation making the table inherently rigid. The triangle is one of the strongest geometric shapes structurally. This Guéridon table is exceptionally strong. The table gives an impression of sturdiness and lightness simultaneously. This example is entirely wood with the exception for the powder-coated tubular steel strut connectors. Vitra produces two sizes—a small and large table measuring, H 29½" diameter 35½", base diameter 30", and H 29¼", diameter 41¼", base diameter 34¾", respectively.[75]

The **EM Table, "Entretoise Métallique," 1950**, France, the last Prouvé furniture piece discussed, like the previous Vitra designs, demonstrates his commitment to the essence of materials, connections, and production (Figure 11.12). The EM Table is the embodiment of "poetic functionalism," the term first used by the Swiss architectural historian Bruno Reichlin to describe the work of Prouvé.[76] Prouvé's design approach compares more closely with that of a design engineer.[77] Important to Prouvé's design is communicating how the EM Table adheres to structural principles. He demonstrates how the material bears its load, and the distribution and disengagement of energies are made visible through an intensive reshaping of elements.[78] Visually, the EM Table design illustrates the flow of forces and stresses in its construction. The result is an aesthetically successful, visually dynamic relationship between the base and tabletop.

Figure 11.12
EM Table, "Entretoise Métallique," 1950, France. Designed by Jean Prouvé. The medium is sheet metal and wood. The top is supported by metal triangulated legs which are turned out in a diagonal slant and braced with a metal tie creating a visually balance piece.
Source: Courtesy of Vitra.

Its medium is sheet metal and wood, and the triangular table legs are turned out and angled on a diagonal slant braced with a metal tie. Its form—position of the legs supporting its top—exudes a downward flow of energy. The EM Table construction is an incredible sturdy surface for working or dining. Vitra caries a range of sizes with table tops in premium solid wood or HPL laminate. Top sizes measure approximately 79–94½" in length.

CHARLOTTE PERRIAND (1903–1999), PARIS, FRANCE

History

Discussing Charlotte Perriand separately from her collaboration with Le Corbusier and Pierre Jeanneret is imperative to fully understand her as an exceptional personality, a woman committed to leading a veritable evolution, or, perhaps more aptly, a revolution.[79] Her work resonated with changes in the social and political order, the evolution of the role of women, and changes in attitudes toward urban living.[80]

It can easily be said that Charlotte Perriand was a pioneer of "modernity" and leading figure of 20th-century design. It is fortunate for the architecture and design community that Perriand was able to contribute an exceptional length of time, living to the age of 96. To commemorate the 20th anniversary of her death, an exhibition was arranged by the Louis Vuitton Foundation. The exhibition titled "Charlotte Perriand: Inventing a New World" (October 2, 2019–February 24, 2020) paid tribute to her as an architect and visionary, exploring the links between Perriand as artist, architect, and designer.

Charlotte Perriand was a Parisian. She was born in Paris on October 24, 1903, into a world transitioning from 19th-century attitudes and traditions, where creatives—fine artists, architects, designers, and urban planners—were beginning to construct a contemporary model of 20th-century "modernity." This would happen within the context of two World Wars, followed by reconstruction, both physical and moral.

From 1920 to 1925, she studied at the École de l'Union Centrale des Arts Décoratifs, and about two years later she began working as an interior designer based at her studio on Place Saint-Sulpice. Her research and interest in furniture design led her to collaborate with Le Corbusier and Pierre Jeanneret in the 1920s and 1930s, and the trio worked on major projects together.[81] What eventually became an egalitarian effort among the trio was unique at this point in design history. However, Charlotte Perriand recalls in *Une Vie de Creation* (A Life of Creation, 1998) that her initial introduction to Le Corbusier was not encouraging:

> Clutching a portfolio of drawings, I found myself face-to-face one October afternoon in 1927 with Le Corbusier's horn-rimmed spectacles. The austere office was somewhat intimidating, and his greeting rather frosty. "What do you want?" he asked, his eyes hooded by his glasses. "To work with you." He glanced quickly through my drawings. "We don't embroider cushions here," he replied, and showed me the door.[82]

Later, after viewing her designs for the 1927 Salon d'Automne, Le Corbusier hired Perriand, and she worked in his Paris studio for ten years.[83] It was around this time that she joined her contemporaries in the founding of the Union des Artistes Modernes (UAM), which, as mentioned previously, involved Chareau, Prouvé, Le Corbusier, Pierre Jeanneret, and others. Through such interactions, other collaborative opportunities came about, one such opportunity around 1952 with Jean Prouvé to furnish the rooms of the Tunisian students' residence at the International University Campus in Paris, Maison de la Tunisie (Figure 11.14).

Around 1934, she began specializing in prefabricated buildings for leisure pursuits. This was useful in the 1960s for her Les Arcs ski resort project. A seminal work later in her career, Les Arcs resort was conceived and built when, in postwar France, the government sought to expand leisure activities to the masses. Les Arcs resort gave a large portion of the population new access to winter sports.[84] Its uniqueness also resided in its expectation to support a vast number of people: With her expertise in mass production, she led the design team of architects and designers. Perriand, as was her custom, designed functional spaces, with modular kitchen and bathroom units and custom furnishings, adding rich colorful surfaces and textures.

Charlotte Perriand was a visionary and acutely prescient in her consideration for the environment and the way she was enthralled with, inspired by, and sensitive to nature and humans' impact on it.[85] This ideology can possibly be linked to her experience in Japan, living and working in a culture where the relationship between man and nature is considered to be harmonious. In 1940, Perriand was appointed as the official advisor on industrial design to the Japanese government and she stayed in Tokyo until 1946 before returning to France. It became noticeable thereafter that her work displayed a Japanese influence. Charlotte Perriand's vision and embodiment of "modernity" was unique and influenced her work heavily, both intellectually and artistically. After World War II, she developed a new concept for the way of living by increasingly integrating the human dimension into her productions, which lasted throughout her career. This emphasis and original way of thinking was unlike that of her contemporaries. For the remainder of her career, Charlotte Perriand dedicated herself to maintaining a standard for the quality of life: whether working-class housing developments, urban or rural dwellings, mountain refuges and hotels, she always approached her projects with the interests of humankind and environment in mind, by creating furniture that is both comfortable and functional.[86] This unique vision embodied her "modernity" and a forward-facing spirit that continued in her work throughout her life.

Swivel Armchair (LC 7), ca. 1928, France, Bookcase, Maison de Tunisie, 1952, France, Wall Cabinet, 1939, Paris, France

Aesthetics

The visual essence for Charlotte Perriand's designs was entwined with her dedication to efficient design and material use visible in her experimentation with the revolutionizing steel—tubular, flat, chrome-plated, powder-coated, and enameled. She successfully designed several furniture pieces pre-collaboration with Le Corbusier and Jeanneret. The pieces, LC 7, LC 8, and LC 9 were placed in Le Corbusier's collection in 1929. It can be said that Perriand's furniture design was a synthesis between tradition and industry. She accomplished this by a flexible use of materials, as seen in the chaise lounge design (LC 4) (Figure 10.9). A chaise was a common piece at the time for residences, but her reinterpretation of tradition using industrial, black enamel steel and a trivalent articulated chrome-plated steel frame completely freed the form from convention into a highly original design. It is evident in the scale of her designs that she was integrating the human dimension into her pieces. As she continued to design for humankind and the environment, this was kept in mind, therefore creating furniture that is both comfortable and functional. Jean Prouvé used to say that she was among the rare designers blessed with spontaneous harmonic contemporary thought.[87]

Furniture

The first Perriand timeline piece is the **Swivel Armchair (LC 7), ca. 1928**, France. It resides in the collection of the Museum of Modern Art, Department of Architecture and Design (Figure 11.13). The swivel chair was designed in 1927 by Perriand for her apartment in the Place Saint-Sulpice in Paris and was shown in the 1929 Salon d'Automne as part of a collection co-designed with Le Corbusier and Pierre Jeanneret.[88] The medium at this time was chrome-plated tubular steel, but currently the chair is

Figure 11.13 Revolving Armchair (LC 7), 1928, France. Designed by Charlotte Perriand. Chrome-plated tubular steel with leather upholstered crest rail and seat.

Source: Digital Image ©The Museum of Modern Art/Licensed by SCALA/Art Resource, New York.

produced in trivalent chrome-plated steel with leather upholstered seat and crest rail.[89] Its size is H 29¾" × W 22" × D 21¼", seat height 21⅝".[90] The design was partly inspired by an office swivel chair. Perriand softened the rigidity of the tubular frame by introducing stuffed cushions for the crest rail and seat.[91]

The cushions rest on coil springs which was a typical approach for upholstered seating at the time. However, because the frame and the upholstery required considerable handwork, the chair was relatively expensive and manufactured in limited numbers.[92] Today, foam has replaced coil spring seating. The chair is currently in Cassina's collection and features expanded polyurethane and padded polyester filling for back and seat.[93] As mentioned earlier, in 1929 the LC 7 became part of Le Corbusier's collection. The companion stool LC 8 and low table LC 9 made of tubular steel and rattan were used in Perriand's dining room, also becoming part of Le Corbusier's collection in 1929. In 2016, Cassina updated LC 7's structure and this led to it obtaining Italian CATAS certification (Testing Certification Research).

The next timeline piece **Bookcase, Maison de Tunisie, 1952**, France, is an example of one of Charlotte Perriand's collaborations. The bookcase was designed with Jean Prouvé. It resides at the Musée National d'Art Moderne, Centre Pompidou, Paris, France (Figure 11.14). It was originally manufactured by Thonet Frères, Paris, France. The bookcase was produced under the name of Bibliothèque Ateliers Jean Prouvé,[94]

Figure 11.14
Bookcase, Maison de Tunisie, 1952, France. Designed by Charlotte Perriand and Jean Prouvé. The medium is mahogany, aluminum, pine, canvas, and lacquer, with color variations.
Source: Art Resource, Inc. New York. ADAGP, Paris.

The Tunisie bookcase was intended to furnish the rooms of Tunisian students resident at the International University Campus in Paris, Maison de la Tunisie. There were 40 of these bookcases in all.[95] The bookcase incorporates several solutions tried out in the past by both Perriand and Prouvé. For example, the principle of sliding doors was developed by Jean Prouvé for furniture intended for Jan Martel in 1930.[96] The principle of the cube system is derived from a joint production by Pierre Jeanneret and Charlotte Perriand in 1940–1947 in which the cubes are arranged in staggered rows. Finally, in a bookcase designed in 1949, Charlotte Perriand developed cubes in folded aluminum.[97] The variations in color have been devised by several artists—Nicolas Schöffer, Silvano Bozzolini, Sonia Delaunay, and Charlotte Perriand—who produce different sketches, which play on the empty spaces and the colored areas.[98] The alternation of the cubes, colors, and their modulations make the bookcase travel along the wall like a piece of jazz music, regulated and improvised at one and the same time, and bring to life a certain musicality in the elements.[99] Its outcome is a timeless work with an endlessly renewed harmony.

The **Wall Cabinet, 1939**, Paris is the last timeline piece to be discussed for Charlotte Perriand. It also resides at the Musée National d'Art Moderne, Centre Pompidou, Paris, France (Figure 11.15). It was designed for the office of Georges Blanchon, Administration du Bureau Central de la Construction. In 1940 Charlotte Perriand, Jean Prouvé, Pierre Jeanneret, and Georges Blanchon together established an office, in the rue Las-Cases, for study of prefabricated aluminum buildings for l'Aluminium Français.[100]

Figure 11.15
Wall Cabinet, 1939, France. Designed by Charlotte Perriand for the office of Georges Blanchon, Administration du Bureau Central de la Construction, Paris. The medium is fir, aluminum, and lacquered mahogany.

Source: Art Resource, Inc. New York. ADAGP, Paris.

The visual essence of the Wall Cabinet is a testament of Perriand's dedication to efficient design and material use. The form of the cabinet is simple—a box with functional sliding doors raised on legs. Its medium is limited—fir, aluminum, and lacquered mahogany—yet the materials become a distinguishing feature, complementing its form. The efflorescent aluminum sliding doors, the use of the light-toned fir at its top and bottom, the two linear lines emphasizing its length, and the black legs and interior accentuate the rectilinear and eye-catching form.

To conclude Chapter 11 and to provide context for the reader and a total environment, Eileen Gray's villa E-1027 main living area (restored) has been selected (Plate 11.1). In 1999, the villa was bought by the Conservatoire du littoral (a cultural conservatory). Since 2014, Cap Moderne, a non-profit, has managed E-1027 and is dedicated to rehabilitating and opening the building as a cultural destination.[101] Cap Moderne has chosen the direction of reconstruction for the villa. Reconstruction versus conservation can be controversial, as pointed out by Tim Benton, an art history professor specializing in 20th-century architecture and a trustee of Cap

Early Modernist designers and architects

Plate 11.1
E-1027 Interior, 1929, Roquebrune-Cap-Martin, France. Designed by Eileen Gray. Photograph of the main living space restored. Managed by Cap Moderne.

Source: Managed by Cap Moderne. Photography by Manuel Bougot.

Moderne. "Left empty, this is one of 100 important houses of the late Modern period," says Benton. "But the interior is one of [the] four most important Modern interiors in the world."[102] It is fortunate for all interested parties that the villa's fate is looking more optimistic in the 21st century.

This concludes Chapter 11. The next chapter moves to America. Chapter 12 will focus on 20th-century European influence in America and the impact on furniture design and interiors.

NOTES

1. Tim McKeough, "The Magical, Mutable Furniture of Pierre Chareau," *Introspective Magazine*, December 12, 2016.
2. Brian Brace Taylor, *Pierre Chareau: Designer and Architect* (Köln: Benedikt Taschen Verlag, 1992), p.7.
3. Ibid.
4. Ibid.
5. Ibid.
6. Tim McKeough, "The Magical, Mutable Furniture of Pierre Chareau," *Introspective Magazine*, December 12, 2016.
7. Ibid.
8. Ibid.
9. On-line Collection description, Cooper-Hewitt, Smithsonian Design Museum, New York, NY, 2020.
10. Ibid.
11. Brian Brace Taylor, *Pierre Chareau: Designer and Architect* (Köln: Benedikt Taschen Verlag, 1992), pp.23, 25.
12. Ibid., p.25.
13. On-line Collection, Object Label, Virginia Museum of Fine Arts, VMFA, Richmond, VA, 2020.
14. Ibid.
15. Ibid.
16. Ibid.
17. On-line Collection, Object Label, Cooper-Hewitt, Smithsonian Design Museum.
18. Ibid.
19. Ibid.
20. Ibid.
21. William C. Ketchum, Jr., *The Smithsonian, Illustrated Library of Antiques, Furniture 2, Neoclassic to the Present* (New York: Cooper-Hewitt Museum, The Smithsonian Institution's National Design Museum, 1981), p.92.
22. Bard Graduate Center Gallery, Press Brochure, Eileen Gray Exhibition, February 29–July 12, 2020.
23. Jennifer Goff, "In Search of Eileen Gray," *Apollo Magazine* 170, September 2009.
24. Ibid.
25. Joseph Rykwert, "A Tribute to Eileen Gray, Design Pioneer," *Domus* 469, December 1968.
26. Ibid.
27. Bard Graduate Center Gallery, Press Brochure, Eileen Gray Exhibition, February 29–July 12, 2020.
28. Jason Sayer, "The Sordid Saga of Eileen Gray's Iconic E-1027 House," *Metropolis*, September 12, 2018.

29 Ibid.
30 Ibid.
31 Ibid.
32 Ann Harrison, "Eileen Gray Architectural Drawings, 1930–1947." Online Archives of California, OAC, Number 2002.M.25, The Getty Research Institute, Special Collections, LA.
33 Ibid.
34 Ibid.
35 Ibid.
36 J. Stewart Johnson, *Eileen Gray Designer* (New York: Debrett's Peerage, for the Museum of Modern Art, New York, 1979), p.17.
37 Bard Graduate Center Gallery, Press Brochure, Eileen Gray Exhibition, February 29–July 12.
38 Jason Sayer, "The Sordid Saga of Eileen Gray's Iconic E-1027 House," *Metropolis*, September 12, 2018.
39 Bard Graduate Center Gallery, Press Brochure, Eileen Gray Exhibition, February 29–July 12.
40 On-line description, Aram Designs, London, UK, 2020.
41 Ibid.
42 On-line Collection, Object Label, Virginia Museum of Fine Arts, VMFA, Richmond, VA, 2020.
43 Ibid.
44 Ibid.
45 Ibid.
46 Ibid.
47 Victoria and Albert Museum, "Ocean Liners: Speed and Style," February 3, 2018–June 17, 2018, Deckchair design: from ocean liner to Modernist villa.
48 Ibid.
49 On-line description, Aram Designs, London, UK, 2020.
50 Ibid.
51 Ibid.
52 Ibid.
53 On-line description, Bienenstock Furniture Library, High Point, NC, 2020.
54 On-line description, Aram Designs, London, UK, 2020.
55 Ibid.
56 Nils Peters, *Prouvé, 1901–1984: The Dynamics of Creation* (Köln: Taschen, 2006), p.7.
57 Ibid.
58 https://en.wikipedia.org/wiki/Jean_Prouvé.
59 Sarah Medford, "The House Collector," *Wall Street Journal Magazine*, June 2015.
60 Nils Peters, *Prouvé 1901–1984: The Dynamics of Creation* (Köln: Taschen, 2006), p.8.
61 https://en.wikipedia.org/wiki/Jean_Prouvé.
62 Nils Peters, *Prouvé 1901–1984: The Dynamics of Creation* (Köln: Taschen, 2006), p.8.
63 Ibid., p.9.
64 Ibid., p.12.
65 Ibid., p.19.
66 Ibid.
67 On-line Description, Design Within Reach, Jean Prouvé, France (1901–1984), 2020.
68 Ibid.
69 Nils Peters, *Prouvé 1901–1984: The Dynamics of Creation* (Köln: Taschen, 2006), p.10.
70 Online Information, La musée Jean Prouvé, 2020, www.jeanprouve.com.
71 Uta Meistere, Interview with Robert M. Rubin. "Collectors are Born not Made," *Society of Architectural Historians SAH Newsletter*, May 17, 2017.
72 On-line Description Jean Prouvé Collection, Vitra International AG, 2020.

73 Ibid.
74 Ibid.
75 On-line Description Jean Prouvé Collection, Vitra International AG, 2020.
76 Uta Meistere, Interview with Robert M. Rubin. "Collectors are Born not Made," *Society of Architectural Historians SAH Newsletter*, May 17, 2017.
77 Nils Peters, *Prouvé 1901–1984: The Dynamics of Creation* (Köln: Taschen, 2006), p.40.
78 Ibid.
79 Online Description, Louis Vuitton Foundation, "Charlotte Perriand: Inventing a New World" (October 2, 2019–February 24, 2020), Paris, France, 2020.
80 Ibid.
81 Online Description, Louis Vuitton Foundation, "Charlotte Perriand: Inventing a New World" (October 2, 2019–February 24, 2020), Paris, France, 2020.
82 On-line, Collection Object Label, Museum of Modern Art, New York, NY, 2020.
83 Ibid.
84 Elizabeth Fazzare, "Charlotte Perriand's French Modernist Les Arcs Comes to the United States," *Architectural Digest*, April 26, 2018.
85 Online Description, Louis Vuitton Foundation, "Charlotte Perriand: Inventing a New World" (October 2, 2019–February 24, 2020), Paris, France, 2020.
86 On-line, Description, Gallery Patrick Seguin, Paris, France, 2020.
87 Ibid.
88 On-line, Description, Casina S.p.A., Meda, Italy, 2020.
89 On-line, Collection Object Label, Museum of Modern Art, New York, NY, 2020.
90 Ibid.
91 Ibid.
92 Ibid.
93 On-line, Description, Casina S.p.A., Meda, Italy, 2020.
94 Christie's, Paris, Online information, LOT 29, Design, Charlotte Perriand (1903–1999), Bibliothèque "Tunisie," Le Modèle Créé En 1952 Réalisé Dans Les Ateliers Jean Prouvé, November 19, 2019.
95 Ibid.
96 Christie's, Paris, Online information, LOT29, Design, Charlotte Perriand (1903–1999), Bibliothèque "Tunisie," Le Modèle Créé En 1952 Réalisé Dans Les Ateliers Jean Prouvé, November 19, 2019.
97 Ibid.
98 Ibid.
99 Ibid.
100 On-line, Description, Gallery Patrick Seguin, Paris, France, 2020.
101 Jason Sayer, "A Sordid Saga of Eileen Gray's Iconic E-1027 House," *Metropolis*, September 12, 2018, www.metropolismag.com/architecture/e1027-villa-eileen-gray-crowdfund-preservation
102 Ibid.

12 Modernism in America and the European connection

12.1
Pictorial timeline—Modernism in American and the European connection.

TIME PERIOD OVERVIEW

When discussing Modernism in America and the European connection, it is helpful to look at the time frame in segments: early Modernism occurring before World War II and mid-Modernism postwar—1945 through the late 1960s. In America, this postwar period has been dubbed the Mid-Century Modern movement or style. This descriptor is reflective of architecture, interiors, urban design, product design, and graphic design. Mid-Century Modern furniture is typically characterized by clean, simple lines and honest use of materials, and it generally does not include decorative embellishment. This characterization is exactly like that of early Modernism.

Before World War II, early Modernism, the European connection is not one particular happening but several occurrences that take place—the preeminent Chicago Tribune Tower Competition of 1922 is one such event. The story of its origin has proved to be one of the most enduring influential narratives in 20th-century architecture, key to understanding the skylines of cities all over the world.[1] The Tribune Tower has stood for nearly a hundred years at the heart of Chicago's cultural heritage and symbolizes the rise of the "city of big shoulders."[2]

Hoping to project an aura of international prestige, Colonel Robert R. McCormick, the powerful publisher of the *Chicago Tribune*, a burgeoning media empire, organized a competition. The brief he compiled asked architects to create "the most beautiful office building in the world." The competition was international and attracted architects from 23 countries.[3] There were nearly 300 entries for the competition.[4] The European architects included were those furthering the vision of the Modern movement such as Adolf Loos (Nice, France), Bruno Taut, Walter Gunther, and Kurz Schutz (Magdeburg, Germany), Walter Gropius and Adolf Meyer (Weimar, Germany), Max Taut (Berlin, Germany), and Eliel Saarinen (Helsingfors, Finland) who won second prize.

Saarinen's project received a financially generous second premium.[5] This 1922 Chicago Tribune Tower Competition brought Eliel Saarinen suddenly to American's attention. In 1923, he and his family immigrated from Finland to the United States using the acclaim and $20,000 he received for his second-place entry.[6] In 1924, Saarinen became visiting professor of architecture at the University of Michigan.[7] One of his architecture students, Henry Booth's father, George Booth, dreamed of building on his private estate in Bloomfield Hills, Michigan, a community of art, science, and education—Cranbrook Academy of Art.[8] Booth hired Eliel Saarinen as chief architect to help with the master plan and the design of the campus, in which Saarinen designed multiple buildings. But his impact on Mid-Century Modernism stems less from building a master plan for Cranbrook than for his philosophy about design education and his progressive curricula.

The intertwinement of his ideas about education and his Finnish background inspired and produced some of the preeminent prewar architects, interior designers, and furniture designers who would shape the mid-20th century. Eliel Saarinen was president of Cranbrook Academy of Art from 1932 to 1946.

> Saarinen wanted students to be able to envision, create, and understand all aspects of design, from architecture to furniture to metalworking, and to engage in experimentation, not so unlike the German Bauhaus school's precepts. Thus, the campus and curriculum were created as a massive laboratory for the graduate students, giving them free rein to work as they pleased.[9]

This proved a perfect scenario for maturing designers since Cranbrook was for advanced students who came for postgraduate work. From 1937 to about 1941, a host of future architects and designers crossed in and out of each other's paths, studying and teaching at the wooded campus[10]—designers such as Florence Knoll,

Charles and Ray Eames, Jack Lenor Larsen, Harry Bertoia, Eero Saarinen, and others. Several of these individuals will be discussed further in the chapter. Mid-Century Modernism has become recognized as one of the most significant design movements, taking into consideration its influence on architecture, interior design, and industrial design.

Equally important to Modernism in America and the European connection as the 1922 Chicago Tribune Competition were occurrences affecting prewar Europe. As mentioned in Chapter 10, the emerging European Modern architecture style of the 1920s and 1930s would greatly influence American "modernity." Additionally, the onset of World War II and the escalating persecution of artists and intellectuals resulted in the Bauhaus closing in 1933. The staff left Germany emigrating all over the world, but in particular the United States. As previously mentioned, émigrés to the US included Walter Gropius and Mies van de Rohe who became heads of two eminent architecture schools, the GSD and IIT, respectively; another Bauhaus colleague Josef Albers and his wife, Anni Albers, were invited to the renowned experimental North Carolina college founded in 1933, the Black Mountain College, becoming esteemed faculty leaders of the art program. The College is a pivotal institution and its impact on US cultural heritage is immeasurable. Josef and Anni Albers were instrumental in ensuring this position. Many of the school's faculty and students were or would go on to become highly influential in the arts including Buckminster Fuller, Robert Motherwell, Susan Weil, Robert Rauschenberg, Merce Cunningham, Franz Kline, and Willem and Elaine de Kooning. The College closed in 1957, yet its powerful influence continues to reverberate.

Two other events that connect Modernism in American to Europe were already mentioned in Chapter 10—first, the 1932 Museum of Modern Art "International Style" exhibition (Hitchcock and Johnson), the genesis of the "International Style" moniker, and second, the writings of George Nelson, architect, industrial designer, author, and teacher for the magazine *Pencil Points*. The magazine was a leading voice in architectural and graphic design when Modernism flourished, introducing key players from America and Europe. While based in Rome, for the Rome Prize, Nelson traveled through Europe where he met a number of the Modernist pioneers whom he interviewed for articles in the magazine. Through his articles in *Pencil Points* he introduced the work of Walter Gropius, Mies van der Rohe, Le Corbusier, and Giovanni "Gio" Ponti to North America. Gio Ponti is the founder of the *Domus* magazine for architecture and design, headquartered in Rozzano, Milan, which is still published today.

In respect to Modernism in America and the European connection, there were many creatives who influenced the direction of mid-century design within the US and Europe. The task to narrow the list is daunting. To assist in abbreviating the list for the sake of this book, the author has taken into account the broad cultural and economic context of postwar America which had immense impact on the Mid-Century Modern movement. This section will focus on two eminent postwar furniture companies, Herman Miller Furniture Company and Knoll International. Between them, these two companies recruited and hired many of the country's renowned postwar designers such as Florence Knoll, Eero Saarinen, George Nelson, Charles and Ray Eames, and Alexander Girard. These companies led design forward for the contract furniture industry and commercial interiors in the 1950s and 1960s, and these icons are currently flourishing today. Herman Miller Furniture Company and Knoll International designers are instrumental in shaping and perpetuating the mid-century ethos regarding all types of design, architecture, interiors, industrial design, textile design, and graphic design.

To grasp the cultural and economic context for postwar America, it is important to understand that the years following World War II were characterized by enormous change economically and culturally. The America postwar era reflected a new optimism—filled with the promise of the future.[11] Pent-up consumer demand fueled exceptionally strong economic growth.[12] The automobile industry successfully converted back to producing cars, and new industries such as electronics and aviation grew by leaps and bounds.[13] Commercial jet travel was introduced in 1957, and ease of travel in the "jet age" encouraged a growing fusion of cultural influences.[14]

The development of industries and a rising economy had positive effects on residential design and public design. The war ended, leaving a new worldwide generation of veterans with young families struggling to rebuild their lives. The pressing need for inexpensive housing and furnishings spurred a boom in design and production. Companies large and small were building facilities or remodeling existing facilities to meet the demands of the growing workforce for both corporate worker and factory worker.

This chapter will address public design and the rise of "contract design" and the America postwar corporate office. It will examine how Herman Miller Furniture Company and Knoll International influenced the appearance of postwar American interiors and furniture. Contract design has come to refer to all interior or design work that is not specifically related to residential design.[15] A synonymous term "commercial design" is used interchangeably in the architecture and design community. The public interior—non-residential design—tends to have a different character. These projects are larger, sometimes huge. Public interiors are accessible to a large range of users and include highly visible and even spectacular spaces.[16] Herman Miller Furniture Company and Knoll International have been committed to Modern design and understanding the nature of the workplace. Through the 1940s, the 1950s, and the 1960s, the companies were crucial players in generating a fleshed-out form of furniture design characterized by the Modern movement.[17] Much of this is attributed to their willingness to experiment with new technologies and materials developed during wartime such as cellulosic, acrylic, nylon, and polyethylene, and the introduction of foam padding in the late 1950s. New materials and technologies helped free design from tradition, allowing for increasingly abstract and sculptural aesthetics as well as lower prices for mass-produced objects.[18] At this point, the Mid-Modern movement is not solely linked to rationalism and its rational roots.

As mentioned above, Herman Miller Furniture Company and Knoll International recruited and hired many of the world's renowned postwar designers who have become synonymous with American mid-century design and their contributions are invaluable to American cultural heritage. The rest of the chapter will examine the work of George Nelson, Charles and Ray Eames, Alexander Girard, Florence Knoll, Eero Saarinen, and Harry Bertoia.

HERMAN MILLER FURNITURE, ZEELAND, MICHIGAN, 1923

History

Herman Miller began in 1905 as Star Furniture Company, a high-quality manufacturer of traditional-style bedroom suites, which opened for business in Zeeland, Michigan. The company was renamed Michigan Star Furniture Company in 1909 and at that time hired 18-year-old Dirk Jan (D.J.) De Pree as a clerk. By 1919, D.J. De Pree had become president of Michigan Star Furniture Company. Within the next several years he convinced his father-in-law, Herman Miller, to purchase the majority of shares of Michigan Star Furniture Company, and in 1923 the company becomes the Herman Miller Furniture Company.[19] De Pree was the first president of the Herman Miller Furniture Company, which continued to manufacture reproductions of traditional home furniture. However, by 1930 amid the turmoil of the Great Depression, like many companies, Herman Miller faced failure.[20] Around this time, De Pree came in contact with furniture designer Gilbert Rohde from New York. Rohde convinced De Pree to move away from traditional furniture and to focus on products better suited to the changing needs and lifestyles of Americans.[21] Herman Miller debuted Rohde's furniture designs at the 1933 Century of Progress Exposition in Chicago.

Not necessarily forgotten, but the name and contribution of Gilbert Rohde (1894–1944) to Modernism in America is not overtly obvious. Yet, few designers did more to influence the appearance of postwar American interiors than the furniture designer Gilbert Rohde.[22] He brought an industrial design perspective to the Herman Miller Furniture Company and, in the process, introduced Modernism to a broad range of Americans, especially through his modular furnishings.[23] Rohde's focus on comfort, informality, multifunctionality, and flexibility transposed European design antecedents into furnishings suitable for American lifestyles. A champion of modular components, he experimented with new industrial materials, including Plexiglas, and produced furniture with biomorphic forms. Not only did Rohde introduce Modern designs, but he also devised a complete merchandising strategy for their promotion.[24] Gilbert Rohde designed Executive Office Group (EOG) in 1942, which was modular and versatile. This design was Herman Miller's entry into the office furniture market. EOG is a precursor of systems furniture. Several years after this trailblazing design, Gilbert Rohde died, in 1944, and De Pree began searching for a new design leader. After seeing an article in *Life* magazine on George Nelson and his Storagewall design, D.J. De Pree hired him to serve as the company's first design director. Nelson was an ideal choice for De Pree, and they developed a warm personal and professional relationship which yielded a stunning range of products.[25] The Marshmallow Sofa used as a practice example in Chapter 4 is one such product (Figure 4.17).

■ An Illustrated Guide to Furniture History

Nelson served as design director from 1945 to the early 1970s and simultaneously founded his own firm, George Nelson Associates in New York in 1947. George Nelson's firm/studio designed for Herman Miller for more than 25 years as they shepherded design into the Modern era.[26] George Nelson Associates partnered with most of the forward-thinking mid-century designers of the time. Together with Nelson's staff, these designers would design for Herman Miller under Nelson's supervision—designers such as Ray and Charles Eames, Harry Bertoia, and Isamu Noguchi, and his staff designers Irving Harper, George C. Mulhauser, Don Chadwick, Suzanne Sekey. Nelson's studio designers were true forward-thinking pioneers of Mid-Century Modernism in their own right.

Aesthetics

This Mid-Century Modern style aesthetic description will pertain to both mid-century furniture leaders, Herman Miller Furniture Company and Knoll International. It is relevant to the understanding and ability to distinguish features of the style to remember that, like early Modernism, the Mid-Century Modern movement supported mass production and factory-made objects. By mid-century, this notion was incorporated with new methods of construction and new materials, with an objective of affordability, versatility, and well-made furniture. Furniture generally possessed an uncluttered profile—clean lines. There is an emphasis on simplicity and functionality. The form can be either organic or geometric, and typically minimal ornamentation. The designs demonstrated a propensity for exploration of traditional and non-traditional materials. Visible is a liberal use of traditional materials, such as wood, and non-traditional materials such as metal, glass, vinyl, plywood, Plexiglass, and Lucite. Plastics dramatically influenced later Mid-Century Modern designs. Importantly, the use of color in designs becomes significant and a vast range of color is used, from neutral to bold. Due to these distinguishing features and original character, the Mid-Century Modern movement's furniture today has become timeless classics and most desirable within popular culture.

George Nelson (1908–1986), New York City, United States

Furniture

The first Herman Miller timeline piece to be discussed is the **Swag Leg Armchair**, 1956, produced 1958–1964. The chair is designed by George Nelson for Herman Miller Furniture Company. This authentic design celebrates the use of the relatively new mid-century material fiberglass and tubular steel from the early Modern repertoire.

The expressive form appears to vacillate between elegant and playful (Figure 12.1). Its name derives from a method of using pressure to taper and curve metal tubing, known as *swaging*.

Figure 12.1 Swag Arm Chair, 1956, U.S., Herman Miller Furniture Company, produced 1958–1964. Designed by George Nelson (1908–1986). The shell is fiberglass-reinforced plastic, with legs which are steel 16-gauge adjustable glides.

Source: Courtesy of Herman Miller.

Upon discovering the solution in swaging, Nelson began design of the chair with its four gently angled and curved tubes.[27] The next question became how to connect the curved tubes/chair legs. He received permission from Charles and Ray Eames to use their patented process developed for molding plastic.[28] He adapted this process to suit the Swag Leg Armchair and created separate shells for the seat and back. With the original design, the shells were made of fiberglass-reinforced plastic. Today the shells are made of recyclable polypropylene, consistent with the Herman Miller commitment to being a good steward of the earth's resources.[29] The Swag Leg Armchair flexes with the sitter and allows comfortable air circulation through the opening between the seat and back. The armrests which are formed as part of the back piece are ample size, allowing for a comfortable repose. The dimensions are H 32″ × W 28″ × D 22″, arm H 26½″ and seat H 18″.[30]

George Mulhauser (1922–2002), New York City, United States

Figure 12.2 Coconut Chair, 1958, U.S., Herman Miller Furniture Company. Design by George Mulhauser (1922–2002), for George Nelson Associates. Seat formed of fiberglass-reinforced polyester with steel legs.

Source: Courtesy of Herman Miller.

Furniture

The next timeline piece from the Herman Miller Collection is the **Coconut Chair**, 1958, designed by George Mulhauser, staff designer and associate at George Nelson's office/studio (Figure 12.2). The chair was created for Nelson's studio and was produced by Herman Miller from 1955 to 1978, then reintroduced in 2001. Past history credited the chair to George Nelson. But today the credit for a design is given to the designer himself or herself, not the studio and or company. Since 1988, the chair has also been produced by Vitra.[31] The playful name of the chair is in alignment with the relaxed character and form. This chair can be for the office or the home. This relaxed and playful quality at mid-century became an important feature for home furnishings as well as for the office.

There have been changes to the chair structure as stated by the George Nelson Foundation.

> The armchair was first produced with a seat of bent steel that was cushioned with foam and covered with fabric or Naugahyde. Later, Herman Miller produced the seat using fiberglass-reinforced polyester. The frame was at first strengthened using bent steel rods that echoed the form of the chair. Later, the legs feet of the frame were screwed individually into the seat. Today, the chair is offered with a leather covering and additional circulation holes on the bottom of the seat.

Charles Eames (1907–1978) and Ray Eames (1912–1988), California, United States

Furniture

The inventive designs and collaborative projects of dynamic couple Charles and Ray (Kaiser) Eames have become synonymous with the postwar Mid-Century Modern movement. They took on commissions both large and small including toys, film, urban planning, furniture, and architecture—the trailblazing Case Study House No. 8 Pacific Palisades, Los Angeles. Their work has influenced almost every aspect of late 20th-century design. Charles, an architect, and Ray, a painter, met at Cranbrook where Charles was head of the Experimental Design Department ca. 1937–1940. Cranbrook unleashed the creativity and skill of these design pioneers—which Saarinen had imagined Cranbrook's curricula would do for those who wanted to design. The school's structure allowed students and faculty to envision, create and collaborate. After Cranbrook, the couple married and moved to California where they began their joint practice, initially focusing on furniture and interior design. They strove to dispel the belief that Modern design was uninviting and created interiors that were warm and informal.[32]

The next timeline piece is the **DCW (Dining Chair Wood)**, 1946, designed by Charles and Ray Eames. The boldly original molded plywood chairs marked the beginning of their long and legendary relationship with Herman Miller in 1946 (Figure 12.3). The chair's form, made of molded plywood, was designed to comfortably fit the body. The aesthetic integrity, enduring charm, and comfort of the chairs earned them recognition from *Time* magazine as the Best Design of the 20th Century.[33] *Time* called the design "something elegant, light and comfortable. Much copied but never bettered."[34]

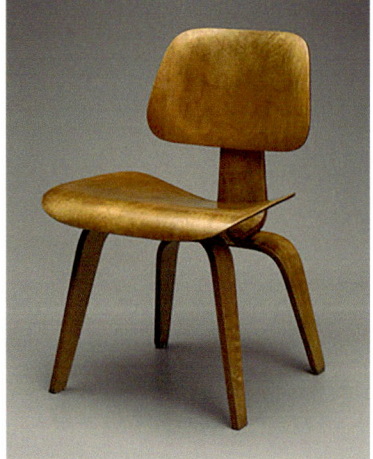

Figure 12.3 DCW (Dining Chair Wood), Herman Miller Furniture Company, ca. 1946. Designed by Charles Eames (1907–1978) and Ray Eames (1912–1988). The medium is molded birch plywood, rubber, steel, and resin.
Source: Courtesy of Herman Miller.

In their search for a better way, Charles and Ray Eames developed an innovative technique for molding plywood. The process allowed them to bend wood in new directions and give hard materials a soft look. The contours from the molding process created out of plywood fit the body's shape. The plywood has five plies, with hardwood inner plies. Natural rubber shock mounts absorb movement.[35]

The DCW's medium is birch plywood, rubber, steel, and resin. The overall size H 29½″ × W 19¼″ × D 21½″.[36] Today, finish choices are richly grained birch veneer in bright colors that recall the times when the chairs were introduced. The environmentally friendly aniline stains Herman

Miller uses allow the wood's natural characteristics to show through. The chairs are also available in natural cherry, walnut, and light ash.[37]

The next timeline piece from the Herman Miller Collection designed by Charles and Ray Eames is **No. 670/671 Lounge Chair and Ottoman**, 1956 (Figure 12.4), referred to as the 670/671, after the Herman Miller part numbers used to make the seating. By the design community, the pair is simply referred to as "Eames Lounge Chair and Ottoman." Today the chair and ottoman are distributed by Herman Miller and Vitra.[38]

Deemed a 20th-century interpretation of the 19th-century English club chair, this seating instantly became a symbol of comfort—and comfort was one of Charles and Ray's key objectives for this product.[39]

The Eameses believed that design addressed itself to the need. In this case, the need was "a special refuge from the strains of modern living." The chair combines factory technologies with intricate hand labor and craftsmanship. The Eameses wanted their Lounge Chair and Ottoman to have the "warm receptive look of a well-used first baseman's mitt."[40] Its comfort is provided by its reclining and sitting position, pivoting, padding, contouring, and flexing. The original materials (1956) were rosewood-faced molded plywood with leather upholstery cushion and cast aluminum base. The current medium, seven-ply walnut, santos palisander, ebony-stained ash, or white ash veneer, with molded plywood frame and premium-quality leather upholstery in a wide array of colors and grains. Also included is urethane foam padding, die-cast aluminum braces, and stainless-steel

Figure 12.4
670/671 Lounge Chair and Ottoman, 1956, U.S., Herman Miller Furniture Company. Designed by Charles Eames (1907–1978) and Ray Eames (1912–1988). The medium is molded plywood and rosewood veneers, case aluminum, black leather-covered latex foam, and down upholstery.
Source: Courtesy of Herman Miller.

■ An Illustrated Guide to Furniture History

glides. The size of the Lounge Chair is H 32" × W 32¾" × D 32¾", seat height 15", and the Ottoman is H 17¼" × W 26" × D 21½".[41] This 60-year-plus-old chair and ottoman have become a timeless iconic design, highly desirable and celebrated by architects and designers.

Alexander Girard (1907–1993), New York City, United States

Alexander Girard, architect, interior designer, furniture designer, industrial designer, and textile designer, was hired by Herman Miller (1952–1973) to head the fabric and textile division. He created fabrics for the designs of George Nelson and Charles and Ray Eames. Initially, Girard established a fabric collection based on his architectural training, consisting of plain upholsteries and geometric prints. But his later collection transformed the mid-century vision of fabrics and textiles for the office and contract design. He called his approach "aesthetic functionalism."[42] This collection was largely inspired by folk art and the relationship built with a 19th-century Mexico textile mill. Through his interaction with the mill, he was able to produce handwoven 100% cotton fabrics of an excellent quality and array of colors—polychromatic, highly saturated, in a variety of patterns and textures. This direction was unprecedented, since at this time mid-century solids and varying grays were the predominant Modernist choices.[43] During his tenure at Herman Miller, he created over 300 textile designs in multitudes of colorways—wallpapers, prints, furniture, and objects.[44]

Alexander Girard developed a furniture collection for Herman Miller in 1967 based on his designs for Braniff International Airways 1948–1965. For Braniff, Girard designed the lounge and office furniture. This collection is highly collectible and rare due to being produced for a limited time period. Unlike his colleagues at Herman Miller, whose work and personalities retained public prominence in the latter part of the 20th century, Girard's contributions did not remain obvious, which was a shame. In 2000, Cooper-Hewitt held a retrospective exhibition on Girard's career, "The Opulent Eye of Alexander Girard," and since then there has been a resurgence of interest in his work.[45]

Furniture

The next timeline pieces discussed for the Herman Miller Collection are from the **Girard Group, 1967**, a sofa and chair designed by Alexander Girard (1907–1993) (Figure 12.5 and Figure 12.6). The pieces were the original Braniff line of furniture created when Girard did the design overhaul for the Braniff Airline in 1965. The pieces were so well received that he created the

Figure 12.5
Sofa, The Girard Group, 1965, U.S. Designed by Alexander Girard (1907 –1993) for Braniff Airline. Re-created in 1967 for Herman Miller Furniture Company. The outer shell may come in a variety of fabrics or painted, and the welt selected from one of three colors. The inner shell and cushion may be upholstered in a variety of fabrics. The shell rests on steel legs with a circular disk pad for the floor.
Source: Girard Studio, LLC.

314

Girard Group for Herman Miller two years later.[46] Alexander Girard's explanation is exquisitely stated about the group of furniture he created. The following is an excerpt of the explanation for the Group by Alexander Girard from Herman Miller's promotional material:

Figure 12.6
Chair, The Girard Group, 1965, U.S. Designed by Alexander Girard (1907–1993) for Braniff Airline. Re-created in 1967 for Herman Miller Furniture Company. The outer shell may come in a variety of fabrics or painted, and the welt selected from one of three colors. The inner shell and cushion may be upholstered in a variety of fabrics. The shell rests on steel legs with a circular disk pad for the floor.
Source: Girard Studio, LLC.

My Group of furniture designs resemble the chameleon: its character remains intact yet its skin texture and color change to suit the environment. A low sight line is maintained which is highly desirable in contemporary low-ceilinged spaces. In groups, the lowness and resulting small scale create a feeling of space and repose and do not interrupt wall spaces. The outer shell may be upholstered in a variety of fabric or painted and the welt selected in one of three colors. The inner shell and cushion may be upholstered in a variety of fabrics. The permutations are infinite. The following design details were basic to my concept: soft rounded corners, maximum choice of fabrics, simple shell components easily assembled, attachment between seats and backs is simple and direct.

Figure 12.7
Fabrics designed by Alexander Girard for the Herman Miller Furniture Company. Demonstrating his signature designs and color palette *(left)* Circles—Barberpole, 1957 *(right)* Palio, 1964.
Source: Girard Studio, LLC.

Alexander Girard was the first Modern designer to define textiles as being more than just functional but with the purpose to further emphasize form through the application of color and pattern.[47] During his career, Girard energized the furniture designs of his Herman Miller colleagues with a new, vibrant color palette and an oeuvre of folk-inspired textiles (Figure 12.7). Within the architecture and design community, Girard is considered the greater colorist and textile designer of modern time.[48] The colorful, whimsical folk art objects inspired his fabric designs' color, texture, and pattern.[49] This inspiration translated to designs with primary colors, concise geometric patterns, and a touch of humor, with which he injected joy and spontaneity into his designs.[50] These qualities are clearly demonstrated in the textile examples (Figure 12.7).

Knoll Associates, Inc., New York, 1938—Knoll International Ltd, Milano, Italy (SpA)

History

German-born Hans Knoll (1914–1955) was a member of a prominent furniture-making family. His father Walter C. Knoll, one of the pioneer makers of Modern furniture in pre-Hitler Germany, produced early Mies van der Rohe designs in his Stuttgart factory. Disenchanted with Europe, Hans Knoll came to New York in 1937 after a brief stay in England. With his background in the production of furniture, an entrepreneurial spirit, and zeal for good design, he was ready in 1938 to form the Hans G. Knoll Furniture Company in a small space on East 72nd Street.[51] As Hans expanded the scope of his company to include interior design projects, in 1941 he hired a young Danish designer, Jens Risom (1916–2016), to help with space planning. Risom then designed a collection of furniture which helped Knoll launch the new company—the original Knoll furniture.[52] Risom was one of the first designers to introduce Scandinavian design to the US. An exemplar of Mid-Century Modern design, he would go on to develop an esteemed reputation and his own company producing Scandinavian designs.[53]

While the company grew quickly in its first few years under Hans's leadership, it was Knoll's association with Florence Schust, beginning in 1943, that propelled the company toward unparalleled excellence.[54] Florence (Schust) Knoll's life prior to meeting Hans Knoll was distinctive for a woman of that time. Her educational and employment opportunities were diverse, placing her in contact with mid-century architect and design virtuosos. In her youth, she attended Kingswood School for Girls (1932–1934), part of the Cranbrook educational community.[55] At Cranbrook, she developed a close relationship with the Saarinens, where Eliel Saarinen served as first president of Cranbrook Academy of Art. She spent summers with the family in Finland.[56] In 1935, Florence Schust went to Columbia University's School of Architecture and studied town planning.[57] She explored furniture-making with Eero Saarinen and Charles Eames, and in 1938 met Finnish architect Alvar Aalto, which resulted in her attending the Architectural Association in London due to his high regard for the school.[58] In 1940, she moved to Cambridge, Massachusetts, to apprentice in the architecture office of former Bauhaus educators, Walter Gropius and Marcel Breuer.[59] After these experiences, she settled to study architecture under former Bauhaus director Mies van der Rohe, at Armour Institute, where he was the head of the architecture program. In 1941, she received her bachelor's degree in architecture from Armour Institute.[60]

Florence and Hans were married in 1946. Over the next nine years, and until Hans's untimely death in a 1955 auto accident, the company grew substantially both in the US and abroad. Founders Hans and Florence Knoll embraced the creative genius at the Bauhaus School and the Cranbrook Academy of Art to create new types of furniture and environments for the workplace. With the development in 1946 of the Knoll Planning Unit, an interior planning arm of what was then called H.G. Knoll Associates, Florence Knoll developed the idea of the modern office and pioneered the commercially focused interior design profession. The Planning Unit team worked on projects for some of the biggest corporations in America.[61] It grew to become the leading innovator of modern interiors and furnishings in the 1950s and 1960s, transforming the CBS, Seagram, and *Look* magazine headquarters in Manhattan, the H.J. Heinz headquarters in Pittsburgh, and properties across the United States, Europe, Asia, and South America, including American embassies.[62]

By 1955, Hans and Florence had established one of the preeminent international design houses. Florence worked on strategic planning for the company and reinforced the idea of collaboration. Throughout her tenure at Knoll, she recruited, hired, and collaborated with many pioneering modernists—colleagues, friends, and former teachers such as sculptor Harry Bertoia, Isamu Noguchi, Eero Saarinen, and Mies van der Rohe, as well as designing pieces for the collection herself. This collaborative vision continues today. For more than 75 years, Knoll has teamed up with celebrated architects and designers to offer creative, groundbreaking furniture, textiles, and accessories. A listing and chronology of Knoll designers can be found on their website.

Through the decades, Knoll has remained true to the Bauhaus design philosophy that Modern furniture should complement architectural space, not compete with it. Knoll is recognized internationally for creating workplace and residential furnishings that inspire, evolve, and endure. Ideas essential to Knoll's work include how people interact with their environments and how their environments impact what they do. Modern design has been the guiding principle for Knoll in offering thoughtful, inventive products—furniture, accessories, textiles, felts, and leathers that stimulate the senses, respond to individual work styles, and transcend multiple generations.

Florence Knoll was a pioneering designer and entrepreneur, and developed the idea of America's postwar office by creating the Modern look and feel of the mid-century corporate office, the descriptor being sleek furniture, artistic textiles, and an uncluttered, free-flowing workplace environment. At Knoll, Modern design has been the guiding principle since its inception, and Florence Knoll nurtured this point as the company trademark. Over 75 years, the company has consistently produced an array of products that combine a Modernist aesthetic with residential appeal for the workplace.

Drawing on her background in architecture, Florence Knoll introduced Modern notions of efficiency, space planning, and comprehensive design to office planning. She initiated the Planning Unit concept, a team of Knoll designers that collectively designed a corporate project presenting a comprehensive design package informed by principles of Modernism. As mentioned earlier, Florence and her Planning Unit team were responsible for the interiors of some of America's largest mid-century corporations. Not only did she fulfill the role as interior designer, but she designed furniture for the Knoll catalog as part of her work with the Planning Unit. She humbly referred to her furniture designs as the "meat and potatoes" filler among the standout pieces of Bertoia, Mies, and Saarinen.[63] However, her designs have become as revered and celebrated as those of her colleagues. Her sofa and chair suite (Figure 12.7 and Figure 12.8) and table series are Mid-Century Modern classics and readily utilized today.

In 1984, Paul Goldberger, then the architecture critic of *The Times*, wrote that Ms. Knoll "probably did more than any other single figure to create the modern, sleek, postwar American office, introducing contemporary furniture and a sense of open planning into the work environment."[64] It is fortunate for the architecture and design community to have Florence Knoll Bassett as a member for an unprecedented number of years. Florence Knoll Bassett passed away on January 25, 1919 at the age of 101.

Florence Knoll Bassett (1917–2019), New York, United States

Furniture

The first piece on the timeline from the Knoll Collection is from the **Standard Florence Knoll Lounge Collection**, 1954, New York, designed by Florence Knoll (Figure 12.8). She referred to the collection as the "fill-in-pieces that no one else wants to do."[65] If that was the case, it has not distracted from the collection's reputation through the decades as defining examples of Mid-Century Modern furniture design.

The Collection's rectilinear form, angular profile, and material reflect Knoll's time spent in the company of Mies van de Rohe. The collection further exemplifies the objective perfectionism of Modern design in the early 1960s.[66] The medium is a metal frame with six legs in heavy-gauge steel with polished chrome finish. The seat and back covering is tufted and covered with polyester fiberfill to enhance comfort.[67] The back cushions are attached with a zipper and can be removed.[68]

Figure 12.8
Sofa, Knoll Lounge Collection, 1954, U.S., Knoll International. Designed by Florence Knoll (1917–2019). Modern rectilinear form, angular profile. With six legs in heavy gauge steel with polished chrome finish. Seat and back covering is tufted and covered with a polyester fiber fill.
Source: Courtesy of Knoll International

Knoll introduced the **Relaxed Sofa and Settee** in celebration of the designer's 100th birthday.[69] This version has four legs, seat suspension with springs, and arm, seat, and back cushions with multi-density foam. For the upholstery choice there is a range of KnollTextiles and Spinneybeck® leathers available. The buttons only come with leather upholstery, not fabric. The overall dimensions are H 31¼" × W 63" × D 35", seat H 18¼".[70]

The next piece is the **Florence Knoll Lounge Chair**, 1954. The Lounge Chair, like its sofa companion, has an angular profile. Its form is a perfect square, the

Figure 12.9
Lounge Chair, Knoll Lounge Collection, 1954, U.S. Designed by Florence Knoll (1917–2019). Modern, rectilinear form, angular profile. Metal base is heavy gauge steel. The chair frame is wood construction. The back and seat cushions are tufted.

Source: Courtesy of Knoll International

dimensions being W 32¼" × D 32¼"[71] (Figure 12.9). The metal base is also a heavy-gauge steel with polished chrome finish—a perfect expression of the Modern aesthetic. The inner frame is solid wood.[72] The back and seat are tufted and, like the sofa, can be upholstered in a range of KnollTextiles and Spinneybeck leathers. In the 21st century, the seat suspension consists No-Sag springs.[73] The overall dimensions are H 31¼" × W 32¼" × D 32¼", seat H 17½", arm H 23½".[74] Knoll International's description states that it is "a scaled-down translation of the rhythm and proportions of mid-century modern architecture." It is not typical that furniture is thought of as a translation of architecture, yet this sentiment seems appropriate in this case.

Eero Saarinen (1910–1961), New York, United States

Furniture

The next items from the Knoll Collection, designed by Eero Saarinen, are the **Pedestal Chair** and the entire **Pedestal Furniture Collection**, 1956 (Figure 12.10). The chair resides in the Yale University Art Gallery, The Mabel Brady Garvan Collection. The Pedestal Furniture Collection is also informally referred to as the Tulip Series. The photograph is from the Knoll's archives, ca. 1955–1956 (Figure 12.11). As seen in the photograph, Saarinen's single Pedestal Furniture series includes the side chair, armchair, and a variety of tables.

Figure 12.10
Side Chair, Knoll International, Pedestal Collection (Tulip), 1956, U.S. Designed by Eero Saarinen (1910–1961). Its medium is an aluminum base, with a fused plastic finish, molded plastic shell reinforced with fiberglass, and an upholstered seat cushion.

Source: Yale University Art Gallery, New Haven, Connecticut. American Decorative Arts, Mabel Brady Garvan Collection. Photo credit: Yale University Art Gallery.

Eero Saarinen and Florence Knoll had a long and established history, beginning at the Cranbrook Academy of Art. As Hans and Florence established their Knoll Furniture Company, she reached out to her friend and colleague, as she would do with other architects and designers, to design furniture for the company. Eero Saarinen's designs involved the use of modern materials such as polymers and plastics, which could produce graceful and organic shapes. His oeuvre included the Single Pedestal Series, 70 series Executive Seating Collection, the Womb Chair, Womb Sofa,

■ An Illustrated Guide to Furniture History

and other pieces. His early designs, now considered Mid-Century Modern classics, helped establish the identity of Knoll as a mid-century progressive company during the formative years.[75] He worked with Knoll from the late 1940s through the 1950s. Today, many of his designs are the most recognizable Knoll pieces.

The medium of the Single Pedestal Furniture Series is molded fiberglass for the seat shell with a base made of heavy molded cast aluminum finished with a powder coat paint. Although the seat of the chair is plastic and the base aluminum, they appear to be one material. The size of the armless version is H 32″ × W 20″ × D 21¼″, seat H 18½″.[76] With the Single Pedestal Furniture Series, Saarinen's intention was to eliminate the "slum of legs" found under four-legged chairs and tables.[77] He worked first with hundreds of drawings, followed by quarter-scale models.[78] The model furniture was set up in a scaled model room.

Figure 12.11
Coffee Table, Pedestal Group Collection (1955–1956), U.S., Knoll International. Designed by Eero Saarinen (1910–1961). The Collection's medium is an aluminum base with a fused plastic finish, molded plastic shell reinforced with fiberglass, and an upholstered seat cushion.
Source: Courtesy of Knoll International.

Harry Bertoia (1915–1978), United States

Furniture

The next timeline pieces from the Knoll Collection are the **Side Chair**, 1955, and **Small Diamond Chair**, after 1952. The two chairs were designed by Harry Bertoia. Italian-born Arri Bertoia (Harry Bertoia) was an American artist—painter, sculpture, metal worker, print maker and furniture designer (Figure 12.12 and Figure 12.13). These chairs are from the Virginia Museum of Fine Art's Decorative Arts after 1890 Collection.

Bertoia received a scholarship to study at Cranbrook Academy of Arts in 1937. In 1943, Bertoia departed Cranbrook to join Charles and Ray Eames in California to pursue ongoing experimental work on molded plywood.[79] The Eameses sent Harry to a welding class in Santa Monica where he learned the skill that would carry him through life.[80] He departed the company in 1946 out of frustration when he received no credit for his innovative chair solutions which made production of the chair possible and were adopted by Eameses.[81]

Figure 12.12
Knoll International, Side Chair, 1955. Designed by Harry Bertoia (1915–1978). The medium is a steel frame with black lacquered metal and plastic.
Source: Courtesy of the Virginia Museum of Fine Arts, Richmond, Virginia, Decorative Arts After 1890 Collection. Gift of Barry Friedman and Patricia Pasto.

Modernism in America and the European connection

Figure 12.13
Knoll International, Small Diamond Chair, after 1952. Designed by Harry Bertoia (1915–1978). The medium is a steel frame, covered in vinyl, with upholstered Naugahyde cushions.

Source: Courtesy of the Virginia Museum of Fine Arts, Richmond, Virginia, Decorative Arts After 1890 Collection. General Operating Fund.

In the 1950s, former Cranbrook classmate Florence Schust Knoll invited Bertoia to work with her and husband, Hans Knoll, in Pennsylvania.[82] Bertoia and his wife agreed and moved to Pennsylvania and set up shop under the auspices of Knoll. The agreement between Bertoia, Florence, and Hans Knoll was that Bertoia would receive credit for all designs he created and the chair rights would remain permanently with Knoll. Knoll produced the first Bertoia chairs in 1952 and is still producing the Bertoia collection today.

Bertoia chose metal as the material of choice for his chair and table designs. Bertoia explored and manipulated the material until he arrived at the wire grid concept that could be shaped at will. The chairs are characterized by their lightness and transparency. Harry Bertoia liked to think of the chairs as being "mainly made of air."[83] The chair construction was comprised of bent and welded steel rods. The finish treatment for the welded steel could be either vinyl-coated or chrome-plated. The idea to construct furniture of welded wire and a springy feel was totally innovative. Bertoia not only created the airy design of the chairs, but also devised the production molds used for mass manufacturing. The Side Chair (Figure 12.11) medium is black lacquered metal and plastic. Its size overall is H 31" × W 21" × D 17½".[84] The Small Diamond Chair (Figure 12.12) medium is vinyl, steel, and Naugahyde. Its size overall is H 29" × W 21¼" × D 25½".[85]

To conclude Chapter 12, the room chosen to give the reader an idea of the context and a total mid-century environment is the Virginia Museum of Fine Arts, Richmond Virginia, Membership Suite, 1950s and Rare Book Room, Library (Plate 12.1).

The mid-century interior, especially pertaining to public space, appears reductive and paired down. A sense of minimalism pervades the overall atmosphere, yet obviously apparent will be selective decorative art objects and art—the controlled placement giving the interior the perception of minimalism. The mid-century commercial building is typically planned on a grid with glass walls. The Museum's Membership Suite's rectangular shape with glazed walls looking onto the terrace and garden alludes to this quality. Bertoia's wire grid side chairs are placed on the terrace, although not seen in this view. Typically, both furniture and interior envelope emphasize the orthogonal and rectilinear as well. The furniture has a lightness in scale and form, as does the color palette used on the wall planes.

The interior architecture and space plan demonstrate mid-century principles excellently, yet the most compelling feature in the narration of the space is the

■ An Illustrated Guide to Furniture History

Plate 12.1
Virginia Museum of Fine Arts Membership Suite, 1950s, and Rare Book Room, Library. *(above)* Members' lounge area, *(below)* Rare Book Room.

Source: Virginia Museum of Fine Arts, Membership Suite, 1950s, and Rare Book Room, Library.

Photo Archives © Virginia Museum of Fine Arts.

inclusion of furniture pieces from the Knoll Collection. The pieces and their placement work splendidly—Eero Saarinen's three executive armchairs that surround the round table in the corner, and in the main conversation grouping. Adjacent to the grouping are Mies and Lilly Reich's Barcelona Chairs. And lastly Florence Knoll's sofa and marble-top end tables. The result of the orthogonal arrangement begets a most compelling space. Regarding the drapery treatment, seen on both glazed walls are pinch-pleat draperies which were very common mid-century. Another mid-century feature is the use of a screening device instead of a partition/wall. This is visible in the foreground where the textured panel is used in this manner. Regarding artwork, the inclusion of a mid-century Alexander Calder mobile is most fitting for an art museum suite. The architecture, interior, furnishings, and art all render a remeberable mid-century interior and exterior environment.

Lastly, the adjacent Rare Book Room, Library, has all the qualities of a historical referenced library—wood-paneled walls, built-in wood shelving, fireplace, seating for one to read, and tables. But what is spectacular is how these traditional elements are reinterpreted using a Mid-Century Modern vocabulary. The traditional characteristic elements are pared down, ornament free, clean lines, rectilinear—just like the Knoll furnishings which embody the same quality.

This concludes Chapter 12. It is good to keep in mind that the public will use the term "modern" to refer to something that is non-traditional or not historically recognized in anyway. However, the reader should comprehend at this point in the book that from the early 1900 the term "Modern" came to refer to a particular approach by a group of architects, designers, and craftsman who sought to cast off historical precedent and develop something entirely new and different for their own time. The final Chapter 13—Movements after Modernism—considers the period around the 1970s, when divergent reactions to Modernism begin to manifest.

NOTES

1. Ibid.
2. Leo Shaw, "How Chicago's Tribune Tower Competition Changed Architecture Forever," *2017 Chicago Architecture Biennial*, October 3, 2017.
3. Ibid.
4. William J.R. Curtis, *Modern Architecture Since 1900* (New Jersey: Prentice-Hall. Simon & Schuster, 1996), p.220.
5. Henry-Russell Hitchcock and Philip Johnson, *The International Style* (New York: W.W. Norton & Company, 1932), p.483.
6. On-line Description, Cranbrook Center for Collections and Research, Bloomfield Hills, Michigan, 2020.
7. Ibid.
8. Ibid.
9. On-line Description History of Cranbrook Academy of Art, Bloomfield Hills, Michigan, 2020.
10. Patrick Sisson, "Cranbrook's Golden Age: How a Freewheeling School Changed American Design," *Curbed American Real Estate and Urban Design Blog Network*, November 7, 2015.

■ **An Illustrated Guide to Furniture History**

11 Jared Gross, *Design, 1950–75*, Exhibition narrative, Metropolitan Museum of Art, New York, New York, October 2004.
12 Michael Moffat, *Post War U.S. Economy*, Thought Company, www.thoughtco.com, January 27, 2020.
13 Ibid.
14 Jared Gross, *Design, 1950–75*, Exhibition narrative, Metropolitan Museum of Art, New York, New York, October 2004.
15 John Pile, *Interior Design* (New Jersey, Prentice Hall, Simon & Schuster, 1995), p.499.
16 Ibid.
17 Judith Miller, *Furniture World Styles from Classical to Contemporary* (New York: Dorling Kindersley, 2005), p.454.
18 Jared Gross, *Design, 1950–75*, Exhibition narrative, Metropolitan Museum of Art, New York, New York, October 2004.
19 On-line Description Herman Hiller History, Zeeland, Michigan, 2020.
20 Ibid.
21 Ibid.
22 Phyllis Ross, *Gilbert Rohde: Modern Design for Modern Living* (New Haven: Yale University Press, 2009).
23 Ibid., Book Introduction.
24 Ibid.
25 On-line Description Herman Hiller History, Zeeland, Michigan, 2020.
26 Ibid.
27 On-line Description, Herman Miller Store, 2020.
28 Ibid.
29 Ibid.
30 On-line Description, Herman Miller Furniture Company, Zeeland, Michigan, 2020.
31 On-line Description, George Nelson Foundation, 2020.
32 On-line Description, Cranbrook Museum.
33 On-line Product Description, Herman Miller Furniture Company, Zeeland, Michigan, 2020.
34 Ibid.
35 Ibid.
36 Ibid.
37 Ibid.
38 On-line Description, Eames Office Website.
39 Ibid.
40 Ibid.
41 On-Line Object Label, Yale University Art Gallery, New Haven, Connecticut, 2020.
42 On-line Description, Cooper-Hewitt Museum.
43 Alex. Girard Foundation.
44 On-line Description, Our Designers, Herman Miller, Zeeland, Michigan, 2020.
45 On-line Object Label, Cooper-Hewitt Museum, New York, NY, 2020.
46 Aleishall Girad Maxon, Girard Studio, Email-Braniff furniture description, September 20, 2020.
47 On-line description, Design within Reach San Francisco, California, 2020.
48 Ibid.
49 Ibid.
50 On-line description, Our Designers, Herman Miller, Zeeland, Michigan, 2020.
51 On-line Description, Knoll Designer Bios, Hans Knoll, Knoll International, 2020.
52 Ibid.
53 https://en.wikipedia.org/wiki/Jens_Risom.
54 On-line Description, Knoll Designer Bios, Hans Knoll, Knoll International, 2020.

55 https://en.wikipedia.org/wiki/Florence_Knoll.
56 On-line Description, Knoll Designer Bios, Florence Knoll, Knoll International, 2020.
57 On-line, Knoll News Detail, "Florence Knoll Bassett, Design Pioneer and Guiding Light of Knoll, Dies at 101," 2019.
58 Ibid.
59 Robert D. McFadden, "Florence Knoll Bassett, 101, Designer of the Modern American Office, Dies," *New York Times*, January 25, 2019.
60 https://en.wikipedia.org/wiki/Florence_Knoll.
61 www.knoll.com/story/shop/the-planning-unit.
62 Robert D. McFadden, "Florence Knoll Bassett, 101, Designer of the Modern American Office, Dies," *New York Times*, January 25, 2019.
63 On-line Description, Knoll Designer Bios, Florence Knoll, Knoll International, 2020.
64 Robert D. McFadden, "Florence Knoll Bassett, 101, Designer of Modern American Offices, Dies," The New York Times, January 25, 1919, www.nytimes.com/2019/01/25/style/florence-knoll-bassett-dead.html.
65 On-line Description, Knoll Products, Knoll International, 2020.
66 On-line Description, Knoll Designer Bios, Florence Knoll, Knoll International, 2020.
67 Ibid.
68 Ibid.
69 Ibid.
70 On-line Description, Knoll Products, Knoll International, 2020.
71 Ibid.
72 Ibid.
73 Ibid.
74 Ibid.
75 On-line Description, Knoll Designer Bios, Eero Saarinen, Knoll International, 2020.
76 On-line Description, Knoll Products, Knoll International, 2020.
77 Ibid.
78 On-line Description, Knoll Designer Bios, Eero Saarinen, Knoll International, 2020.
79 On-line Information Description, Harry Bertoia Foundation, St. George, Utah, 2020.
80 Ibid.
81 Ibid.
82 Ibid.
83 Ibid.
84 Ibid.
85 Ibid.

13 Movements after Modernism
High-tech, Postmodernism, Deconstructivism

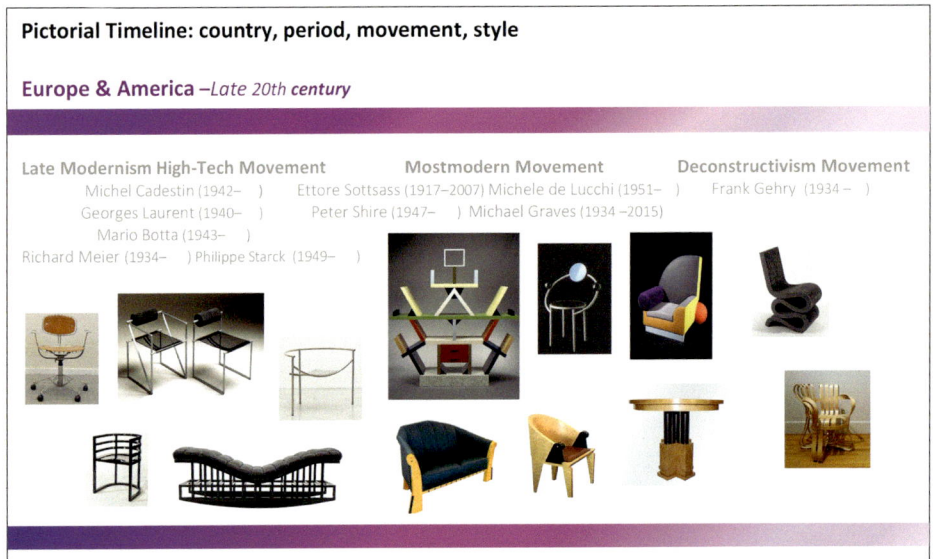

13.1
Pictorial timeline—Movements after Modernism: High-tech, Postmodernism, Deconstructivism

TIME PERIOD OVERVIEW

This concluding chapter will discuss in brief the impact on furniture design by movements that evolved from the 1970s characterized by a loss of faith in the forward momentum of Modernism, to the 1990s, driven by the advance in the computer and telecommunications industries. The categorization of furniture in relation to a specific movement and time period toward the end of the 20th century is indistinct, compared with other time periods. Notice that in the pictorial timeline for this chapter the pieces appear less zoned.

By the time the 1970s arrived, there was a shift in the ground of architectural thinking that had an impact on all areas of design—interiors, industrial, furniture design and decorative arts. The 1970s was a decade of experimentation. Pluralism reigned. Multiple influences, principles, and practices coexisted, impacting the design of furniture. Late in the century, categorization of furniture becomes nebulous. By the time the 1970s arrived, there was vocal skepticism about the tenets of "modern architecture," and movements and "isms" were debated.[1] By the end of the decade, it was common enough to hear the refrain "modern architecture is dead."[2] Although history rarely gives precise dates for the end of an era, architectural historian, cultural theorist, and critic Charles Jencks (1939–2019) anointed a particular event as the end of the Modern movement. The implosion of the Pruitt-Igloo housing project in St. Louis (March 16, 1972, at 3 p.m.) is the date that Jencks declares an iconic blow to the primacy of modern architecture.[3] In the 1970s, the socioeconomic state of the West was precarious. In 1973, oil supplies from the Middle East were cut, sparking a world-wide energy crisis, a crippling blow to the West by the oil-rich Arab nations. Consumer confidence plummeted, and by 1975 a global recession was underway.[4] Cynicism regarding the global economy prevailed.

Taking a step back to the early 1930s, Modernist pioneers envisioned a mechanized future, embracing the machine and mass production, and rationalizing that elements of human culture must be understood in their relationship to a broader system. It was assumed that architecture and design defined that system and complex form in which the simplest definable components would exist—cultural norms, ways of living and working. In regard to the Modernist tenets, one could say that prewar Modernism was utopian and theoretical, and postwar Modernism ca. 1950 saw a continuation and exploration of Modernist principles, forms, and technological inventions, but was practical and applied, no longer utopian.[5]

The term "Postmodern" will appear twofold in the chapter—the literal interpretation is exactly what it states: movements that come after the Mid-Modernist period. But this term by the 1980s also applies to a distinctive approach in architecture, interiors, and furniture design, and takes on the moniker "Postmodern Movement." The chapter's survey will begin with High-tech—referred to as a Late Modern architectural movement. Following High-tech will be the Postmodern Movement, and lastly the Deconstructive movement. It is important to be aware that in many cases the architects and designers themselves reject the labels given to designate movement and/or styles.

HIGH-TECH MOVEMENT, CA. 1970s

History

High-tech architecture, also known as Structural Expressionism, is a type of Late Modern architectural style that emerged in the 1970s. It burgeoned from the Modernist ethos and aimed to avoid links to the past, moving away from building materials commonly used in traditional architecture. The term "tectonic" as pertaining to architecture is defined as "the science or art of construction, both in relation to use and artistic design."[6] The High-tech building celebrates utilizing new advances in technology and building materials—high-performance systems and materials such as steel, glass, and concrete. Toward the end of the 20th century, construction systems and materials became more advanced and available in a wider variety of forms. High-tech architecture makes extensive use of the advancement in systems and materials also referred to as high-performance systems. The formal emphasis for High-tech was on transparency in design and construction. Evident visually is the desire to communicate the underlying structure and function of a building. High-tech architecture readily exposes the mechanical systems as well as structural systems throughout its interior and exterior. So in respect to furniture design, the same ideology was applied and expressed aesthetically. Recommended architecture and interiors to investigate are the Centre Pompidou, Paris (Piano and Rogers, 1977), Herman Miller Factory, Bath, England (Terry Farrell and Nicholas Grimshaw, 1976), HSBC Building, Hong Kong, China (Norman Foster Associates, 1979), Lloyd's building, London (Richard Rogers Associates, 1986).

Aesthetics

In the design and construction of furniture, there is an emphasis of a technical nature. In a furniture piece, the structural support is often exposed, revealing how the piece is assembled. This approach is similar to High-tech architecture communicating both form and function. Also similar to architecture, with furniture design there is an emphasis on the externalization of structural components. The selected medium for furniture design is reminiscent of industrial production—materials such as steel, aluminum, cable, wire, exposed hardware, welts, bolts, rivets. The form preference typically is the use of a strong simple geometry. Its design conveys an ethos of science and progress—the overall aesthetic appears tectonic. Additionally, in regard to aesthetics, the dynamic appearance of the furniture piece, like a High-tech building, relies on light and shadow, and color can also play an important role to accentuate certain functional or technical features.

Michel Cadestin (1942–), Georges Laurent (1940–)

Furniture

The first timeline piece is the **Beaubourg Desk Chair, ca. 1976,** Paris. The designers are architect and designer Michel Cadestin and architect and designer Georges Laurent. The chair was created for the Centre Pompidou (Figure 13.1). The Pompidou Centre is named after French President Georges Pompidou (1969–1974), and is a High-tech building located in the Beaubourg area of Paris. The building is known

Figure 13.1 Beaubourg Desk Chair, ca. 1976, France. Designed by Michel Cadestin and Georges Laurent. Galvanized steel-wire frame, steel star-shape base, and leather seat.

Source: Courtesy of Destijds Design VOF, Elfde Wijk 40, 7797 HH, Rheezerveen, Netherlands.

locally as the "Beaubourg." It is a complex building which includes a modern art museum, public library, music center, and exhibition space. The building design was the result of a much-publicized architecture competition. The winning team was Richard Rogers (1933–) and Renzo Piano (1937–). The Beaubourg opened in January 1977.

The Beaubourg Desk Chair possesses similar qualities to High-tech architecture. The design communicates form and function with an emphasis on the externalization of structural components such as the galvanized steel-wire frame reminiscent of industrial production. And the steel star shape chair base recalls the steel truss used for structural support within a building—in this instance, supporting the chair seat, back, and sitter. The leather back cushion and seat cushion is an ideal solution for comfort, adding softness and visual approachability. Its overall size is H 34¼" × W 18½" × D 20".[7]

Mario Botta (1943–)

Furniture

The next timeline pieces are the **Seconda Chair**, **1980**, Italy, and the **Prima Chair**, **1982**, Italy (left and top, Figure 13.2) and (right, Figure 13.2). Both chairs were designed by Italian architect Mario Botta and originally manufactured by Alias.

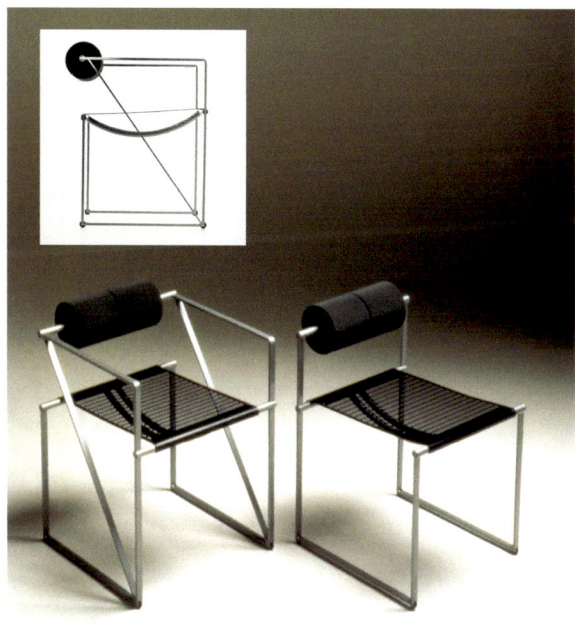

The top image of the Seconda Chair is an exquisite view of the clear use of geometry seen in the chair's overall rectilinear shape, triangle, and circle/cylinder. As with High-tech architecture, there is an emphasis on design and construction for both chairs. Also, as with the architecture, Mario Botta communicates the underlying structure and function. The structural frame for both models is clearly articulated. Both the structure and clear geometric parts define the chairs' aesthetic appearance.

The medium for the chairs is metal used for the frame and rectilinear metal perforated seat with polyurethane foam cylinder for the back rollers. The overall dimension for the Seconda Chair is H 28¾" × W 20¼" × D 15¾", seat H 19".[8] The overall dimension for the Prima Chair is H 27 15/16" × W 18⅞" × D 20 1/16".[9]

As mentioned in the introduction, classification of furniture near the end of

Figure 13.2
(*left and top*) Seconda Chair, 1980, Italy. *(right)* Prima Chair, 1982, Italy. Designed by Mario Botta. The medium for both chairs is a metal frame with perforated metal seat and polyurethane foam cylinder back rollers.

Source: Courtesy of Mario Botta Architetti.

the century is indistinct. It is not unusual for these chairs to be listed as Postmodern since they were created ca. 1980s. However, given the tectonic appearance and structural approach, High-tech is appropriate. A final mention: the form of both the Seconda Chair and Prima Chair resembles the simple, serene geometry found in Mario Botta's buildings.

Philippe Starck (1949–)

Furniture

The next timeline piece, **Dr. Sonderbar Chair, ca. 1983**, France, was designed by architect, designer, inventor, and entrepreneur Philippe Starck. The chair was made by XO Design between 1983 and 1989 (Figure 13.3). XO Design was founded in 1984 by Philippe Starck and Gérard Mialet. The ambiguous XO was chosen with care—an abbreviation with multiple interpretations. An old cognac? An symbol for kisses and hugs? It can be read as "cross the line"—or the boundaries.[10]

The goal of the brand was design innovation and new ways of selling and moving beyond the invisible line defining the design industry.[11] The brand strove to merge the rich lexicon of makers, time-honored wood joiners, mold-makers, plastic injectors, metal workers, and so on. XO Design crossed frontiers, and the world of contemporary furniture is the beneficiary.[12]

This three-leg sculptural chair is rumored to have been inspired by the seat of a pilot.[13] Its form is an exquisite exercise in restraint. The forming of the tubular steel gracefully moves between radial line and straight. Its shape is visually delicate but the triangulated form makes it structurally very strong. Its straight-on view reveals the radial lines and elliptical form superbly (top, Figure 13.3). What is fascinating about this view is that it very easily can be read as a two-dimensional work. The medium is nickel-finish tubular steel with perforated sheet metal used for the seat.

The chair was fabricated via welding. The connections are partially visible in the details (below, Figure 13.3). The chair's size is H 25" × W 35½" × D 18½", seat H 16".

Figure 13.3 Dr. Sonderbar Chair, ca. 1983, France. Designed by Philippe Starck for XO Design. The medium is nickel-finish tubular steel frame and perforated steel seat and welded fabrication.

Source: Courtesy of Béton Brut, London, UK. Photography, Gareth Hacker.

Richard Meier (1933–)

Furniture

This timeline piece is the **Reading Room Chair, ca. 1978,** US (Figure 13.4). Although designed by Richard Meier in the late 1970s, it is not clearly definable as High-tech furniture but can be readily addressed as Late-Modernist movement furniture.

As stated in Knoll's literature about the collection: "The epoch of modernism was firmly deemed still alive in the case with the Richard Meier Collection for Knoll." And yet, by combining the woodwork of the traditional American craftsmen with his own contemporary style, Meier came up with a collection that spoke of the past, present, and future all at once.[14]

Figure 13.4 Reading Room Chair, ca. 1978, U.S. Designed by Richard Meier for Aye Simon Reading Room, Solomon R. Guggenheim Museum, New York City. The chair became part of the "Richard Meier Collection" for Knoll. The medium is wood with a black lacquered finish.

Source: Courtesy of Richard Meier & Partners Architects LLP. Photo Credit, Steven Sloman.

The chair was created for the Aye Simon Reading Room on the second floor of the Solomon R. Guggenheim Museum, New York. Richard Meier & Partners Architects designed the space and custom furniture (1977–1978).[15] Meier brought the chair to Knoll to see if it could be taken further. The company accepted, and the result was the Knoll Richard Meier Collection, consisting of the chair, several tables, and a chaise lounge.[16] Meier mentions about the design, "The simple idea of the chair emerged from a double cube, one on top of the other. The bottom, from the seat downwards, is carved out of the lower cube; an upward extension, the curve of the arms, is formed from the implied upper cube."[17] The medium is black lacquered wood but can be specified in other finishes. Its overall size is H 17½" × W 21" × D 20".

The next timeline piece also from the Meier Collection for Knoll is the **Rocking Chaise, 1982** (Figure 13.5). Again, there is an emphasis on combining the woodwork of traditional American craftsmen using the black lacquered wood frame and

Figure 13.5 Rocking Chaise, 1982, U.S. Designed by Richard Meier for the "Richard Meier Collection" for Knoll. The medium is wood with a black lacquered finish.

Source: Courtesy of Richard Meier & Partners Architects LLP. Photo Credit, Steven Sloman.

leather upholstered cushion, yet in a Modernist way via an articulate display of geometry expressed by use of the grid-like rectilinear base—and emphasis on the curve line both with the upholstered cushion and slightly curved base. As with the chair design, the Rocking Chaise concurrently blends the past, present, and future. The overall size of the Rocking Chaise is H 27½" × W 28" × D 72", seat H 17½". It is designed to rock when when one sits or lies in either direction, and is wide enough for two people. This Meier piece is an unusual and fascinating approach to the convention chaise lounge some what reminiscent of Charlette Perriand's LC4 design (Figure 10.9 and Figure 10.10).

POSTMODERN MOVEMENT, CA. 1980S

History

Postmodernism is a broad movement marking a departure from Modernism. It gained momentum in the late 1970s, reached its height in the 1980s, and began to wane in 1990s. Postmodernism occurred across a variety of academic disciplines—theoretical, including cultural studies, philosophy, linguistics, and literary criticism, and design disciplines, including architecture, interior design, furniture design, and industrial design. Its theoretical premise, regardless of discipline, centered on rejection of what is described as the grand narratives and ideologies associated with the Modern movement. Pertaining to architecture, the impetus was the belief that the Modern movement resulted in a bland architecture and failed utopianism. Postmodernism is the antithesis of the streamlined Mid-Century Modern style. It replaces the Modernist style through us of diverse aesthetics, borrowed elements, and references from the past. This occurs in furniture design as well as architecture.

In the creation of Postmodern furniture, as in architecture, it is not unusual for distortion and exaggeration of motifs or for a form to be adopted for its own sake. Color and symbolism also play an important role. Postmodern buildings appear dramatic and grand, and in appearance Postmodern furniture is sympatico. Pertaining to architecture, interiors, and other areas of design, inherent in the Postmodern ethos was encouraging new ways of viewing the familiar.

As seen at certain points in design history, there is a collective that makes it the goal to produce work that is for the most part physically similar and expresses a specific ideology. At the beginning of the 1980s, architect, designer, artist Ettore Sottsass (1917–2007) founded the Memphis Group in Milan. This Italian-based design and architecture collective included international participants as well, and was active from 1981 to 1988. Both founder and group became an emblem of Postmodernism. The group designed Postmodern architecture, furniture, lighting, fabrics, carpets, and ceramics. The decadence and elaborateness of the Italian designer's work was in tandem with the 1980s zeitgeist in the US, yet at the same time the playful colorful geometric style was an insouciant break from that zeitgeist. This indifference was in line with the kind of Reagan-era rebellion seen in other areas of arts—such as the onset of MTV.

The 1980s in the United States was a decade known for indulgence—conspicuous consumption. The decade is often remembered for its materialism and consumerism. Many Americans embraced a new conservatism in social, economic, and political life during the 1980s, characterized by the policies of President Ronald Reagan who was president for most of the decade (1981–1989). The designs that emerged from the Memphis Group defined the boundary—pushing Postmodernism through the 1980s. The abstract decorations, asymmetrical shapes, angular furniture, and colorful graphics, like the architecture, might be construed as irreverent to the tenets of the Modernist movement. The Postmodern ethos reared its head against the perceived banality of Modernism and strove to develop its own lexicon. Although architects and design professionals interpreted the Postmodern lexicon with parochial enthusiasm, it is noticeable that with US architecture, interiors, furniture, and decorative arts, this interpretation was typically less playful and flamboyant than the Memphis Group. By the 1990s, Postmodernism was waning. Yet, during the 1980s in which the Memphis Group flourished, indisputably the collective created for popular culture a Postmodernism both fashionable and fun.

The work of architect, designer, educator Michael Graves at a point shifts to Postmodernism, and Graves is credited with designing what is considered a seminal Postmodern work, the Portland Municipal Service Building (1982). During this period of working, he also produced original and influential Postmodern furniture (Figure 13.9 to Figure 13.11). Recommended architecture and interiors to investigate are Michael Grave's Fargo-Moorehead Cultural Bridge, Fargo, North Dakota (1978) and the Portland Municipal Service Building, Portland, Oregon (1982), James Stirling and Michael Wilford's Neue Staatsgalerie, Stuttgart, Germany (1984), and Philip Johnson & John Burgee, AT &T Building, New York City (1984).

Aesthetics

Postmodern furniture design and construction, like the architecture, replaces the streamlined Mid-Century Modernist style through use of diverse aesthetics, borrowed elements, and references from the past. However borrowed, it is not unusual for manipulations to occur, and distortion and exaggeration of the vocabulary and motifs is common. Also normative is the manipulation in scale for certain furniture features and parts. Additionally, symbolism can play an important role in furniture design, as in Postmodern buildings. Visually, it can appear as if the symbolism and/or form is adopted for its own sake. Color is also generously utilized as are a variety of materials and finishes. The abundance of materiality plays an important role in respect to appearance, often lending a sense of the dramatic. Postmodern furniture, like the buildings, can readily appear dramatic and grand. A critical premise encouraged by Postmodern design, regardless of whether it is architecture, interiors, furniture, or product design, is communicating the freedom to exercise the ability of adapting new ways of viewing the familiar.

Ettore Sottsass (1917–2007)

Furniture

The first pictorial timeline piece is the **Carlton Room Divider**, 1981, Italy. This Postmodern piece is designed by Italian architect, artist, and designer Ettore Sottsass, founder of the Memphis Group (Figure 13.6). This Postmodern room divider is a seminal piece for the movement and one of the most striking and memorable furniture designs created by the Memphis Group. This example resides in the Metropolitan Museum of Art. The piece calls into question conventional furniture forms by combining a space divider, bookcase, and chest of drawers.[18] This spir-

Figure 13.6 Carlton Room Divider, 1981, Italy. Designed by Ettore Sottsass for the Memphis Group. A seminal Postmodern furniture piece. Manufactured by Memphis Milano. The material is medium-density fiber board (MDF) and plastic laminate.

Source: Metropolitan Museum of Art New York, New York. John C. Waddell Collection, Gift of John C. Waddell, 1997.

ited tiered bookshelf and cabinet combined different colors and finishes. The form appears anthropomorphic, recalling the head and arms of an ancient idol or totem. The material is a medium-density fiber board (MDF) and plastic laminate. Its size H 76½" × W 74¾" × D 15¾". This Room Divider was intended for the higher end of the market and finely handcrafted.[19]

Michele De Lucchi (1951–)

Furniture

The next pictorial timeline piece, the **First Chair**, 1983, Italy, was designed by architect, designer, writer, and educator Michele De Lucchi. The chair was created during the period of Michele De Lucchi's involvement with the Memphis Group collaborative (Figure 13.7). The First Chair, like other Memphis Group creations, can be found in museums throughout the world. Currently, Michele De Lucchi resides in Milan, overseeing his atelier AMDL Circle, an interdisciplinary practice working on projects around the globe.

In respect to the chair's design, its form communicates lightness in scale and overall appearance. The design is articulate in its implementation of geometry—linear line and

Figure 13.7 First Chair, 1983, Italy. Designed by Michele De Lucchi for the Memphis Group. A Postmodern design. The medium is powder-coated steel with lacquered wood.

Source: Courtesy of Architetto Michele De Lucchi.

circle. Formally, the circle is addressed on multiple levels; flat when it becomes the back rest and seat, spherical as it accentuates the tubular frame arm area equivalent, and lastly, completing the pattern, the tubular frame's profile becomes circular. Its medium is powder-coated steel, with lacquered wood. The addition of color creates visual hierarchy and excitement. The overall size of the chair is H 35 7/16″ × W 23⅗″ × D 17⅝″, seat H 17⅝″.

Peter Shire (1947–)

Furniture

The next Memphis Group piece is the **Bel Air Chair**, 1982, manufactured 1984, Italy (Figure 13.8). Designed by American artist, ceramicist, and furniture designer Peter Shire, the iconic Bel Air Chair was the most important contribution of the Californian designer to the Memphis Group and became a signature object for the collective.[20] It was used on the cover of the most widely distributed book on the group authored by Barbara Radice—*Memphis: Research, Experiences, Results, Failures and Successes of New Design* (Rizzoli, 1984).

Figure 13.8 Bel Air Chair, 1982, manufactured, 1984, Italy. Designed by Peter Shire for the Memphis Group. A Postmodern design. The medium is a wood frame with cotton upholstery over foam and painted wood.

Source: Courtesy of Peter Shire.

Although the chair fits into the Memphis aesthetic, Shire creates a design that is pure West Coast. Shire's style was influenced by the Los Angeles culture of surfing and hot rodding, as well as Art Deco and 1950s Space Age architecture in Southern California and the state's mass culture.[21] The chair's asymmetrical back is based partly on shark fins and partly on the Stevens House, a late 1960s masterpiece by architect John Lautner, located on the beach in Malibu, California (1968).[22] The title "Bel Air" was taken from the name of a luxury five-star hotel in Beverly Hills, California. This colorful chair's back is made of a wood frame with cotton upholstery over foam and painted wood. The overall size is H 50″ × W 48⅜″ × D 42½″.[23] The iconic Bel Air Chair has been in constant production since its creation.

Michael Graves (1934–2015)

Furniture

This Postmodern piece is the **Sunar Hauserman Loveseat**, 1980, US (Figure 13.9). It is the design of architect, designer, and educator Michael Graves. It was designed as part of the Sunar Hauserman furniture collection including Postmodern chairs and tables for the Sunar Hauserman company showrooms. At this time, Michael Graves was the architect commissioned to design and update the firm's furniture showrooms as well as the furniture. Sunar Hauserman was a well-established contract furniture company, considered one of the leaders in contract furnishings at this time. By the 1980s, increased competition challenged the company greatly, affecting the firm's business; sadly, by 1989 the company closed its doors.[24]

Figure 13.9 Sunar Hauserman Loveseat, 1980, U.S. Designed by Michael Graves for the Sunar Hauserman company. A Postmodern design. The medium is a bird's eye maple frame, with ebony inlays and vibrant peacock-blue upholstered back and seat.

Source: Courtesy of Michael Graves Architecture & Design.

Graves's furniture designs for Sunar were truly original and were the epitome of Postmodern furniture. When Sunar Hauserman unveiled their showrooms across the country, it was difficult for even the architects and designers not in favor of Postmodernism to pass up the accolades. The loveseat's form is borrowed from the early 20th-century ubiquitous overstuffed rolled-arm sofas most often found in homes. However borrowed, notice how the translation of the overstuffed upholstered arm is replaced with a wood arm which emulates the shape in profile. Also note how the wood frame has an exaggerated flair as it reaches the floor, recalling the flare of the skirt at the bottom of a traditional sofa. When wood is used for traditional sofas, often there is decorative carving on the wood. For this Postmodern sofa, the concept is replicated by small triangles in a contrasting material. The contrasting material is also used to accentuate the base of the leg and mark the center of the rolled arm. The design is the opposite of Modernist minimalism and machine aesthetic, purposely so. It is original and has a strong visual presence. Its form is balanced visually and the material selection and color palette is inviting to the sitter. The medium is a bird's eye maple frame, with a vibrant peacock-blue upholstered back and seat with ebony inlays in the frame.[25] The overall dimensions H 30" × W 32" × D 53½", seat H 16".[26]

The next piece the **Parrot Chair**, 1980, Italy is a Postmodern design also created by Michael Graves. It was manufactured by Sawaya Moroni, Milan. For more than 40 years, the company has been a highly regarded Italian design partnership which focuses on architecture, interior design, and product design (Figure 13.10). The Parrot Chair is from the Sunar Hauserman period. The use of the circular shape back resembles the elegant Art Deco style barrel-back chair. The Parrot Chair also exudes an elegant presence. Visible in its overall form is the elliptical back appearing both visually soft yet erect and dignified. The back slants downward and gracefully defines the arm area which is terminated by the contrasting black lacquered rolled end.

Figure 13.10 Parrot Chair, 1980, U.S. Designed by Michael Graves. Manufactured by Sawaya Moroni, Milan. A Postmodern design. The medium is curly maple, with black lacquered rolled arms and burgundy leather seat.

Source: Courtesy of Michael Graves Architecture & Design.

The black triangular block with the rolled end visually and physically terminates the elliptical back. The leg profile has a flatness and mimics the use of the triangular shape, which appears fitting for the chair, yet unusual. There is no applied ornament, yet the individual parts as an ensemble seem ornamental. The outcome is visually captivating—the impeccable curly maple, with a black lacquered arm area and burgundy leather seat.[27] The result of the design and chosen materials is aesthetically powerful. The overall size is H 33" × W 21½" × D 19".[28]

The **Arcadia Table**, 1990, Italy, is the last Michael Graves design on the timeline (Figure 13.11). Originally manufactured by Meccani Arredamenti, Italy, its form is classically derivative and is an example of the Postmodern tendency to borrow features from past. The form recalls Greco-Roman Classicism which is apparent in the tripartite arrangement of its design. Its base, central column area, and table top with apron resemble a Classical building's columns resting on a dado, with cornice and pediment. The diameter of the table is W 43 9/10" and it is 29½" high.[29] Its medium consists of lavish materials, in arable with ebony inlays and black lacquered wood columns.[30] The table appears stable and regal—very much the same quality attributed to Classical architecture.

Figure 13.11 Arcadia Table, 1990, Italy. Designed by Michael Graves. Manufactured by Meccani Arredamenti, Italy. A Postmodern design. The medium is arcadia, in arable with ebony inlays, and black lacquered wood columns.

Source: Courtesy of Michael Graves Architecture & Design.

DECONSTRUCTIVISM MOVEMENT, CA. 1980S–

HISTORY

Deconstructivism is a Postmodern movement which appeared in the 1980s. Its genesis is linked to Algerian-born French philosopher Jacques Derrida and his development of a form of semiotic analysis known as "deconstruction" which he discusses in numerous texts and developed in the context of phenomenology, the study of structures of experience and consciousness. The summarized goal of Deconstructivism according to some critics is "Removing the essence of architecture."[31] In 1988, Philip Johnson and Mark Wigley curated an exhibit for MoMA, Deconstructivist Architecture, which crystalized the movement and brought fame and notoriety to its key practitioners—Peter Eisenman, Frank Gehry, Zaha Hadid, Rem Koolhass, Daniel Libeskind, Bernard Tschumi, and the architecture firm Coop Himmelblau (Plate 13.1). Deconstructivism architecturally is characterized by the use of fragmentation, manipulation of the idea of a structure's surface or skin, redefinition of shapes and forms, and radical manifestation of complexity in building.[32] Architects' projects often described as applying Deconstructionism equate to an absence of harmony, continuity, or symmetry, giving an overall impression of the fragmentation. The finished visual appearance characterized by unpredictability and controlled chaos aims to perplex the visitor, making the stay in the space an experience worth remembering. Recommended architecture and interiors to investigate are Frank Gehry's house, Gehry Residence, Santa Monica, California (1977), considered one of the earliest Deconstructivist buildings, although Gehry denies this,[33] and Daniel Libeskind's Jewish Museum, Berlin, Germany (1989). Libeskind's design won the competition in 1989 for the extension of the Berlin Museum with a Jewish Museum Department; it opened in 2001.[34]

Aesthetic

As noted at the start of this chapter, late 20th-century furniture is rather nebulous, and that which falls within the parameter of Deconstructionism is the most indistinct. Noticeable is that furniture associated with this movement applies a non-rectilinear approach. Valued are radical shapes and forms, no different than the architecture. The focus appears to be on freedom of form rather than functional concerns. An audacious move toward the extraordinary and innovative is welcome.

Frank Gehry (1929–)

Furniture

Side chair, "Easy Edges," 1971, manufactured ca. 1982, US. Designed by architect Frank Gehry (Figure 13.12), the chair resides in the Decorative Arts Collection, Brooklyn Museum of Art, New York. The chair's form recalls the shape of old-fashioned ribbon candy commonly seen during the Christmas Holiday. Its uniqueness, besides its folded form, is its contact with the body of the person seated beyond the back and seat—the Easy Edges Chair's contouring form and material come in contact with the sitter's calves and heels.

Figure 13.12 Side Chair "Easy Edges," 1971, U.S. Manufactured ca. 1982. Designed by Frank Gehry. Design emphasis Deconstructivism.

Source: Brooklyn Museum of Art, Brooklyn, New York. Creative Commons-BY. Decorative Arts Collection, Gift of Paul F. Walter. Photo: Brooklyn Museum #83.108.1

In regard to the form, it is constructed from a single length of cross-laminated corrugated cardboard (27 layers), folding back and forth.[35] Visible in profile is the double *S*-curve. The upright back forms the beginning of the top *S*, the sides covered with a thin layer of pressed board. A wooden dowel serves as glide across the rear of the base. Its overall size is H 33⅜" × W 14" × D 23¼".[36]

The last timeline piece designed by Frank Gehry is the **"Cross Check" Chair**, 1989–1991, US (Figure 13.13). In a Santa Monica workshop established by Knoll Associates in 1989, Frank Gehry began experimenting with creating furniture forms out of thin laminated strips of bent wood. The design of this chair

Movements after Modernism ■

Figure 13.13 "Cross Check" Chair, 1989–1991, U.S. Designed by Frank Gehry for Knoll Associates, 1989. The chair was part of a collection and series. The medium is laminated strips of bent maple.

Source: Brooklyn Museum of Art, Brooklyn New York. Creative Commons-BY. Gift of Joan H. and David E. Bright, in honor of their daughter Jennifer M. Bright B.A., 2013.

was inspired by the woven construction of apple crates that Gehry had played on as a child. The ribbonlike elements presented an essential challenge of integrating materials and structure. Three years later, Gehry's ground-breaking collection of laminated maple chairs and tables previewed at the Museum of Modern Art in New York. The collection has playful names, such as Hat Trick Chair, Face Off Table, High Sticking Chair, Power Play Chair and Ottoman, which seems emblematic of childhood since the ideas stem from childhood play and memories. Beyond the exhibit, the collection subsequently won numerous design awards. The medium is laminated strips of bent maple and the overall size is H 33⅝" × W 28½" × D 24¼".[37] It is fortunate as a creative individual to be able to carry an experience or memory from childhood and develop it into a successful creative work and marketable product.

The survey and book have now come to an end. For this chapter, placing the furniture design into a context was the most challenging since for the 1970s–1990s multiple influences, principles, and practices coexist, impacting furniture design as well as architecture. It is a period in history during which the integral relationship of furniture, interiors, and architecture was not necessarily consonant. Not that the relationship is one of total dependency, for there has always been a degree of autonomy. At this point in history, the dissonance in furniture, interior, and architecture design make it a challenge to distinctly place furniture within a given movement or style. The project chosen to give the reader some idea of context is one featured in the MoMA's 1988 Deconstructivist Architecture exhibition (Plate 13.1). The furniture in the large meeting room, although appropriately selected, is not of Deconstructivist design. The chairs appear to be the Eames Soft Pad Group Management Chairs and the conference table a custom wood top boat-shape table. Although not visible in the photograph, in the adjacent reception area Wassily Chairs designed by Marcel Breuer are used. What is compelling about the mid-century and early 20th-century furniture selected for the project is that these designs define "modernity" in a movement that has abandoned the tenets of "modern architecture." The idea that a furniture's design can travel through time and find its appropriate place in any movement or style is something to contemplate.

The following excerpt from the exhibition publication by Wolf D. Prix, Partner, seems to encapsulate the design concept impeccably: "a source of lift—but also a leading edge—a cutting edge, a blade—which slices through the corner and springs outside."[38] The project is a Deconstructivist rooftop renovation by architects Coop Himmelb(l)au, Vienna, for the law firm Schuppich Sporn & Winischhofer. The preliminary design began 1983. The construction took one year and

An Illustrated Guide to Furniture History

Plate 13.1 Schuppich Sporn & Winischhofer, Renovation 1983–1988, Vienna, Austria. Designed by Coop Himmelb(l)au Architects.

Source: Coop Himmelb(l)au Architects. Photography: DuccioMalgamba.

was completed on December 23rd, 1988.[39] The project is in a traditional Viennese building at the corner of Falkestrasse and Biberstrasse in the inner city. The client's program was 4,300 square feet of attic space, which included a large meeting room, office space, reception area, and adjacent rooms.[40] The architects state: "While designing, we envisioned a lightning bolt reversed and a taut arc." The firm further explains the design concept:

> The open glazed surfaces and the closed, folded or linear surfaces of the outer shell control the light and allow or restrict the views. Both directions of view, that from outside and that from within, which are captured in one of the early drawings, define the complexity of the construction's special relations. The differentiated and differentiating constructional system, which is a cross between a bridge and an airplane, translate the special energy into constructional reality.[41]

I would argue that furniture pieces selected for the space appropriately respond to the Deconstructivist architecture impeccably, taking a secondary position, for there is no doubt the stellar Deconstructivist architecture is primary.

NOTES

1. William J.R. Curtis, *Modern Architecture Since 1900* (New Jersey: Prentice-Hall, Simon & Schuster, 1996), p.589.
2. Ibid.
3. Mark Hinchman, *History of Furniture: A Global View* (New York: Fairchild Books, A Division of Condé Nast Publications, 2009), p.590.
4. Judith Miller, *Furniture: World Styles from Classical to Contemporary* (New York: Dorling Kindersley), p.504.
5. Mark Hinchman, *History of Furniture: A Global View* (New York: Fairchild Books, A Division of Condé Nast Publications, 2009), p.581.
6. Robert Maulden, *Tectonics in Architecture: From the Physical to the Metaphysical*. Thesis, Massachusetts Institute of Technology, 1986, p.3.
7. Destijds Design VOF, Online description, Beaubourg Desk Chair by Michel Cadestin and Georges Laurent, 1stDIBS, 2020.
8. On-line information, First Dibs, www.1stdibs.com/furniture/seating, 2020.
9. Ibid.
10. www.Connox.com/xo-design.html.
11. Ibid.
12. Ibid.
13. www.Catawiki.com.
14. On-line Description, Richard Meier Collection for Knoll, Knoll International, 2020, www.knoll.com/knollnewsdetail/the-richard-meier-collection.
15. On-line Description, Richard Meier & Partners Architects LLP, *Aye Simon Reading Room, New York, New York, 1977–1978*, Richard Meier & Partners Architects LLP, New York, 2020.
16. On-line Description, Richard Meier Collection for Knoll, Knoll International, 2020.
17. Ibid.
18. On-line Object Label, Metropolitan Museum of Art, New York, 2020.
19. Ibid.

20 On-line Object Label, Victoria and Albert Museum, London, England, 2020.
21 Ibid.
22 Ibid.
23 Ibid.
24 Encyclopedia of Cleveland History, Cas Wester Reserve University-Case.edu/article/sunar-hauserman.
25 www.1stdibs.com/furniture/seating/sofas/michael-graves-postmodern-sofa/id-f_18354742.
26 Ibid.
27 Ibid.
28 Ibid.
29 www.pamono.com/arcadia-table-by-Michael-graves-for-meccani-arredamenti-1990s.
30 Ibid.
31 Bob Lansroth, "Deconstructivism in Architecture and Its 10 Most Amazing Buildings." Widewalls, December 6, 2015.
32 Ibid.
33 https://en.wikipedia.org/wiki/Gehry_Residence.
34 https://en.wikipedia.org/wiki/Jacques_Derrida.
35 On-line label, Brooklyn Museum of Art, Brooklyn New York, 2020.
36 Ibid.
37 On-line label, Brooklyn Museum of Art, Brooklyn New York, 2020.
38 Philip Johnson and Mark Wigley, *Deconstructivist Architecture* (New York: The Museum of Modern Art, distributed by New York Graphic Society Books, Little Brown and Co., 1988), p.80.
39 On-line Description, www.coop-himmelblau.at/architecture/projects/rooftop-remodeling-falkestrasse, 2020.
40 Ibid.
41 On-line Description, www.coop-himmelblau.at/architecture/projects/rooftop-remodeling-falkestrasse, 2020.

14 Conclusion

OUTDOOR FURNITURE

In conclusion, there is one last salient area to discuss regarding furniture history—outdoor furniture. What is obvious today is the blurring of the lines between indoor and outdoor spaces, and the growing desire to connect with nature. Outdoor space, regardless of whether it is public or private, a park, garden, patio, terrace, or deck, has become synonymous with good health—wide-ranging health benefits result from spending time outdoors. Outdoor furniture is categorized within the "Casual Furniture" market which includes all things related to outdoor and casual living.

Currently, one of the most common materials used in the design and construction of outdoor furnishings is *polyethylene*, a lightweight thermoplastic which becomes soft when heated and hard when cooled. It can be manufactured as a one-piece product—seamless and with smooth surfaces. The advantage is an absence of cracks and crevices, allowing for easy cleaning of the entire product using just a damp cloth, water, and soap. Also, a tremendous advantage is its durability and longevity.

Over the last several decades, notable architects and designers have been invited and/or commissioned to design outdoor furniture collections. For example, Philippe Starck designed the Bubble Collection for Kartell, and Maya Lin designed the Stone Collection for Knoll's 60th anniversary. Although, today, the material used for design is typically polyethylene, the author has selected for this chapter an example of an outdoor furniture collection designed using a material other than the ubiquitous polyethylene. The collection is designed from aluminum and steel imparts with a powder-coated finish. Award-winning architect Margaret McCurry designed the Windmark Collection for the company Landscape Forms. The collection draws inspiration from architecture, landscape, iconic furniture, history, and poetry.[1] McCurry mentions, "Like my architecture, I wanted this furniture to be contemporary with links to the past," (Figure 14.1 and Figure 14.2). The collection reveals visual lightness with structural strength and heft enough to hold to the ground in wind.[2]

The first model from the Windmark Collection for Landscape Forms designed by Margaret McCurry is the **Grass Armchair** (Figure 14.1). During the design process, McCurry took a fascinating approach in designing the collection. Cardboard models were made, as might have been done for an architecture project. Then the scaled models were manipulated through means of Photoshop software into a natural outdoor setting. The compositional outcome appears surreal—artfully linking the tangible living grass of the terrain with the grass cutouts—the nontangible. Notice on the cardboard model the cutouts on seat of the chair grow into fronds on the chair's back (left, Figure 14.1). On the other side is the view of the actual chair and table placed outdoors (right, Figure 14.1).

Noticeable with both chairs is that the Windmark Collection's forms are derived by bending and folding material in inventive ways, creating shapes that are simple but arrestingly new.[3] The patterns in the metal are interactive in spirit.[4]

The next Windmark piece is the **Gingko Leaves Armchair** model (Figure 14.2). The design development and process happened also via cardboard model and

Figure 14.1 Grass Armchair, 21st century, U.S. Windmark Collection for Landscape Forms, designed by Margaret McCurry. The medium is aluminum steel with a powder-coat paint finish.

Source: Courtesy of Margaret McCurry.

Figure 14.2 Gingko Leaves Armchair, 21st century, U.S. Windmark Collection designed by Margaret McCurry. Outdoor furniture Armchair, the medium is aluminum steel with a powder-coat paint finish, color: buttercup.

Source: Courtesy of Margaret McCurry.

Photoshop manipulation. The white cardboard model appears in an unexpected dreamlike state floating among white blossoming foliage (left, Figure 14.2)—a strange and unexpected beauty. To the right is the chair in a buttercup yellow paint, featured in an actual outdoor setting (right, Figure 14.2). McCurry states about her vision, "The gingko leaves tumble. Rain falls and splashes against the seat in drops expressed as a series of little holes."[5]

To provide an abbreviated background and some insight to the genesis of outdoor furniture, walking through time will be beneficial in order to understand the history. For outdoor furniture, the history is best explained through materiality rather than style, although the two are intertwined.

Stone furniture

Beginning with stone furniture from Antiquity, archaeologists uncovered formal garden designs in the Roman city of Pompeii. In ancient Rome, the most prevalent style of outdoor furniture was stone. Stone slabs were used for benches and tables. The symmetrically designed garden–outdoor room was designed for recreation, rest, and worship, and shows evidence of benches and statuary, along with walkways and fountains.[6] Eerily, archaeologists in Pompeii uncovered well-preserved garden furniture existing from the eruption of Mount Vesuvius in A.D. 79.[7]

Turf bench

During the Middle Ages (around the 15th century), gardens contained earthen seating, which historians call turf benches. Turf benches were among the most distinctive features of Medieval gardens and are depicted in many paintings and tapestries.[8] This earliest form of seating in gardens were constructed of mounded earth or brick, stone, wood, or woven branches.[9] Once formed, the frames were filled with soil and surfaces were topped with grass.[10] In Medieval paintings and tapestries, turf benches are shown to be rectangular, circular, L-shaped, or U-shaped. Arbors or trellises were sometimes built into the seat to provide shade and shelter, while circular benches were constructed around single trees.[11]

Wicker furniture

Archaeologists uncovering the forgotten civilizations of Egypt discovered dozens of examples of wicker furniture made from reeds and swamp grasses. A plentiful and hardy resource, these materials grew in abundance along the banks of the Nile river. The furniture they made was used indoors and out, and included pieces such as storage chests, chairs, and baskets.[12] Over the centuries, many cultures and civilizations have contributed to the different styles and patterns of weaves. Materials used include willow, bamboo, rattan, and a variety of grasses. The wicker furniture styles that are recognized today are mostly from Victorian England (1798–1901). Characterized by being artistically beautiful, with delicate weaves, they are very fragile, so makes it rare to find one of the original English antiques in perfect condition in the 21st century.

According to tradition, the first wicker furniture piece came to America on the *Mayflower*, a cradle from Holland for Peregrine White. The child was born on board the *Mayflower* in Provincetown Harbor, in November 1620. Now in the collection of the Pilgrim Hall Museum, Plymouth, Massachusetts, descending through the White family.[13] Scholars have found evidence that such cradles were also imported into Plymouth later in the century.[14]

In the US, wicker came into vogue in the 1850s thanks to Cyrus Wakefield, a Boston native who discovered loads of rattan used for securing cargo at Boston's shipping docks. Wakefield realized that rattan had more possibilities than just cushioning goods and started importing it for furniture making. Wakefield partnered with the Heywood brothers, who had created a loom that would make wicker furniture faster and replace the slow process of handwork. The partnership became the Heywood Wakefield company. Together, they dominated the industry until 1920s, when the fashion of wicker furniture began to decline. A resurgence wouldn't happen until the 1960s and 1970s when the first cost-effective synthetics became available.

Metal furniture, cast iron, and wrought iron

The earliest iron furnishings in gardens coincided with public parks. Early examples of metal garden furniture were cast iron and lacked an adequate finish, causing rust and deterioration. Metal furniture susceptible to rust must be treated to withstand the elements. Early iron garden furniture took its cue from indoor furnishings.[15] Many early designs are still replicated today. Cast-iron furniture was produced in the United States in the mid-1800s. The process entailed pouring molten steel into molds, cooling it, and putting it together.[16] The furniture was poured in parts so that when the iron had cured, the pieces would be assembled into a finished piece.[17] The cast-iron process allowed for very intricate designs and shapes reflective of the Victorian era.[18]

However, over time wrought iron proved to be the more durable iron and preferred choice for outdoor furniture. Wrought iron is a specific type of iron, and the traditional material of the blacksmith, deriving its name from the word "wrought," which is the Medieval past tense of the verb "to work." Wrought iron literally means "worked iron," which refers to the method of manufacturing the metal by working it repeatedly under a hammer.[19] It is an iron alloy with a very low carbon content, and this is what makes it durable. It is an impure mix of glass-like slag within the iron. As it melts together, the impurity becomes a conservator of the metal as it ages.[20] Wrought iron is tough, malleable, ductile, corrosion resistant, and easily welded. Today, wrought iron is used for contemporary outdoor designs as well as traditional.

Wood furniture

With public parks, public greens, and public squares gaining popularity in 18th–19th-century England and America, along came benches for sitting and conversation. The demand for outdoor furniture in private homes and gardens increased as well.

Conclusion

Figure 14.3
Almodington Bench, ca. 1750, Somerset County, Maryland. "Garden seat" for Almodington Plantation. Medium yellow pine, paint. Dimension LOA 96¼", HOA 45½", DOA 28".

Source: Courtesy of Munder-Skiles Outdoor Furniture, Garrison, New York. Replica of the Almodington Bench, ca. 1750, Somerset County, Maryland.

Figure 14.4
Munder-Skiles Outdoor Funiture replica, Almodington Bench, ca, 1750, Somerset County, Maryland.

Source: Courtesy of Munder-Skiles Outdoor Furniture, Garrison, New York. Replica of the Almodington Bench, ca. 1750, Somerset County, Maryland.

One of the earliest known wooden garden bench examples in America was made for the Almodington Plantation house in Somerset County, Maryland, ca. 1750. The Almodington bench can be seen in the collection of the Museum of Early Southern Decorative Art (MESDA), North Carolina (Figure 14.3). These bench types were referred to as "garden seats" by their 18th-century makers.[21] Benches similar to this are pictured in William Halpenny's *Rural Architecture in the Chinese Taste* (London, 1755).[22] The design of the Almodington Plantation bench is a diagonally slatted four-panel back, with solid wood seat, cross-braced arm, and simple rectilinear stretchers at its base. The bench is compelling, a precision of simple wood diagonal, vertical, and horizontal members harmoniously composed, rendering a visually poetic outdoor furniture piece. It is fortunate that Munder Skiles, makers of the finest handmade exterior furniture for over 25 years, has produced a replica of the bench for their collection (Figure 14.4). The company's hand-building of exterior furniture relies on historically researched, traditional methods along with the most advanced modern techniques.[23] A phenomenal asset for American cultural heritage.

Before the creation of what we now consider wood furniture appropriate for outdoor living, people would take their interior furnishings outside to enjoy the temperate seasons. What is recognized today as the Windsor chair is one such piece that began this tradition. In the 16th century, the first Windsor chairs were made in Great Britain, but evidence of origin is not certain. The design was possibly a development of West Country, Welsh, and Irish "stick-back" chairs. The Windsor chair production eventually moved to High Wycombe and these chairs were of the comb-back variety. By the 18th century, steam bending was being used to produce the characteristic "bow" of the Windsor chair which is most recognizable.

There are various theories of how the "Windsor chair" label derived. One is an association with the garden at Windsor Castle. Another is that the chairs were shipped to the town of Windsor for distribution to London. No matter the legend, they became popular garden seats throughout the country. By the 1750s, the English Windsor chair was ubiquitous indoors as well as outdoors and would have been used everywhere from inns and taverns to libraries and meeting houses. The delegates of the First Continental Congress, which met at Carpenter's Hall in Philadelphia on September 5, 1774, used "sack back" Windsors for the signing of the papers; among the delegates were Patrick Henry, George Washington, John Adams, and John Jay (Figure 14.5).[24]

Physically, the Windsor chair is constructed of turned (on a lathe) slender spindles that are socketed into a solid, saddle-shaped wooden seat. Spindles extending downward form the legs and those extending upward form the back and arm rest. There are several variants to the chair's back—low back, high back, bow back, sack back, and comb back, to name a few. One of the major selling points of the Windsor chair was its portability—light and easy to carry. It was extremely popular in both England and in North America.

Figure 14.5 Windsor Chair, "Sack Back." Similar to the design as the chair at Carpenter's Hall, 1774.

Source: Author's illustration.

Specific to North America, the Adirondack chair today has become an outdoor emblem in popular culture. In the 21st century, there are many variations ranging from wood, colorful plastic, and even two-person benches. The Adirondack chair is named after the northeastern New York State Adirondack Mountains (Figure 14.6). However, the name is all that connects the Adirondack chair to this mountain region. The exact birthplace of the Adirondack chair is still a mystery. Many feel the Adirondack chair may have evolved from the older Westport chair, Westport, New York (Figure 14.7).[25] The main difference between the two chairs is that the Westport chair is constructed with large wide boards while the more traditional Adirondack chair is constructed with smaller board slats. The two features that are considered hallmarks for both chairs are the raked, slanted back and the large, broad armrests. The fact that the Westport chair has a slanted back and wide, broad armrests makes it easy to see why the older Westport chair could very well have been the original Adirondack chair.[26] However, there is no definitive proof.

Figure 14.6 Adirondack Chair, East Coast. U.S. Similar to the design of the early 20th-century traditional Adirondack Chair.

Source: Author's illustration.

Figure 14.7 Westport Chair, Westport, New York. Similar to the design of an early 20th-century original Westport Chair.

Source: Author's illustration

Lastly, a mention of teak outdoor furniture whose origins begin mid-century when Scandinavian design appeared in the US from Denmark, Sweden, Norway, and Finland. Over the centuries, due to the countries with teak forest being colonized by European governments, teak's reputation spread throughout Europe, and teak furniture made in Scandinavia became a valued commodity. Scandinavian furniture makers made great use of the larger pieces of wood, and hand sculpting gave their pieces decorative curves that fit right into the Scandinavian mid-century modern ethos of the cleanest and simplest designs—functional minimalism.

Historically, the Dutch colonial power at the time (19th century) planted seedlings of teak and started teak plantations in Indonesia. The government of

Indonesia has since taken over and developed the plantations to what they are today. Teak is a tropical hardwood species and particularly resistant to different climates, making it suitable for shipbuilding and outdoor furniture. It is found in southeast Asian nations such as Thailand, Burma, and Malaysia. When introduced in the US in the 1950s during the Scandinavian design wave, it quickly became a popular choice for outdoor furniture because of its attributes. It can be left unfinished or protected, and as it weathers over time, the wood goes from a honey-brown color to a silvery gray. Los Angeles designer, Kay Kollar Design, sums up the aesthetic and functional benefit of teak poignantly: "Teak is beautiful, simple wood that works well outside without a tremendous amount of maintenance."[27]

The journey through *An Illustrated Guide to Furniture History* has come to an end. By the completion of Chapter 13, the intention was that the power of the unconventional approach—Analysis of Form: Nine-Step Methodology—had resonated and that the value of the ninth step and crucial part of the process—the use of visual notes, which are the connective tissue between learning furniture history and visual literacy—has been understood. The goal is that you are now becoming adept at using visual notes as an analytical tool. It is also important to keep in mind what was mentioned in Chapter 5 regarding the use of sketching, drawing, diagramming, and rendering for analytical documentation. For this purpose, the utility of sketching is stressed—sketching as a tool without expectation of artist talent and creating a work of art (although you might strive for this eventually). The expectation for this book is to use sketching, drawing, diagramming, and rendering to imprint on your mind the key features of the furniture piece chosen to investigate so you can distinguish these pieces and place them appropriately within a timeframe and place of origin.

A list of recent scientific publications from active scientists and theorists focused on recall and recognition and the relationship between drawing and memory has been provided on the following page for your reference. Additionally, with this list are several notable books about drawing that are good resources. As the reader continues with this approach as a personal learning tool, a valuable thing to remember is that, as a graphic analysis tool, the drawing/sketch is a conversation between you and the designed piece or artifact. You determine what to sketch. The sketch is to organize and visually record your thoughts—getting the information down for reference.

Lastly, do not hesitate to pick up the book without the intension of traveling through Part III. The other sections can be excellent for reference. Part I can continually be referred to in regard to understanding the historical perspective (Chapter 1), construction principles (Chapter 2), and how to place furniture categorically (Chapter 3). And in Part II, the visual note examples (Chapter 4) and professional graphic narrative examples (Chapter 5) can be guides for building drawing, sketching, and rendering skills.

Thank you for taking this journey with me and I wish you a successful future of lifelong learning.

PUBLICATIONS: DRAWING AND MEMORY, AND BOOKS ABOUT DRAWING

Books

Norman Crowe and Paul Laseau, *Visual Notes for Architects and Designers* (Hoboken, NJ: John Wiley & Sons, 2012).

Rudy De Reyna, *How to Draw What You See* (New York, NY: Watson-Guptill Publications, 1970).

Betty Edwards, *Drawing on the Right Side of the Brain* (New York, NY: Jeremy P. Tarcher/Penguin, 1979).

Bert Dodson, *Keys to Drawing* (Cincinnati, OH: North Light, 1985).

Darren R. Rousar, *Memory Drawing: Perceptual Training and Recall* (Excelsior, MN: Velatura Press, 2013).

Recent publications on drawing and memory

Myra A. Fernandes, Jeffrey D Wammes, and Melissa E. Meade, "The Surprisingly Powerful Influence of Drawing on Memory," *Current Directions in Psychological Science*, August 30, 2018.

Melissa E. Meade, Jeffrey D. Wammes, and Myra A. Fernandes, "Drawing as an Encoding Tool: Memorial Benefits in Younger and Older Adults," *Experimental Aging Research*, 44, 2018, 5.

University of Waterloo, "Drawing is Better than Writing for Memory Retention," *Science Daily*, December 6, 2018.

Jeffrey D Wammes, Melissa E. Meade, and Myra A Fernandes, "Creating a Recollection-Based Memory Through Drawing," *Journal of Experimental Psychology: Learning, Memory, and Cognition*, 44(5), 2018.

Beth Morling, Cindi May, and Gil Einstein, "Teaching Current Directions in Psychological Science," Association for Psychological Science (APS), March 29, 2019.

J.D. Wammes, T.R. Jonker, and M.A. Fernandes, "Drawing Improves Memory: The Importance of Multimodal Encoding Context," *Cognition*, 191, 2019

Adrian S. Banning, "The Art of Memory: Benefits and Mechanisms of Drawing," *The Journal of Physician Assistant Education*, 30(2), June 2019.

NOTES

1 Landscape Forms Brochure PDF, 2020.
2 Ibid.
3 On-line Brochure, PDF, Landscape Forms, Kalamazoo, Michigan, 2020.
4 Ibid.
5 Ibid.
6 Summer Classics, "A Short History of Outdoor Furniture," May 24, 2016, https://summerclassics.com/blog.

7 Ibid.
8 Metropolitan Museum of Art, The Cloisters Museum & Gardens, The Medieval Garden Enclosed, March 15, 2010, Blog 2000–2011.
9 Ibid.
10 Ibid.
11 Ibid.
12 Ibid.
13 On-line Collection Label, Pilgrims Hall Museum, Plymouth, Massachusetts, 2020.
14 Ibid.
15 Summer Classics, "A Short History of Outdoor Furniture," May 24, 2016, https://summerclassics.com/blog.
16 Jean McClelland, "Vintage Iron Furniture Deemed Authentic with Makers Mark," *The Herald-Dispatch*, October 17, 2015.
17 Ibid.
18 Ibid.
19 On-line Description, The Real Wrought Iron Company, North Yorkshire, UK, 2020.
20 Jean McClelland, "Vintage Iron Furniture Deemed Authentic with Makers Mark," *The Herald-Dispatch*, October 17, 2015.
21 On-line Label, Museum of Early Southern Decorative Arts (MESDA), North Carolina, 2020.
22 Ibid.
23 On-line Description, Munder-Skiles, Garrison, NY, 2020.
24 Mike Dunbar, "Famous Furniture Sack Back Windsor Chair." *Woodcraft Magazine*, 75, July 27, 2017.
25 On-line Information, C.J. Gross, "The Westport Adirondack Chair Story," Clarks Original Westport Adirondack Chair, Lexington, Kentucky, 2020.
26 Ibid.
27 Jill Krasny, "How teak worked its way into modern design," 1st Dibs, July 19, 2017, www.1stdibs.com/blogs/the-study/teak.

Index

Locators in *italics* refer to figures, though where figures are interspersed with related text these are not distinguished from principal locators.

Adam, James 12
Adam, John 12
Adam, Robert 12, 62–64, 66–67, 70, 226
Adirondack chair 348
aesthetic functionalism 314
aesthetics: 18th-century 214–216, 218, 219; ancient Egypt 184, 185–186; ancient Greece 186–187; Art Nouveau 246–248; deconstructivism movement 338; early Modernist designers and architects 283–284, 288, 293, 298; English Renaissance 206, 208–209; Europe Arts and Crafts Movement 240–241; high-tech movement 328; Italian Renaissance 200; Modern movement 310; Neoclassical design 235; Philadelphia, America 232; postmodern movement 333; Queen Anne furniture style 229–230, 231; Vienna Secession 250
Affleck, Thomas 93–98, *94–95*
Alberti, Leon Battista 198
Almodington Plantation house, Maryland 347
American Arts and Crafts Movement *238*, 239, 252–259
American furniture: 17th- and 18th-century *31*, 75–79; Charleston, South Carolina 107–117; Colonial period 75–76, 107, *214*, 229–235; high chest of drawers example 128–137; international style *261*, 263, 270–272, 307; Newport, Rhode Island 79–88; Philadelphia, America 88–107; piece categorization 75–79; post-war migration 307; postmodern movement 333; Rococo style 88–89, 91, 94, 96–98, 229
animal legs, ancient Egypt 183, 185–186
Anne, Queen of England 224–225; *see also* Queen Anne furniture style

antiquity: Egypt 182–186; Greece 186–188; outdoor furniture 345; pictorial timeline *181*; Rome 189–193; time period overview 181–182
Arad, Ron 156–157
Arcadia Table 337
Art Deco 262–263
Art Nouveau *238*, 239, 244–248, 257–259; *see also* German Jugendstil
Arts and Crafts Movement: in America *238*, 239, 252–259; in Europe *238*, 239–244
Asian traditional lacquer 286
Austria, Vienna Secession *238*, 239, 248–252

Baillie Scott, Mackay Hugh 241, 242, 244, 257
ball and claw leg design 32, *33–35*, 77, 82, *85*
Barcelona chair, Spain 272–273
Baroque period 43, 214–215, 217
Bates, Elizabeth 70
Bauhaus *261*, 262, 266–268, 272–273, 317
Beaubourg Desk Chair 328–329
bed headboards 36, *37*, *39*, 208–209
bedroom, Roman *192*, 193
beds, English Renaissance 208–209
Behrens, Peter 262, 271
Bel Air Chair 335
Benton, Tim 300–302
bergère 42–43, *44*
Bertoia, Harry 320–323
birch wood 312–313
Blackburn, Graham 231
block-and-shell furniture 231–232
block-front chests 81–82, 231–232
boiserie 51, *51–52*
bonnet-top secretary 86–87, *87*, *88*, 229–231
Botta, Mario 329
Boudin, Léonard *47*, 223, *223*, 224
breakfront bookcases 113–114, *115–116*, 226–227
Breuer, Marcel 262, 267, 268, 273
bronze doré 46

352

buffet cabinets *241*, 241
bull's leg design 183
Burgundian style 202–203

C-scrolls *101*, 107, 223
cabinetmakers: American 80–94; Charleston, South Carolina 108–109; English 12, 24, 54–60; French 223–224
cabinets, French 202, 203–204
cabriole 43, *44*, *53*, *101*
Cadestin, Michel 328–329
Cadwalader residence, Philadelphia 94, 95, 102, 233
camelback sofa 66–67
Campbell Bench 164–165
canapé 47, 49
caquetoire 202, 204–205
card tables 90, 94
Carlton room divider 334
Carolingian period 75
carpentry 12–14; *see also* construction
cartouche 43, *44*, 218, 219
carving: 18th-century 217–218, 219; ancient Egypt 183, 186; ancient Rome 191; ball and claw 32, *33–35*; France 202–203, 204–205; Philadelphia Rococo 88–89, 91, 94, 96–98, 232; postmodernism 336; Queen Anne style 230; the Renaissance 198–199, 200, 203–204, 207; Rococo style 229
case goods 70
case piece: 18th-century 70; in America 77, 231–232; breakfront 227; chest-on-chest 77–79, 96, *98*, 108, *112–113*; Neoclassicism 223–224; piece categorization 5
cassone (chest) 198–199, *199*, 201
cast iron 346
categorization *see* piece categorization
Catholic Counter-Reformation 214–215
chaise lounge 274–275
Chareau, Pierre 280–285
Charleston, South Carolina 107–117
chest design 82–84, *83*
chest-on-chest: analysis of form 128–137; as case piece 77–79, 96, *98*, 108, *112–113*; characteristics 97–99
Chicago Tribune Tower Competition 306
Chinese Chippendale camelback sofas 66–67
Chinese Chippendale chairs 64, *64*, 94, 227
Chippendale chairs *57*, 77
Chippendale, Thomas: "big three" 12, 54; biographical details 54–55; Dumfries House, Scotland 60–63; Dundas residence, England 227; Harewood House, England 67–68; influence in America 76–77, 88–89, 102, *103*, 109
Christie's UK 70–74
citron 190
CJK Design 162–163
Classical aesthetic 216; American furniture 77, 96, *98*; chest-on-chest 77; Georgian period 57; Greek furniture 182, 186–187, 188; Harewood House, England 68; Louis XVI 45; the Renaissance 199–205, 208; Rococo style 62, 64, 70, 216; Roman furniture 193
Classical temples 77, 96, *98*
claw design *see* ball and claw leg design
Coconut Chair 311
Colonial America 75–76, 107, *214*, 229–235
commercial design 308
commode: English 64, *65*; French *46*, 46–47, *47*, 223
Congrès Internationaux d'Architecture Moderne (CIAM) 263
console tables *46*, 46–47, *48*, 217–218, 221–222
construction: 18th-century principles 5, 12; 21st century craftspeople 32, *33–35*, 36, *37*; joinery 13–14, *15–17*
contract design 308, 314
court cupboards 206, 207
Cross Check Chair 338–339
Crowe, Norman 156
Curtis, William J. R. 244
curvilinearity 230, 248

da Vinci, Leonardo 202
DCW (Dining Chair Wood) 312–313
De Lucchi, Michele 334–335
De Pree, D. J. 309
De Stijl *261*, *262*, 269–270, 288
deconstructivism movement *326*, 337–341
découpage 219, 220
del Sarto, Andrea 202
Delafosse, Jean-Charles *49*
Derrida, Jacques 337
design professionals: analysis of form 123; Arad, Ron 156–157; graphic narratives 155–156; Herold, Karen 157–159; Jóhannesson, Dennis 172–173; Karim Rashid Inc. 168–171; Knoll Bassett, Florence Marguerite 159–162; Koules, Chris 162–163; Krueck, Ron 163–164; Lee, Gary 164–165; Pheasant, Thomas 165–166; Piretti, Giancarlo 166, *167*; Prouvé, Jean 168; Rashid, Karim 168–171; Sexton, Mark 163–164; Sigurgísladóttir, Hjördís 172–173; Sinoway, Morlen 173–177

■ **Index**

desks (secretary) *80*, 80, 219–220
Deutscher Werkbund *261*, 262, 263–266
d'hôtel particulier 50
Diamond Chair 320, 321
display cabinets, Art Nouveau 245–247
double chests, Charleston, South Carolina 108–114
dovetail joints 13, *18*
Dr. Sonderbar chair 330
Ducal Palace, Gubbio 210, *211*
Dumfries House, Scotland 60–63
Dundas residence, England 68–69, 74, 227
Dundas sofas *69*, 225–226

Eames, Charles 312–314
Eames, Ray 312–313, 314
Easy Edges Chair 338
ebony 12, 185, 190, *336*, *337*
edge joints 13, *19*
Egyptian furniture 182–186, 345
Elfe, Thomas 108–111
Elmslie, George Grant 254–255
EM Tables 295–296
English furniture: 18th-century *214*, 216, 224–229; Arts and Crafts Movement 239–244; cabinetmakers 12, 54–60; Georgian period 54–58, 216; non-upholstered 65–66, 70–74; Queen Anne *30*, 76–77; the Renaissance *196*, 205–211; upholstered 56–69
Europe Arts and Crafts Movement *238*, 239–244; *see also* American Arts and Crafts Movement
Executive Office Group (EOG) 309
exhibitions, 20th century 263

Fairbanks, Jonathan L. 70
fauteuil 43, *44*, *45*, *138*, 222–223; Grand Comfort 274; Modernism 273–274, 289
First Chair 334–335
flat-top secretary *80*, 80, *81*
Florence, Italy 197
Florence Knoll furniture 159–162, 318–319
form, analysis of 123; French armchair example 138–145; high chest of drawers example 128–137; learning outcomes 124–126; Marshmallow sofa 146–154; nine-step process 123, *125*, 125–126, 349; practice examples 123–124; visual notes 124, 125
Foullet, Pierre-Antoine *47*, *223*, 223–224
Francis I 201–202, 205–206
free-hand drawings 155–156
French furniture: 18th-century *214*, 220–224; analysis of form on French armchair 138–145; Art Deco 262–263; Art Nouveau *238*, 239, 244–248, 257–259; golden age of 42–53; Louis XIV *29*, 43, 45; Louis XV *29*, 42–53, 138–145, 216, 221; Louis XVI *29*, 45; Modern movement 271–272, 274; piece categorization 42–53; Régence *45*, 215, 220, 221–222; the Renaissance *196*, 197, 201–205; Rococo style 47, 50, 220–221, 222, 224
Frothingham, Benjamin 20, 85, *86*
fruitwood 43, 225
furniture: historical perspective 3–4; pictorial timeline 3–4, *6–10*
furniture categorization *see* piece categorization

garden benches 346–347
Gary Lee Partners 164–165
Gehry, Frank 338–339
Gehry, Residence, California 338
gender: changing role of women 221; early Modern women designers 286
George I 216, 224
George II 54, 96, 216, 225
George III 54, 216, 225
George Nelson Associates 310
Georgian period: aesthetics 225–228; cabinetmakers 12, 54–57; Chinese Chippendale 227–228; Classical aesthetic 57; classification of styles 225, 228–229; "Golden Age" 225; Rococo style 54, 55, 216, 229; time period overview 224–225
German Jugendstil 262
Germany: Bauhaus *261*, 262, 266–268, 272–273, 317; Deutscher Werkbund *261*, 262, 263–266
Getty Research Institute (GRI) 271
gilt gold sofas *69*, 225–226
Gingko Leaves Armchair 344–345
Girard, Alexander 314–316
Girard Group 314–315
Goddard, John 80–81, 85
Gothic form *60*, 197, 202, 203
Gottshall, Franklin 28
Grand Comfort 274
graphic narratives 155–156
Grass Armchair 343–344
Graves, Michael 333, 335–337
Gray, Eileen 280–281, 286–291, 300, *301*
Great Bed of Ware, England 208–209
Greek Classicism 182, 186–187
Greek Klismos chair 165–166, 186–188
Gropius, Walter 262, 271
Gubbio Studiolo 210, *211*
Guéridon tables 295
Guimard, Hector 247–248

Harewood House, England *67*
Hatnefer's chair, Egypt 184–185
headboards 36, *37*, *39*, 208–209
Henry II 202, 203
Henry VIII 205–206
Hepplewhite, George: "big three" 12, 54; biographical details 57, 58; Kittinger Company *72*; Neoclassical design 57–58, 70; shield-back chairs *58*, *60*, 60, 70
Herman Miller Furniture Company 307–311, 314–315
Herold, Karen 157–159
Heyward-Washington House 111–112
Heywood Wakefield company 346
high-back chair with oval back-rail 242–244
high-back chairs 242–244
high boy cabinets 14, 102
high chest, analysis of form 128–137; *see also* chest-on-chest
high-tech movement *326*, 327–332
Hitchcock, Henry-Russell 270–271
Hoffmann, Joseph 250

ideation 155–156, 163, 166, *167*
Independence Hall, Philadelphia 99–100, *100*
Industrial Revolution 239–240
intarsia 198, 201, 210, *211*
international style 261, 263, 270–272, 307
iron 241, 346
Italy: 18th-century *214*, 217–220; the Renaissance *196*, 197–201

Jacobean period 75
Jeanneret, Pierre 273–274, *276*
Jencks, Charles 327
Jóhannesson, Dennis 172–173
Johnson, Ken 49–50, 53
Johnson, Philip 263, 270–271, 337
joinery: construction principles 13–14, *15–17*; Egypt 183, 184–185; types of joint 13–14, *15–20*

Karim Rashid Inc. 168–171
Killen, Tim 110–111
Kirtlington Park, England *234*, 235
Kittinger Company *71–73*
Klismos chair, Greece 165–166, 186–188
Knoll Associates 159–162, 316, 321–323
Knoll Bassett, Florence Marguerite 159–162, 316–319
Knoll, Hans 316–317, 321
Knoll International 307–309

Kohn, Josef 250
Koules, Chris 162–163
Krueck, Ron 163–164

La Maison Tropicale 292–293
lacca contrafatta 219
lacca povera 219
lacquer work: 18th-century Italy 217, 220; Asian traditional lacquer 286; Campbell Bench 165; high-tech movement 331–332; Louis XV furniture 52, *53*; Modernism 288–289, 290; postmodernism 336–337
Laseau, Paul 156
Late Baroque Period 43, 217
lathes: historical perspective 21, *22–23*; leg design 26, *27*, 32; period furniture design 28, *29–31*
Laurent, Georges 328–329
Le Corbusier (Charles-Édouard Jeanneret) 271–272, 273–274, *276*, 280–281, 297
Lee, Gary 164–165
leg design: 18th-century 24, *25*, *27–28*; ancient Egypt 183; ball and claw 32, *33–35*; English Renaissance 207–208; use of lathes 26, *27*, 32
Leonards 36, *37*, 38, *39–40*
Lin, Maya 343
Louis XIV *29*, 43, 45
Louis XV: aesthetic direction 216; French armchair analysis of form 138–145; influence in Italy 220; reign and golden age of furniture 42–53; role of women 221; stylistic characteristics *29*, 42, *45*, 45, 52
Louis XVI *29*, 45

Mackintosh, Charles Rennue 242–244
Madame de Pompadour 221
mahogany: "age of" 54, 229; breakfront bookcases 226–227; Georgian period 225; wood grain 227, 230, 232
Maison de Verre 282, 283
maple 190, *336*, 339
Marshmallow sofa, analysis of form 146–154, 309
Masson, Charles 257–259
McCormick, Robert R. 306
McCurry, Margaret 343–345
McIntire, Samuel 60, *61*
Medieval furniture 202, 241
Meier, Richard 331
Memphis Group 332–335
metal frames 274, 318, 329–330
metal use in furniture: Arts and Crafts Movement 240–241, 242; Chareau, Pierre 283; international style 273; outdoor furniture 346

Index

metal work 285, 291, 321
Metropolitan Museum of Art, Gubbio 210, *211*
Metropolitan Museum of Art, New York 44, 50, *51*, 218
Michelozzo di Bartolommeo 198
middle class: 18th-century France 221; Arts and Crafts Movement 240; Colonial America 75–76, 100, 229
Mies van der Rohe, Ludwig 262, 271, 272, 273, *277*, 316
Miller, Herman 309–311
Modernism: in America *305*, 305–309; Bauhaus *261*, 262, 266–268, 272–273; De Stijl *261*, 262, 269–270, 288; Deutscher Werkbund *261*, 262, 263–266; early designers and architects *280*, 280–281; interior design 275, *276–277*; international style *261*, 263, 270–272; Modern furniture 261–262, 305–306; movements after *326*, 326–327; origins 238–239, 253; pictorial timeline *261*
Morlen Sinoway Atelier 173–177
Morris, William 239–240
mortise-and-tenon joints 13, 14, *17*, 184–185
MR Chair 273
Mulhauser, George 311
Museum of Early Southern Decorative Art (MESDA) 79, 108, *112*, 347
Muthesius, Hermann 262

Nelson, George 310–311
Neoclassical design: aesthetics 235; characteristics 223–224; Dundas residence, England 68–69; Georgian period 57, 58; Harewood House, England 68; Pheasant, Thomas 165; popularization 70; Rococo style 62, *63*, 70, 74, 216
Neoclassical movement 216
the Netherlands, De Stijl *261*, 262, 269–270, 288
New England, America 79–88
Newport, Rhode Island 79–88, 231–232

oak: Arts and Crafts Movement 241, 242, 243–244, 257; Medieval furniture 202
ogee feet 82, *84*
Orientalism 220
ormolu 46, *46*, 50, *53*
outdoor furniture 343–349

Parrot Chair 336–337
pattern books: Colonial America 79, 228–229, 233; English Renaissance 208, 209; Georgian England 54, 60, 65, 216; Neoclassical style 70; Pompadour Highboy 102

pedestal chair 319–320
Perriand, Charlotte 271–274, *276*, 280–281, 296–301
Pheasant, Thomas 165–166
Philadelphia, America 88–107, 232–235
Philippe II 215
pickers (buyers) 38, *39*
pictorial timeline 3–4, *6–10*; 18th-century *214*, 214–217; analysis of form 123, *127*; antiquity *181*; early Modernist designers and architects *280*; Modernism *261*; Modernism in America *305*; movements after Modernism *326*; Renaissance *196*; time periods 179
piece categorization 5, 42 *see* more detail see under individual country headings; American furniture 75–114; English furniture 54–74; French furniture 42–53
piecrust tables 101
Piretti, Giancarlo 166, *167*
polyethylene 343
Pompadour Highboy 102
Pompeii excavation 216
Pompidou Centre 328–329
Port Royal estate 114, *117*
Portland Municipal Service Building 333
postmodern movement *326*, 327, 332–337
Prairie Style 253–257
Pre-Raphaelites 239–240
press cupboards 206
Prima Chair *329*, 329, 330
Prix, Wolf D. 339
professional organizations, 20th century 263
Protestant Reformation 214–215
Prouvé, Jean 168, 280–281, 291–296, 299–300
provenance 42; *see also* piece categorization
Puritans 79–81

Quakers 79–80, 79–81
Queen Anne furniture style: aesthetics 229–230; in America 30, 76, 77, 86, *87–88*; furniture 230–231; Rococo style 216, 224–225

Randolph, Benjamin 89–93, 95, *96*
Rashid, Karim 168–171
reading room chair 331
Régence *45*, 215, 220, 221–222
Reich, Lilly 273, *277*
Reichlin, Bruno 293, 295
the Renaissance: England *196*, 205–211; France *196*, 197, 201–205; Italy *196*, 197–201; time period overview 196, 214
Reniseneb's chair, Egypt 185–186
residential design 308

ribband-back chair 62, *63*, 228, 229
ribbon-back chair 228
Riemerschmid, Richard 262
Rietveld, Gerrit 262
Rinascimento 197; *see also* the Renaissance
Rock, Orlando 70–74
rocking chaise 331–332
Rococo armchair 222–223
Rococo style: aesthetic direction 215, 216; in America 76–77, 88–95, 102–104; in England 55, *56*, 61, 62, 64, 224–225; in France 42–43, 47, 50, 220–221, 222, 224; French armchair analysis of form 138–145; high chest of drawers analysis of form 128–137; in Italy 217, 218, 220; ornamentation 235; Philadelphia Rococo 89–95, 232; Rococo style 42–43
Rohde, Gilbert 309
Roman architecture 189
Roman banquet couch 189–190
Roman bedroom *192*, 193
Roman couches and footstools 190–193
Ron Arad Associates 156–157
room dividers 334

S-scrolls 60, *101*, 107, 223
Saarinen, Eero 306, 319–320
Saarinen, Eliel 306
Salle à Manger Masson 257–259, *258*
satinwood 190, 225
Savery, William 99–107
savonarola chairs 199–200, 201
Scandinavian teak furniture 348–349
Schuppich Sporn & Winischhofer 339–341, *340*
Schust, Florence 316, 321; *see also* Knoll Bassett, Florence Marguerite
Scotland: Arts and Crafts Movement 239–244; Dumfries House 60–63
scroll feet *44*, 63, 223
Secession movement *238*, 239, 248–252
Seconda Chair *329*, 329–330
Sexton, Mark 163–164
sgabello chairs 200, 201
Sheraton, Thomas: "big three" 12, 54; chair back designs 58, *59*, 60; Kittinger Company *71*; Neoclassical design 58, 70
shield-back chairs *58*, 60, *60*
Shire, Peter 335
side chairs: American Arts and Crafts Movement 254–256; Art Nouveau 247–248; deconstructivism movement 338; Georgian England 228; Knoll Collection 320; Philadelphian furniture 232–235; Vienna Secession 249–251

Sigurgísladóttir, Hjördís 172–173
Sinoway, Morlen 173–177
sketching 156
slab tables *107*
slant-front desks *86*, 86
Sling Chair, France 273–274
Societé des Artistes Décorateurs (SAD) 262–263, 282
Sottsass, Ettore 332, 334
South Carolina, America 107–117
splat-back designs *60*, 60
spline joints 14, *20*
spring pole 21
standing livery cupboards 207
Star Furniture Company 309
Starck, Philippe 330, 343
Statton Furniture Company 86–87
Stickley, Gustav 255–256
stone furniture 345
Structural Expressionism 327–332
Studio K Creative 157–159
styles, overview of furniture history: pictorial timeline 3–4, *6–10*, 179; piece categorization 5, 42
Sunar Hauserman Loveseat 335–336
Sutton Fine Furniture 79, 101
swag leg armchair 310–311
swaging 310–311
swivel chairs 298–299
Synistor, P. Fannius, villa *192*, 193

tassel-back chairs *101*, 102, *103*
tea tables 100–101, 102, *106*
teak outdoor furniture 348–349
tenon 13, *17*; *see also* mortise-and-tenon joints
textiles: Girard designs 314–316; Knoll Associates 317, 318–319; Modernism 315, 317; Renaissance beds 208; Roman banquet couch 190
Thonet company 274
through-tenon 13
Townsend, John 80–85, 231–232
treadle lathe 21
tripod tables 100–101, 102
turf benches 345
turning (construction) 21, 207

Union des Artistes Modernes (UAM) 263

Vallin, Eugène 257–259
van Doesburg, Theo 262
Venetian design 215, 218–220
Victoria and Albert Museum (V&A) 64, 208–209
Victorian era 239–240

Index

Vienna Secession *238*, 239, 248–252
Virginia Museum of Fine Arts 321–323, *322*
visual acuity 156
visual expression 156
visual images 5, 123–124; *see also* pictorial timeline
visual literacy 156
visual notes 123–124; *see also* form, analysis of

Wagner, Otto 251–252
walnut: decline in use 225; French furniture 43; French Renaissance 203, 204; Italian Renaissance 198, *199*, 200, 201; Medieval furniture 202
Watson, Thomas 109
Westport chair 348

Whitley Company 99
wicker furniture 345–346
Wiener Werstätte *see* Vienna Secession
Wigley, Mark 337
Windmark Collection 343–345
Windsor chairs 347–348
Winterthur Museum 114, *117*
Winterthur Museum collection *18*, 91, 96
women, changing role of 221
women designers, early Modern design 286
wood grain 227, 230, 232
wood-inlay technique 210, *211*
wooden outdoor furniture 346–347
World War I 271, 291
World War II 271, 292, 297–298, 307, 308
wrought iron 241, 346